The Cultural Cold War in Western Europe

ALSO IN THE INTELLIGENCE SERIES

Secrets of Signals Intelligence during the Cold War and Beyond edited by Matthew M. Aid and Cees Wiebes

British Military Intelligence in the Palestine Campaign 1914–1918 by Yigal Sheffy

British Military Intelligence in the Crimean War, 1854–1856 by Stephen M. Harris

Signals Intelligence in World War II edited by David Alvarez

Knowing Your Friends: Intelligence Inside Alliances and Coalitions from 1914 to the Cold War edited by Martin S. Alexander

Eternal Vigilance: 50 Years of the CIA edited by Rhodri Jeffreys-Jones and Christopher Andrew

Nothing Sacred: Nazi Espionage against the Vatican, 1939–1945 by David Alvarez and Revd. Robert A. Graham

Intelligence Investigations: How Ultra Changed History by Ralph Bennett

Intelligence Analysis and Assessment edited by David Charters, A. Stuart Farson and Glenn P. Hastedt

TET 1968: Understanding the Surprise by Ronnie E. Ford

Intelligence and Imperial Defence: British Intelligence and the Defence of the Indian Empire 1904–1924 by Richard J. Popplewell

Espionage: Past, Present, Future? edited by Wesley K. Wark

The Australian Security Intelligence Organization: An Unofficial History by Frank Cain

Policing Politics: Security Intelligence and the Liberal Democratic State by Peter Gill

From Information to Intrigue: Studies in Secret Service Based on the Swedish Experience 1939–45 by C. G. McKay

Dieppe Revisited: A Documentary Investigation by John Campbell

More Instructions from the Centre by Andrew Gordievsky

Controlling Intelligence edited by Glenn P. Hastedt

Spy Fiction, Spy Films and Real Intelligence edited by Wesley K. Wark

Security and Intelligence in a Changing World: New Perspectives for the 1990s edited by A. Stuart Farson, David Stafford and Wesley K. Wark

A Don at War by Sir David Hunt K.C.M.G., O.B.E. (reprint)

Intelligence and Military Operations edited by Michael I. Handel

Leaders and Intelligence edited by Michael I. Handel

War, Strategy and Intelligence by Michael I. Handel

Strategic and Operational Deception in the Second World War edited by Michael I. Handel

Codebreaker in the Far East by Alan Stripp

Intelligence for Peace edited by Hesi Carmel

Intelligence Services in the Information Age by Michael Handel

Espionage and the Roots of the Cold War: The Conspiratorial Heritage by David McKnight

Swedish Signal Intelligence 1900–1945 by C.G. McKay and Bengt Beckman

The Norwegian Intelligence Service 1945–1970 by Olav Riste

Secret Intelligence in the Twentieth Century edited by Heike Bungert, Jan G. Heitmann and Michael Wala

The CIA, the British Left and the Cold War: Calling the Tune? by Hugh Wilford

The Cultural Cold War in Western Europe 1945–1960

Editors

GILES SCOTT-SMITH
HANS KRABBENDAM
Roosevelt Study Center, the Netherlands

Routledge
Taylor & Francis Group
LONDON AND NEW YORK

First published in 2003 in Great Britain by
by Routledge
2 Park Square, Milton Park, Abingdon, Oxon, OX14 4RN
270 Madison Ave, New York NY 10016

Transferred to Digital Printing 2010

Website: www.routledge.com

British Library Cataloguing in Publication Data

The Cultural Cold War in Western Europe, 1945–1960. – (Routledge series. Studies in intelligence)
1. Cold War – Social aspects – Europe, Western 2. Social control – Europe, Western – History – 20th century
3. Propaganda, Anti-communist – Europe, Western – History
4. Europe, Western – Cultural policy – History – 20th century 5. Europe, Western – Social conditions – 20th century
I. Scott-Smith, Giles, 1968– II. Krabbendam, Hans, 1964–
303.3'75'094'09045

ISBN 0-7146-5308-X (cloth)
ISBN 0-7146-8271-3 (paper)

Library of Congress Cataloging-in-Publication Data
has been applied for

This group of studies first appeared in a Special Issue on The Cultural Cold War in Western Europe, 1945–1960, *Intelligence and National Security* 18/2 (Summer 2003) published by Routledge (ISSN 0268-4527).

Publisher's Note

The publisher has gone to great lengths to ensure the quality of this reprint but points out that some imperfections in the original may be apparent.

Contents

Foreword

DAVID CAUTE

Certain perils now beset Cold War cultural studies, and I would be inclined to judge any conference or seminar in this field by its ability to avoid these perils. Briefly, they are:

1. Bogus attachment of the fashionable label 'Cold War' to some work of literature, cultural event, artistic movement or film sequence which could equally well have happened even if the Romanovs had crushed the Bolsheviks in 1917 and ruled Russia for a further 50 years, with the monk Rasputin in charge of ideology. Examples: 'Hitchcock's film "Rear Window" and the Cold War.' Or: 'Moby Dick and the Cold War'. Or: 'The Lesbian Novel and the Cold War'. Or: 'Home, Garden and the Bikini – Cold War and Gender Stasis.' (I have invented these examples, but not out of thin air.)

2. Strangulation of the subject under discussion by means of esoteric jargon clogged with abstraction, nouns tortured into verbs, cinematic metaphors, or website prose. 'Cold War culture' has become something of a playground in Critical Studies departments where closed linguistic systems thrive. I have not invented the following examples, all noted down in the course of a single conference in the USA: 'Lacanian overview', 'surplus surveillance', 'modes of enframement', 'process of eventuation', 'the single-basket effect', 'alternative orders of credulity' [sic. 'credibility'] and, of course, the ever-present, all-purpose 'hegemonic gaze'.

3. The 'covert action' and (related) 'secret state' mythologies. For Cold War liberals, conservatives and anti-communist historians, the entire Soviet experience and its Western believers more or less boil down to Hiss, the Rosenbergs, the Cambridge Five, the KGB, the Venona tapes and archival exposure. For revisionists and heirs to the New Left, it is much the same thing in reverse: the Western position in the Cold War

boils down to the CIA, the FBI, covert subsidies, false fronts, dummy foundations, and Machiavellian expropriation of innocent art by the pax (or pox) americana.

4. Following on from (3), it is not the book, painting or symphony which counts in the last analysis, but who paid for the printer's ink, the canvas and the orchestra's travelling expenses. Scholars should therefore devote themselves to archival exposure of who paid the piper, and more or less forget about the tune, the big ideas which dominated Cold War culture in the 1950s and 1960s.

5. Presentation of a cultural Cold War from which one side (the Russians, their satellites and their friends in the West) have strangely vanished. No sign or sound of them. It is America vs Amerika.

Broadly speaking, the October 2001 conference held at the Roosevelt Study Center, Middelburg, entitled 'Boundaries to Freedom: the Cultural Cold War in Europe, 1945–60', emerged with 90–100 per cent scores in avoiding Perils 1 and 2 (pseudo-subjects and jargon), probably achieved 50–50 with respect to Perils 3 and 4 (the covert action/secret state domain and the 'who paid the piper?' domain), and scored really low only in terms of Peril 5 –*gdye Russkii Vopros?*

This deficiency was mentioned by more than one participant during the final discussion; clearly it has been taken to heart by the organizers, who have restyled the conference 'the Cultural Cold War in Western Europe' for the purposes of publication. I do not think this solves the problem. As many of the best contributions to the conference demonstrated, one cannot understand the cultural Cold War in Western Europe without constant attention to America's role, purposes and influence. Still less can one understand the culture of Britain, France, Italy and Germany in the age of Orwell, Sartre, Guttuso, and Brecht without studying how the 'Meeting on the Elbe' (*Vstrecha na Elba*, as Grigorii Aleksandrov called his film) turned sour.

Absent Russians and East Germans are not merely temporarily missing characters (displaced persons) in the drama; by their absence they invite us to re-invent a Cold War and its attendant culture in a tradition set in motion by the revisionist historians of the New Left era; a Cold War instigated exclusively by a belligerent, expansionist USA and its client states, a Cold War which was really about retaining overseas empires, expanding global markets, suppressing blacks, battering workers, and keeping women in their place. I have to say that in my experience this kind of 'Cold War' invariably yields to the real one as soon as the Russia and East Europe specialists show up. They can spell 'gulag'. Unfortunately, they were not among us at the Roosevelt Study Center.

At the risk of tedium, I want to restate this from a slightly different angle. At any Cold War culture conference organized by the heirs and successors of the Congress for Cultural Freedom, or Americans for Democratic Action, or the Royal Institute for International Affairs, the Soviet and East European component would be exceedingly prominent. Therefore the composition of such a conference becomes an ideological question — even if unintentionally and on the back of what appear to be a series of personal accidents. A Cold War conference without 'the Russians' (I mean, of course, experts on the Soviet Union) is invariably inclining towards becoming an anti-American, anti-Western convocation before the first word is uttered.

As soon as we hear from Zhdanov's legions, the fierce voices of *Literaturnaia gazeta*, *Sovetskaia muzyka*, *Iskusstvo*, *Kul'tura i zhizn'* and *Neues Deutschland*, we begin to ask ourselves the currently unfashionable question: was the cultural Cold War about — perhaps very much about — what Orwell and those CIA-funded, Congress for Cultural Freedom bastards like Arthur Koestler and Sidney Hook said it was about? Were Merle Fainsod, Isaiah Berlin, Hannah Arendt, George Kennan and Bertram Wolfe and the other proponents of 'totalitarian' theory perhaps more right than wrong?

I came away from the Roosevelt Study Center conference richly rewarded and much stimulated by new contacts and friendships. I am much indebted to Hans and Giles for their hospitality and excellent arrangements.

[David Caute's book *Cold War Culture. Stage, Screen, Music, Ballet, Expo, Art and Ideology. USA-USSR-Europe*, will be published by Oxford University Press in 2003.]

Illustrations

Acknowledgments

The origins of this volume lie with a conference co-organized by the Roosevelt Study Center, a research institute on twentieth-century American history located in the Netherlands, and the Netherlands Institute for War Documentation (NIOD). It was held in Middelburg in October 2001.

The NIOD and the RSC are 'sister institutes' that share a single parent who is their main sponsor: the Royal Netherlands Academy of Arts and Sciences. The Royal Academy has stimulated the initiative of joint programs between these institutes. The conference was the first result of this co-operation.

A conference is never a product of one person, or in this case one institute. The conference organizers Hans Krabbendam and Giles Scott-Smith greatly benefited from the expertise of Peter Romijn, Paul Koedijk, and Jolande Withuis. Special thanks also to those who gave their support to this project from the very beginning: Scott Lucas, Frances Stonor Saunders, Hugh Wilford, and especially Richard J. Aldrich.

Financial support was granted by the Royal Netherlands Academy of Arts and Sciences, the American Embassy in The Hague, the Franklin and Eleanor Roosevelt Institute in New York, the Netherlands Institute for War Documentation, and the Roosevelt Study Center.

Abbreviations

AAPC	Anglo-American Productivity Council
AAUW	American Association of University Women
ACUE	American Committee on United Europe
AFL	American Federation of Labor
ATA	Atlantic Treaty Association
BP	Bureau Politique (of the PCF)
BPC	British Productivity Council
CCF	Congress for Cultural Freedom
CGIL	Confederazione Generale del Lavoro [Italian]
CGT	Confédération Générale du Travail [French]
CIA	Central Intelligence Agency
CIERP	Centre Intersyndical d'Etudes et de Recherche de Productivité [French]
CIO	Congress of Industrial Organizations [American]
CISL	Confederazione Italiana Sindicati Lavoratori [Italian]
COSEC	Coordinating Secretariat [of ISC]
CPN	Communistische Partij Nederland [Dutch]
CRD	Cultural Relations Department [British]
DAU	Declaration of Atlantic Unity
DGB	Deutsche Gewerkschaftsbund [German]
DKP	Danmarks Kommunistiske Parti [Danish]
ELEC	European League for Economic Cooperation
EPA	European Productivity Agency
ERP	European Recovery Program
FBI	Federal Bureau of Investigation [American]
FDJ	Freie Deutsche Jugend [East German]
FO	Force Ouvrière [French]
FRUS	Foreign Relations of the United States
FTUC	Free Trade Union Committee
FYSA	Foundation for Youth and Student Affairs
GDR	German Democratic Republic
HIACOM	Harvard International Activities Committee [American]
HICOG	High Commission in Germany [American]

HMG	His Majesty's Government
IAW	International Alliance of Women
ICD	Information Control Division [American]
ICFTU	International Confederation of Free Trade Unions
IFBPWC	International Federation of Business and Professional Women's Clubs
INU	Inostrannoye Upravleniye (Foreign Intelligence Service of the MGB)
IOJ	International Organization of Journalists
IPD	Information Policy Department [British]
IRD	Information Research Department [British]
ISC	International Student Conference
IUS	International Union of Students
IUSY	International Union of Socialist Youth
KGB	Komitet Gosudarstvennoi Bezopastnosti (Committee of State Security)
MFA&A	Museum, Fine Arts, and Archives Section [of OMGUS]
MGB	Ministerstvo Gosudarstvennoi Bezopastnosti (Ministry of State Security)
MI5	Security Service [British]
MoMA	Museum of Modern Art [New York]
NALSO	National Association of Labour Student Organisations
NATO	North Atlantic Treaty Organization
NCFE	National Committee for Free Europe
NCSS	National Council for Social Service
NGO	Non-Governmental Organization
NPC	National Productivity Center
NPC	NATO Parliamentarians Conference
NSA	National Student Association [American]
NUS	National Union of Students [British]
OECD	Organisation for Economic Co-operation and Development
OMGUS	Office of the Military Government of the United States, Germany
OPC	Office of Policy Coordination [American]
ORIT	Interamerican Organization of Workers
PCF	Parti Communiste de France
PCI	Partito Comunista Italiano
PEN	Poets, Essayists, and Novelists
PPMI	Perhimpunan Pemuda Mahasiswa Indonesia [student union]
PTAD	Productivity and Technical Assistance Department [American]
PWE	Political Warfare Executive [British]

RFE	Radio Free Europe
RIAS	Radio in the American Sector [of Germany]
RKW	Rationalisierungs Kuratorium der Deutschen Wirtschaft
ROTC	Reserve Officer Training Corps [American]
SFC	Society for Freedom and Culture [Danish]
SED	Sozialistischen Einheitspartei Deutschland [East German]
SFS	Sveriges Förenade Studentkårer [Swedish]
SIS	Secret Intelligence Service [British]
SMAP	Student Mutual Assistance Program
SOE	Special Operations Executive [British]
SOE	Special Operations Executive [British]
TUC	Trade Union Congress [British]
UIL	Unione Italiana del Lavoro
UJRF	Union de la Jeunesse Républicaine de France
UNESCO	United Nations Education, Scientific and Cultural Organization
UNR	Union pour la Nouvelle République [French Gaullist Party]
USIA	United States Information Agency
USIS	United States Information Service
VDS	Verband Deutscher Studentenschaften
VoA	Voice of America
WAY	World Assembly of Youth
WFDY	World Federation of Democratic Youth
WFTU	World Federation of Trade Unions
WIDF	Women's International Democratic Federation
WOMAN	World Organization of Mothers of All Nations
WSSF	World Student Service Federation
WUUN	Women United for United Nations

1

Introduction: Boundaries to Freedom

HANS KRABBENDAM AND
GILES SCOTT-SMITH

In recent years, aided by the end of the Cold War itself, there has been a renewed interest in the wider social, political, and cultural implications and consequences of Cold War policies in the West. In particular, this has generated a re-evaluation of the relations between cultural activities and political agendas, and a broader understanding of the uses (and abuses) of power. As historian Tony Shaw has put it in a recent review article, 'virtually everything, from sport to ballet to comic books and space travel, assumed political significance and hence potentially could be deployed as a weapon both to shape opinion at home and to subvert societies abroad.'[1]

The predominant focus of this volume is on the relationship between the United States and the countries of Western Europe, since the anti-communist security alliance between them affected a broad range of policy areas. The essays are thus connected by the issue of what freedom and free society actually meant in opposition to the Soviet-communist alternative, and how Western Europe in the period 1945–1960 was a battleground for the shaping of democratic societies. This was the phase during which the infrastructure of the Cold War was created: the organizations, the policy directives, the mobilization of groups in civil society – processes often put in motion by veterans from World War II who saw the Cold War as an extension of the same struggle. It was a time that represented idealism and creativity as much as fear and risk, motives which mingled in an unprecedented expansion of governmental activity and private initiative that began to blur the lines between state and civil society. In the words of Scott Lucas, while billions may have been spent on military hardware, 'all this was meaningless if populations did not endorse and, in some cases, proselytize the values that proved their superiority'.[2] The powers of persuasion (and manipulation) were certainly employed by both East and West, however different the end goals, levels of subtlety, and relative merits actually were.

In 1947, Melvin J. Lasky, Berlin correspondent for the *Partisan Review* and in 1950 co-founder of the Congress for Cultural Freedom, expressed his conviction about the commitment of western opinion leaders to the Cold War effort as follows: 'The mere announcement of fact and truth is, unfortunately, not enough. The facts must illustrate, must dramatize, must certainly be timed; our truth must be active, must enter the contest, it cannot afford to be an Olympian bystander'.[3] Twenty years later, historian Christopher Lasch criticized this involvement of intellectuals in an article reflecting on the allegations of their CIA connections: 'The campaign for "cultural freedom" revealed the degree to which the values held by intellectuals had become indistinguishable from the interests of the modern state – interests which intellectuals now served even while they maintained the illusion of detachment.[4] Yet the positions of Lasky and Lasch should not represent the whole debate. As Michel Foucault recognized, power is not simply a negative force: 'What makes power hold good, what makes it accepted, is simply the fact that it doesn't only weigh on us as a force that says no, but that it traverses and produces things, it induces pleasure, forms knowledge, produces discourse.'[5] Such an insight highlights the complexities involved when examining the culture-politics relationship. It can also offer paths for alternative interpretations of the Cold War and its cultural consequences.

HISTORIOGRAPHY

Historiographically, the Cold War has moved through several phases. The orthodox view in the West that the Soviet Union and the ideology of communism were wholly to blame, the dominant perspective up until the early 1960s, was eventually challenged by critiques from New Left and other historians who focused their attention instead on the American military-industrial complex as an equally important cause of the confrontation. Revelations about the covert actions of the CIA, which began to emerge in the late 1960s and early 1970s, also contributed to the sense of mistrust in the US government and marked this period off from the black-and-white perspectives of the initial post-war years. This 'revisionism' was itself followed by so-called post-revisionism and corporatism in the 1970s and 1980s, which skirted the issue of blame in favor of in-depth policy analysis, particularly on the American side, in order to balance the revisionist claims. The 1990s saw further shifts in perspective. The triumphalist attitude in the West after the communist downfall was combined with a widespread belief that the newly accessible archives in the former Eastern bloc would hold many of the answers to Cold War questions. Instead, these archives have produced as many new conundrums as they have offered glimpses of the 'truth'.[6] In contrast, in the last few years there has been a gradual increase in studies that have made use of American and European sources for a more in-depth look at the complex mix of public and private organizations that operated from the 1940s onwards. This new wave of publications have shown a more sophisticated approach, revealing the complexity of the issues, the diversity among the various nations involved, and the uses of contributions from different academic disciplines, with end results that represent a move beyond the simple question of right and wrong in the Cold War. The entry into this field by scholars from disciplines such as sociology, literature, and media studies has been complemented by a gradual (if at times surprisingly reluctant) 'cultural turn' on the part of diplomatic historians themselves, for long sufficiently occupied with the examination of inter-governmental relations alone.[7]

The papers collected in this volume represent a further development of this latest trend in historical research. The contributors here represent current European and American research that offers an important cross-section of case studies highlighting the connections between overt/covert activities and cultural/political agendas during the early Cold War. It therefore provides a valuable bridge between diplomatic history and intelligence research, fields which usually work in isolation from each other.[8] Several questions lie at the center of these contributions. What were the boundaries to freedom in the West in the early phase of the Cold War, and how were they set? Did the defenders of the principle of a free society find a balance between 'truth', freedom of information, and efforts to direct and influence opinion? How far could 'freedom' be instituted and promoted by official powers without it collapsing under its own contradictions into only a semblance (or representation) of freedom? Again to quote Tony Shaw: 'Was all culture, on both sides of the Cold War, merely an extension of politics? If so, how should this alter our perception of the conflict?'[9] This collection contributes to the increasing debate on these issues within the realms of Cold War research.

CULTURE

Using the word 'culture' for an exercise of this sort inevitably threatens definitional vagueness. Three definitions were dominant in providing a basis for this volume: firstly, the general notion of culture as a recognizable set of norms and beliefs by which a society might define itself; secondly, the forms of political culture by which different political systems define their basic values and the roles of participants; and thirdly, the domain of 'high culture', involving the positions of intellectuals and developments in the arts. As with any definitions of culture, these three dimensions are not mutually exclusive and intermingle throughout the articles presented here. The risk of having too wide a concept of culture will therefore be taken.[10] The important and multivaried dimensions of popular culture, a research area that demands a separate volume all to itself, are only represented here via references to the promotion of a more consumer-orientated society in western Europe.[11]

It must be said that the increasingly inter-disciplinary character of Cold War studies has not necessarily contributed to a greater agreement on the main issues involved. Neither has the increasingly multi-dimensional study of the cultural Cold War, as opposed to culture *in* the Cold War, been accepted by everyone as a legitimate enterprise. David Caute forcefully argues in his foreword that such research has led to a confusion, if not a *falsification* of culture and its importance, because of the constant determination to find a cold war 'smoking gun' behind all cultural activity. His critique is important, since at a certain point 'culture' collapses under the weight of investigation into merely another term for 'propaganda'. Opposing positions have arisen between those who view culture as an area of (semi-)autonomous activity, influenced by political machinations but nonetheless demonstrating its 'own' paths of development, and those who focus more on the (attempted) control of cultural messages through government- or elite-inspired behind-the-scenes manipulation. These two sides to the debate are both represented here, the former most strongly by Jessica Gienow-Hecht and the latter by Scott Lucas and Frances Stonor Saunders. The rest of the articles fall somewhere in between, but the emphasis of most of the contributors is on the attempts to 'organize culture', be that by promoting a certain belief system, establishing 'networks of influence' via institution-building, or by simply displaying cultural production as a symbol of 'freedom'.

INTELLIGENTSIA

The collection is subdivided into five parts, each covering particular aspects of the politics-culture mix in Cold War Western Europe. The first part focuses specifically on issues of autonomy and control in the cultural and political realms. In an interview with Scott Lucas, Frances Stonor Saunders talks frankly about her book, which has done so much to open these topics up for renewed debate amongst scholars and within the media, and the research that lay behind it.[12] Emphasis is given to the problem of integrity for intellectuals, and especially those connected with the management of the Congress for Cultural Freedom, who talked freedom while simultaneously walking within the lines of control as set by the CIA. Saunders argues that while one can appreciate the effects of Stalinism in causing such a balancing act in the early Cold War years, after the mid-1950s the intellectual positions taken became more and more untenable.

Opposing this view is Hugh Wilford, who has reached different conclusions from his research on the efforts of the US government to influence the British intelligentsia and the political left. Concentrating on developments in the trade union movement, in the cultural world, and in politics, Wilford demonstrates that American attempts to call a tune were often used by the British for their own ends. While it is possible to argue that American funding and organization did help British intellectuals rise to a level of international influence that they might not otherwise have reached, for instance via *Encounter* or Bilderberg, Wilford denies that this entailed a reduction in autonomy for British cultural and political life.

STATE-PRIVATE NETWORKS

Part two extends the arguments laid out in part one. Scott Lucas adds to the perspective of Saunders by confronting head-on the connection between culture, ideology, and Cold War discourse. For Lucas, much Cold War historiography has failed to grasp the scale and extent of the ideological campaign being waged by the West against the East. By developing his concept of 'state-private networks' (a theme which runs through this book), Lucas presents an analysis that flattens the state-civil society boundary and points towards the need for a more reflective understanding of what 'freedom' meant, and how 'freedom' was supposed to be secured on both sides of the Atlantic.

The next two contributions follow on from this perspective by emphasizing the difficulties of actually creating a transatlantic region based on the same values. Anthony Carew offers an overview of how the 'politics of productivity' was pursued in Western Europe via the Economic Recovery Program (Marshall Plan), and the resulting tensions between national traditions, business and labour interests, and the American drive for monetary stability and the modernization of work practices. Carew also demonstrates that although the American labour unions were essential for projecting the ERP message to European workers, the differences in opinion and approach between the American Federation of Labor (AFL) and Congress of Industrial Organizations (CIO) were considerable. American initiatives stumbled not only against European resistance but also as a result of internal divisions within their own ranks.

Valerie Aubourg complements this position with her analysis of Bilderberg and the Atlantic Institute. Both organizations have often been represented in Cold War historiography as discreet fora where the transatlantic elites could influence policy-making agendas away from democratic scrutiny. Aubourg's study instead outlines how both groups took several years to be established because of the general lack of elite interest, particularly on the side of the Americans. Even then, these efforts to create an organizational basis for 'Atlanticism' often provided an outlet for disagreement rather than agreement. Nevertheless, this offers a window onto the elite-level contacts that were established, and the interests that were at stake, in these efforts to solidify a consensus of opinion on both sides of the Atlantic.

TARGET GROUPS

Part three focuses on two target groups which the government information agencies of the leading western countries considered particularly susceptible to communist propaganda: youth and women. While there was some continuity between wartime (anti-fascist) and post-war (anti-communist) agencies, such as Britain's Cultural Relations Department (CRD), the Western initiatives after 1945 were largely a response to the already-existing networks of Soviet influence within various international civil organizations.[13]

In his essay on CRD, Richard Aldrich demonstrates how the response to Soviet influence in world youth groups shifted from aiming to influence the heavily-infiltrated World Federation of Democratic Youth towards the founding of an alternative organization. The result was the formation of the World Assembly of Youth (WAY) in 1948. Originally the CRD intended that this youth organization should become financially independent, but instead an ongoing dependency on government disbursements was established. Yet internal disputes between governmental departments, and the lack of a substantial financial commitment, led the British controlling interest in WAY to decline in the early 1950s, inevitably to be replaced by the more flush Americans.

Concerning the involvement of the United States, Karen Paget provides a detailed reconstruction of the relationship between American officials and national and international youth organizations. Of particular interest here is the claim that covert interest in youth groups began soon after World War II and not in the late 1940s as is often thought. Paget also offers an insight into the difficulties of covertly influencing democratically-controlled bodies such as the National Student Association, which occurred mainly through the recruitment of student leaders and, in the early years, via the controlling interest of the Harvard 'apparat', the International Activities Committee (HIACOM). This process led to the formation of the International Student Conference and the establishment of its Coordinating Secretariat (COSEC) in Leiden in 1952. The argument that the CIA's covert activities were a necessary measure in order to avoid the public blandishments of McCarthyism therefore does not hold for Paget, since clandestine activities in the youth field had begun much earlier than the Red Scare of the early 1950s.

It is on this point that Paget's position conflicts with that of Joel Kotek, who exactly ascribes an important role to McCarthyism in forcing a secret anti-communist agenda to be put together outside of regular democratically-monitored channels in the United States. The key event in this development was the massive Soviet-sponsored 1951 Berlin youth festival, which highlighted the influence of the USSR amongst the world's youth and offered a direct challenge to western attitudes of moral and material superiority. While the East declared triumphantly that it had gathered over one and a half million participants from around the world, the West responded by assembling a 'counter-festival' and inviting the visitors to see 'the other side'. The result was that both sides claimed 'victory' afterwards, but more significant was how the festival gave an impetus to the CIA's investment in youth affairs, mainly via the International Student Conference.

Simultaneously with the youth operations, American women also became involved in the international debate about peace, as Helen Laville explains. The experience of World War II caused many women to become involved in peace movements, yet internationally the Soviet Union again had considerable influence in this area and the response from the West took some time to develop. A significant step in this direction was the Memorial Day Statement issued in 1951 by a variety of women's groups, in direct response to the Soviet-led Peace campaign. Once an 'official' position on the definition of peace (and the vital role for women in achieving it) had been established, 'free-lance' efforts by women outside of this development (such as Dorothy Thompson's plan for a congress of women's organizations in Berlin) were frowned upon by government and 'authorized' women's groups alike. Laville's chapter offers another good example of civil society groups co-ordinating with government in order to define the limits to acceptable action and acceptable discourse within the context of the East-West confrontation.

TARGET AREAS

The essays in part four offer contrasting examples from western European countries of the importance of national social conditions for the diffusion of ideas. Marc Lazar focuses on the political and social regimes of the strongest communist parties in western Europe – in France and Italy. While outlining the different themes of these two national parties, Lazar demonstrates how the communists sought to create their own distinct 'culture' separate from (and in defiance of) the modernization/consumerist ethos being introduced from the United States. Yet despite this, polls of communist workers showed a bare preference for life in the USSR as opposed to life in the USA, and the popularity of Hollywood movies in working class areas demonstrated the pervasiveness of American popular culture and its plentiful images of satisfaction.

David Ellwood provides a useful addition to Lazar's analysis by concentrating on the American effort to modernize Italian society, politics, and industry via the European Recovery Program (ERP). Yet despite a massive investment in information programs and organizational initiatives in order to propagate the short- and long-term benefits of the Marshall Plan, the Italians remained relatively immune to the propaganda bombardment. The ERP came up against considerable resistance from sections of the government, from the Catholic Church, and from employers associations as much as from trade unions. Nevertheless, considering how Italy was widely expected to be the first West European country to go communist after World War II, it would be a mistake to write off the American efforts as having had no effect on Italian society.

The following two essays concentrate on the particular national circumstances surrounding the Congress for Cultural Freedom's efforts to establish itself in Denmark and the Netherlands. Although the Society for Freedom and Culture was founded in Denmark in 1953 by Arne Sejr, Ingeborg Philipsen argues that Sejr was effectively expanding his own covert network and was not specifically interested in the actual goals of the CCF itself. It was only after 1956 that CCF representative Jorgen Schleimann began to transform the Danish Society more towards the outlook of the CCF. However, Philipsen gives enough evidence to make it clear that the Congress was unable to establish much of a foothold in Scandinavia as a whole, and the lack of success in Denmark is demonstrative for the whole region.

Tity de Vries provides a counterpoint to Philipsen's work by concentrating on the lack of Dutch involvement within the Congress for Cultural Freedom. Via an in-depth study of the career paths of four prominent Dutch intellectuals – Alfred Mozer, Sal Tas, Henry Brugmans, and Abraham Hammacher – de Vries is able to pinpoint the deciding factors that caused the Dutch to be 'absent' from the CCF. This was in spite of the repeated efforts by the Congress in the 1950s to establish a Dutch branch. The lack of a tradition of public debate, ambivalence towards American culture, and the peculiarities of Dutch social organization all contributed to this situation. The few intellectuals with a more cosmopolitan, internationally-based outlook found themselves isolated within the Netherlands itself.

HIGH CULTURE

The final part comprises three studies in the fields of music (Jessica Gienow-Hecht), art (Cora S. Goldstein) and drama (David Monod), and their relevance within the complex nexus of cultural production and Cold War politics. Beginning with an overview of how 'culture' has been situated within Cold War historiography, Jessica Gienow-Hecht takes the example of cultural ties between Germany and the United States and argues that it is a mistake for an analysis of cultural relations in the Cold War to begin in 1945. Without an understanding of previous, pre-World War II associations, which in the American-German case went back to the mid-nineteenth century, no worthwhile understanding of international cultural relations in the Cold War can be achieved. This sets up a contrast between the cultural message of the United States to Western Europe in the 1950s – 'we are just like you' – and the Marshall Plan's socio-economic 'you can be like us' message of the late 1940s.

Concentrating on visual art, Cora Goldstein highlights the relatively late conversion of the American authorities in western Germany after the war to using the visual arts as a means to enhance the relations between Germany and the West. Goldstein asserts that the initial American sponsorship of modernist visual art in western Germany only came about through an unofficial group of American officials known as Prolog, at the end of 1946. As the struggle for allegiance in Germany increased in the late 1940s, so the American authorities there began to take a more direct involvement, in doing so stimulating free artistic expression and aiding the development of German art away from both fascist influences and the impact of the war. But the initial impulse for this support had been a private initiative, demonstrating again that the use and importance of culture in the Cold War should not be studied wholly from the perspective of governmental involvement.

David Monod provides the closing contribution with his study of the *Porgy and Bess* musical and its State Department-sponsored European tour of 1952. This production was chosen, not just because it was a fine dramatic display, but also for its theme (Afro-American culture) and for the opportunity to demonstrate the artistic prowess of Afro-Americans themselves on stage. State Department officials declared the tour to have been a great success, and on artistic grounds it was. However, the complexity of this piece of art, the specific objectives of the actors, directors, and owners, the violence of the storyline, and the autonomous interpretations of European audiences, all prevented *Porgy and Bess* from becoming purely a piece of American *agitprop*. Culture may often be put to specific uses for political reasons, but the autonomous nature of cultural production means that it just as often escapes the straightjacket of interpretation that political interests would like to impose.

CONCLUSIONS

Based on the analyses presented in this collection, the following observations can be made regarding the questions posed earlier.

First, World War II experiences provided the means and ends for fighting the Cold War, such as the determination to fight totalitarianism, the acceptance of expanded government activity, the necessity of state-private co-operation in the anti-communist campaign, and a continuity of personnel in the post-war intelligence effort. Moreover, historians of the Cold War will benefit from a longer-term perspective of cultural relations between Europe and the United States which provided a framework for post-war mutual understanding.

Second, the communist control of international civil organizations, backed by Soviet financial and administrative aid, called forth an initially defensive reaction from Western countries. This involved attempts to either wrest control from the Soviets or establish alternative organizations.

Third, the American strategy to lead and engage European countries and organizations in combating Communism was frequently thwarted by private initiatives, national elites, and local conditions. Equally important is the fact that initiatives were taken by Europeans themselves, such as the Bilderberg Group.

Fourth, in spite of the willingness of government agencies to use civil organizations for the 'battle of ideas', they also realized there were boundaries to the manipulation of independent bodies. After all, voluntary civil organizations needed to avoid the impression of political and/or state control. However, some organizations themselves wanted to support the Cold War effort of their governments on their own accord. The growing awareness of the importance of cultural factors in the Cold War confirms the interpretation that the State was only one protagonist (albeit the most powerful one) among various others.

Fifth, the seeming lack of concern about the boundaries between acceptable and unacceptable financial support offered by the CIA at the time might have been a result of the generation of the 1940s and 1950s being less suspicious of the Agency's motives, in contrast to the breakdown of the Agency's reputation in the 1960s.

Finally, the essays confirm that, in terms of interpretation, high culture occupies its own realm that cannot be easily manipulated into a propaganda device.

NOTES

1. Tony Shaw, 'The Politics of Cold War Culture', *Journal of Cold War Studies* 3/3 (2001) p.59.
2. Scott Lucas, 'Beyond Diplomacy: Propaganda and the History of the Cold War', in Gary Rawnsley (ed.) *Cold War Propaganda in the 1950s* (London: Macmillan 1999) p.11.
3. Melvin J. Lasky, 'On the Need for a New Overt Publication, Effectively American-Oriented, on the Cultural Front', 7 December 1947, OMGUS Information Control Division, National Archives RG 260 Box 246.
4. Christopher Lasch, 'The Cultural Cold War', *The Nation* (11 September 1967) p.198.
5. Michel Foucault, 'Truth and Power', in Colin Gordon (ed.) *Michel Foucault: Power/Knowledge* (New York: Harvester Press 1980) p.119.
6. See 'Soviet Archives: Recent Revelations and Cold War Historiography', *Diplomatic History* 21/2 (Spring 1997).
7. Recent symposia in *Diplomatic History* have highlighted this turn. See 'The American Century: A Roundtable (Part II)', 23/3 (Summer 1999); 'Roundtable: Cultural Transfer or Cultural Imperialism? "Americanisation in the Cold War"', 24/3 (Summer 2000).
8. On this point see for instance the argument put forward by Kenneth Osgood, 'Hearts and Minds: The Unconventional Cold War' (book review), *Journal of Cold War Studies* 4/2 (Spring 2002).
9. Shaw, 'Politics of Cold War Culture' (note 1), p.61.
10. In the words of Melvin Lasky himself, deriding the word's overuse, 'if everything or everyone has a culture, then nothing and no one has a culture'. Melvin J. Lasky, 'The Banalization of the Concept of Culture', *The Republic of Letters* 11 (2001) p.40.
11. On popular culture in the Cold War see Rob Kroes, Robert W. Rydell & Doeko F. J. Bosscher (eds.) *Cultural Transmissions and Receptions: American Mass Culture in Europe* (Amsterdam: Free UP 1993); Reinhold Wagnleitner & Elaine Tyler May (eds.) *"Here, There and Everywhere": The Foreign Politics of American Popular Culture* (Hanover, NH: UP of New England 2000).
12. Frances Stonor Saunders, *Who Paid the Piper? The CIA and the Cultural Cold War* (London: Granta 1999).
13. On Soviet influence abroad see F.C. Barghoorn, *The Soviet Cultural Offensive: The Role of Cultural Diplomacy in Soviet Foreign Policy* (Princeton UP 1960); Fernando Claudin, *The Communist Movement: From Comintern to Cominform* (Harmondsworth: Peregrine 1975); Clive Rose, *The Soviet Propaganda Network: A Directory of Organisations Serving Soviet Foreign Policy* (London: Pinter 1988); Stephen Koch, *Double Lives: Stalin, Willi Münzenberg, and the Seduction of the Intellectuals* (London: HarperCollins 1995).

PART I

Intellectuals between Autonomy and Control

2

Revealing the Parameters of Opinion: An Interview with Frances Stonor Saunders

W. SCOTT LUCAS

In 1999 Frances Stonor Saunders published Who Paid the Piper? The CIA and the Cultural Cold War *(London: Granta); in the United States the book was called* The Cultural Cold War: The CIA and the World of Arts and Letters *(New York: New Press). The book received much attention from the media and from academics. On 17 January 2002, Scott Lucas, author of* Freedom's War: The US Crusade against the Soviet Union, 1945–56 *(New York 1999) interviewed Frances Saunders about the methods of the CIA, the role of intellectuals in the political and cultural battles of the Cold War, the question of their autonomy, the need for financial support of cultural activities in the early and advanced stages of the Cold War, and the debate about the principles of intellectuals. In the second part of the interview Saunders talks about her research methods, the responses to and reception of her book in various parts of the Western world, the effects of the revelations of CIA funding, and contemporary parallels regarding (American) culture and international politics.*

* * *

WSL: In the introduction to your book you write, 'The defence mounted by custodians of the period – which rests on the claim that the CIA's substantial financial investment came with no strings attached – has to be seriously challenged. Amongst intellectual circles in America and Western Europe there persists a readiness to accept as truth the idea that the CIA was merely interested in extending the possibilities for free and democratic cultural expression. 'We simply helped people say what they would have said anyway', goes this 'blank cheque' line of defence'. (p.4) And on the next page you raise it with a question mark, 'Did this not risk producing, instead of freedom, a kind of ur-freedom, where people think they are acting freely, when in fact they are bound to forces over which they have no control?' I think it is that question of control that has been raised. Are you intending to argue in the book that it is a controlled relationship with the CIA controlling the private sphere?

FSS: It is a complex answer to a fairly direct question. I think what I try and say is that from the CIA's point of view from the very first – I quote Tom Braden, the first head of the Agency's International Organizations Division – 'When we launched in 1950, if the question of Korea had come up and if a private operation had been brought up in a sort of context that was negative to or seen to be undermining our current policy, then we would have vetoed it.' In other words, he was very clear that they had built into the equation, and as a theoretical control at least, the idea of veto.

Now I looked for concrete examples of that veto being exercised but didn't find very many. Initially, I was not disappointed but puzzled because I thought that the nature of the CIA would have been more likely, at least more tempted, to fight for some form of direct control. Then I realised the further I went on that the more I looked at these private letterheads, the more of these characters turn out to be CIA who were in fact using their covers as writers or administrators or accountants or whatever it might have been. The Congress for Cultural Freedom was flooded with CIA personnel so from an administrative level at least the Agency had absolute and effective control; at least it thought it did, and when it didn't, there are instances where they sought to re-establish it, whether it be with money or guidance, airing the themes that it wanted to have played.

It was clear from the very beginning that they had these meetings. They were very civilised and they were very much like you would expect at high table at campus: here's the theme, what do we think, and they would all have an argument about it, but the bottom line to the people who were sitting around those tables was that the CIA were very clear about what the themes were they wanted heard and more or less how they wanted them to be played. So the instances that I do uncover of control, of articles being vetoed, to me are a huge indictment because they disprove the blank cheque argument concretely.

But much more subtly and more importantly, I think, than those individuals and the limited numbers of episodes of direct control from Washington, is the way the relationship evolves between the Congress, and indeed some of its CIA personnel within it, principally Michael Josselson and his cohorts and the International Organizations Division and in turn between the IOD and the Congress's apologists in the CIA and the rest of the CIA in Washington.

I was fascinated to discover that the CIA was having to really push its case, particularly towards the early to mid 1960s, to protect its assets with other departments of the CIA and with high-level strategists in Washington. That would suggest that, in the CIA's consortium, the magazines were actually kind of developing themes in a certain way that the rest of Washington found antipathetic or uncomfortable. Its ultimate resolution lay in the theory, which I certainly was not able to prove but happen to believe it is true, that President Lyndon Johnson ordered this operation to be silenced. Now there is one of two reasons for that: either because the operation was on the verge of being exposed and the best way to deal with that kind of flak is just to cut it off yourself and carry out a damage limitation exercise, which is what Tom Braden believes, or the other line is that Johnson was deeply uncomfortable with the adherence of some of these intellectuals to CIA-funded projects at a time when dissent was growing over Vietnam, his war. 'What do you mean, these writers, they're my writers, my magazines, and they're talking out against my war?'

The second explanation is harder in a way to believe because if you look at *Encounter* and the other magazines, there is nothing, at least with hindsight that seriously challenges the American foreign policy of the period, including Vietnam. I suppose at the time that people thought that even muted criticism was pretty far out, and maybe it was in the context of *Encounter*, but it was resolutely integrated into American Cold War thinking if you read it as a political journal. People of the time didn't necessarily read it this way because it was so brilliantly disguised as a cultural journal with a capital C which also had a kind of political side. But it was a political journal with a capital P: Every document you can find about *Encounter* written by the people giving it institutional support is unequivocal about what they expected it to do. They expected *Encounter* to be a bridgehead and a vehicle, gathering accommodation for and acquiescence to the American proposition. I have no doubt about that.

So the issue of control has been used, I think, as a stick to beat me with. Tom Braden said, 'We didn't have to exercise it that often because the operation was running smoothly. We were very happy with it, we were very proud of it.'

There is stuff on Steven Spender, the British poet who was co-editor of *Encounter,* that I didn't put in the book. He's sent off at the beginning in the middle to late 1950s because they want to go to India, they want to go to all these places where *Encounter* was designed to get the biggest readership. And they're forever saying, 'God, he's going off like a loose cannon and we really ought to prepare his speeches for him and, actually, let's not send him anymore, let's get somebody else. We'll only send him if he reads from a prepared text and does not depart from it.' Where private people had information or whether it was lack of preparedness or whatever it might have been to lead them to strike out on their own, they were very, very nervous about it and tried to rein them in all the time.

WSL: Irving Kristol, the editor of Encounter, *always vehemently argued that he was independent going into the project, that he wasn't controlled. Is that a fair point?*

FSS: That probably is. It is evident from the beginning that the appointment of Kristol probably was a misjudgement on behalf of the CIA backers because he did not have the temperament to be easily controlled. You see straight away that he is disillusioned and highly irate at the idea that Paris, the headquarters of the Congress for Cultural Freedom, is dictating the editorial line to London, and there is an exchange of fiery letters between Kristol and Josselson, the chief CIA operative working with the Congress in which Kristol says, 'What are you up to? I'm choosing my own editorial line, that's why I was appointed.' What's interesting about Kristol is that he seems to quieten down for a bit after they say, 'You can piss off', basically. They threatened him with his job. And he clings on for another year and a half and he is much more quiet in that period. He is ultimately replaced with Melvin Lasky.

So he wasn't, I do not think, as far as Michael Josselson and Washington were concerned, a great appointment. It was also considered that the Rosenberg piece, the Fiedler piece, was a huge mistake. Those comments about the acoustic being wrong, about the meanness of the article, were felt by people for the whole life of the magazine. Some people never really recovered from that Rosenberg piece. So those who were not quite ready to sing from the same hymn sheet were thoroughly disenchanted. They lost – not readers, they had a fantastic readership, they had a big hit on that first issue so commercially it was a great idea – but they lost possible friends for *Encounter*. I think that was held against Kristol for a long time.

What is interesting about Kristol afterwards, though, is that he gets support from Josselson for his *Public Interest*, the magazine he sets up. Still, once he's kind of cracked what the Congress is all about, he's very happy to use it to go and suck from the teats.

WSL: Is it a negotiation between Kristol and the CIA through Josselson?

FSS: The problem with Kristol was not that he was going to undermine or veer from the line. The fact is that he wasn't as political as Josselson wanted him to be. Kristol was quite bemused by the cultural aspect of the magazine, by the idea of grafting on to the European tradition this idea of engaged

American intellectual. I do not think that he felt it was necessary in *Encounter* – though not elsewhere – to be as political as Josselson wanted him to be.

But Kristol was meant to be the Political Editor and that situation was resolved by putting Lasky, who clearly had the chance to carry not just the right political line, but the right degree of political content. There is that very, very real letter from Josselson to Spender, where Spender says, maybe it is Kristol, that this is a cultural magazine with a capital 'C'. It is not.

WSL: So that conflict between what is political and cultural is a fundamental problem in the Cold War?

FSS: That's one of my main problems with *Encounter* magazine. People who were supplying these fantastic articles – you know, no one can argue with the sort of calibre and memorable contributions on the cultural front – were there to supply a kind of veneer, a cultural window dressing. The culture was the Trojan horse and within it was the secretly carried political agenda.

WSL: So Josselson got it right in the end? Politics and culture are connected.

FSS: Absolutely, but for those who wrote for *Encounter* who wanted to resist the politicisation of every aspect of culture, they felt there was a place they could go and just write about the great Russian writers and they could write in a way that wasn't beholden to any kind of party. What they didn't realise, and this is what the great deception was, was that the context within which those articles were placed firmly established them as political even if they were written with a disengaged cultural view. So the engagement of people who didn't necessarily want to be engaged in that struggle or on that agenda, that was the problem. And of course these people made it very clearly felt when the whole thing was revealed. In some cases before it was revealed.

WSL: So I guess an example would be Bertrand Russell being named as an honorary president of the Congress for Cultural Freedom?

FSS: Absolutely. They were so clever. All of those invitations to grace the letterhead were incredibly carefully considered.

WSL: Let me ask you about the 'they' because this is a little bit unclear to me. We can definitely go and say when the International Organizations

Division is set up, here's Braden. Beyond Braden, we could probably identify Allen Dulles, but I become a little bit unclear when we get beyond Braden who the 'they' are. Who are the strategists?

FSS: Braden is, by his own admission, not the kind of person who really knows Braque from a bale of hay. He's worked in the Museum of Modern Art, he's certainly a cultural sophisticate in terms of the European intellectual scene, but he wasn't the one gifted with these great contacts and insights, it was Josselson. The early group, I think, is quite clearly identified in the book, it is Josselson, it is Lasky, it is Koestler initially. It is that inner core, that *apparat* that organizes and launches the Congress in 1950. Others like Denis de Rougemont then fall away because they are marginalized like Koestler. Koestler was ruthlessly treated.

WSL: By the CIA or by other intellectuals?

FSS: By the Congress for Cultural Freedom *apparat*, I'm sure responding to the CIA's concerns, Frank Wisner in particular, that this guy was far too vocally hard-line anti-communist, and that he was driving away that heart of the constituency they were trying to appeal to, which is the moderate non-communist Left group. So he was got rid of straight away. This was his baby, he worked incredibly hard on this, and straight after the launch in 1950, you see signs that Koestler is being got rid of and he is disposed of quite thoroughly.

WSL: Is it Josselson leading this or is it people like Brown (European representative of the American Federation of Labor) and other 'private' members of the apparat?

FSS: Brown wasn't private. He was the first CIA link man. He funnelled the CIA dollars in these brown envelopes handed over at these gay night clubs in Paris. He financed the Congress until the CIA was able to get a proper cover and a proper financing apparatus in position. There are all sorts of stories, very well researched by Tony Carew, about how Brown himself was a loose cannon and he was going off with his own agenda and Brown loved stirring CIA triangles. It is a fascinating story, full of tension and distrust and suspicion and all those things.

His role at the beginning of the Congress is absolutely crucial. Again, I do not think Brown is saying, you have to get rid of Lasky in 1950. He might have been the messenger boy, but he's not the person making those decisions. Diana Josselson, wife of Michael Josselson, was very clear about Brown's significance to Josselson, who sort of had a sneaking admiration and fondness for him although Brown was absolutely antipathetic to everything Josselson stood for and everything he believed in. The guy was organizing thuggery in Marseilles. He was just not up Josselson's street.

I almost feel like apologising for descending to the level of character and motivation to the degree that I am, but actually this is a story about, for me, what motivated these people, what their psychological backgrounds and make-up were, why they made the decisions that they did. I think that personalities may be very unfashionable in academic histories, but I think personalities are hugely important.

I do not think that there is any doubt that Josselson was not going to take any advice from Brown. Josselson may have taken orders indirectly from Washington, in terms of 'here's the money, now do this, that, and the other', and then Josselson would have fought his corner. You know Josselson fought very hard to maintain and evolve the Congress' interest against what he thought, rightly in some cases, was the leaden, flat-footed approach of some of his colleagues in Washington. He had a heart attack at one point, he has such a ferocious row with these guys who are trying to tell him what to do and he knows that they are wrong.

WSL: The book seems to be very sympathetic to Josselson.

FSS: Yes.

WSL: You actually seem to like Josselson.

FSS: There was one criticism, I cannot remember by whom, one reviewer who said that it was too sympathetic to Josselson, and that this was because I was relying too heavily on Diana Josselson as a source, which I suppose is true. I was very clear when I interviewed her that I wasn't going to give her any control over what I said, but I would take on board her comments or whatever. And I did. I showed her some pieces and she made valuable corrections. Factual errors I had made, whatever.

I think that Josselson was in an impossible position. If you read his testimony, it is very moving, his 20, 30 pages that he left in his personal papers which are now in the Harry Ransom Center at the University of Texas. He wrote that for future consumption, obviously. He confesses to his gross disillusionment with the misdirection of US foreign policy in the mid to late 1960s. He's in a terrible position, and all he is trying to do is salvage the reputation of the Congress and indeed the people within it from the savaging that he knows they're going to get when these sorts of things are exposed. One of the reasons he knows it's all going to crumble is because the foreign policy is going in a direction that these magazines and this organization cannot carry, they just simply cannot carry the argument any more. And he says, we started with a great sense of – he never uses the crude terms of manifest destiny – this great promise, a manifest sense of the good that could be achieved.

We end with reckless, misguided, wanton mistakes in US foreign policy. Here's a man who's sick to the heart of what's happening. I think he was an idealist, and I think he was naive in lots of ways. That sets him back in wanting to replace, you know, the West's dependence on the Middle East for oil with atomic power, which is wonderfully idealistic.

WSL: To take it back to control, it is not simply that Washington is handing down the guidelines and they are implemented just like that. Josselson is interpreting or trying to interpret.

FSS: Braden is a very good delegator. He sets this thing up, he has got his man in Paris, he's got his case officers on his man in Paris, he's quite happy with the operation. Fine. He gets replaced by someone called Cord Meyer who cannot work like that, who issues directives left, right, and centre, who is known as being a kind of ruthless operator. He's a very different mould to Braden. And this is where the problem starts for Josselson. Suddenly, having been almost autonomous, he's in a chain of command, and where you see the kind of mushrooming of CIA personnel and controls where the foundations are put in place rather than this haphazard set-up, where there is no accounting at all, just the cash is being handed over – Marshall Plan counterpart funds, all of that stuff – where you see all of these things becoming much more systematically and ruthlessly established is under Cord Meyer.

WSL: I assume that Meyer's staff in Washington, rather than Josselson, would become the controlling element.

FSS: Absolutely. Diana Josselson says at one point there is all these CIA people all over the place, and he's having to deal with them. They're just sort of arriving in the Paris office saying, 'I'm here to do this, that, and the other', and he's like, 'These people are getting in my hair.'

WSL: I had always dated the increased CIA control from the late 50s.

FSS: Well, Josselson starts playing a game. He starts trying to give them the impression that they're getting what they want. So they can report back to Washington and file their secret report and everything else but he is just giving them a bit of pablum to chew over, so he is a clever operator. You know, if anyone should be identified as difficult to control, in a sense it was Josselson. Do not forget that Josselson is not the only one, Lasky is involved.

Lasky is a very sharp sword with which to sort of cut around the Gordian knot of Josselson's manoeuvring with Washington. Lasky is answering to Washington, there is no doubt in my mind about that. Why else would the CIA man who recruited him tell me he recruited him? I do not understand why the CIA would bother to invent the recruitment of Lasky.

WSL: But is Lasky a contract officer?

FSS: He is fully paid, his salary is paid by the CIA through *Encounter* magazine, prior to that through *Der Monat,* the monthly journal in Germany edited by Lasky.

WSL: So you call it contract in the sense whether it is on a rolling basis or whether he is on a more permanent basis, Lasky is definitely being paid. He is a CIA officer.

FSS: Braden says – the quote is in the book – that 'he's working for me and he is paid by me.'

WSL: So when Braden says, 'We did put our own man into Encounter*', it is Lasky whom he put in in 1958?*

FSS: Yes.

WSL: More generally, beyond the Encounter *case, I am wondering if the CIA moves more aggressively in the late 1950s to put its own people inside organizations.*

FSS: Another very interesting thing about control, this whole idea about patronage and what does it mean. Here's a very good example which I think reinforces my case. International PEN, an organization promoting the freedom of the writer, exists. It is exactly the kind of organization that the CIA said it wanted when it created the Congress for Cultural Freedom. So there is already an organization that's dedicated to the putative aims of the Congress for Cultural Freedom. It is not *parti pris*, it is there to defend freedom of expression, writers regardless of their political, ethnic, religious, or whatever hue. There it is, languishing due to lack of funds, but by the mid 1960s, it is really well-established as the most significant international writers' organization despite the competition from the Congress.

They, the CIA, are all over it like a rash. Suddenly they want to get Arthur Miller elected President. They have their guy, David Parker in

London, who is being controlled by Keith Botsford. The question is: if this organization already exists and is doing its good work, why are they trying to penetrate it, why are they tumbling in with personnel trying to buy in to PEN with quite significant donations to the American Centre in order to get the first meeting in 42 years of International PEN in the United States, which it does in New York in 1965–66 when Conor Cruise O'Brien makes that fantastic counter-appearance at New York University and makes the speech about the Jekyll and Hyde nature of the US government? I'm not sure how one can defend the altruistic line if you see an organization like PEN, which is well able to stand up on its own two feet by then, being penetrated by the CIA which also seeks to control its agenda.

WSL: Some might find it strange that the CIA would try to promote Miller, who is usually seen as a critic of US foreign policy.

FSS: He's got the best explanation for it. He suspects, he says in his memoirs, that they were using him as a kind of bridgehead to get into the Eastern Bloc, which they failed to do. PEN is ahead of the Congress in terms of this intellectual détente and the necessity of genuine proper exchange going into Eastern Europe and vice versa and talking to people. Because when the Congress has tried to do it, they have got these guys in their serge suits and they are clearly stooges. Quite rightly so, the Eastern European representatives say we do not want to talk to these guys, these are not genuine representatives of our intellectual brothers behind the Eastern bloc, behind the Iron Curtain. So what PEN offers is a way in that the Congress has not been able to achieve and Arthur Miller is a perfect figurehead for that, because he has good credibility.

WSL: Just to be clear. Is Miller witting or unwitting?

FSS: I believe he is unwitting and he expresses reservations about it in his memoirs and he reflects that he had reservations at the time. It is interesting that he never goes back to them. He says, 'Our guys, our boys from the State Department or possibly the CIA might be stirring the stew.' He does not go back to it later in the memoirs. Go back for one second to Hugh Wilford. What is his argument in his work on British intellectuals in the Cold War?

WSL: It is interesting because it is not a straightforward dismissal of 'Who Paid the Piper?'. What I think he is doing is two things: one, he is making the argument that certain officials who were instrumental in liaising with the British were not in fact CIA, so he is saying there were other levels of government co-operation...

FSS: Overt?

WSL: Yes, the Labour Attaché was indeed the Labour Attaché in these operations and that is not a CIA involvement. The second level is to argue that there is an autonomy on the part of the British and that those people, whether they be British politicians, whether they be British writers or whatever, did maintain a level of their own interest and that they could...

FSS: But that is not controversial. That's built into the very first provision of the CIA involvement, which is that autonomy, not just the semblance of it, but autonomy should be preserved because autonomy is going to give the greatest credence to the independence of these organizations. But it is also quite clearly defined, that if the autonomy takes people into areas of direct conflict with American interest, then that autonomy should in some way be curtailed. And I have always said that this was not some sort of ventriloquist act except in some cases – there are clearly some pieces planted as certain times and they actually were penned by CIA agents, but that's minimal and almost insignificant.

Of course there is autonomy and it was built in from the beginning. That's why I say the autonomy is part of the equation and it is ringed, even if the individual writer does not know that one step beyond the views he's expressing is an invisible ring or wall or fence that says, 'Beyond this, you do not go.' The argument is that he hasn't got to that stage and he's fine and expressed what he wanted to express freely. The problem that lots of writers had was knowing that in theory if they'd gone beyond that, they would have been stopped or their articles would have been dropped. It is interesting that since I published this book, I have had countless letters from people saying, 'I never really understood why my piece against party policy on the labour market wasn't accepted. I always just got fobbed off and I now realise or believe that the reason why it wasn't accepted was because they didn't want to hear that.'

There was a kind of censorship by omission if you like. It never actually often came to that, you just didn't run the piece, you just said the pages were full. Magazines do that all the time, they have their own sort of culture, but what I'm saying is that most magazines have a culture which is quite easy to identify, and if you agree with it, you go with it, and if you do not agree with it, you do not. If you want to write for Rupert Murdoch that's fine, I have got no objections to that, you know what you're doing. But if Murdoch is hiding behind subsidiaries and you do not know he is there, then you have the right to say, 'I'm one of those people who do not want to take Murdoch's side and I do not like the overall agenda even if the piece I was writing would have been accepted and would have been accepted in its entirety without a single cut. I do not want to contribute to that overall agenda.' That's the issue.

WSL: So the parameters of opinion are set?

FSS: Some writers would say, 'I never had anything published in *Encounter* I didn't mean, I didn't want to stand by or believe in and want to see printed.' The self-same writers would say, 'However, if I'd known at the time what *Encounter*'s institutional backing was, I would not have published it there.'

WSL: That's interesting because you're saying that some people could be autonomous, but it is not just a question of whether they're automonous but whether they're cognizant of State involvement.

FSS: I think so. It is not just about the words you put on paper. It is also about where they're put, the context.

WSL: So if Encounter *had been funded overtly by the US Government and if the CCF had been overtly supported by the US Government...*

FSS: I would have no problem with that.

WSL: You would have no problem with it?

FSS: No problem with it. I have no problems with the United States Information Agency – I would not have been personally interested in going on a USIA tour of the Soviet Union or wherever it might be, but that's a personal choice. If intellectuals wanted to, as Dwight Macdonald said, choose one lesser evil over the other, I choose the West – fine. And if that's the way they felt it was best to put forward their views and acquire an international audience for their ideas which they would not otherwise have had, that would be fine. And those options were available.

There is another argument which is that the institutions like the USIA suffered hugely as a result of this competition from this covert CIA operation, which was milking the best writers and the best performers and the best names to these more secret endeavours simply because these people had no problem writing for *Encounter* when they didn't know it was CIA but they might have a problem writing for the USIA. There was also glamour attached to *Encounter* that USIA by definition could never achieve. So those forms are out there, they are available. Let people say, 'This is what we think is best about what we have.' But of course we know why they didn't, because if you did openly and you did it in the democratic fashion, then democracy produces its own checks and balances and then Congressman George Dondero would have got up and said, 'We're not spending taxpayers' money on this type of stuff.' The CIA's own argument for going covert is that its own democratic procedures had to be suspended, because it didn't allow for this kind of operation.

WSL: I was going to put to you Braden's argument, 'We weren't being evil, we weren't being manipulative. We had to go covert because we couldn't go overt.' So he presents it as a defence.

FSS: Yeah, he does, and I think that you could make that argument. I think I am fairly magnanimous in giving voice to or reflecting, as much as I can, the view that in those early years that it was important to do it and that, if the only way to do it was covertly, then it had to be done covertly, because otherwise nothing would be done at all and everyone was a Cold Warrior then. My argument and my problem is that no one ever sat down and really considered the philosophical, the moral, not to mention the practical kind of dyslexia that was built into the whole proposition, the Jesuitical means justify the ends argument. And at no point did anybody successfully say, 'If we go on doing this, we will end up jeopardizing the very things we are trying to attain.'

WSL: Even Josselson?

FSS: Josselson had great misgivings by the end, and I accept there were some other people within the CIA who were going back to Washington and saying, 'Let's pack up our tent now.' After Soviet leader Nikita Khruschev came to power, as early as that, they were saying, 'Let's pack up, let's cut the strings, and let these people out on their own. They're launched, and if we stay with them, we'll end up sinking them by association.' Which is exactly what happened. Now those voices weren't listened to.

WSL: You may have sympathy for Josselson not just because you interviewed his widow...

FSS: He genuinely understood. He was trying, from quite an early date, to keep his CIA colleagues and paymasters at bay, from putting their grubby hands all over the Congress. Now they couldn't keep from doing it, why? Having defended it so vigorously, they had to make sure their investment, intellectual and otherwise, in this operation was closely protected, but secondly, at a time when the CIA was just losing quids down on everything and its public image was black, this was the only operation they had, at least internally, that they could be proud of, that they thought was working. That's why they won't let go of it.

WSL: You can understand what Braden does. I assume you do not really have a problem with an unwitting intellectual who is in CCF or Encounter, *but is it safe to say then that you have problems with the witting intellectual?*

FSS: Yes. I do for a whole variety of reasons. One, because as well as the intellectual inconsistency – you can make it more if you want, but let's just call it intellectual – is it possible to defend Ezra Pound by separating his verse from his persona? Saying they are two separate things and that an autonomous aesthetic has to be defended by any freedom-loving democracy, this is essential and this is the opposite to what totalitarian structures do. Right, and so let's defend him, he's the only American accused of treason at wartime, he's been sitting in this cage at Pisa, and he's brought over and he ends up in the loony bin or whatever. So there you go, they give him the Bollingen Award for Poetry in 1948.

Likewise when Herbert von Karajan wants to come and conduct in New York and the Jewish lobby gets up and says, 'This man has a hugely ambiguous relationship, as yet unresolved with the Nazi party, et cetera, et cetera, we do not want him to conduct,' the leading American officials say, 'No, no, these are two completely separate issues, you do not understand, that's one thing that should be dealt with in one respect, and this is another thing.' The opposite is the case with this smear campaign against the poet Pablo Neruda, a vocal Marxist. 'In a war, all is fair,' says John Hunt, the CIA officer overseeing the Congress for Cultural Freedom. This guy Neruda was apparently using his poetry to celebrate the values and agenda that we were fighting against tooth and nail, therefore, it was absolutely fair to smear the man and his poetry and to link the two.

I just do not think you can think both ways. I think you either have an absolute standard whereby you say the aesthetic is autonomous or you do not. There is a kind of opportunism there which makes me distrust those kinds of intellectual. Now most of those, not all of them but most of them, were also the ones who, where they were witting, could make the same argument for wittingly accepting CIA patronage, which was, 'This is a war, you know. Nothing's perfect but in a war, it is perfectly alright to oppose unfreedom and state manipulation and intervention with a kind of diluted form of that, which is taking money from the government and saying that you're not, which is taking a degree of control from the US State and saying you're not'. This is what they were wittingly engaged in doing, they knew when they sat down at the table with CIA people that the CIA people were at the very least hoping to have that guidance acted upon in the magazines. The money did not come unconditionally. There is plenty of evidence for that. When the CIA thought it wasn't getting a return on its investment, there were problems with money.

WSL: So Nikolas Nabokov, the General Secretary of the CCF is witting?

FSS: Definitely, yeah. Loved it, yeah, wanted to be in the game. He didn't pass the security test for employment by the US Government – so this was a kind of palliative.

WSL: Raymond Aron?

FSS: Yes.

WSL: Denis de Rougemont?

FSS: Absolutely. De Rougemont was, I'm sure, witting from the very beginning, he was brought in, he was told what was going on, because he also had that European Centre of Culture which was receiving support, he was closely involved with the technical financial apparatus. Aron, on the other hand, I think was probably told by French intelligence because at one point they come in and say, 'The Congress is rumbled.' It is rumbled and Lawrence de Neufville – the CIA officer supervising operations from the Paris station – is very good on this, he says, 'What happens if we go into Paris and technically we have this arrangement like we do with the Brits which is that we're allies and we cannot just order all these covert operations on French soil without at least informing the French government,' and they do not, and they get blown. The kind of deal is that the French have been allowed to put two people in the Congress, but I cannot think of either of their names at this moment.

John Hunt is clear when they had that final meeting to tender his and Josselson's resignation, come clean about what had happened, there was a furious argument and Aron went out and slammed the door. Because the problem for him was that his reputation in French cultural and political spheres was now seriously undermined.... Hunt left me in no doubt that Aron knew, but whether he knew from Day One I do not know.

WSL: The new book by Giles Scott-Smith, if I read it correctly, seems to make a slightly different argument on the control and autonomy issue, that there was a genuine wish to defend the cause of intellectual freedom amongst European intellectuals.

FSS: Absolutely.

WSL: Although he is not explicit in his book, I think there is an implicit response to what you are saying, that the focus on the CIA's role denigrates this as a motive.

FSS: I can see that there is some justification to this point. I said early on that this book was a corrective to the official history of the Congress for Cultural Freedom by Peter Coleman. He had access to the Congress for Cultural Freedom papers and the *Encounter* papers, which have never surfaced by the way. I have to make an assumption that Melvin Lasky has a lot of the *Encounter* papers. Stephen Spender had some but was haphazard in keeping an archive, and in fact when this whole debacle happened concerning revelations of CIA support of *Encounter* in the mid-1960s, someone said to Stephen, 'Get your stuff out of the loft'. You know, his loft was broken into.

I found some papers in Reading University, which Coleman does not refer to, and which provide a link with Warburg. Coleman says, almost in his opening page, that having tried to investigate the CIA link and got nowhere with the Freedom of Information Act, this was in any case immaterial because the Congress existed in and of itself and has to be viewed on its own merits. So I said I didn't think it was right, unless you bought into the myth of the blank cheque – which if you do, then fine, do not bother spending weeks and weeks in archives in Abilene, Kansas, I do not recommend it to anyone, but if you do, you do not have to go any further – and that's the line Coleman took, and my book was an attempt to correct that. I didn't believe the CIA was different from any other big government department or indeed private corporation, they make an investment and they seek a return. And I couldn't believe the sort of naiveté or the disinterest, if you like, of Coleman when he said that he didn't think it was truly important, the CCF got the money and that was it. And I just didn't believe it, and I'm sure I was right not to believe it.

Does it denigrate the CCF? I do not know. There is an incredible sensitivity because at one point intellectuals say, 'It is immaterial what we did, we would have done it anyway, it was in no way tainted by association with the CIA', and then they say that my book revealing the associations with the CIA is an attempt to denigrate and taint what they did. I think this reveals a great degree of sensitivity. I do not ever say that *Encounter* didn't exist, in and of itself, as a worthy magazine. All I say is look at it and read it in the context that it was published by its managers and its backers.

WSL: Is it fair to say that Encounter *would not have existed without the CIA?*

FSS: Financially it was never ever self-supporting. Lots of magazines can stumble on for years. *Encounter* might have gone on with some official sponsorship from the British Government openly. It might have been one of those magazines that received an Arts Council grant or a Ford Foundation grant. Truth is, it needed to double its circulation to even get into the financial black, and huge numbers of copies were distributed courtesy of... You know, the deal was that in order for the British Government to get a hand in, they would get to distribute through the Information Research Department, established in 1948 to conduct 'grey' propaganda to India, Pakistan, and all those other countries where no one could afford to buy it anyway.

WSL: And if it had been supported by the British Government openly, it would have been a different magazine? In defence of intellectual freedom?

FSS: What do you think? I think so. The testimony is there of the people who did object to funding mechanisms even without having any notion or idea of control. These people's initial response was, 'I acted freely, independently, I wasn't controlled by anyone. Nonetheless, had I known I would not have been played for a sucker, I would not have written for this magazine.'

WSL: They certainly would not have published the Leslie Fiedler 1953 article on the Rosenbergs.

FSS: Exactly. I admire, am kind of bolstered by those very intellectuals who make the case for autonomy because they say, nonetheless, they would have preferred to have gone somewhere else. Dwight Macdonald famously says to Josselson, 'I say what I want to say. Do you think I'd have said it there if I'd known of covert CIA support?'

And look at that McDonald piece. I got fobbed off by everybody on that, everybody, that it was a badly-written truculent piece of anti-Americanism of the worst kind, because Dwight was drunk on olive oil and his romantics of the moment. Nonsense, it was all about the repetition, a reprise of the Kincaid Report on US prisoners in the Korean War, which they were desperate to bury, deeply embarrassed by.

Kristol, I'm sure in his own mind but he was conveniently in line with Washington on this, was determined that those reports on collapse of POW morale in Korea were not going to be aired, and the correspondence is there to prove that. But to me, he said, no, no, no, no, no, the suppression of the Macdonald essay had nothing to do with that. I have him on film saying that.

WSL: I want to pick up on the question of reception...

FSS: There is one thing I want to say, and I really want to make this clear, and I hope the book does. I completely understand the context, at least at the beginning of the Cold War, of the pressure, often self-induced, on the part of intellectuals to feel that they had to fight for the right side, that they had to speak up for the right causes. But I unequivocally say you can not have it both ways, you can not say nigh on 20, 25 years, that it is possible to go on pumping money and support into an apparatus which is claiming to be free and independent and privately sponsored. They were clear deceptions. Privately sponsored does not mean in anybody's mind State-sponsored, does it? I feel really unhappy about it.

You can wriggle around as much as you like and be very very academic about it – I do not mean that as a slight on academics, but you can be academic about how those principles can be diluted or changeable or subject to different conditions. If you make the principled stand, well, stand by it! I think that was the most important thing, the best advertisement for American intellectuals or intellectuals on the side of the West, for Pax Americana, would have been to be honest.

WSL: If I can raise a qualm about that, which has come from certain authors you have raised, you may question in retrospect the motives of the organization, but the CIA did facilitate, did foster intellectual and cultural life in Europe. Are you arguing that the CIA distorted the intellectual cultural environment?

FSS: Yes, I take the Jason Epstein line from an article in 1967 on the revelations of CIA funding. What he expresses much better than I do is that it fostered an anti-Communism that did contribute to Vietnam, an anti-Stalinism that became so rigorous and so dogmatic once it set that it made intellectuals, except those that had abandoned it dramatically, unable to accept the possibility that US foreign policy in Vietnam and China was wrong, simply wrong.

WSL: But is that a distortion in Europe as well?

FSS: Well, yes. I think the bridgehead that had been built provided US apologists with the kind of European consensus that it would not have had otherwise or would not have been so sustained and so well-nurtured and so graciously appointed, if you like. These were very, very well-established, strong journals and institutions of some public opinion by the time we get to the disastrous departures in American foreign policy, no not departures, culminations if you like. Fulbright says it and Epstein says it – I haven't invented this but it is certainly the line I take and agree with – I think that what it did, was to confuse deeply the issue of intellectual independence with the need for, which I never doubted, opposition to the Soviet Union. It confused, muddied the intellectual rules. Again, look at internal critique of the Congress itself, when they come out of that General Assembly with the statement that what's happened is they've poisoned the wells of intellectual discourse. Now, I think that if that's the Congress's own self-signed epitaph, I do not have a great opinion of it.

What I saw in Germany was really fascinating, the talks I gave, the questions that were asked, and the kind of response in the press. The Cold War is definitely still being fought there in a way that is only comparable to the way it is still being fought by a tiny, tiny calcified intellectual group in America. The Cold War is sustained still by Horowitz, Kristol, et cetera, et cetera. In Germany, unlike Spain, or France, or Italy or the UK where there is already a kind of historical resolution, the Cold War is, for the older generation certainly, still vividly felt and lived. Arguments would start between very elderly, articulate, feisty people about who did what, what it meant, and about all these issues, still very contemporary, about patronage and government support, the idea and possibility of projecting a nation through culture, et cetera, et cetera. There isn't the kind of detachment that I probably had from operating from the UK, from being a kind of innocent, if you like, in this whole story.

WSL: To my mind, you set out to write about how the CIA organized the effort, how it worked with American 'private' functionaries and with certain European allies like Nabokov, but you didn't set out to write about the European cultural scene.

FSS: No, no, and I think the two are totally inter-linked and, crucially, I do not think you can ignore one at the expense of the other. But I wanted to just kick the door in on this story and then leave the building open for everyone else to glance at the archives and come with histories of their own. Whether you agree with the line I take in the book or not, it opens up the possibility of doing these other bits of research that need to be done. I could have written exactly the same book on Latin America, on Japan, on Africa.

I realized as I went on that I was writing a kind of incitement for publication. However nice you are about it in academic terms, it is a story that's full of human motivation that rests on thorough archival research, and I have a point of view to make and you can disagree with the point of view as much as you like, but the material is there, and much, much more of it that needs to be looked at. There is still this huge gap in the examination and analysis of how intellectual ideas in Europe developed post-war because nobody has, apparently, gone through every issue of *Der Monat*, gone through the careers of the individual writers.

WSL: An example of that 'individual' approach was a paper at the Middelburg conference by Ingeborg Philipsen on this one person who is trying to be a covert operator and set up a Danish chapter of the CCF.

FSS: The danger of this kind of operation, of course is that it attracts the kind of people who want to go in for a bit of derring-do. Koestler certainly had a bit of experience in this area, but Nabokov never really made the grade so he gets the next best thing. There is definitely a kind of an appeal for these people, a lot of them didn't fight, wore glasses and didn't pass the tests, the medicals or whatever. So they had this kind of urge, after the war, to get in there and do something. Some of the strategies employed by the Congress were guerrilla strategies.

WSL: The issue I have with the book: it was too successful in the sense that it covers so thoroughly, in terms of research, the CIA's relationship with high culture, intellectual movements, literary magazines, art, that there is a dimension in the story that does not quite come out. I'll give you an example, the labour operations.

FSS: I think that's right. In a sense I think I may have deferred to or been cowed by the prestigious research that Tony Carew has done, and others. And I think you're right, and I think you could also say where's the youth movement, where's the feminist movement. And I think Malcolm Bradbury made a very good point in his review, and he wrote the sequel to my book in his review. A sequel which was the relationship between the US government and popular culture at the time, all the jazz and all the jazz tours and that stuff. So that dimension was sort of missing.

WSL: The reason I put up the labour case is for a specific question. I have already read the labour case differently from what you set out in the book in that it was the private sphere, it was the boys in labour who were pushing the government to do something, give us money, do something and the government only slowly came around to respond.

FSS: The impression I got, from the papers that I saw and the interviews I did, was that, at least as far as the Congress was concerned, there was no shortage of cash coming out of Irving Brown's budget and that he had no shortage of cash at the beginning. But Brown was either smeared in

Washington or his opponents were rightly bringing up or bringing to light some of his operations or methods that they didn't like. And I know that he was marginalized and after that went off all over the place, going off to South America. So I think he was a bit of a buccaneer and that there were moments and actually a cut-off point, there were a couple of times when his backer – the CIA, US government – said no.

WSL: And the Carmel Offie affair may have had something to do with it?

FSS: Carmel Offie had something to do with it, and George Meany's position too. It is a very complex story, and I'm sure I haven't nailed it and to be frank I didn't try to and I was sort of alluding to the much bigger picture there and hoping that Tony Carew would fill in the gaps in his work. And I'm sure he will.

WSL: But no sequel from you?

FSS: I'm very tempted. I had the huge advantage of having no past, no back story, no obvious axe to grind, and frankly I must have looked like a complete idiot to the people I met, at least the first time round. Because I didn't know much about it. I didn't do anything as strategic as to cultivate this aura of stupidity, but I know that people talked to me on sufferance but largely sort of ignored me and forgot about me. And what happened was that, when the book came out, people like Kristol and Lasky and various others, they were really taken aback. I do not know if they thought I would ever pursue it or was serious about it.

And anyway, what happened as a result was, just before the book was published and I was seeking permission to quote and everything else, people suddenly realised that I was serious and I had finished this work and so they started withholding permission and then they wanted to see everything that I was writing and it was six months of really difficult, bitter struggles to get vital permission. John Hunt went from being incredibly frank and open. Suddenly he clammed up and would not allow me to quote direct from his papers – in fact, he was the only one who would not and I had to go and paraphrase. There was a body of letters going to various interviewees who it was felt by other people had been too co-operative, had told me too much, and they were frankly at times quite intimidated.

It was such a mess that, to be honest, when I finished it I swore to myself that I would never ever go through that again. And I'm now thrilled to be doing something completely out of copyright 600 years back. But I have not left it, the caravan hasn't moved on by any means. I'm still actively researching and trying to thrash out my research. I have just been told recently of an unfortunately failed effort to bring a court case in the US to get the CIA to respond to a Freedom of Information Act request on Stephen Spender and T.S. Eliot. And they refused to acknowledge or deny any existence of any files, blah, blah, blah.

It is very much an ongoing thing but there is not a sequel in the offing yet. And also my interest in this was not the CIA and how it works and who these people are. I do not find them interesting or attractive enough. I was fascinated by the context of the story, but I didn't want to be painted as a kind of CIA buff, I'm not.

My interest was in the point at which, the moment at which politics and culture and patronage collide, and the complications they cause. That to me was the fascination as well as the individual motivation. It is a people history. It is about people who I just wanted to find out more who they were.

WSL: I get the impression that the book was generally well received in Europe.

FSS: In Germany it was loved or hated. I was accused of British anti-semitism, which I think was due to Lasky and his mates. When I went to Germany to promote the book, I was asked, 'How do you respond to this charge of anti-semitism?', and I thought that it was so weak and so utterly ridiculous unless it was the German publishers wanting me to remove a reference to Lasky's oriental-shaped eyes – well, I think I changed it to almond-shaped, but I was simply trying to describe his look.

All I did was raise the issue that had been voiced by WASPs and Jews and Brits. It was an observation from Washington that there was some kind of difficulty at times in dealing with cosmopolitan, ruthless European intellectuals like Josselson, like Lasky, by the WASPish elite, Protestant elite in Washington. And that was one of the things that Diana Josselson raised as an issue when her husband Michael was getting into trouble with the apparatchiks back in Washington, they didn't really trust this guy, they couldn't really get a handle on him.

What was most striking was the calcification of Cold War positions in Germany and in America, which wasn't the same anywhere else. It certainly was not the same in Spain. Remember, when I started researching this book, if you had looked in various encyclopedias or reference books under Cold War, it would say see US International Relations, US Foreign Policy, whatever. There was not really a Cold War feel. It is now burgeoning. Now just five years later, under Cold War, it says see labour relations, British government, Frenchwomen, the whole long list of entries. It is just interesting to see how the Cold War as a historical exercise is taking shape.

And the response in America was that it has still got a long way to go because it is still so polarized and much more now since 11 September when we have had a huge revival of the kind of pious polarities which were dominant in the Cold War.

One thing I wanted to say about the National Security Council. The National Security Council Directives and the definitions of propaganda and all that early manual stuff, none of them have been replaced yet, none of them have been seriously challenged. These institutions that were set up in the late 40s and these foreign policy plans, none of this structure has been dismantled since the end of the Cold War. All these things have been reinforced, in terms of just the basic grammar but also in terms of how these bodies work. That's one of the things that astonishes me. The Cold War, although it is history, is still – all these revelations from the documentation of the kind of architecture of Cold War in terms of American/US foreign policy thinking, the architecture is still exactly the same.

WSL: The book closes with really interesting conclusions with the sense of tragedy, the personal tragedy of Josselson, the sense of betrayal by the intellectuals. But chronologically, it closes down in the late 60s.

FSS: That was my gravest misgiving, having to close it down there. And I did because I had got that far with that many pages. If there is a sequel or a real dimension missing from the book it is that what I have done is set up a discussion for what happened in the intellectual climate post '67, which is really interesting. So definitely someone else should write that book.

WSL: Do these covert operations continue post-'67 in some other form, despite the Ramparts *revelations, despite the Katzenbach report, despite the highly publicized shift of operations?*

FSS: The Katzenbach report is important. When it is circulated to the CIA, someone in the CIA says, 'We will have to stop applying these strategies and tactics and operations domestically. But in the international field we have to re-double our efforts.' It is very clear they get the green light to go on, so there is no theoretical impediment to them carrying on. On the contrary, there seems to be encouragement that they should keep on doing it.

WSL: They simply could not support domestic organizations, even if they had international activities.

FSS: No, I think it is clear that they could support the international operations even of American groups but they could not provide any kind of funding or support to US-based initiatives.

WSL: The National Student Association? You cannot continue to fund them, but you could continue...

FSS: You could perhaps pay the mortgage on an office.

WSL: I am interested about the extent that, in the 1980s, the National Endowment for Democracy, quasi-public, fills that gap with domestic organizations.

FSS: I always thought that the CIA was already in USIA. You see, there is one crucial pattern to this book. People were on the whole quite open and quite easy to talk to if I could produce, from archives or from other interviews, evidence. They were often terribly reluctant to be the first person to say something – 'I do not know or you need to ask so and so about that' – but if I had something and I could go and say, 'I now know that XYZ, can you tell me a bit more?', they would be quite willing to elaborate.

But whenever I touched on USIA or abstract expressionism or control, the denials were vigorous and unequivocal. The issue of control I think bruised the image but there is tons of stuff you should look at which suggests a much greater degree of CIA infiltration of USIA although they said they had nothing to do with it at all.

So I always thought USIA would have become the channel that the CIA would have used after '67. All that Peace Corps stuff as well, unless they just cut it straight off, which I do not believe they did. I think they would have gone through probably other channels that were already there, where they already had some sort of inroad and simply expanded their presence. Those are the things I would look at. I would probably look at anything that's 'free' or 'independent' or 'private'.

WSL: So we're in 2002. It is supposedly a new era. Do we have that same kind of involvement by the American state in trying to manipulate or control foreign opinion?

FSS: I think what would have happened post-September 11th is that a lot of veterans of this cultural warfare programme sat back and said, 'We told them. We told them the level of anti-Americanism abroad has reached unprecedented heights to the degree where people come out and celebrate the attack on the World Trade Center, or even if they're not that extravagant in their approval of the deaths, they can murmur about America asking for it. And this is a vivid demonstration of exactly what we were trying to curtail or diminish or erode. There is naturally a kind of an envy of the US and this has built itself up now to a head of steam – what we were doing was trying precisely to project the very best of who we were and what we had to offer. If they'd let us go on, blah, blah, blah.' I'm sure there were people who felt vindicated for their part in cultural warfare programmes in the Cold War post-September 11th and would have said, 'We need now to renew this, to do this again.' I think there would have been people in overt government institutions like the National Endowment for Democracy or what's left of it or Voice of America or whatever's left of it, saying, 'We have these facilities but we are underfunded, under-recognized, and very much ridiculed in Washington, and we should be having now more money, more budget.'

What do they do? They go and give, what is it, $1 billion straight off to the CIA? They raise, I'm sure, they have raised the ban on assassinating Bin Laden and a few of the Al Qa'eda. So whether or not Bush formally lifts the ban on assassination is immaterial now because the precedent has been established. It is alright to go and kill individuals.

I was asked in an interview after September 11th, 'Isn't this exactly the time when culture is the best weapon to answer the kind of knee-jerk, ignorant, reactionary anti-Americanism, not just of the Arab states but also of our own allies?' And there was a lot of anti-Americanism in the UK and in France and is still now.

My answer is that there is a constructive anti-Americanism, one that everybody, particularly Americans, should be involved in which says, 'America is now the only superpower. And at a time where it has the capacity to police the world with less opposition than ever before, it is exactly the time when intellectuals and monitors and historians and whoever they might be....' I'm not calling for radical history, I think the intellectuals who may want to stay out of it, should stay out of it. I think that for those who want to sort of do something, there should be an honourable form of anti-Americanism, which is simply something which tries to provide the corrective to the enormous concentration of power and resources. You have to be sure that there are certain kinds of mechanisms whereby America is held up to its own exalted standards. The same for the British government, the French government, and everyone else. It just happens to be that America needs it more than anyone else because America is bigger and more powerful than anyone else.

I think a lot of the anti-Americanism is the kind that so exacerbated Cold Warriors in the 1940s and 50s, that kind of fashionable Left Bank sort of excrescence that all Americans are bad. That's just nonsense, completely destructive, but to hold America to account for its foreign policies, to hold it to account for its ideas about democracy, to hold it to account for the idea that it can Xerox democratic forms and institutions and just sort of drop them on other people is appropriate. And the fact is that America does not seem to know its enemy. It seems to be profoundly ignorant of who its enemies are. If America demonstrated more tolerance and interest in the sources of those anti-Americanisms and thoughts... It should just say, 'Take it or leave it, this is what we have to offer, not just the kind of gross consumerist, globalist image you get from watching American sitcoms.'

All the cultural sophistication in America is widely known by the people at large in the countries that are opposing America's foreign policy. They should have access to it – if you put the CIA in, you are guaranteed to get into trouble, so do not make the same mistake again. Put the money where it is needed and where people overtly and honestly are able to state what they are doing, which is trying to project a positive national image.

WSL: And bomb Al-Jazeera when it criticizes American foreign policy?

FSS: Yes, absolutely. That great moment, that great opportunity. Here was an independent TV channel, a kind of reed, a lonely reed standing in Middle and Far East politics, and it is like, 'Bomb the shit out of it.'

America needs to spend a lot more money, less on bombs and baked bean tins and peanut butter and much more on open cultural warfare. I have no problem with cultural warfare if it is open, and no problem in saying we will attack you with Mark Morris [Dance Group] or Boston Symphony Orchestra. This is what will work – not with Noriega where they tried to use music as a form of torture – but why aren't they airlifting in tapes of the BSO and stuff?

There is nothing wrong with culturalism if the artists are cognizant and willing. Britart – the New British Art movement – Damien Hirst, Tracey Emin, whatever, gave cutting-edge kudos to New Labour. They did it wittingly, knowingly, and they could stand up to the criticisms. What's the problem with that? People, critics, and other artists say, 'Well, linking artistic work to the reputation of the government degrades the art of the movement or the idea of artists working free of the iron grip of the state. It is their choice, their choice, no problem with that.' And it is also other people's freedom to say, 'You know, I do not think you should have done that.'

3

Calling the Tune? The CIA, The British Left and the Cold War, 1945–1960

HUGH WILFORD

In addition to a series of revelations about Soviet espionage, the last ten years have seen a steady drip of new information about American covert operations in western Europe during the early Cold War period. In 1999, for example, the British writer Frances Stonor Saunders published an enterprisingly researched history of the CIA's effort in the 'Cultural Cold War', the secret struggle between the Americans and Soviets for the 'hearts and minds' of the world's intellectuals, under the intriguing title, *Who Paid the Piper*?[1] What follows is an attempt to piece together newly available evidence about the CIA's covert operations during the late 1940s and 1950s as they affected specifically the British non-communist left, a category defined broadly to include trade unionists, left-wing intellectuals and Labour Party politicians.

In the small amount of literature published on this subject to date, the tendency has been to portray the CIA as fatally compromising the independence of the British left, reducing it to a state of tame ideological obedience in the Cold War. This, at least, was the interpretive thrust of a pioneering piece of investigative journalism by Richard Fletcher published in 1977, 'How CIA Money Took the Teeth Out of British Socialism'.[2] A similar verdict on the CIA's campaign in the Cultural Cold War is implied in the title of Saunders's book, with its tacit suggestion that the Agency succeeded in calling the tune of those intellectuals who received its secret support. A close examination of the impact of American covert operations on the British left, however, reveals a rather more complicated picture.

LABOR DIPLOMACY

American attempts to influence the politics of Cold War British trade unions were part of a much broader effort to sway the political allegiance of

European labour generally, reflecting a dawning American realization that the left was to play an important if not dominant role in reconstructing the war-torn continent. Hence the creation during the late 1940s of a massive apparatus of 'labor diplomacy', which included the Labor Attaché programme, Labor Information Officers and exchange schemes for trade unionists. It is possible to detect two main impulses at work here: one was to ensure that European unions were anti-communist; the other was the more positive goal of spreading the so-called 'productivity gospel' – the values of non-political trade unionism, labour-management co-operation and modern working practices - so as to buttress the economies of western Europe against communist destabilization and at the same time anchor them more securely within the American economic orbit.

Clearly Britain was a less important target of this campaign than countries such as Italy and France, where economic and political conditions were more unstable. Nonetheless, there was enough official American concern about the strength of communism in British unions and the backwardness of UK industry for the US Government to dispatch a number of 'labor diplomats' to Cold War Britain. The first and, arguably, most effective of these was Samuel Berger, who had come to London earlier as a student at the London School of Economics in the 1930s, returned in wartime as the labour expert in W. Averell Harriman's Lend-Lease mission, then stayed on after the War in the newly created post of Labor Attaché. Thanks to his previous experience of British labour affairs, Berger now enjoyed better access to the leadership of the Trades Union Congress (TUC) and members of the Attlee cabinet, including the Prime Minister himself, than any other American diplomat. Next came the Marshall Plan Labor Information Officer in London, William Gausmann, who circulated widely in British labour circles throughout the 1950s, albeit at a slightly lower level than the Labor Attaché. Finally there was Joseph Godson, Attaché from 1953, who was on surprisingly close personal terms with Sam Watson, powerful president of the Durham Miners, and Hugh Gaitskell, from 1955 leader of the Labour Party (then in opposition) whom Godson supported in his factional battles with the left-wing followers of Aneurin Bevan.[3]

In addition to their public duties, all three of these labour diplomats engaged in covert anti-communist political warfare, for example working behind the scenes against the Soviet-influenced World Federation of Trade Unions, helping to distribute the propaganda of the Foreign Office's secret anti-communist unit, the Information Research Department, and co-operating with Labour Party and TUC officials in their campaigns against communists within the British labour movement. Perhaps not surprisingly, this has led to speculation that one or other of them was a CIA officer operating under cover. The evidence for this is inconclusive, but in an important sense the question is academic anyway. Even if they were not actually on the CIA payroll, all three men had links with Jay Lovestone, a former head of the American Communist Party who by the late 1940s had become both the leading foreign policy adviser to the American Federation of Labor (AFL) and the key agent in the CIA's international labour operations. Admittedly, relations between this fanatical anti-communist and Gausmann were distant, even hostile; but Berger and especially Godson dealt closely with him, the former acting for a time as his liaison with the CIA, and the latter sending him reports from London couched in the coded language favoured by 'Lovestoneites' when discussing Agency business. Considering Godson's proximity to Lovestone, it is small wonder that there was some disquiet in left-wing British circles about the activities of the Labor Attaché, which included attending anti-Bevanite caucuses organized by the Gaitskellites and, it has recently emerged, receiving confidential Labour Party and TUC papers from Sam Watson. This is to say nothing of Lovestone's other British contacts, among them prominent journalists such as Hugh Chevins of *The Daily Telegraph* and Richard Lowenthal of *The Observer*, as well as less well-known figures like the ex-communist Jack Carney, whose regular reports to his American friend found their way into the notorious 'JX Files' kept by the CIA's chief of counter-intelligence, James Jesus Angleton.[4]

Quite what effect all this activity had on Cold War Britain is less clear. Perhaps the least successful element of the whole American campaign to influence the British left was the 'productivity gospel'. As later decades of industrial unrest would attest, neither British labour nor management ever paid anything more than lip-service to the positive, productivist message of US labour diplomacy. To the extent that British industry did buy into the American model, it was probably as much the result of growing dependence on Marshall aid and private American investment as any conversion to the methods or goals of productivity policy.

Turning to the negative, anti-communist mission of the labour diplomats, however, the balance sheet appears more favourable: the British labour movement entered the 1960s with communism under control and the Atlanticist Gaitskellites to the fore. How much this had to do with American labour diplomacy, though, is debatable. The right-wing leadership of the TUC and Labour Party was probably capable of keeping its own house in order without US assistance; certainly anti-communist British unionists were no less ready than their American cousins to resort to covert political warfare against communism when circumstances seemed to demand it, as is shown by evidence of links with the Information Research Department and private anti-communist bodies such as Common Cause and Industrial Research and Information Services.[5]

Ultimately the impression one forms after studying US labour diplomacy in Cold War Britain is less of a highly successful ideological intervention than an enterprise dogged by internal division and conflict. There was, for example, constant tension between the official and private diplomatic players involved – Jay Lovestone, far from being a passive pawn of the CIA, was forever trying to get one over on his intelligence bosses, whom he regarded as raw novices in the war on communism (he referred to them sneeringly as the 'Fizz Kids') – while the two rival wings of the American labour movement, the American Federation of Labor and the Congress of Industrial Organizations, fought for control of the diplomatic machinery throughout the period. If the US ever did succeed in establishing an ideological 'hegemony' over British labour, it was at best a highly fractious, volatile one.

THE CULTURAL COLD WAR

The CIA's effort in the 'Cultural Cold War' shared a number of features in common with the 'labor diplomacy' campaign. It too was prompted by a growing awareness of the power of the left in post-war Europe, in this instance left-wing intellectuals, who were viewed not only as important opinion-formers but also as particularly vulnerable to Soviet propaganda. Second, the cultural campaign had a positive as well as a negative aspect: pointing out the dangers to intellectual freedom posed by communism, but also celebrating the cultural life of the western democracies. Finally, although the effort was focused mainly on the continent, there was sufficient neutralist sentiment in the UK for British intellectuals to become targets as well.

The most important American weapon of the Cultural Cold War in Britain, as elsewhere, was the Congress for Cultural Freedom (CCF). Founded in 1950 at a conference held in Berlin with secret backing from the CIA, and subsequently head-quartered in Paris, the intellectual citadel of European neutralism, the CCF engaged in an extraordinary array of activities, including festivals, seminars and concerts, all designed to demonstrate to intellectuals the cultural advantages of political freedom. A British affiliate, the British Society for Cultural Freedom, was established in January 1951 under the leadership of such prominent literary intellectuals as Stephen Spender, Malcolm Muggeridge and Fredric Warburg. Young political thinkers on the right wing of the Labour Party, including Anthony Crosland, Roy Jenkins and Hugh Gaitskell, were drawn into the organization's sphere of influence through their involvement in such events as the Future of Freedom conference held in Milan in 1955. The CCF even established a presence in British universities in the shape of the Committee on Science and Freedom at Manchester.[6]

However, the organization's most successful venture in Britain was undoubtedly its magazine *Encounter*. Launched in London in 1953 under the joint editorship of Stephen Spender and the young New York intellectual, Irving Kristol, *Encounter* rapidly established a reputation as the foremost journal of 'serious' political opinion and cultural expression in the English language, securing contributions from a remarkably wide cross-section of the British intelligentsia, again including the likes of Crosland, Gaitskell and Jenkins. Throughout it remained financially dependent on secret subsidies from the CIA.

The initial response of British intellectuals to these cultural blandishments was one of resistance. The CCF's founding Berlin conference was disrupted by the mischievous antics of two Oxford dons, Hugh Trevor-Roper and A. J. Ayer, who objected to what they perceived as the excessive anti-communism of the event's organizers. The British Society for Cultural Freedom never really got off the ground, hampered as it was by internal doctrinal and factional conflicts, and was effectively replaced as the CCF base of operations in Britain by *Encounter* in 1953. *Encounter* itself also had to overcome latent cultural snobbery and suspicions that it was a Cold War 'Trojan horse'. Later in the decade, Bertrand Russell was at the centre of a series of embarrassing public rows with the Congress's US affiliate, the American Committee for Cultural Freedom, concerning domestic American anti-communism and its effects, which culminated in 1957 with his noisy resignation from one of the CCF's Honorary Chairs.

For the most part, however, British resistance to the American Cultural Cold War effort had died out by the mid-1950s, as was confirmed by the amazing success of *Encounter*, the Gaitskellites' attendance at the 1955 Milan conference, and the staging in Britain of such events as the Changes in Soviet Society seminar, held at St Antony's College, Oxford, in 1957. Whether this means, though, that the CIA had succeeded in colonizing the consciousness of Britain's left-wing intellectuals, as some commentators have concluded, is very much open to question. For one thing, such a verdict overlooks evidence of British intellectuals attempting to use the US cultural apparatus for their own domestic selfish purposes. Sometimes such acts of appropriation were literal and crude, as when officers of the British Society for Cultural Freedom took their friends out to lunch joking that 'the American taxpayers are paying!' At other times they were more subtle: witness Stephen Spender's constant campaigning to reduce the American, political side of *Encounter*'s coverage, and transform the publication into a latter-day version of the British 'little magazine' he had helped edit during the 1940s, *Horizon*.[7] In both cases, the basic impulse was the same: the British were exploiting the covert patronage of the CIA for their own ends.

Finally, one needs to take into account the possibility of collaboration, that is British intellectuals co-operating with the American Cultural Cold War effort because they naturally shared its values and goals. Knowledge of the CIA's role in covertly funding the CCF was probably more widespread in British intellectual circles than has generally been admitted. Spender might indeed have been 'unwitting', but both Warburg and Muggeridge were in on the secret, as they later made plain. Indeed, Muggeridge helped arrange counterpart funding for *Encounter* from British Intelligence, a fact which hints at the extent of behind-the-scenes collusion between the US and UK secret services.[8] It is also worth remembering that the British Government was waging its own Cultural Cold War through the Foreign Office's Information Research Department, which similarly involved the participation of left-wing British intellectuals, including no less a socialist icon than George Orwell. In sum, then, the British response to the cultural campaigns of the CIA was more complex than some accounts would have one believe, involving as it did resistance, appropriation and complicity.

LABOUR, THE ACUE AND BILDERBERG

Finally, to turn to American attempts to influence what is still, of course, a contentious political issue today, namely Labour Party policy on Europe, it is well known that both the Truman and Eisenhower administrations supported the notion of a United States of Europe. A strong European union promised a solution to the 'German problem' and a bulwark against Soviet expansion, as well as the flattering prospect of a continent made over in the image of America. Less well known is the fact that, in order to expedite the process of unification, the CIA secretly funded the group of pro-federalist organizations in Europe known as the 'European Movement'.

As has recently been revealed by intelligence historian Richard J. Aldrich, the main conduit of CIA funds to the European Movement was a body called the American Committee on United Europe (ACUE).[9] Launched in early 1949 by OSS luminaries William Donovan and Allen Dulles, the ACUE was run out of offices in New York by Tom Braden, future head of the CIA division in charge of such front organizations as the Congress for Cultural Freedom. Although also responsible for a domestic propaganda campaign designed to persuade American public opinion of the need for a more united Europe, Braden's main duty was to arrange discreet American financial assistance for the European supporters of such federalist initiatives as the Council of Europe, the Schuman Plan and the European Army. By the mid-1950s the CIA (whose first disbursement had arrived in the form of a bag containing $75,000 dumped on Braden's desk in 1951) was funding the ACUE to the tune of about one million dollars a year, making it one of the US's most expensive covert operations of the early Cold War period.[10]

Although the federalist option enjoyed some support in Britain – indeed, the leadership of the European Movement, with which Braden liaised closely, was drawn, initially at least, from senior British political circles – the ACUE soon realized that the greatest obstacle in the path to European federation was opposition from the governing Labour Party. The sterling area, the Commonwealth and, ironically, a growing attachment to the concept of Atlantic union: all these strategic preferences caused the Attlee government to reject federalism in favour of a loose form of confederation in which member states retained their sovereignty. The ACUE attempted to combat Labour anti-federalism by funding a variety of federalist measures: a public demonstration across the street from the Council of Europe in Strasbourg intended to put British delegates 'in a mood for compromise'; the publication of a pamphlet by leading French socialist André Philip encouraging dissent from the Party line amongst Labour supporters; and the 'Mackay Plan', a proposal for transforming the Council of Europe into a European parliament drawn up by the federalist Labour MP R.W.G. Mackay.[11] None of these ventures made much difference to the official Labour position, however. For example, despite feeling pressurized and isolated, the British delegation to Strasbourg in 1951 strongly opposed – and eventually succeeded in wrecking – the Mackay Plan.[12]

A rather different picture is presented by Labour participation in the so-called Bilderberg Group, the notoriously secretive council of western political leaders, industrialists and financiers which derived its name from the hotel in which it met for the first time in 1954, with funds provided by the CIA.[13] Hugh Gaitskell, a founder member of 'the Group' and of the Steering Committee formed in the wake of the 1954 meeting, performed a number of duties on behalf of Bilderberg's organizers, preparing a paper for the follow-up conference at Barbizon, France, in 1955, arranging for the attendance of other Labourites such as Alfred Robens, Douglas Jay and George Brown at subsequent gatherings, and even helping to raise financial donations from British industrialists when the Group met at Buxton, Derbyshire, in 1958.[14] Following Gaitskell's decision to stand down from the Steering Committee in the same year, his function as Bilderberg's Labour point-man was taken over by the Party's chief international strategist, Denis Healey, who proved no less energetic in the role than his predecessor.

The warmth of Gaitskell and Healey's attitude towards Bilderberg would seem to suggest that, as with the Congress for Cultural Freedom, the CIA had succeeded in winning the Labour leadership over to its cause. Such an interpretation, however, fails to take into account several factors. First, the CIA subsidy of the 1954 meeting was a one-off – the funds for later conferences came from genuinely private sources – and was granted only after sustained European lobbying. Indeed, there were suspicions among the Americans that Bilderberg was the brain-child of the British intelligence services: C. D. Jackson, President Eisenhower's chief adviser on 'psychological warfare', believed that the Group's principal organizer, the Polish-born Joseph Retinger, was a 'British secret agent'.[15] Second, while the published reports prepared by Retinger after each conference create the impression of remarkably consensual discussions, notes taken during the meetings by American participants indicate that in fact a great deal of argument took place, usually involving British Labourites. In 1954, for example, C. D. Jackson was perturbed by the 'brilliantly executed British hostility to every American point of view' he encountered at Bilderberg. Three years later, when the Group convened at St Simons Island, Georgia, he was similarly dismayed by Denis Healey's proposals to neutralize Germany or, as he put it, 'Munichize NATO'.[16] Finally, it is important to acknowledge the possibility that Labour politicians attended Bilderberg because it served their interests to do so. They were, after all, out of government at home and therefore, understandably, did not want to be excluded from a powerful new international forum. Bilderberg also signified an American shift away from a European strategy towards a more Atlantic one, which was naturally congenial to Labour's Atlanticist inclinations. Finally, there were the high standards of hospitality on offer, a not unimportant consideration for a group of politicians which included such celebrated *bon viveurs* as Tony Crosland and Roy Jenkins.[17] While it might well be true that Bilderberg reveals the likes of Gaitskell and Healey at their least attractive – the meetings arguably appealed to a Gaitskellite penchant for secrecy and elitism – nonetheless it does not prove that they were dupes of the CIA.

CONCLUSION

Since the end of the Cold War it has become clear not only how closely the Soviet Union controlled national communist parties in the West but also how extensively the western non-communist left was penetrated by American covert operatives. As the evidence has emerged, it is not perhaps surprising that some commentators have leaped to the conclusion that the CIA succeeded, by dint of Machiavellian cunning, in reducing the left to a state of ideological subjugation in the Cold War. Clearly, the secret sponsorship of bodies ostensibly devoted to the ideal of cultural freedom raises deeply troubling ethical questions. Similarly, the realization that the CIA was active in so many fields on the non-communist left invites some fascinating but disturbing counterfactual speculation. Had it not been for secret American support, for example, would the Gaitskellites in the British Labour Party have seen off the ideological challenge of Bevanism as easily as they did? Still in Britain, but on a more cultural front, would such Bloomsbury *literati* as Stephen Spender, who had first come to prominence in the 1930s, still have wielded the literary authority they did in the 1950s without the covert backing of the CIA?

In other words, the recent findings about the CIA's operations do open up the possibility that covert American influence was more influential in shaping the politics and culture of the post-war British left, and therefore British political and cultural life in general, than has previously been supposed. That said, careful scrutiny of the new evidence also suggests that in calculating the precise extent and nature of American influence, we would be well advised to avoid resorting to simplistic notions of American 'cultural imperialism' or crude conspiracy theories. This was in fact an extremely complex historical situation. For one thing, the American campaign was itself ridden with internal contradictions, its public and private elements conflicting as much as they co-operated. More importantly, the British response to the US intervention, far from being one of passive subordination, was characterized variously by willing collaboration, creative appropriation and straightforward resistance. It might well have been the case that the CIA tried to call a particular tune; but the piper did not always play it, nor the audience dance to it.

NOTES

1. Frances Stonor Saunders, *Who Paid the Piper? The CIA and the Cultural Cold War* (London: Granta 1999).
2. Richard Fletcher, 'How CIA Money Took the Teeth Out of British Socialism', in Philip Agee and Louis Wolf (eds.) *Dirty Work: The CIA in Western Europe* (London: Zed Press 1978) pp.188–200.
3. See Hugh Wilford, 'American Labour Diplomacy and Cold War Britain', *Journal of Contemporary History* 37 (2002) pp.45–65.
4. On Lovestone and his alliance with the CIA, see Ted Morgan, *A Covert Life. Jay Lovestone: Communist, Anti-Communist, and Spymaster* (New York: Random House 1999); also Anthony Carew, 'The American Labor Movement in Fizzland: The Free Trade Union Committee and the CIA', *Labor History* 39 (1998) pp.25–42.
5. On Labour's links with the Information Research Department, see Hugh Wilford, 'The Information Research Department: Britain's Secret Cold War Weapon Revealed', *Review of International Studies* 24 (1998) pp.353–69.
6. See Hugh Wilford, ''Unwitting Assets?' British Intellectuals and the Congress for Cultural Freedom', *Twentieth Century British History* 11 (2000) pp.42–60.
7. See Saunders, *Who Paid the Piper?* (note 1) p.112.
8. See Saunders's revelatory account, ibid. pp.165–80.
9. For more on ACUE, see Richard J. Aldrich's pioneering account in *The Hidden Hand: Britain, America and Cold War Secret Intelligence* (London: John Murray 2001) Chap.16.
10. Thomas W. Braden, interview with author, 18 June 2001, Woodbridge, Virginia; John D. Blumgart, 'ACUE: Notes on organisation and finances', 15 April 1957, Paul Hoffman

Papers, Harry S. Truman Library, Independence, Missouri.

11. Thomas W. Braden to Walter Washington, 4 January 1951, Allen Dulles Papers, Seeley G. Mudd Manuscript Library, Princeton University; William P. Durkee, ACUE Annual Report, May 1952, ACUE Papers, Lauinger Library, Georgetown University; see 'The Mackay Plan', R.W.G. Mackay Papers, British Library of Political and Economic Science, London.
12. William P. Durkee, ACUE Annual Report, May 1952, ACUE Papers.
13. See Aldrich, *Hidden Hand* p.369.
14. Meeting in Paris minutes, 6 December 1954, Hugh Gaitskell Papers, University College London; Hugh Gaitskell to Victor Cavendish-Bentinck, 11 March 1958, Gaitskell Papers.
15. C. D. Jackson to Edward Littlejohn, 5 August 1954, C. D. Jackson Papers, Dwight D. Eisenhower Library, Abilene, Kansas.
16. C. D. Jackson, diary log, 29–31 May 1954, Jackson Papers; C. D. Jackson to Henry Luce *et al*, 19 February 1957, Jackson Papers.
17. See Lawrence Black's valuable discussion of these factors in his 'The Bitterest Enemies of Communism: Revisionists, Atlanticism and the Cold War', *Journal of Contemporary British History* 15 (2001) pp.26–62.

PART II

Public-Private Partnership

4

Beyond Freedom, Beyond Control: Approaches to Culture and the State-Private Network in the Cold War

W. SCOTT LUCAS

'Culture' is now part of historians' Cold Wars. In the last decade, they have belatedly considered a conflict which was more than geopolitics and military deployments, more than Presidents and General Secretaries, summits and treaties, economic competition and the Bomb. 'Culture' has brought examination of concepts such as race, gender, and class in relation to foreign policy as well as documentation of cultural diplomacy. It has broadened the Cold War to include Abstract Expressionism, basketball, and tourism amongst other activities. The 'new diplomatic history' is beyond the 'new' to the point of cliché.[1]

Any success has been partial, however, for even as 'culture' was being elevated to a place in the narrative of US foreign policy, it was being limited. Much of the 'cultural diplomacy' scholarship has restricted itself to the official, with an often anodyne focus on the US Information Agency, the Voice of America, and exhibitions and fairs.[2] An organization is sketched and cultural output listed but often unconsidered. The broader American crusade, with its covert sponsorship of 'culture' and informal collaboration between the state and the private sphere, is never portrayed, let alone examined. Most significantly, the 'new diplomatic historian' has yet to confront the challenge set by theorists such as Edward Said:

> Culture serves authority, and ultimately the nation state, not because it represses and coerces but because it is affirmative, positive, and persuasive.... [Culture] is a historical force possessing its own configurations, ones that intertwine with those in the socio-economic sphere.[3]

Nor is it in the interests of many US-based historians to consider these issues. A 'culture' which is simply an extension of diplomacy and a simplistic American ideology, rather than one which might be an integral part of power and economic structures, is far more manipulable. In the most pernicious development, the triumphalist school, winning the Cold War of the past to exalt the United States of the present, has stepped in to claim an unproblematic, naturally superior 'culture'. Tony Smith opened a roundtable on the 'American Century' in 1999 with the proclamation:

> America's victory in the struggles against fascism and communism between 1939 and 1989...has resulted for much of the globe in a fundamental reorganization of political power in a morally positive direction. For the moment, if democratic government is the only unchallenged form of state legitimacy virtually everywhere in the world, if social questions such as the rights of women and minorities are so widespread on almost everyone's political agenda, if economic questions concerning the relative roles of state and society everywhere have common themes, then sure it is because of the worldwide impact of a philosophical – some might prefer to say an ideological – conviction that mobilized American resolve to win the struggles against fascism and communism.[4]

'Americanization' is presented, squeaky-clean, as a one-way process in which foreign peoples welcomed the commodities as well as the values of liberal democracy. Geir Lundestad, in the guise of his work on the 'invitation to empire' extended to the United States by Europe, has announced, 'In the 1990s Europe remained culturally as attached to the US as it had ever been; as measured in everything from the popularity of American movies and television programs to the increase in sales of Coke in Central and Eastern Europe.'[5] Volker Berghahn makes the declaration, 'While there is still some European criticism of [American] culture, often using well-worn arguments going back as far as the 1920s, the fear of it has largely disappeared. On the contrary, intellectuals and the educated bourgeoisie of Europe have long joined in its enjoyment.'[6]

This is an exalted 'culture' which, having vanquished old communist enemies, slays other enemies from the past. Even dissident scholars are not safe. In a colloquium in *Diplomatic History*, the house journal of US diplomatic historians, Jessica Gienow-Hecht asked, 'Shame on US?', to make straw men of those scholars who had asserted and challenged an American 'cultural imperialism'. At one point, she reduces the appeal of 'left' arguments to the allegation, propagated in the polemics of Paul Hollander, that their proponents 'often settled in university towns'.[7]

On one level, analysis of aspects such as race and gender in foreign policy has challenged this rah-rah 'culture'. By connecting the 'domestic' and 'foreign' more effectively than a simple account of propaganda and projection, such analysis establishes that culture is more than an explicit adjunct to diplomacy. Negotiated and established implicitly in the language of policy-making and implementation, 'culture' is the setting but never the resolution of tensions and contradictions within a society as well as a state.[8]

Yet the value of this cultural analysis is also its limitation in the evaluation of US strategy in the Cold War, for at some point strategy demands an explicit, unchallenged mobilization of cultural concepts. Constructions of gender in Hollywood film or gendered depictions in US policy towards postwar Germany are significant on a number of levels, but in the battle for hearts and minds, the foremost issue was the establishment of the superior position of women in the 'West' and the use of women in other battles such as the claiming of 'peace'.[9] Cases such as the Justice Department's intervention, based on Cold War considerations, for the right decision in *Brown v. Board of Education* and Louis Armstrong's State Department-sponsored tour are only individual episodes in the long-running strategic contest with the Soviet Union over race. Amidst the domestic ramifications, such as the purging of W.E.B. DuBois from the NAACP leadership and the prosecution of the Civil Rights Congress, civil rights at home would continue to have a high place in overseas psychological strategy throughout the early Cold War.[10]

TAKING THE DOOR OFF THE HINGES: A BROADER APPROACH TO US CULTURE AND THE COLD WAR

It is in this environment – the 'culture' of yesterday, the 'culture' of today – that Frances Stonor Saunders' *Who Paid the Piper?: The CIA and the Cultural Cold War*, published in 1999, was such a valuable intervention. Some authors, bucking the general academic trend, had begun to incorporate the neglected tale of the US government's covert support of 'culture' in wider contexts such as the relationship between ideology and foreign policy, but Saunders' was the first extended account of the CIA's systematic campaign. The book not only posed a serious challenge to easy assertions of US victory in the past; it threatened to expose the political motives of present-day historians. As Edward Said noted, 'The contemporary cultural climate in the United States is dominated by the corporate-government nexus, which no longer lurks in the shadowy organizations or behind the front foundations that Saunders inventories with compelling tenacity.'[11]

Saunders, preferring to let a lively story speak for itself, never focuses on a nuanced interpretation of the CIA's interaction with private allies. Thus it is easy to read the text as one of the CIA's 'control' of cultural activity, an impression reinforced by attention-grabbing ploys such as the British title of the book and Saunders' identification of the unexplored story, 'Did [the

CIA's intervention] not risk producing, instead of freedom, a kind of *ur*-freedom, where people think they are acting freely, when in fact they are bound to forces over which they have no control?'[12]

The risk is that such sweeping language, largely reliant on narrative, leaves analytic hostages to fortune. Even scholars sympathetic to Saunders' criticism of US foreign policy take up the issue of precision in the state's relationship with the private sphere. Hugh Wilford writes incisively, 'It might well have been the case that the CIA tried to call a particular tune; but the piper did not always play it, nor the audience dance to it.'[13] Giles Scott-Smith's recent book, while never directly challenging Saunders, sets out that 'the starting point for interpreting the CCF [Congress for Cultural Freedom], therefore, should not be the outlook of the CIA but the views of the post-war intelligentsia, and how the Congress both emerged as a consequence of those views and *simultaneously* represented their political co-optation within the conditions of the Cold War'.[14]

Actually, Saunders' story holds up well against this critique, at least in regard to 'cultural production'. At every 'free' gathering of intellectuals seeking 'freedom', the state's operatives were in the shadows. Sidney Hook may have challenged the 'communist'-inspired Waldorf Conference through the formation of the Americans for Intellectual Freedom, the forerunner of the Congress for Cultural Freedom, but the CIA and labour leader David Dubinsky secured Hook's headquarters in a Waldorf suite and paid the bills while Frank Wisner, the head of the Office for Policy Coordination, despatched Michael Josselson to monitor the festivities. The initial meetings of the CCF's 'steering committee' in summer 1950 established 'First priority: France, Italy' which, remarkably, happened to be the US government's priorities for political warfare.[15] By 1954 more than 80 per cent of the CCF's million-dollar budget was coming from the Agency; in 1966, just before the public revelation of the covert funding, more than $2 million was channeled to the CCF.[16] Still, the claim is maintained that this covert state involvement is no more than an irrelevant trifle. Peregrine Worsthorne, who wrote for the CIA-subsidized journal *Encounter*, insisted in a review of *Who Paid the Piper?* that there was 'nothing worse than very occasional CIA interference in the editorial decisions [of *Encounter*], rows and vendettas between Spender and Kristol, etc, which, although fun to read about, do not begin to do justice to the invaluable contribution made by that journal to the London literary scene, which would have been immeasurably less distinguished and colourful if it had not existed.'[17]

However, the reaction to Saunders' book (or, in another sense, the ignorance of it by the academic 'mainstream' in the United States) is far more than a critique of its scholarly merit. Instead, it raises a broader issue of politics and scholarship, one which goes beyond a reasoned critique such as Wilford's. If doubts can be raised about the CIA's 'control', then it might be possible to remove the Agency from the scene with a tribute to the 'autonomy' of private institutions and individuals. Doing so, the ideological normality of 'free' Americans making their choices to fight the Cold War can be restored.

What then is to be done to prevent this elision of the cultural crusade from historical debate and, equally important, from consideration of current issues? Rather than enter upon yet another cycle of punch and counter-punch on 'control' v. 'autonomy', perhaps one might begin with Barbara Sussex's concise statement, regarding the journal *Encounter*, 'one should be careful not to exaggerate the amount of control which *had* to be exerted over [editor Irving] Kristol ... and instead consider the question of whether [state] censorship was needed at all'.[18] Provided the private actor's point of view helped further the objectives of the state, there was no need to curb 'autonomy'. Kristol put it nicely when he wrote to Michael Josselson, 'I know the kind of magazine that you and the Congress want, and I shall do my best to deliver', and once more when he asserted, 'We have to create our Asian writers.... We get them to conceive of their material, and to write it up, in a *certain way – our way.*'[19]

Instead the first step, far from restricting Saunders' vision, is to expand it through full consideration of the state-private network and the 'mobilization of culture'. Now that Saunders has opened the door on the covert dimension of the Cold War crusade, albeit in selected areas of 'high' culture, others can take it off the hinges by documenting the Agency's involvement with all aspects of 'mid', if not 'mass', culture through support of women's groups, youth organizations, academic departments, labour unions, film productions, and professional bodies as well as showpieces from *Encounter* magazine to the Boston Philharmonic to the paintings of Jackson Pollock.

The CIA would always be essential to this cultural crusade. The fiction of the US ideology of 'freedom', with free individuals making free choices, could only be maintained if most government support for 'private' initiatives was covert. And, at least in the early 1950s, there was the spectre of Congress quashing the Executive's open backing of cultural programmes as a waste of money if not, in the ironically warped vision of the time, 'socialist'.[20] Yet, if the CIA led the implementation of the government's cultural strategy, it was a 'total' strategy which involved all agencies in the Executive. The State Department, the US Information Agency, and the CIA as well as the Department of Defense, the Joint Chiefs of Staff, the Treasury, the Atomic Energy Commission, the Psychological Strategy Board, and the Operations Coordinating Board all were involved in the effort.

POLITICAL WARFARE AND THE DYNAMICS OF THE STATE-PRIVATE NETWORK

The 'cultural' has to be acknowledged as part of a US campaign which had been developing since 1947. The overt and covert dimensions might have been separated by the newly-created National Security Council, with the NSC giving the State Department responsibility for 'overt propaganda' and the top-secret annex, NSC 4-A, mandating the CIA to oversee 'covert psychological operations'.[21] The distinction was a device, however, to meet Secretary of State George Marshall's request 'that [he] should not be identified with' covert efforts,[22] rather than a fundamental division within the Executive. The operations were part of an integrated strategy, both for the emergency case of the French and Italian elections in spring 1948, and for the long-term plan of 'political warfare'. As George Kennan's Policy Planning Staff, which led the development of the strategy, defined it:

> What is proposed here is an operation in the traditional American form: organized public support of resistance to tyranny in foreign countries. Throughout our history, private American citizens have banded together to champion the cause of freedom for people suffering under oppression.... Our proposal is that this tradition be revived specifically to further American national interests in the present crisis.[23]

There was no shortage of funds for the campaign. Under the counterpart provisions of the Marshall Plan, millions of dollars were available for propaganda and covert operations, first by the Economic Cooperation Administration, then the Office of Policy Coordination, the specialist agency established in 1948 for covert operations.[24]

It is in this context that the state-private network was created and developed. Significantly, this occurred before the formation of the CIA's International Organizations Division, responsible for support of 'private' initiatives, in 1951. The best-known creation of the network, the National Committee for Free Europe, was the idea of George Kennan's Policy Planning Staff. Kennan and his assistant, Robert Joyce, liaised both with upstanding citizens (and former government officials) such as Dean Acheson, Allen Dulles, and Joseph Grew and with the Office of Policy Coordination to set up the venture.[25]

Even more significantly, in the context of the 'cultural' argument, the impetus for the state-private network often came from the private side. The CIA and Office of Policy Coordination might have been present at every step of the path to the Congress for Cultural Freedom, but it was still Sidney Hook's determination that started the process. The perception of well-placed women in New York that the US should be 'engaged in the Battle for

Women's Minds (which is a pleasanter term than Psychological Warfare)' would lead to the CIA-sponsored Committee of Correspondence.[26] Film and television executives such as directors John Ford and Cecil B. DeMille, NBC's David Sarnoff, and CBS's William Paley would volunteer their services.[27]

Perhaps the best example of this 'private' dimension in the early Cold War is the battle of the trade unions. From 1942, the American Federation of Labor had pressed the government to develop 'free' labour organizations overseas. Well before the 'official' US conflict with the Soviet Union in the Cold War, the head of the Free Trade Union Committee, Jay Lovestone (a former leader of the US Communist Party in the 1920s), was demanding a vigorous campaign against communist-led unions in Western Europe. With the State Department reluctant to pursue an aggressive strategy, implementation was left to the private sphere, supported by some *ad hoc* arrangements with benefactors within the government. CIA funding for a full campaign was not arranged until 1949.[28]

Nor was the state-private relationship necessarily a harmonious one. In the case of the AFL and the CIA, Lovestone's impatience and irascibility was the primary source of discord. In his unique code, he wrote, 'The Fizz kids [the CIA] have continued their marked anti-Labor and anti-Semitic tendencies in addition to their incompetence.... Any new field we will enter, we will do so without them.'[29] In fact, it was the CIA that would begin to distance itself from the Free Trade Union Committee, finding new 'private' outlets for its labour activity and relegating Lovestone and Irving Brown, the European representative of the American Federation of Labor, to the margins.

Kristol and Josselson's interchanges over the content and approach of *Encounter* provide another example of tensions. Kristol's vision of creating 'a certain kind of intellectual cultural milieu, which would in turn have far-reaching, but indirect, effects'[30] did not satisfy Josselson's desire for an political publication openly challenging communism. In a somewhat sinister tone, he sharply rebuffed the editor:

> [You say] that the Congress is in the publishing business to just give readers what they want to read... Your theory is absurd... You will remember that at our Executive Committee meeting everyone was in agreement that the period spent so far by *Encounter* in overcoming covert and overt resistance ... was time well spent, but now it [is] time to go one step further.[31]

The dispute over approach was serious, with an abortive attempt to replace Kristol as editor in 1955, but it was mitigated by Kristol and Josselson's unity over the objective to forge a Euro-American intellectual axis and by the reality, despite Kristol's assertion, that the 'cultural' and the 'political' were not separate areas of activity. *Encounter* would continue to be guided by Kristol's vision for the first five years of its existence.

Private initiative was not produced by a state puppet-master pulling strings; the mobilization of culture in the Cold War came through negotiation. At the same time, this was not 'autonomy'. To put it bluntly, if the US government had not covertly funded the 'private' efforts (or, in some cases, assisted in their funding through foundations such as Rockefeller and Ford),[32] they would not have existed. The significance of the state was not in creating the cultural crusade but in providing a strategic vision and the organization for a crusade which went beyond the efforts of any individual or group. State agencies, including the CIA, did not 'control' the private sphere but directed it in the pursuit of this vision.

Consider the development of the National Committee for Free Europe. NCFE's relationship with the State Department and the CIA was never an easy one. Like its counterparts in the US labour movement, the NCFE leadership and its staff chafed at government caution. From Radio Free Europe's launch in 1951 beyond the demise of the Hungarian Revolution in 1956, NCFE pressed for an aggressive campaign of 'liberation'; its founding fathers were more hesitant. By 1952 NCFE president C.D. Jackson (later President Eisenhower's Special Assistant for Psychological Strategy) was complaining:

> I think that the NCFE, the Committee for Free Asia, the Psychological Strategy Board, and the VoA [Voice of America] should go out of business because what we are doing is handling [psychological warfare] like something you pick up at [the toy store] F.A.O. Schwarz. We are neither conveying America, nor freedom for the future, and all we will eventually succeed in doing is get some damn good guys killed.

The State Department's Charles Bohlen responded by turning Jackson's words against him. It was not the Department's caution that was risking lives; rather, 'the present end result of the [aggressive] operations of VoA and RFE would be to get people killed'.[33]

Yet NCFE never acted in defiance of the strategy and aims of the state. To the contrary, it was fulfilling the guidelines of the National Security Council, issued in 1948 and reiterated on several occasions, for 'the gradual retraction of undue Russian power and influence from the present perimeter areas around traditional Russian boundaries and the emergence of the satellite countries as entities independent of the USSR'.[34] While the highest levels of the Truman and Eisenhower Administrations might have been indecisive about the pursuit of liberation, working-level officials, including those at the CIA, always had a general mandate to work with the NCFE. In this manner 'liberation', contrary to the assertions of most historians, was a goal of the US government precisely because of the state-private network.[35]

Other examples of the state's organization and direction are less dramatic but no less important. The intervention of the Office of Policy Coordination not only shaped the US delegation for the founding conference of the Congress for Cultural Freedom in Berlin in 1950, but also removed potentially troublesome leaders such as Arthur Koestler and, for a time, Melvin Lasky. Behind the pretext that officials of the National Student Association approached the US government because they were 'virtually paralyzed by lack of funds...to propagate in other countries the distinctly liberal but anti-totalitarian ideals which they were soon to defend at home against McCarthyism', the CIA ensured 'proper' international activity by the NSA through funding and operatives inside the organization.[36]

By the late 1950s, the CIA was tightening the system of direction by placing operatives inside organizations. In 1958 Kristol was replaced as editor of *Encounter* by Melvin Lasky, who had worked with US intelligence for more than a decade on 'cultural' operations. Trade union efforts turned to areas like Latin America where Serafino Romualdi, a US intelligence officer in World War II, directed ORIT (Interamerican Organization of Workers) and then launched the American Institute for Free Labor Development. Even the 12 women of the Committee of Correspondence received attention, as Anne Crolius, who had had contacts with US intelligence since the war, became Executive Secretary.[37]

'AMERICANIZATION' AND OVERSEAS 'RECEPTION'

The projection of culture and freedom in the Cold War is only a starting point for analysis, however; a full examination of the state-private network requires consideration of its reception. Whatever the level of co-operation between the US government and its private allies at home, the cultural crusade would come to nothing if it had no effect overseas. As early as 1946 leading executives as well as the government were fretting:

> We have failed to recognize that we must advertise and sell the American economic system as well as the products of that system. It is our job to explain and sell the rightness of private competitive enterprise both at home and abroad. If we don't, we shall be in very real danger of losing it.[38]

The problem arises, in part, because of the divide between 'political' and 'cultural' approaches to American intervention in Europe. Saunders' exceptional work is largely confined to the relationship between state officials such as Josselson and private operatives such as Kristol. The 'foreign' only appears in the accounts of British funding of *Encounter*, an episode involving Malcolm Muggeridge and the magnate Victor Rothschild, and of the relationship between the composer Nicolas Nabokov, the General Secretary of the Congress for Cultural Freedom, and Josselson.

In contrast, a body of work on 'Americanization' has emerged in the last decade. Much of the analysis is two-dimensional, however, describing the dissemination of American cultural products abroad with little consideration of the complexity of the 'local' response.[39] For example, scholarship has yet to contend with Peter Conrad's sharp assertion that the process has not been a simple projection and reception of American qualities:

> America – God bless its credulity, God damn its credulity – was more effectively promoted by the glossy, metricious lies of Dallas and Dynasty than by the abstruse art of Rothko and Charles Ives. What made American culture globally irresistible was its acquisitive vices, not its civic virtues.[40]

It should also be noted that the studies are almost exclusively on 'Americanization' in Western Europe, with the 'developing' world, as in much scholarship on the Cold War, remaining firmly on the periphery. A difference in perspective might bring far different conclusions. When the CCF ventured to India in 1951 to present the dangers of neutralism, it was rebuffed by the local audience and 'branded widely as a U.S. propaganda device'. The CCF did not hold another major gathering in the developing world until 1958 and, on that occasion, it focused on the less contentious issue of economic development.[41]

Most importantly, the analysis of much work on 'Americanization' is incomplete because, with the absence of the state from consideration, 'culture' is separated from the total political environment. The pretence is maintained that culture is freely transmitted, rather than being mobilized and manipulated for goals which are perhaps not so innocent or laudable.[42] Thus, scholars who attempt to link the political and cultural in the reception of the American crusade face the difficult question of 'autonomy'. Scott-Smith's book is a valuable examination of theory and practice in the development of the CCF but he devotes little space to the evolving thought of European intellectuals even as he claims their 'agreement with [the] 'timeless' principles of intellectual freedom'.[43] Such an assertion has to contend with Christopher Lasch's challenge, published 35 years ago, that 'freedom' was far from a simple matter for the CCF's leading voices: 'The defense of freedom merged imperceptibly with the dogmatic attack on historical materialism which, in another context, had done so much to impede historical and sociological scholarship in the period of the Cold War.'[44]

A case for examination is that of the first systematic deployment of 'culture' in pursuit of a specific political goal, the blocking of communist accession to power in the French and Italian elections of 1948. James Miller, Irving Wall, David Ellwood, and Frank Costigliola have described aspects of the American campaign but the development and reception of culture as political warfare is not considered. Scholarship remains at a level as superficial as the immediate assessment of the US government, after the communists were shut out of the French and Italian ruling coalitions, that American activity had 'aided materially – perhaps decisively' the final result.[45]

If, as Ellwood has shown, the Italian response to the subsequent Marshall Plan was far from simple acceptance of American objectives as well as aid,[46] such a simple conclusion is inadequate. Were the 'local' editors and publishers of US-subsidized newspapers controlled or did they negotiate their own cultural space? *Ninotchka*, the 1939 film starring Greta Garbo, may have been re-released thanks to the campaign of anti-communism, but did its distribution have any impact? How does one evaluate, with its ethnic, social, economic, and 'national' dimensions, the cultural significance of the Letters to Italy campaign? And what of the interaction with the 'political', such as the millions of US dollars supporting the Christian Democratic Party, and with quasi-state institutions such as the Vatican and the Mafia?[47]

The case is even more significant because the US intervention, initially developed as an 'emergency' measure, was far more than temporary given the 'massive popular support which continue[d] to be given the communists'.[48] One of the first missions of the Psychological Strategy Board, created in 1951, was to devise a comprehensive plan for US influence in France and Italy, using 'aggressive propaganda, including an information program, co-ordinated with that of the Italian/French government, and having the appearance of being of Italian/French, rather than U.S. inspiration'.[49] Throughout the 1950s, the CIA station in Italy was distributing 'several million dollars' annually to private allies. Plans were still active in the 1960s, and their legacy may have been long-lasting.[50] Allegations of covert links with 'far-right' Italian movements have been raised in cases such as the kidnapping and slaying of Aldo Moro in 1978 to the bombing of the Bologna train station two years later.

Marc Lazar has evaluated the politico-cultural relationship between a Soviet-defined communism and local parties and institutions in France and Italy.[51] What is needed is a parallel study on the 'non-communist' side, one which goes beyond vague characterizations of 'Americanization' removed from political and economic environments and frameworks. The approach is needed not only for national but also for international and transnational movements such as the Congress for Cultural Freedom.

THE STATE-PRIVATE NETWORK AND THE CULTURAL 'WAR AGAINST TERRORISM'

An examination of the state-private network and the cultural crusade, both through its production and its reception, is far more than a project to fill in a missing history. The current international crisis has not only demonstrated the continuing central place of the state in culture as well as politics; it has also shown that the perceived mission, in the 'war on terrorism', goes beyond the geopolitical. Once again, a not-so-subtle battle for hearts and minds is invoked, as in President George W. Bush's proclamation, 'If ... you don't hold the values we hold dear true to your heart, then you, too, are on our watch list.'[52]

Such an invocation raises fundamental comparisons with the state-private network in the Cold War. The US government might have enlisted advertising executives to promote a Coalition against Terrorism[53] but domestically there appears to be no need for a formal structure to the new crusade, as there was in the 1950s,[54] because of a general unity of belief in 'Americanism' forged over the half-century of the Cold War. That ideology may be vague, even contradictory in its tenets, but it is tangible in the flags, the speeches, the newscasts, the unofficial national anthem 'God Bless America', even the code names of the military operations ('Infinite Justice', 'Enduring Freedom') since 11 September. David Halberstam, formerly known as an incisive critic of the American adventure in Vietnam, framed the ideology in 'Who We Are': 'I have seen the resilience of American democracy time and again ... and I have come to admire the loyalty and energies and resolve of free men and women freely summoned.'[55]

Abroad, cultural projection appears to be a far more difficult proposition. As the Congress for Cultural Freedom soon found in India in 1951, the complex cultural negotiation, with its religious, ethnic, racial, and gendered aspects, is beyond any simple imagery of America and the world. Even the 'special relationship' with Britain could only go so far: a survey in December 2001 found that 'British consumers have become more distrustful of overtly American brands.... The survey found more than two-thirds of British consumers are concerned the world is becoming too Americanized.'[56]

After 11 September 2001 and televised reactions which ranged from celebrations in the West Bank to placards in Pakistan reading, 'America: Think Why You Are Hated', the US government scrambled to project a new campaign for hearts and minds. The press were informed at length about Charlotte Beers, the former director of the advertising company J. Walter Thompson whose nomination to become Undersecretary of State, held up for six months by the Congress, was rushed through after 11 September 2001 so she could 'look after the US's image abroad'. Beers, touted for her campaigns for Uncle Ben's rice ('Perfect every time'), Head and Shoulders shampoo ('Helps bring you closer') and American Express ('Don't leave home without it'), 'would really connect with the hearts and minds of those people'; after all, Secretary of State Colin Powell stated, 'She got me to buy Uncle Ben's rice.' Beers told NBC News about her new task selling the US to the Muslim world, 'This is definitely the most elegant brand I – I've ever had to work with, and I have a lot of facets of the brand. First it's President Bush and Secretary Powell embodying the brand. That's a pretty inspiring place to start.'[57]

There were other clear signs both of the assumption that foreign audiences would embrace all the symbols of 'Americanism' and of the worry that it might not be so. Having failed with public condemnation and appeals to the government of Abu Dhabi to remove the television station Al-Jazeera from the airwaves, the US government declared that it would win the day by putting Secretary of State Powell before Al-Jazeera's cameras. (Nevertheless, in the last bombing of Kabul before its fall to the Northern Alliance, US planes struck Al-Jazeera's office, and Al-Jazeera's correspondent in Washington was arrested. A week later, key Congressmen launched Initiative 911, earmarking $500 million for an Arabic-language satellite television station.[58])

In another echo of US efforts in the Cold War, the government allocated $25 million for Radio Free Afghanistan. The new station would be modeled upon Radio Free Europe and Radio Liberty, which broadcast 'freedom' into the Soviet Union.[59] President Bush's special advisor, Karl Rove, held a 'war summit' in Los Angeles with 40 media executives 'to enlist the creative energies of the television and film industries in winning the propaganda war for the US'.[60] Columnist Thomas Friedman chipped in with an idea for the Saudi Arabian monarchy 'to endow American Studies departments in all Saudi universities', an echo of the US-sponsored development of American Studies throughout Europe in the 1950s.[61]

The desperation of the US state to maintain a grip on world opinion culminated in the self-exposure of a new generation of covert operations. The *New York Times* revealed in February 2002 that the Pentagon's recently-established Office of Strategic Influence, with a multimillion-dollar budget, was 'developing plans to provide news items, possibly even false ones, to foreign media organizations as part of a new effort to influence public sentiment and policy makers in both friendly and unfriendly countries'. According to officials, the OSI would have 'a broad mission ranging from 'black' campaigns that use disinformation and other covert activities to 'white' public affairs that rely on truthful news releases'. The private sector was playing its part in the plans: the Pentagon was paying the Rendon Group, a Boston public relations firm, $100,000 per month for advice on techniques and presentation.[62]

THE LIMITS OF AMERICANIZATION

Yet it is here that 'Americanization' reaches its limits, both in the history of the Cold War and in current international affairs. It is one thing to welcome American cultural products, a far different matter to embrace an entire cultural and ideological system.[63] Bodies such as the Congress for Cultural Freedom could succeed only if there was a negotiation of an 'international' cultural identity, but Cold War America, no less than the Cold War Soviet Union, could not accept an 'autonomy' which did not fully embrace its objectives:

> Unwillingly our free society finds itself mortally challenged by the Soviet system. No other value system is so wholly irreconcilable with ours, so implacable in its purpose to destroy ours, so capable of turning to its own uses the most dangerous and divisive trends in our own society, no other so skillfully and powerfully evokes the elements of irrationality in human nature everywhere, and no other has the support of a great and growing center of military power.[64]

For a time, the Soviet challenge and the Manichean nature of the conflict, as well as the scale of US efforts, obscured these limits. In the 'core' area of US interest, namely Western Europe, the American cultural strategy would parallel that of allies such as Britain, with its elaborate system of 'gray' propaganda disseminated by witting 'private' allies of the state. The CCF could point to immediate advances amongst an intellectual vanguard and initiatives such as the Bilderberg conferences could extend the state-private network across the Atlantic. The 'periphery' was a different matter. Long before the case of Vietnam became a catalyst for dissent from the American cultural as well as political mission, the CCF's unity was being fractured by the changing nature of the Cold War and by the geographical diversity of the organization.[65]

When the illusion of an 'Americanized' world was shattered, the response from US-based intellectuals was one of condemnation rather than understanding. As early as 1954, Leslie Fiedler was panicking in *Encounter* about the Western European 'core', 'The self-distrust of the [European] intellectuals, their loss of faith in their function and in the value of their survival, blends with the Marxist dogma that one's own bougeoisie (if you are a bourgeois, yourself!) is the worst enemy. Conditioned by this principled self-hatred, the European intellectual finds it hard to forgive America for being willing and able to let him live; and even harder to forgive himself for knowing that he could be, in our "McCarthy-ridden" land, if not happy at least unhappy in his customary way. Both these resentments he takes out on a mythicized image of all he hates, which he calls America.'[66]

Irrespective of blithe academic statements about Americanization, the state-private network's projection of America faces the same problems today. After the bombing of Afghanistan began in October 2001, a leading CNN anchorman was lost for words when a correspondent informed him that 81 per cent of Pakistanis polled favoured the Taliban in the military conflict vs. only 3 per cent support for the United States. Academic experts commented, 'While we may be quite supreme on the technological battlefield, we've left the war for people's hearts and minds unoccupied and given Osama bin Laden and his cronies really free reign at manipulating mindsets', while President Bush exclaimed in exasperation, 'I'm amazed that there is such misunderstanding of what our country is about that people would hate us. I am – like most Americans, I just can't believe it, because I know how good we are.'[67] Perhaps more ominously for the US, even the 'core' was not secure. Leading European politicians labeled American foreign policy 'simplistic' and insisted, 'Gulliver can't go it alone', and the British government, usually the last ally to wobble, was warned that it was 'time to stop being America's lap-dog'.[68]

As with Fiedler's 'Good American', the state-private cultural crusade has collapsed in frustration with a deficient 'other'. Francis Fukuyama, still trying to declare the 'end of history', offered, 'Perhaps the hatred [of the US] is born out of a resentment of western success and Muslim failure', while Professor David Forte asserted, 'Most Muslims have been given a diet of socialist propaganda for decades, of hatred of the United States for a long time. They have never had the experience of a secular regime which is open and free by which they can understand the United States for what it is.'[69] Even the British were considered beyond redemption, as political journalist Joe Klein sneered:

> A sad truth: while all the carping [over US treatment of 'unlawful combatants' detained at Camp X-Ray at Guatanamo Bay] pains an Anglophile like me, most Americans don't give a fig about what you think. There is the old American bias toward seeing Europe as tired, flaccid and hopelessly parochial. And there is an old American saying which I think I've just invented: Before you get up on your high horse, be sure you are not riding an ass.[70]

It is to Saunders' credit that we are always far behind her work. American academics may still debate history, as well as current events, on the artificial premise of a US 'freedom' in which there is a division between the state and the private sphere, but they have been left behind. Instead the issue is how 'America', the nation constructed by the state-private network, will be received abroad in the twenty-first century.

For there is a tension, never to be resolved, between American exceptionalism and a universal ideology. In the end, Halberstam's 'Who We

Are' turns upon the fundamental assertion, 'We remained very different from the rest of the world.'[71] And, if that is true, why should the rest of the world continue to welcome the American cultural crusade, especially when that crusade obscures other, less altruistic motives? The words of George Kennan, one of the architects of political warfare and the state-private network, still ring ominously:

> We have about fifty per cent of the world's wealth, but only six point three per cent of its population.... In this situation, we cannot fail to be the object of envy and resentment. Our real task in the coming period is to devise a pattern of relationships which will permit us to maintain this position of disparity without detriment to our national security.... We need not deceive ourselves that we can afford the luxury of altruism and world benefaction.... We should cease to talk about vague objectives such as human rights, the raising of living standards and democratization. The day is not far off when we are going to have to deal in straight power concepts. The less we are then hampered by idealistic slogans, the better.[72]

NOTES

1. Noted examples of the new approach include Frank Costigliola, '"Unceasing Pressure for Penetration": Gender, Pathology, and Emotion in George Kennan's Formation of the Cold War', *Journal of American History* 83/4 (1997) pp.1309–39; Emily S. Rosenberg, '"Foreign Affairs" after World War II: Connecting Sexual and International Politics', *Diplomatic History* 18/1 (1994) pp.59–70, and subsequent commentaries; Cary Fraser, 'Crossing the Color Line in Little Rock: The Eisenhower Administration and the Dilemma of Race for U.S. Foreign Policy', *Diplomatic History* 24/2 (2000) pp.233–64. For further evaluation, see Scott Lucas, 'Culture, Ideology, and History', *Global Dialogue* 3/4 (2001) pp.45–58.
2. See, for example, Walter Hixson, *Parting the Curtain: Propaganda, Culture, and the Cold War* (New York: St. Martin's Press, 1997).
3. Edward Said, *The World, the Text and the Critic* (London: Vintage 1991) p.171. The quotation is also used to introduce Giles Scott-Smith's recent study, *The Politics of Apolitical Culture: The Congress for Cultural Freedom, the CIA and post-war American Hegemony* (London: Routledge 2002) p.2.
4. Tony Smith, 'Making the World Safe for Democracy in the American Century', *Diplomatic History* 23/2 (1999) pp.174–88.
5. Geir Lundestad, 'Empire by Invitation' in the American Century', *Diplomatic History* 23/2 (1999) pp.189–218.
6. Volker Berghahn, 'Philanthropy and Diplomacy', *Diplomatic History* 23/3 (1999) p.419. See also Volker Berghahn, *America and the Intellectual Cold Wars in Europe* (Princeton UP 2001).
7. Jessica Gienow-Hecht, 'Shame on US? Academics, Cultural Transfer, and the Cold War – A Critical Review', *Diplomatic History* 24/3 (2000) p.478.
8. See, for example, the analyses in Frank Costigliola, ''I Had Come as a Friend': Emotion, Culture, and Ambiguity in the Formation of the Cold War', *Cold War History* 1/1 (2000) pp.103–28 and Penny von Eschen, *Race Against Empire: Black Americans and Anticolonialism, 1937–1957* (Ithaca, NY: Cornell UP 1997) as well as Petra Goedde's forthcoming book, *GIs and Germans: Culture, Gender, and Foreign Relations*.

9. See Helen Laville, *Cold War Women* (Manchester, UK: Manchester UP 2002).
10. See the work of Gerald Horne, notably *Black and Red: W.E.B. DuBois and the Afro-American Response to the Cold War, 1944–1963* (Albany: State Univ. of New York Press 1986), and Helen Laville and Scott Lucas, 'The American Way: Edith Sampson, the NAACP, and African-American Identity in the Cold War', *Diplomatic History* 20/4 (1996) pp.565–90.
11. Edward Said, 'Hey, Mister, You Want Dirty Book?', *London Review of Books* 21/19 (30 September 1999) p.55.
12. Frances Stonor Saunders, *Who Paid the Piper? The CIA and the Cultural Cold War* (London: Granta 1999) p.4.
13. Hugh Wilford, 'Calling the Tune? The CIA, The British Left, and the Cold War', paper at the Annual Conference of the Society for Historians of American Foreign Relations, June 2001. See also Wilford's essay in this volume.
14. Scott-Smith, *Politics* (note 3) p.22.
15. Ibid. p.113; Scott Lucas, *Freedom's War: The US Crusade against the Soviet Union, 1945–56* (New York: New York UP 1999) pp.94–6.
16. In addition to the detailed account of financial arrangements in Saunders, see Scott-Smith, *Politics,* 123. The July 1950 report of Melvin Lasky, one of the most important (if problematic) 'private' operatives for the state's covert efforts, on the formation of the CCF is illuminating. His high-minded assertion of 'the intelligentsia of the civilized world … join[ing] together freely, to discuss, to criticize, to formulate an independent program for the defense of their common democratic ideal' is immediately undermined by his implicit call for state direction: 'a comparison with communist-controlled organizations of the 1930's and early 40's should indicate the potential force of a structurally similar, politically opposite (i.e. anti-totalitarian) International Intellectuals' Organization today'. [Scott-Smith, *Politics*, p.114].
17. Peregrine Worsthorne, 'How Western Culture was Saved by the CIA', *Literary Review* (July 1999), reprinted at <www.users.dircon.co.uk/~litrev/reviews/1999/07/Worsthorne_on_Saunders.html>
18. Barbara Sussex, '*Encounter*: Forming a Euro-American Cultural Bloc?' (MPhil (B) thesis, University of Birmingham, 2002) p.19. Kristol later wrote, 'It will be said that my own frequently expressed political opinions were so clearly 'safe', from the CIA's point of view, that censorship was superfluous.' [Irving Kristol, *Looking Back, Looking Ahead: Reflections of a Neoconservative* (New York: Basic Books 1983) p.17].
19. Kristol to Josselson, 15 September 1953, International Association for Cultural Freedom Papers (University of Chicago), Box 94, Folder 7 (author's italics) and Kristol to Josselson, 16 February 1955, IACF Papers, Box 95, Folder 3 (author's italics). I am grateful to Barbara Sussex for these references.
20. See Tom Braden's explanation in 'I'm Glad the CIA is Immoral', *Saturday Evening Post*, 20 May 1967.
21. NSC 4-A, 9 December 1947, reprinted at <http://www.fas.org/irp/offdocs/nsc-hst/nsc-4.htm>
22. James Lay oral history, 17 December 1952, US National Archives, Records of the CIA, History Source Collection of the CIA Historical Staff, Box 12, HS/HB 800C, Interviews K-R.
23. Policy Planning Staff report, 'The Inauguration of Organized Political Warfare', 4 May 1948, *Foreign Relations of the United States, 1945-1950: Emergence of the Intelligence Establishment*, Document 269, <http://www.state.gov/www/about_state/history/intel/260_269.html>
24. See Scott-Smith, *Politics* (note 3) p.71.
25. See Lucas, *Freedom's War* (note 15) p.67 and pp.100–4.
26. Executive Director's report, 27 August 1953, Lena Phillips Papers (Schlesinger Library, Radcliffe College, Cambridge, Massachusetts), Carton 7, Committee of Correspondence.
27. Lucas, *Freedom's War* (note 15) pp.118–20.
28. See the accounts in Federico Romero, *The United States and the European Trade Union Movement, 1944–1951* (Chapel Hill: Univ. of North Carolina Press 1992) and Anthony Carew, 'The American Labor Movement in Fizzland: the Free Trade Union Committee and the CIA', *Labor History* 39/1 (1998) pp.25–42.

29. Lovestone to Brown, 26 March 1951, Lovestone Papers (Hoover Institution, Stanford University, Palo Alto CA), Box 381, Irving Brown.
30. Kristol to Josselson, [undated – February 1955], IACF Papers, Box 95, Folder 3.
31. Josselson to Kristol, 13 February 1955, IACF Papers, Box 95, Folder 3 (author's italics).
32. In addition to Saunders' exposé of Foundation funding for CIA-backed projects, see Kathleen D. McCarthy, 'From Cold War to Cultural Development: The International Cultural Activities of the Ford Foundation, 1950–1980', *Daedalus* 116/1 (1987) pp.93–105.
33. Record of Princeton Meetings, 10–11 May 1952, *US Declassified Document Reference System*, 1988, p.1164.
34. NSC 20/4, 23 Nov. 1948, *Foreign Relations of the United States*, 1948, Volume I, pp.662–9.
35. In addition to Lucas's argument in *Freedom's War*, see his 'The Myth of Leadership: Dwight Eisenhower and the Quest for Liberation', in Constantine Pagedas and Thomas Otte (eds.) *Personalities, War, and Diplomacy* (Basingstoke, UK: Macmillan 1997).
36. CIA memorandum, 'American Students in Post-war International Affairs', undated, *US Declassified Reference System*, 1994, p.1781; CIA memorandum, undated, *US Declassified Document Reference System*, 1992, p.12.
37. On ORIT, see Philip Agee, *Inside the Company: CIA Diary* (Harmondsworth: Penguin 1975). On the Committee of Correspondence, in addition to Laville's *Cold War Women* (note 9) the assertion is based on an interview by Laville and Scott Lucas with Anne Crolius in 1993.
38. Reed to Benton, 3 October 1946, Hulten Papers (Truman Library, Independence, Missouri), Box 15, Voice of America 1946–47.
39. See, for example, Reinhold Wagnleitner and Elaine Tyler May (eds.) *'Here, There, and Everywhere: The Foreign Politics of American Popular Culture* (Hanover, NH: UP of New England 2000).
40. Peter Conrad, 'What did John Wayne do in the Cold War, Daddy?', *The Guardian* (London), 4 July 1999, <http://www.guardianunlimited.co.uk/Archive/Article/0,4273,3880329,00.html>
41. Christopher Lasch, 'The Cultural Cold War: A Short History of the Congress for Cultural Freedom' in Barton Bernstein (ed.) *Towards a New Past* (New York: Pantheon 1968) pp.332–4.
42. This is my greatest concern with the excellent work of Rob Kroes, perhaps the foremost European scholar on 'Americanization'. See his 'Advertising: The Commodification of American Icons of Freedom', in Wagnleitner and May *Here, There* (note 39) pp.273–308.
43. Scott-Smith, *Politics* (note 6) p.166.
44. Lasch in Bernstein (ed.), *Towards* (note 41) pp.326–8.
45. Acheson-Bevin meeting, 14 September 1949, *Foreign Relations of the United States*, 1949, Volume VI, 415.
46. See Ellwood's contribution to this collection and his 'The Impact of the Marshall Plan on Italy; The Impact of Italy on the Marshall Plan', in Rob Kroes *et al.* (eds.) *Cultural Transmissions and Receptions: American Mass Culture in Europe* (Amsterdam: VU UP 1993).
47. On US intervention in Italy, see James Miller, *The United States and Italy, 1940-1950: The Politics and Diplomacy of Stabilization* (Chapel Hill: Univ. of North Carolina Press 1986) and Lucas, *Freedom's War* (note 15) pp.43–7 and pp.136–8.
48. Bonbright to Matthews, 7 July 1951, Harry S Truman Papers (Truman Library), Staff Memorandum and Office Files, PSB Files, Box 11, 091.4 Europe #1.
49. 'Plan 'B' Action Checklist', 22 October 1951, *US Declassified Document Reference System*, 1991, p.1617.
50. William Colby, *Honourable Men: My Life in the CIA* (London: Hutchinson 1978) pp.108–40; 'Italy: Department of State Guidelines for Policy and Operations', January 1962, *US Declassified Document Reference System*, 1992, p.1393.
51. See Lazar's contribution to this collection.
52. George Bush, 31 January 2002, quoted in 'Bush Warns Nations that Sponsor Terrorism', <http://www.cnn.com/2002/ALLPOLITICS/01/31/ bush/index.html>
53. Claire Cozens, 'US Attempts to Shore Up Support for War', *The Guardian* (London), 30 Oct.

2001, <http://www.guardian.co.uk/Archive/Article/0,4273,4288135,00.html>

54. 'A large measure of sacrifice and discipline will be demanded of the American people. They will be asked to give up some of the benefits which they have come to associate with their freedoms. Nothing could be more important than that they fully understand the reasons for this. The risks of a superficial understanding or of an inadequate appreciation of the issues are obvious and might lead to the adoption of measures which in themselves would jeopardize the integrity of our system.' [State Department/Department of Defense report (NSC 68), 7 April 1950,*US Declassified Document Reference System*, Retrospective 71D].
55. David Halberstam, 'Who We Are', *Vanity Fair*, Nov. 2001, p.9.
56. Claire Cozens, 'US Brands Suffer as Anti-American Feeling Runs High', *The Guardian* (London), 21 Dec. 2001, <http://www.guardian.co.uk/Archive/Article/0,4273,4324034,00.html>
57. 'Publicity Queen Sells America to the Muslims', *The Times* (London), 16 Oct. 2001, p.3; 'Bush hires advertising executive to pour out PR messages over Afghanistan', *NBC Nightly News*, 7 Nov. 2001, <http://www.prfirms.org/resources/news/bush_hires_110701.asp>. The most extravagant (and culturally-blind) linkage of commerce, propaganda, and 'Americanism' came in the advice of a London-based US advertising executive on 'Selling the Stars and Stripes', even as he protested, 'Most Americans really have no idea why they are hated (aside from the obvious, that we're happier, better looking, and own 25 per cent of the world's wealth). After months of trying to figure it out, we have yet to land upon a set of nefarious actions or deeds that would justify such sentiments.' [Ashley Alsup, 'Selling the stars and stripes', *The Observer* (London), 2 Dec. 2001, p.7].
58. Duncan Campbell, 'US Plans TV Station to Rival Al-Jazeera', *The Guardian* (London), 23 Nov. 2001, <http://www.guardian.co.uk/Archive/Article/0,4273,4305529,00.html>. In Jan. 2002, CNN.com launched its Arabic-language service. A CNN official denied that the timing of the initiative had anything to do with US government efforts. (Private information, 4 Dec. 2001).
59. For a discussion of Radio Free Afghanistan, see Lauren Langbaum, 'The Truth Will Set You Radio Free', HotlineScoop.com, 30 November 2001, <http://hotlinescoop.com/web/content/features/matchup/matchup011130.htm>
60. Andrew Gumbel 'Bush Enlists Hollywood to 'help the war effort', *The Independent* (London), 12 Nov. 2001, <http://www.independent.co.uk/story.jsp?story=104472>; Duncan Campbell, 'Hollywood Hopes for War Role', *The Guardian* (London), 14 Nov. 2001, <http://www.guardian.co.uk/Archive/Article/0,4273,4299166,00.html>
61. Thomas Friedman, 'Pay Attention: We Don't Buy Your Dangerous Lies', *The Guardian* (London), 17 Oct. 2001, <http://www.guardian.co.uk/Archive/Article/0,4273,4278706,00.html>
62. James Dao and Eric Schmitt, 'Pentagon Readies Efforts to Sway Sentiment Abroad', *New York Times*, 19 February 2002, <http://query.nytimes.com/search/abstract?res=F30C1EF6345B0C7A8DDDAB0894DA404482>. Embarrassed by the leak of the plans, the Bush Administration emphasized in the following days that the plans had not been approved.
63. Perhaps the most egregious conflation of cultural product and system occurred in *The Times* of London in Feb. 2002. The newspaper's editorial asserted that the desire of Iran's young people to eat pizza pointed towards a desire for a revolution, to be led by the late Shah's son, to join the West. ['Inside Iran: A Regime that may not be as Secure as It Looks', p.13].
64. State Department/Department of Defense report (NSC 68), 7 April 1950, *US Declassified Document Reference System*, Retrospective 71D.
65. See Peter Coleman, *The Liberal Conspiracy: The Congress for Cultural Freedom and the Struggle for the Mind of Postwar Europe* (New York: The Free Press 1989) pp.199–211.
66. Leslie Fiedler, 'The Good American', *Encounter* 2/3 (March 1954) p.54.
67. Wolf Blitzer, *CNN Late Edition*, 14 Oct. 2001; Jerrold Post, George Washington University, *CNN Late Edition*, 14 Oct. 2001; George Bush speech quoted in *CNN Late Edition*, 14 Oct. 2001, available at: <http://www.cnn.com/TRANSCRIPTS/0110/14/le.00.html>
68. Vedrine quoted in 'Peremptory tendencies: France fires a warning shot at the US', *The Guardian* (London), 7 Feb. 2002, <http://www.guardian.co.uk/Archive/Article/

0,4273,4351220,00.html>; Jonathan Freedland, 'Patten lays into Bush's America', *The Guardian* (London), 9 February 2002, p.1; Will Hutton, 'Time to stop being America's lap-dog', *The Observer* (London), 17 February 2002, p.30.

69. Francis Fukuyama, 'The West Has Won', *The Guardian* (London), 11 Oct. 2001, <http://www.guardian.co.uk/Archive/Article/0,4273,4274753,00.html>; David Forte, Cleveland State University, *CNN Late Edition*, 14 Oct. 2001, <http://www.cnn.com/TRANSCRIPTS/0110/14/le.00.html>
70. Joe Klein, 'It's interrogation, not torture', *The Guardian* (London), 4 Feb. 2002, Section G2, p.2.
71. Halberstam, 'Who We Are', p.5.
72. PPS 23, 'Review of Current Trends in US Foreign Policy', 24 Feb. 1948, in Anna Kasten Nelson (ed.) *The State Department Policy Planning Staff Papers*, Volume II: 1948 (New York: Garland 1983) p.122.

5

The Politics of Productivity and the Politics of Anti-Communism: American and European Labour in the Cold War

ANTHONY CAREW

> 'Endless efforts have been made to increase productivity without coming to grips with this problem [i.e. the role of organized labour]. Foremen have watched workers. Engineers have measured workers. Personnel technicians have cajoled workers. Industrial psychologists have tested workers. And the latest group, the psychiatric sociologists have brought psychoanalytic techniques to the workbench and, where others have failed, they now offer to mesmerize workers.'[1]

In this contribution I want to discuss the 'politics of productivity' within the Marshall Plan and to locate it within the wider politics of anti-communism as it affected the labour movement during this early phase of the Cold War. It involves looking at the American agenda for Europe and the European reaction to this. It also means examining the differences within the American labour movement over how communism should best be fought.

Historians have constructed various over-arching concepts to explain the forces at work in the Cold War, the 'politics of productivity' being one such. The expression was coined by Charles Maier to describe America's attempt to shape the post-war international economic order in such a way that political issues were transformed into problems of output. It would result in a political settlement with an emphasis on subordinating class conflict to consensus around the pursuit of economic growth through productivity, a state of affairs characterized by 'consensual American hegemony'.[2] In the field of labour it meant that economies were more likely to succeed if class-based labour relations were abandoned, with employers and workers becoming partners in the non-ideological pursuit of technical efficiency. Maier describes an approach that was plainly visible within the Marshall Plan and its successor aid programmes which ran throughout the years 1948-60.[3] Organized labour was, of course, a key player in this phase of the

Cold War, sometimes as an agent of change, often as the object of other people's programmes and strategies.

POLITICS OF PRODUCTIVITY

A programme focusing on productivity issues appeared first in Britain in the early months of the Marshall Plan with the creation of the tripartite Anglo-American Productivity Council (AAPC). Its initial emphasis was on sharing technical know-how in the interests of efficiency, though it was to become much more than this. But it was in the second half of the Marshall Plan, with rearmament following the start of the Korean War in 1950, that an increase in productivity throughout Europe became a general objective. Productivity in Europe had been on an upward trend between 1947 and 1950, largely as a result of the re-imposition of managerial discipline that was made possible by conservative financial disciplines. Now a more concerted approach was needed, one that would involve the active support of workers. It was no longer good enough simply to increase production, it was essential to produce more with greater efficiency. A new productivity and technical assistance department (PTAD) was created within the Marshall Plan with a budget rising from four million dollars in 1949 to 43 million in 1952 and earmarked for technical assistance – the transfer of technology and know-how. Americans saw themselves as the fount of knowledge in this area: they would be the disseminators of 'the truth'. This was the period when American productivity consultants and efficiency experts began to descend on Europe in numbers, 900 of them by 1954. It was also the period when study visits to America by European workers and managers moved into high gear, with 7,000 people crossing to the United States over the next three years.

The productivity programme that ran for most of the next decade had a variety of elements that could be broadly grouped into three categories. At the forefront were schemes intended to increase the productivity of labour through the reorganization of the labour process and the wage system. Central to these were campaigns to spread the use of work study. Marshall Plan officials would later describe the Work Study Training programme as 'the number one technical assistance programme of all time'. It aimed to bring 2,000 young European workers to the United States for a year's training while instructing many more at home. Secondly there were programmes to raise more generally the professionalism of management in all areas on the basis of ideas deriving from the notion of 'scientific' management. Thirdly there was a broad education and information programme with a highly ideological thrust involving study visits, publications, films, and training courses designed to instil into Europeans an awareness of the virtues of a consumer oriented, mass production, managerially driven free enterprise system on the American model.

For the Americans the productivity programme was about more than imparting an awareness of some common-sense facts of economic life: it was about wrenching Europeans away from their traditional values and convincing them of the virtues of a world of market-led growth, competition and unceasing change – the 'growth society' as Raymond Aron termed it.[4] Recognizing that organized labour in Europe had always strongly adhered to socialist ideas, the Marshall Plan strategy was that 'with increased wages ... resulting from the Production Assistance Drive, labour should see that its best future is with private capitalism and a free enterprise economic system.'[5]

Following the model of the AAPC, from mid-1951 each Marshall Plan country came under pressure to establish a National Productivity Centre (NPC). The driving force behind the launch of the NPCs was the Benton-Moody programme under the Mutual Security Act, commonly known as Conditional Aid, which earmarked 100 million dollars for purposes of nurturing in Europe American concepts of free enterprise. Funded largely by Marshall Plan counterpart funds, these centres were the partner bodies of the US aid agency and had responsibility for organizing study visits of workers, managers and technical staff to America, and within their own territory publishing literature on productivity while conducting training and education programmes in a variety of subjects under the general rubric of management science.

In Britain, there was no great difficulty in the transformation of the AAPC into the British Productivity Council (BPC), and here the productivity programme proceeded reasonably smoothly across the full range of activities. They included a productivity advisory service; a factory visits programme to spread information of best practice that would organize 10,000 inter-factory visits for the workers and managers of 500 firms; a publicity programme with a budget of $500,000 which allowed the production of a monthly productivity bulletin, tens of thousands of copies of occasional pamphlets and financing of nine television films on productivity; a loan facility to help small businesses to re-equip and re-organize, and a three million dollar fund for the promotion of training and research on productivity. Most important of all was the BPC's Work Study Unit which organized large conferences throughout the country. Much of the teaching material used was straight from the work study courses developed by ICI, a firm not noted for its embrace of trade unions. On the one occasion when the Trade Union Congress (TUC) did put forward a nominee to join the panel of lecturers, he was rejected for being 'too political'. Even so, the TUC continued to support this programme and only drew the line when the BPC proposed to introduce a work study advisory service for individual firms.

Americans working on the aid programme were critical of the Trades Union Congress for not publicizing more vigorously its own positive report on American industrial practices and productivity achievements. They recognized that British union leaders did not want to appear to their members to be under undue American influence. But Marshall Plan staff believed that the British labour leaders were privately more enthusiastic about the campaign than they dared admit in public. Clearly the hope of the TUC leaders was that the beneficial effects of increased productivity would outweigh undesirable aspects such as the spread of unilaterally imposed work-study programmes. But they could not escape the fact that at rank and file level there was often great suspicion of the campaign and at best a weariness born of constant exhortation to do better. The day when workers would enjoy the pay-off for greater productivity always seemed as far away as ever. And as long as unions feared the effects of the Conservative government's labour policies, they were unlikely to advocate an end to restrictive practices. The mounting press campaign from the mid-1950s highlighting restrictive practices of workers and their general restrictive spirit may be taken as evidence of the limited appeal of the productivity propaganda during this decade.

In other European countries it proved more difficult to establish effective national productivity centres. Governments were not overly enthusiastic about the initiative and often responded by simply going through the motions. Employers were wary of this new, intensified phase of interest in productivity. In a sense they were taking their cue from American businessmen associated with the National Association of Manufacturers who feared that the productivity programme in Europe would only intensify European union calls for 'co-determination'. The Patronat in France were extremely doubtful about the American approach and felt they were being pressured into a scheme they did not want. Jean Monnet too had misgivings about the programme's emphasis on labour productivity as opposed to the productivity of capital.

A similar lack of enthusiasm was evident in Italy. The NPC, established as part of the prime minister's office, was a weak body, lacking dynamism and in reality little more than a glorified management consulting agency. It met formally only twice a year and signally failed to give the impression that it saw a long-term role for itself. From the outset, manufacturing employers in Confindustria and the management association CITA considered that the establishment of a national productivity centre was unnecessary.

West Germany was the last of the major countries to establish an NPC under the auspices of the economics ministry. There was considerable confusion about its role and how it would relate to the already existing Rationalisierungs kuratorium der Deutschen Wirtschaft (RKW). German unions believed that the extension of co-determination represented a sounder approach to industrial efficiency and feared that American-style productivity would simply add to the unemployment rolls. An initial productivity scheme proposed for the railways would have led to the loss of 50,000 jobs. For these reasons, in the early years German unions remained aloof from the American-led initiative. By spring 1953 the NPC was still barely operational. When launched it was subject to close monitoring by the US aid agency and an American seat on the governing body allowed it a veto over policy. As late as 1955 the Americans considered the NPC to be 'on trial'.

In each of these countries as well as in Belgium and Austria, organized labour complained of being granted only a minority voice in the affairs of the NPC and the elaboration of productivity programmes. This was a fundamental problem that was never rectified.[6] In Germany the Deutsche Gewerkschaftsbund (DGB) protested that the two seats allocated to them out of nine did not amount to co-determination. Trade union representatives on the Italian national productivity centre were greatly outnumbered by businessmen and productivity 'experts', and it was a reflection of the low priority granted to the interests of workers that the labour division was the last element in the NPC administrative structure to be established. In France even the non-communist unions were kept at arm's length from the NPC and given only the right to advise on proposed team visits to the USA through a body subordinate to the NPC.[7] The French unions would later acquire a dedicated research centre, Centre Intersyndical d'Etudes et de Recherche de Productivité (CIERP), to service them on questions of productivity, staffed by experts and financed by the Americans. But within this organization deference to the American paymaster on the part of the French technical staff was evident and their advocacy of policies not approved of by the unions led to internal friction. Within two years there would be a parting of the ways with Force Ouvrière (FO) cutting its ties with the CIERP.

The head of the Marshall Plan Labour Division in France viewed the early phase of the productivity programme with concern and warned his superiors: 'I personally believe that the differences...are so strong that they compel the consideration of whether the programme is worth anything at all.' At a similar stage in the German programme his counterpart in Bonn echoed these sentiments: 'Some time ago I wrote ... recommending that ... the money should be put back in the till, and the intensive and comprehensive productivity programme abandoned.'[8]

THE PILOT PLANT PROGRAMME

Inevitably the programmes of the NPCs were of particular concern to organized labour. Emphasis on the productivity of labour often simply meant pressure on employees to work harder: at best it tended to mean working differently.[9] However, if trade unions were to go along with this in the national interest the whole programme would need to be opened up to the principles of collective bargaining. There might well be scope for improving the organization of work, but the manner of doing so and the objectives for which the improvements were sought needed to be jointly agreed. As a trade union consultant on productivity for the Marshall Plan, William Gomberg believed that his role was to take the techniques of scientific management and convert them from substitutes for collective bargaining into tools of collective bargaining. This was where a major battle would have to be waged.

Despite the scepticism of the Europeans, to American labour officials working independently of the Marshall programme in Europe the productivity focus did seem to open up new possibilities. Hitherto the Marshall Plan had not benefited workers directly, living standards had not improved, and full employment was not a high priority. Within the US labour movement there was growing disquiet over this record. In France and Italy, the two countries where Marshall Aid (and thus economic recovery) were most strongly challenged by the communist-dominated labour movements, collective bargaining was a frail institution little in evidence below national level. The communist-led unions were essentially vehicles for political mobilization – up to 1947 championing the battle for production; after 1947 sabotaging recovery on Cominform instructions. The minority unions that had broken away from the communist fold were weak and no match for the communists when it came to political mobilization. Meanwhile workers were being exploited as productivity rose.[10] But some American trade unionists believed that if the French non-communist unions could be encouraged to engage in detailed negotiation within industries and enterprises over the content of productivity programmes they could prove their worth, gain greater support among workers and thereby increase membership. According to this scenario, successful productivity bargaining would be the arena within which communism would be defeated.

As represented particularly by the CIO wing of the American labour movement, the aim was to foster a form of trade unionism that was militant in its approach to collective bargaining, strongly organized at the base, vigorous in its defence of workers' interests and with a particular focus on the enterprise. The communists could be left to indulge in sloganeering about the class war, but militant non-communist unions would achieve tangible benefits for their members in the here and now. It was not a question of seeking to build a non-political labour movement – the link between politics and trade unionism in Europe was recognized to be too strong for that – but it was a matter of making workers collectively more self-sufficient in their place of work and so less reliant on political mobilization. This was US labour's approach within the productivity programme. In part its point of reference was the hard-nosed bargaining practices of American trade unionists in industries such as automobile manufacturing, but it also borrowed from the unique experience of the US clothing industry where trade union industrial engineers had applied pressure on employers to raise efficiency and so improve wages and job security.

This model of trade unionism was embraced by Marshall Plan labour staff when in 1951 the Americans called for the establishment of a 'pilot plant' programme as a central element of Conditional Aid. Under this, particular industries or enterprises in selected locations were to benefit from American investment and concerted technical assistance in an effort to drive up productivity.[11] For the Americans it was an attempt to effect a cultural change in Europe by challenging the restrictive mentality that impeded the free flow of market forces, whether in the shape of employer cartels, patterns of national collective bargaining and wage uniformity, or worker suspicion of new technology. The hope was to encourage 'maverick' businesses to jettison past practices and explore new ways. If as a consequence they suffered ostracism by employers' associations, the Americans would step in and ensure that they were not disadvantaged in terms of access to supplies and markets. But it would prove to be difficult to break down the sense of collective identity of European employers. As an example, virtually all the men's clothing firms in France offered themselves as pilot plants rather than have to compete with one another.[12]

The main focus of the pilot plant programme was France and Italy. In France such plants were designated in over 100 steel enterprises and were widespread in the clothing and footwear industries. In Italy the 'demonstration areas', as they were called, were proposed for 15 districts with as many as 200 firms involved. In practice only two schemes materialized covering some 50 firms, the main location being Vicenza. Germany's pilot plant scheme was later in preparation and hardly got past the drawing board stage.

The idea of the Marshall Plan labour staff was that collective bargaining would take place between the local employers in the pilot schemes and the non-communist unions especially over the equitable share-out of gains from any increased productivity. In practice from the start of the Conditional Aid programme this issue became a fundamental cause of dispute. It ranged Marshall Plan administrators against European governments, Labor Division staff against PTAD staff and national trade union federations against governments and employers. In the event, European governments balked at the idea of incorporating into their agreements with the Americans on the use of Conditional Aid any specific reference as to how productivity gains should be apportioned. And employers subsequently rejected the trade union claim that gains from increased productivity should be shared on an equal basis by business, workers and consumers. Employers were adamantly opposed to writing such a formula into collective agreements. At best, as in Italy, they were only prepared to exchange with the unions non-binding letters of intent. Many employers made it clear to the Americans that they would abandon the scheme if they were pressed any further on this issue.

Within the aid agency, business interests proved to be more influential than organized labour, and the Americans backed away from insisting that collective bargaining be part and parcel of the pilot schemes, in other words a condition of Conditional Aid. In the absence of such insistence as a condition of participation in the scheme, the French and Italian unions were generally too weak to drive a hard bargain with their employers in the pilot plants. What had therefore been intended as a programme to demonstrate the virtues of collective bargaining within a regime calculated to increase productivity and prosperity went disastrously awry. The correspondence of the Marshall Plan labour staff reveals their anguish and frustration at this turn of events. The Chief of the Labor Division became embroiled in an intense conflict with his superior, the Special Representative in Europe, over their failure to demand fair treatment of workers whose productivity had increased. He argued that there could be 'no appropriate role for the Labor Division in an agency that confesses it has no means available of assuming that a proper share of the benefits of its major industrial programme will accrue to workers.' With the matter unresolved a year later a new Acting Director of the Labor Division was told that if he resisted established policy he would be dismissed forthwith. It was one of the big battles fought within the Marshall Plan administration, and it was one that the labour staff lost.[13]

Marshall Plan officials could never comprehend why, in the case of the French employers, they refused to enter into a bargaining relationship with non-communist unions that might have seen the communists outflanked. Instead industrialists seemed to prefer existing industrial relations practice characterized by periodic CGT-staged insurrectionary strikes and demonstrations. No doubt the employers recognized that the CGT spoke for the greater proportion of organized workers and could not be ignored. But perhaps another consideration was that following its syndicalist tradition, the CGT also avoided any collective bargaining entanglements, conveniently leaving managerial prerogative unchallenged. In Italy the employers' organization Confindustria had its own criticisms of the American approach to productivity, claiming with some logic that it was misplaced in a country with a surfeit of cheap labour.[14] In the demonstration areas benefits accruing to workers were minor and the employment situation continued to be characterized by low wages, bonuses fixed unilaterally by management, non-recognition of unions and discipline maintained by the fear of unemployment.

Despite these problems, the Americans persevered with the pilot plants in the hope that something good would come out of the programme. The attitude seemed to be that any programme was better than no programme. But for the Congress of Industrial Organizations (CIO), the main labour advocate of productivity bargaining, the scheme's failure was insupportable. It therefore called on its trade union allies in France and Italy to withdraw from the programme. The French FO and the Italian UIL did exactly that. At that point, what had been intended to be the centrepiece of the French and Italian productivity programmes effectively died.

The CIO's assessment of this phase of the programme was scathing: 'In France and Italy, and in the rest of Europe to somewhat lesser extent, the productivity programme was implemented with none of the elementary safeguards that American unions would insist on for their own members. It was policed in an inadequate and shoddy way that amounted to nothing less than a speed-up programme that undermined jobs and bolstered...prices.' The American Federation of Labor (AFL)'s representative in Italy judged that the productivity programme was 'a snare and a delusion, a complete waste of time, energy, money and personnel and adds up in my opinion to an A1 scandal.'[15]

From 1953 the physical presence of Americans in Europe began to wane as a process of Europeanization of the aid programme commenced. In 1955 executive control of the programme passed to the European Productivity Agency (EPA). Its ten million dollar budget was still mostly funded by the United States and many American technical staff continued to work for it, but formal administration was in the hands of Europeans within the framework of the OEEC. Under the EPA there was a partial shift in emphasis in that Europeans were now expected to learn from each other about productivity, exchanging team visits in order to disseminate best practice. Yet the United States was still held to be the Mecca for up-to-date management thinking, Europeans continued to cross the Atlantic in large numbers on study visits, many to attend courses at the business schools of Harvard and Columbia University, and consultants from such establishments figured prominently in EPA programmes. It would be fair to say that the spiritual force behind the EPA still remained in America.

During the first two years of the EPA's existence there was no union role in policy making. The programme for labour continued the fixation with work study while promoting 'human relations' techniques, the latest managerial fad for breaking down worker resistance to management.[16] However, by 1956 the position of EPA Deputy Director was awarded to a senior union official and thereafter there was a stronger union voice in the shaping of programmes, with greater stress on the need for agreement between the two sides of industry on the means and ends of sponsored projects. Towards the end of the 1950s European trade unionists associated with the EPA belatedly felt that they were beginning to gain some purchase on projects and were having some influence on the way productivity was approached. However, the frenetic pace of the productivity campaign never let up and even in 1959, the EPA's last full year of operation, its programme for trade unionists enrolled 4,000 trade union officers on 51 national-level training courses and 400 on inter-European study visits.[17] And right until the programme was finally wound up in 1960, there remained in much of the European labour movement a feeling that the productivity drive was something that had been imposed on them by the United States and that all too often it amounted to little more than a vehicle for management propaganda.

Overall one can hazard some generalizations about American policy in Europe. By the late 1950s, assisted by American aid and the growing integration of national economies, western Europe had largely recovered. What contribution had been made by the productivity programme addressed to labour is harder to tell. The sheer weight and volume of propaganda in favour of ever greater effort meant that people throughout western Europe were now familiar with the concept of higher productivity as a 'good thing'. To question the logic of this, for whatever reason, was to go against a tidal wave of received wisdom: doubters left themselves open to charges of 'Luddism'. Because of the managerial slant in the productivity programme, workers found themselves having to debate the issue in terms that supported the agenda of business. The politics of productivity made it easier for management to justify their efforts to control the labour process since the 'science' of industrial efficiency was largely the preserve of capital. The emphasis on the human factor in achieving higher levels of efficiency made it easier to blame the lack of worker effort for inadequate productivity growth, even when, as in Britain, low capital investment was a major culprit.

The 1950s saw the start of the long post-war boom and the spread of a Fordist system that nowadays conjures up for some in the labour movement nostalgia for days when unions were powerful. But if productivity was rising as a consequence of the American-backed campaign, it was certainly not universally a product of a routinized system of harmonious industrial relations based on shared values. Indeed collective bargaining practice in countries such as France and Italy still fell far short of what the Americans had hoped to create. There were labour-management battles here that remained to be fought in the 1960s. It is hard, therefore, to see how, in any direct way, the politics of productivity had much impact in strengthening non-communist unions in these countries. They may have chipped away at communist trade union strength, but they had certainly not dislodged it.

THE POLITICS OF ANTI-COMMUNISM

As this overview of the American productivity programme for Europe reveals, in terms of the involvement of the American labour movement the main player was the CIO. But there is another dimension to the productivity programme which brings into the spotlight the AFL, the other main organization in the US labour movement, indeed the senior body. This constitutes a coda to the history of the productivity campaign and reveals a great deal about American differences over how to fight communism during the Cold War. The AFL remained largely aloof from the productivity programme, sceptical as to its chances of succeeding and sometimes openly hostile to the role played in it by the CIO. What were the issues at work here?

The AFL and the CIO had a very uneasy relationship rooted in the labour history of the 1930s and 1940s. During the Marshall Plan years, there remained deep personal animosities at leadership level and the memory of significant ideological differences. The AFL had always been deeply anti-communist whereas the CIO had included leading communists among its first generation of leaders. The CIO had also spent four years from 1945 to 1949 as a partner of the USSR's trade union federation inside the World Federation of Trade Unions (WFTU), whereas the AFL had adamantly refused to join that body precisely because of Soviet trade union membership. With the Marshall Plan up and running, the CIO had withdrawn from the WFTU by 1949 and in the same year it purged the bulk of its communist leadership. This allowed new scope for the AFL and CIO to participate jointly in the anti-communist International Confederation of Free Trade Unions (ICFTU) and to liaise on aspects of international policy including the Marshall Plan. But there was still considerable mistrust on the part of the AFL, especially over the question of anti-communist policy and practice. Simply stated, the AFL did not believe that CIO leaders had a sufficiently clear understanding of the nature of the problem posed by communism within the labour movement, nor did they believe that they had a real commitment to fighting it. At best they regarded the CIO leadership as woolly and confused and therefore unreliable allies in the anti-communist crusade.

The productivity programme of the Marshall Plan served to highlight the differences in emphasis between the two organizations. The CIO believed, as did many in the Marshall Plan, that economic and social want opened the doors to communism and therefore to resist it meant creating healthy economies, progressive social policies and a socio-economic regime in which democratic trade unions played an integral part. As CIO President Walter Reuther argued: 'There is a revolution going on ... of hungry men to get the wrinkles out of their bellies...The communists didn't start it. They are riding its back ... The communists would have people trade freedom for bread ... In the world that we are trying to help build, people can have both bread and freedom.'[18] The productivity programme fitted neatly into this framework.

Yet to the AFL leaders this was a simple-minded approach, one they dismissed as 'belly communism'. Workers, they insisted, were more interested in 'freedom' than bread and butter issues. They saw communism as a much more virile and dangerous force, not confined to areas of economic hardship.[19] It had to be challenged directly in every conceivable theatre and by every possible means, economic, political, military and cultural. There could be no compromises. What was needed was an unremitting struggle, not simply to contain communism but to roll it back and defeat it. Those who did not share the AFL's uncompromising position were themselves regarded with suspicion, even when they were explicitly anti-communist in their own day-to-day practice. Likewise there was no tolerating those who espoused neutralist sentiments in the Cold War: every organization had to choose which side it was on. Above all there was no room for notions of peaceful co-existence with any brand of communism, even if it did project a 'new look' as in the USSR after Stalin's death.[20]

This perspective within the AFL reflected the thinking of a small group of union leaders who comprised the Federation's Free Trade Union Committee (FTUC). The FTUC's Executive Secretary was Jay Lovestone, one time Secretary of the American Communist Party. With a small field staff, most prominent of whom was his protégé Irving Brown, Lovestone ran the FTUC as an agency dedicated to fighting communism in the international labour movement around the world. In doing so he utilized similar clandestine techniques to those that were the stock-in-trade of the Cominform. In effect it amounted to communist practice in reverse. While the CIO focused their efforts on strengthening collective bargaining machinery in France and Italy, the FTUC conducted a range of international operations from support for strong-arm gangs in Marseilles and Genoa to break up communist-led dock strikes, through to financial support for anti-communist publications; material support for non-communist trade unions in Finland in the ferocious fight with the communists for control of the Finnish national trade union centre SAK; systematic attempts to woo dissident communist Party members in France and Italy; organizational assistance and courier services for the Congress for Cultural Freedom; a network of spies and undercover agents operating in Eastern Europe; material assistance to non-communist trade unionists in Berlin. And beyond

FIGURE 1

Matthew Woll, of the International Photo Engravers Union of North America, flanked by Jay Lovestone (to his right, seated) and Irving Brown (to his left) at a meeting of the American Federation of Labor and the French Force Ouvrière in Paris 1951.

Arthur Deakin file of the George Meany Memorial Archives, Silver Spring, Maryland, USA

Europe the FTUC mounted expensive anti-communist programmes targeted on the labour movement in India, Indonesia and Taiwan.[21] Most of these activities were well hidden from view. The more conventional, open trade union aspects of the AFL's work overseas were left to the far less important International Affairs Committee.

What is important about Lovestone's FTUC operation is that it was generously funded from CIA sources, especially in the early 1950s, and much of the CIA's funding of covert labour programmes was channelled through Marshall Plan counterpart funds. However, Lovestone had a fraught relationship with his CIA paymasters, some of whom he considered too liberal in their politics.[22] As with the leadership of the CIO, he regarded such CIA types as innocents abroad when it came to fighting communism. In this game of cat and mouse between the FTUC and the CIA it was never really clear who was using who, and certainly both were trying to gain the upper hand. Crucially the relationship really began to sour in 1950 when the CIO first sought American government financial assistance for its international work, and especially funding from Marshall Plan sources. With Marshall Plan funds already being tapped by the CIA to pay for the FTUC's covert operations, the CIO now seemed to be vying for access to the FTUC's secret honey pot.

In 1951, as the new phase of the productivity programme began to expand, the CIO decided to establish a permanent presence in Europe. It justified this on the grounds that Marshall Aid had thus far been a disappointment to the working class in recipient countries and so there was need for closer on-the-spot monitoring by representatives of the American labour movement proper who would also mount their own independent support programmes. The CIO believed that it could make a better fist of helping to build the non-communist labour movement in Europe. An important element in its thinking was that the longer-established AFL-FTUC programme was too negatively anti-communist. The CIO view was that under the influence of AFL policies in France and Italy 'the non-communist unions have relied to a dangerous extent on too-simple and too-negative anti-communism. They have, therefore, had some marked success in frustrating communist political strikes, but have lost their own ability to use the strike weapon to further economic demands and have saddled themselves with a reputation for breaking political strikes'.[23] The AFL approach offered no immediate tangible benefits to European trade unionists of the sort that the CIO envisaged through a vigorous regime of collective bargaining, facilitated, they hoped, by the productivity programme.

The emergence of the CIO on the European stage was seen by the AFL as a dangerous challenge and a threat to the viability of its own work. In particular it risked sowing confusion in the all-important anti-communist campaign. The CIO might proclaim its hostility to communism, but its credentials were suspect and the AFL would not allow it to be associated with its own work or privy to the details of these operations. If the CIO were to launch a competing anti-communist programme using funds from broadly the same source there was an obvious risk of confusion and the possibility of 'contamination' of the FTUC's work. And, of course, simply in terms of their long-standing rivalry, for the AFL it would have the undesirable effect of elevating the CIO's international profile.

However, both the CIA leadership and important figures in the Truman administration, notably Averell Harriman, were keen to cut the CIO into the world of secret government funding. To do so meant extending the options available, and if the two labour organizations did subsequently manage to co-operate with one another, the combined impact of their programmes would be all the greater. Yet this was unacceptable to the AFL, and when it became apparent that the CIO were in receipt of 'sugar funds' from the Marshall Plan they began to cut back on their own collaborative work with the Intelligence Agency. It did not amount to a complete severance, but the number of activities they engaged in with Agency funding was reduced and Lovestone distanced himself from CIA Director Allen Dulles.[24]

Funding received by the CIO from Marshall Plan sources was used for more conventional trade union programmes than those undertaken by the FTUC. The CIO was primarily concerned to build the strength of the non-communist wing of the French, Italian and German labour movements for purposes of collective bargaining. Much of its effort therefore focused on leadership training courses for local union officers and educational projects linked to collective bargaining problems such as those associated with the productivity drive. Because of this orientation, it was relatively easy to secure funding from the Marshall Plan productivity programme whose budget had increased significantly in the early 1950s. As far as Marshall Plan administrators were concerned, there need be no secret about such activities, since they were part of the official remit. But for the CIO it was still important that as much secrecy as possible be maintained about the funding source since such information in the hands of French or Italian communists would be a powerful propaganda weapon against the Americans.

The CIO's involvement in trade union training courses in France and Italy became a matter of much scorn in AFL circles. To Lovestone and Brown it reflected the CIO's otherworldliness and their lack of willingness to leave the classroom and confront the reality of the daily threat posed by international communism. Most of the funds acquired by the CIO in this way were channelled to programmes that were being run formally by the ICFTU. The ICFTU itself was content to go along with the fiction that the funds were simply a generous donation from the CIO.

To make it easier to disguise the source of such government funding, the ICFTU established an Educational Foundation from which its training and educational work would be financed. The Foundation was to seek grants and donations from trusts and charities, which would provide a convenient cover for other sums received from Marshall Plan channels. However, although in 1953 the ICFTU got as far as registering the Foundation in New York State, where it expected to tap into most of the available charitable funds, the operation never became a going concern. The reason was simply that AFL President George Meany, who was also a vice-president of the ICFTU, refused to give his consent to the Foundation receiving money from US government sources. It was, he said, a matter of principle in the ICFTU not to accept government funding of any kind. His own organization the AFL, through the FTUC, was still benefiting from CIA funding, but he was determined to ensure that the CIO's source of Marshall Plan finance would dry up.

CONCLUSION

All this is what might be described as the 'politics of the politics of productivity' in the Marshall Plan, and, as such, more complex than the simple aim of a productivity drive to defeat communism through sustained economic recovery. It is, at one level, part of the fraught internal history of the US labour movement in the 1950s and a manifestation of the organizational rivalry between the two wings of the movement. But it is also a prism through which one can grasp the fierce debate that raged within the leadership of the American unions over the best way to fight communism, a debate that was echoed in the disagreements within the American foreign policy establishment between those for 'containment' and the supporters of 'roll back'. It might be claimed that by running two contrasting approaches to the problem of communism the American labour movement covered all the bases and gained the optimum return. But both approaches were of course flawed: the productivity programme did not result in anti-communist French or Italian trade unions outflanking their communist rivals through tangible success at the bargaining table, and the AFL's virulent, inflexible anti-communism often served to alienate the very allies that it sought to win, even among more moderate European trade unionists.

In general it would be fair to say that European trade union leaders often felt more comfortable in dealing with the CIO than the AFL for the simple reason that the former seemed to speak more the language of social democracy. In its ideal form, the CIO's approach to productivity could be reconciled with social-democratic objectives. Its proponents were perceived as having an ideological grounding similar to their own, whereas the AFL were more closely identified with the values of business unionism. The European view was that as long as productivity initiatives were consistent with national economic planning objectives and approached within the context of collective bargaining, they could be judged on their merits. On the other hand, many European union leaders came to regard the strident anti-communism of the AFL as excessive, too redolent of McCarthyism.[25] Even trade unionists from the right of the movement found it politic to dialogue with communists, and their growing tendency to exchange delegations with Eastern-bloc union bodies became the focus of serious friction with the AFL from the 1950s onwards.[26] The AFL's strongest allies among Europe's trade unions were those that were directly dependent on it for undercover finance – FO in France, CISL in Italy, and sections of the Finnish and and Greek labour movements. It was in such countries, where domestic communism was strong, that the AFL had most success in tapping into a well of fierce, uncomprising anti-communism.

However, in the end it was the AFL approach that seemed to have the more lasting effect. With European economic recovery broadly complete at the end of the 1950s, many of those who had favoured the productivity approach in countering communism were now ready for a measure of détente in East-West relations.[27] In the Lovestone camp, however, détente was anathema. It was also recognized that despite valiant anti-communist resistance by workers in Berlin in 1953 and Poznan and Budapest in 1956, there was still a long way to go before communism could be successfully challenged in the Eastern European heartland. The AFL had little doubt that the final prize would go to the party with most staying power. Arguably their crowning achievement was to be able to open an AFL-CIO office three decades later in post-communist Moscow.

NOTES

1. William Gomberg, Marshall Plan Productivity Consultant, International Conference on Social Problems of the Organization of Labour, Abbaye de Royaumont, France, June 1951.
2. Charles Maier, 'The Politics of Productivity: Foundations of American International Policy After World War II', *International Organization* 31 (Fall 1977).
3. Throughout I refer to the aid programme as the 'Marshall Plan' to avoid undue complexity of terminology. In reality it changed its official title several times as the original Economic Co-operation Agency gave way to the Mutual Security Agency and then to the Foreign Operations Agency before finally becoming the International Co-operation Agency.
4. Raymond Aron, *18 Lectures on the Industrial Society* (London: Weidenfeld & Nicolson 1967) p.14.
5. Smith to Scherback, 7 July 1952, Draft Statement Sent to Ambassador Draper, SRE PTAD, Labour Productivity Branch – Subject Files 1950-54, File Productivity General. Marshall Plan files are in Record Groups 286 and 469 at the National Archives and Record Center, Suitland, Maryland.
6. It was also the case outside Europe. In Japan, where a national productivity centre was created in 1954 under strong American influence, the trade union centre Sohyo, which the American military occupation itself had brought into being, adamantly refused to join.
7. French employers tended to have the final say in the choice of workers for team visits to America. Many were not trade unionists at all and frequently foremen were sent as 'workers'. Anthony Carew, *Labour Under the Marshall Plan* (Manchester UP 1987) p.160.
8. Harris, 'Comment on the Productivity Programme', undated, SRE PTAD, Labour Productivity Branch, Country File 1950-54, Box 3, File France; Zulauf to Mahder, 22 September 1953, Mission to Germany, PTAD Labour Advisor, Subject Files 1952–54, File Productivity Institute.
9. Despite the fact that the gap between British and American levels of productivity reflected exactly the difference in horsepower available to shop floor workers, the US Ambassador to Britain suggested that Britain's economic problems were only likely to be overcome by people working harder, and for less. Douglas to Marshall, 12 Aug. 1948, ECA Admin, Box 6.
10. In the words of a joint CIO and AFL investigation of conditions in France in 1950: 'Our productivity programme... carries serious threats to the welfare of the workers and does nothing to protect them – as the communists so accurately charge... There is no protection against wage cuts [resulting from]...the adoption of machine methods... There is nothing to prevent the direct benefits of increased production made possible by Marshall Plan aid from going entirely to the employers.' Carew, *Labour Under the Marshall Plan*, p.118.
11. The idea of pilot plant projects did not originate with the Marshall Plan. Before then, for example, the American Clothing Workers Union (ACWU) hoped to finance one or two clothing ventures in Italy incorporating the best management and labour practices of the United States. In 1946-47 August Bellanca of the ACWU had undertaken two lengthy trips to Italy to help establish a clothing factory in Tuscany. Giuseppe Di Vittorio, General

Secretary of the communist-led CGIL, had tried to have one such plant located in his own hometown. Ambassador Dunn airgram to Secretary of State, 25 Aug. 1947, Michael Ross Collection, Box 5 (15), George Meany Memorial Archives, Silver Spring, Maryland.

12. Fisher to Ozer, 23 August 1951, SRE PTAD, Labor Productivity Branch, Subject Files 1950–54, File Production Assistance Programme.
13. Carew, *Labour Under the Marshall Plan* (note 7) p.170. Goldy to Porter, 17 Sept. 1951, SRE PTAD, Labour Productivity Branch, Subject Files 1950-54: File Production Assistance Programme.
14. 'When the Americans come and tell us that there is a 'modern capitalism' which cares about the workers, the client and public opinion, we may answer that European capitalism has evolved in another way... Americans should remember that they cannot come to our continent and put out unrealistic advice' *24 Ore*, April 1953.
15. Carew, *Labour Under the Marshall Plan* (note 7) p.158; Goldberg to Gomberg, 15 Aug. 1955, William Gomberg Collection, London School of Economics.
16. Following a visit to Europe in 1955 UAW official Jack Conway reported to FOA: 'The EPA ... has laid such stress on achieving productivity increases through the use of incentive pay systems, the use of time and motion study, and other such techniques that most plant level leaders who know anything at all about EPA are extremely suspicious and distrustful of it. If EPA now becomes associated in the minds of these same people with the promotion of these human relations programmes which are essentially anti-union in character, the EPA might just as well fold up shop as far as the labour movement is concerned.' Conway to Meskimen, 28 Oct. 1955, FOA Box 32.
17. Programme of Action of EPA and Part 1 Budget for 1959–60, EPA, 1959.
18. Henry M. Christman (ed.) *Walter P. Reuther: Selected Papers* (New York: Macmillan 1961) p.47.
19. This thinking was reminiscent of Ambassador Walter Bedell Smith's 1947 warning from Moscow: 'We have ... been too preoccupied in the past with feeding the stomachs of people while the Soviets have concentrated on feeding their minds.' See W. Scott Lucas, *Freedom's War: The US Crusade against the Soviet Union, 1945–56* (New York UP 1999) p.48. Bedell Smith was of course later the Director of the CIA when the AFL's covert international programme was at it its height.
20. On the question of equivalence between capitalism and communism, Walter Reuther had famously told the founding congress of the ICFTU that he was for neither 'Standard Oil nor Stalin, but the broad middle way', a formulation that infuriated Lovestone. Following the death of Stalin, Reuther had also argued that the USSR would not resort to nuclear war and that the real battle between East and West would have to take place on the economic front. Thus he welcomed the idea that super power competition in the third world should be over the production of economic aid by the rival economic systems, with the recipients free to choose whichever system suited them best. Anthony Carew, *Walter Reuther* (Manchester UP 1992) p.159, ff. 18. Again the FTUC leadership considered this to be extremely naive.
21. Anthony Carew, 'The American Labour Movement in Fizzland: the Free Trade Union Committee and the CIA', *Labour History* 39/1 (Feb. 1998). The sharp contrast between the CIO and AFL/FTUC approaches can be seen in their respective programmes for Italy. While the CIO were organizing training courses to help unions equip themselves for productivity bargaining, the AFL's Irving Brown was collaborating with FIAT to establish a training school intended to develop a 'counter-apparat' schooled in the theory and practice of Bolshevism and taught by former communists whose aim was to produce 'professionally trained cadres, who are politically and physically ready to fight and resist to the end.' Hand-picked for training, they would be a 'hard core group dedicated to the single objective of constituting an ideological and physical barrier to the Communist Party machine.' Irving Brown, 'Conditions Which the FIAT Management Must Guarantee', undated 1954, Irving Brown Collection, Box 12 (20), George Meany Memorial Archives.
22. Tom Braden, head of the CIA's International Organizations Branch was a particular object of his scorn. Lovestone referred to such Ivy League types derisively as 'fizz kids'. Braden's superior, Frank Wisner, who ran the Office of Policy Co-ordination was, in Lovestone's eyes 'the Park Avenue hillbilly' and stood only slightly higher in his estimation.

23. Carew, *Labour Under the Marshall Plan* (note 7) p.121.
24. But unknown even to his closest collaborators Lovestone was careful to keep alive his unofficial channel to James Angleton, CIA head of counter-intelligence whose brand of anti-communism matched his own. Ted Morgan, *A Covert Life: Jay Lovestone, communist, Anti-communist and Spymaster* (New York: Random House 1999) p.285.
25. Anthony Carew, 'Conflict Within the ICFTU: Anti-Communism and Anti-Colonialism in the 1950s', *International Review of Social History* 41 (1996) p.158.
26. Anthony Carew et al., *The International Confederation of Free Trade Unions* (London: Peter Lang 2000) pp.240, 244–7.
27. Walter Reuther was one of the many western trade union leaders who made highly publicized visits to Eastern Europe in the 1960s.

6

Organizing Atlanticism: the Bilderberg Group and the Atlantic Institute, 1952–1963

VALERIE AUBOURG

The Bilderberg group, which has created an abundant but often polemical literature, and the Atlantic Institute, which has been largely and unfairly ignored by historical works,[1] can be fruitfully compared in their historical development. Both private, transatlantic organizations, they originated in 1952-53, grew in the 1950s and flourished in the early 1960s. Each rested on its own specific, informal, transatlantic networks, which only partly overlapped, and their analysis can help to shed light on the general context of private networks and the Cold War with a particular emphasis on the 'Atlantic Community' concept. Both received funding, at one time or another, from the Ford Foundation. But these two cases also describe a very active European participation, and suggest that the European influence on the formulation of 'Atlanticism' has been more important than is often presented.

THE BEGINNINGS OF THE BILDERBERG GROUP

The project, as is well known in the numerous writings about this group, was conceived in 1952 by Joseph Retinger, a Pole settled in London after an adventurous life, as a high-level, private and transatlantic conference to prevent anti-Americanism in Western Europe, and an isolationist reaction in the United States.[2] He first contacted Paul van Zeeland, the Belgian politician and then Minister of Foreign Affairs, the Dutch industrialist Paul Rijkens and chairman of Unilever, and, through him, Prince Bernhard of the Netherlands. They organized a meeting of important European personalities in September 1952 in Paris to discuss the basis of a general report on American-European relations. The goal was to provoke a constructive American response for future collaboration.[3]

If we consider the milieux in which the Bilderberg group developed, four distinctive elements appear. The circles of the governments-in-exile in

London during the Second World War were essential. Retinger, as counselor and friend of the Polish Prime Minister Sikorski, organized meetings about postwar Europe between the different exiled governments, and took a special interest in several schemes of European integration.[4] Those associated with these discussions included Paul Rijkens, Panayotis Pipinellis, representative of the Greek government in London, Paul van Zeeland, in charge of the CEPAG, the Belgian postwar planning body, and E. N. van Kleffens, the Dutch Minister of Foreign Affairs.

The European League for Economic Cooperation (ELEC) was another crucial network and actually provided a rich breeding ground for the Bilderberg group. Created in the autumn of 1946 by Retinger and van Zeeland, it was their first common project, dedicated to European reconstruction and union. The ELEC offered a pattern used again by both men for the Bilderberg group: discrete discussions in small circles, relying on personal contacts among elites, generally free-trade oriented. Many of the ELEC members were contacted in the early years to attend Bilderberg conferences. Three good examples are the British industrialist Edward Beddington-Behrens, the Belgian politician Etienne de la Vallée Poussin, and the president of the Bank of Brussels, Louis Camu.[5]

The European Movement constituted a third useful network for Retinger, the former secretary-general of the Movement. After his departure in 1951, he kept an active interest in the Council of Europe and often traveled to Strasbourg. It is through this channel that he met Guy Mollet, the secretary-general of the French Socialist Party, who became a founding member of the Bilderberg group in 1952.[6]

Finally, the intelligence circles who had established strong links during the war offered the fourth crucial network. This has been analyzed by Richard J. Aldrich, who concentrated on the American Committee on United Europe (ACUE) and its connections with the European Movement.[7] Retinger, although very probably not himself a member of the SOE, had close relations with that organization because of his contacts with the Polish underground movement for the Sikorski government. He was a close friend of Major-General Sir Colin Gubbins, head of the SOE in 1943, who had a special interest in Poland and later participated in the Bilderberg group from the beginning.

Retinger, as secretary-general of the European Movement from 1948 to 1951, also knew of its financing (and especially the financing of its European Youth Campaign) by the recently-created CIA through the ACUE, and was proud of an arrangement that financially saved the Movement from bankruptcy.[8] He had influential American friends in intelligence and political circles, whom he contacted in 1952, but the decisive contacts seem to have been provided by Prince Bernhard of the

Netherlands – exactly what Retinger had hoped in soliciting his participation in the project.

Bernhard wrote to General Walter Bedell Smith, head of the CIA, and met him, Allen Dulles and Averell Harriman in December 1952 during a trip to the USA also undertaken by Retinger and van Zeeland.[9] During the war, he had met General Eisenhower, Bedell Smith, then his Chief of Staff, and C.D. Jackson, Deputy Chief of Psychological Warfare for the Allied Forces, and had kept in touch from time to time. In December 1952 Bedell Smith was on the verge of leaving the CIA, and of receiving new responsibilities in the recently-elected Eisenhower administration. The winter 1952 contacts of Retinger, van Zeeland and Prince Bernhard with Bedell Smith and Allen Dulles, two major figures of the American intelligence establishment, are often considered as proof of a CIA involvement in the genesis of the Bilderberg group. Actually, a close look at the archives show that the American reaction was at first cold and hesitating.

Due to lack of time in the busy early period of the new administration, Bedell Smith asked C.D. Jackson, an expert in psychological warfare and from January 1953 Assistant to the President for Cold War matters, to deal with the request of the three European fathers of the Bilderberg group, who were in search of unofficial encouragement to build an American section with high-level participants. Writing to Ann Whitman, Eisenhower's personal secretary, who kept the President informed on the question, C.D. Jackson commented that

> Bernhard was getting impatient and a little hurt, and started sending Beedle [Bedell Smith] cables and letters asking him to produce the American counter committee. Finally, in desperation, Beedle asked me, since I knew Bernhard quite well, if I could help him out of this fix, and I agreed to take over the project.... During the winter of 53, there were more important committee assignments for prominent Americans with time to give than answering Bernhard, and while I was stewing about how to get out of this trap, God intervened in the shape of the newly formed Coleman committee.... I wrote him an impassionated letter telling him how important all this was, and how this project seemed to be made to order for the Coleman committee, and blah, and blah, and blah, and to my amazement Coleman agreed to take on the project.[10]

And that is about all for the intervention of Walter Bedell Smith and C. D. Jackson in the genesis of the group. From the fall of 1953, Jackson asked Prince Bernhard to deal directly with John Coleman.

The Coleman Committee, or Committee for a National Trade Policy, therefore provided the American network out of which American participation to Bilderberg grew. Created in September 1953 at the request of the White House to campaign for its policy of trade liberalization, it gathered prominent industrialists, lawyers and bankers dedicated to freer trade, under the chairmanship of John Coleman, of the Burroughs Corporation, a long-time supporter of Eisenhower. George Ball, then a Washington lawyer, was an important figure on the Coleman Committee, and that is how he became involved in the Bilderberg group.[11] It was a typical East Coast, elite organization of the 1950s, with many members associated with the Committee for Economic Development, an influential business planning group, the Council on Foreign Relations, the famous New York think-tank, and the Marshall Plan administration. Some important American members of the Bilderberg group, such as businessman and diplomat George C. McGhee and industrialists H. J. Heinz and James Zellerbach, joined this transatlantic network due to their membership of the Coleman Committee in 1953.

After an American report in November 1953, and a common, general report in the following spring, a conference was held in May 1954 in Oosterbeek, Netherlands, in the de Bilderberg Hotel. It was a success, and the real issue was not so much communism or anti-communism in themselves (rejection of communism was a basic assumption among participants), but the alleged lack of sophistication of American intervention in Europe at the time. In other words, the real problem was anti-Americanism, and especially the old anti-Americanism of European elites, with McCarthy constituting one of the hottest topics.

The same pattern of European pressure and American reluctance is noticeable in 1954–55. The Europeans wanted a big figure (McCloy is often referred to) and a regular mechanism of transatlantic meetings, while the Americans were reluctant to engage in a permanent process. Even C. D. Jackson, very appreciative of the first conference which he attended, did not want to envision a regular series of conferences. Only in late 1954 and early 1955, after repeated European requests, did American participants finally get organized, finding a chairman, co-chairman, and secretary – Dean Rusk (president of the Rockefeller Foundation), Bedell Smith, and Joseph E. Johnson (president of the Carnegie Endowment for International Peace) respectively – raising money among themselves, and applying in October to the Ford Foundation for a grant for one conference to be held in the United States (which actually took place much later).[12]

In September 1955, the third conference, held in Germany in Garmisch-Partenkirchen, was especially satisfactory, and both European and American elites were from that time convinced of the value of the group. It was perceived as a place to get first-hand information on international affairs, to test fresh ideas in a non-official context, and to network at a transatlantic level. The 1956 and 1957 conferences, in Denmark, the United States and Italy respectively, confirmed this development and allowed heated exchanges on colonialism and decolonization, the Suez crisis and the Soviet economic offensive in the Third World. In 1957, the American group was given its definitive shape. Chaired by lawyer Arthur H. Dean and industrialist H. J. Heinz, it was awarded a new $30,000 grant from the Ford Foundation for the St-Simons conference, the first to take place in the United States. By 1957, Bilderberg had become a well-established structure in private, transatlantic relations.

C.D. Jackson always kept an interest in Bilderberg. He attended the conferences of September 1957, September 1958 and May 1960 and followed the development of the group, but Walter Bedell Smith was not a very active member in this formative period. The intelligence community was certainly important for the creation of the Bilderberg group, but more in terms of milieux, personal contacts and shared values than political initiative or funding.

THE FLOURISHING OF THE BILDERBERG MEETINGS

The end of the 1950s witnessed the continuous development of the Bilderberg group, with an increased membership for the steering committee. It is not possible in this short space to give a detailed history of the group, but one can mention important personalities who contributed to the success of Bilderberg in the late 1950s: from Italy the diplomat Pietro Quaroni and businessmen Giovanni Agnelli and Alberto Pirelli; from Germany the industrialists Fritz Berg and Otto Wolff von Amerongen and the Christian Democrat Carlo Schmid; from Britain the Labour politicians Hugh Gaitskell and Denis Healey and the Conservative Reginald Maudling; from Belgium Paul van Zeeland; and the Americans George Ball, H. J. Heinz and C.D. Jackson.

A certain feeling of routine nonetheless surfaced. As C. D. Jackson noted to Prince Bernhard in 1961 about the previous years,

> [t]here were some Conferences of particular interest to the Americans during which the Europeans were somewhat bored, and vice-versa. You will remember that there was even serious talk as to whether or not Bilderberg might not have outlived its usefulness. The Conferences were still fun, because most of the conferees had gotten to know and like each other, but it had developed into something of a 'club' atmosphere rather than solid benefit.[13]

Moreover, the group was reorganized in the early 1960s. In late 1959, Joseph Retinger, in bad health, retired, and was replaced by Ernst van der

Beugel, former Dutch State Secretary of Foreign Affairs and Vice-President of KLM, assisted by another Dutchman, Arnold T. Lamping, a former Ambassador to Germany. The name of 'Bilderberg Meetings' was also adopted to stress the informal nature of a series of conferences with new participants each year, and not the gathering of a closed and structured group. The international context was also more favourable to challenging Atlantic themes, for example the trade negotiations between Europe and the United States, discussed at the St Castin conference in April 1961. This evolution was apparently positive since Jackson felt enthusiastic about the 1961 and 1962 conferences in St Castin, Canada, and Saltsjöbaden, Sweden, for their '*joint* analysis of their *joint* problems, looking toward a *joint* solution'.[14]

The success resulted also from the functions of the Bilderberg group in the late 1950s and early 1960s. First, it integrated the German elites, especially the German SPD elites, in a Western network and a Western-oriented frame of mind. As noted by Shepard Stone, an excellent observer of the German political scene in an internal note for the Ford Foundation, after the 1957 Fiuggi conference the German participants Fritz Erler and Carlo Schmid said that the Bilderberg contact 'would have influence on SPD foreign policy ideas in the future'.[15] This analysis was confirmed by Ernst van der Beugel in a recent interview.[16]

In addition, the Bilderberg group attained a remarkable closeness to the Kennedy Administration through the participation of Dean Rusk, George Ball and George McGhee, three of its founding members who entered the State Department in 1961. They left their responsibilities in the management of the group, but closely followed the Bilderberg debates. Ball in particular attended the conferences when he was Under-Secretary of State, and could provide ideas on the Administration's thinking. The original reluctance of the very beginning had totally disappeared by the early 1960s, and this interest of American elites, both in and out of official positions, was confirmed by new Ford Foundation grants in 1959 ($48,000) and 1963 ($60,000). In view of the policy of the Kennedy administration to encourage a strong Europe, but also to keep it Atlantic-oriented and compatible with American economic interests, the value of Bilderberg as a means of promoting Atlantic understanding was considered very important.

Another characteristic of the Bilderberg group should be noted at the end of our period. It could not integrate the new Gaullist elites. Wilfrid Baumgartner, the former Governor of the Bank of France and then Minister of Finance, was the regular French participant in the steering committee from 1960, but he was not a typical Gaullist. On the contrary, the Bilderberg group became a rallying point against what was perceived as a nationalist challenge to Atlantic values. The Cannes conference, in March 1963, is an excellent example of this. Held just after the famous press conference of 14 January 1963, in which de Gaulle rejected the United Kingdom application for membership of the EEC, the discussions presented a sharp criticism of French policy. As C.D. Jackson later put it, the conference was successful in 'kicking hell out of de Gaulle's representative'[17] – more specifically Jacques Baumel, the secretary general of the Gaullist Party (UNR), who had the hard task of defending French policy decisions. In 1963, this aspect was more important than the anti-communist dimension.

THE PREMISES OF THE ATLANTIC INSTITUTE

Compared to the Bilderberg meetings, the Atlantic Institute evolved at a slower pace from a nebulous idea to a substantial project. It first received regular but marginal attention in the first part of the 1950s. Under the name 'Atlantic Service Bureau', it belonged to the program of the Atlantic Citizens Congress, an organization created by Hugh Moore, a Pennsylvania industrialist whose ambition was to set up an Atlantic Movement modeled after the European Movement. Moore was a member of Clarence K. Streit's Atlantic Union Committee, promoting the radical project of an Atlantic federation, but was looking for a more practical means of building a strong Atlantic Community, especially by educating public opinion.[18] Understood as a kind of Atlantic clearing house, the project never materialized due to lack of funds.

A more classical "Atlantic Community Cultural Centre" was recommended in the same period by the Copenhagen Conference, an international gathering held in August-September 1953 with members of private groups interested in the Atlantic Alliance and the promotion of Atlantic solidarity. It followed the first conference on the Atlantic Community, organized the previous year in Oxford, and led to the creation in 1955 of the Atlantic Treaty Association (ATA), a loose organization of non-official societies supporting NATO and close to official circles. In Copenhagen, the project was understood as a 'monument to NATO and a symbol of Western achievement in purpose, operation, and material actuality'.[19] In 1956, the ATA supported the idea again under the name of an Atlantic Study Centre, although it did not undertake to set up such a body.[20]

From 1954, the idea of an Atlantic Institute was also put forward by the Declaration of Atlantic Unity group (DAU), created by another former member of Streit's Atlantic Union Committee, Walden Moore. Acting as an international correspondence committee, it issued a petition in October 1954 in support of a strengthening of NATO and stronger Atlantic co-operation. One of its suggestions was for a transatlantic Center of Studies, and it was certainly influenced in some way by the ideas of Hugh Moore, who was a friend of Walden Moore and who signed the Declaration. The same influence can be felt in the NATO Parliamentarians Conference (NPC), an unofficial body created in 1955 for the regular meeting of parliamentarians from NATO countries which sought to create a special interest in Atlantic questions among elected representatives. It had important links with and strong support from members of the DAU. It is therefore not surprising that this milieu of private, pro-Atlantic organizations favored the creation of some kind of institute dedicated to the study and promotion of Atlantic questions. In 1956, the DAU, the NPC and the ATA had the opportunity to present the idea to the Wise Men Committee on non-military cooperation in NATO set up by the Alliance, headed by Gaetano Martino, Halvard Lange and Lester Pearson.[21] It was not listed in the final recommendations of the Wise Men, but at least had been discussed within official circles.

The project of an Atlantic Institute properly crystallized in 1957, during a conference on the Atlantic Community held in Bruges, Belgium. Co-organized by the College of Europe and the Foreign Policy Research Institute of the University of Pennsylvania, with financial help from the Ford and Mellon Foundations and the Olivetti group, it connected several private European and transatlantic groups that had appeared in the early 1950s on both sides of the Atlantic. Among the participants were well-known figures such as Paul-Henri Spaak, Robert Schuman, Henry Brugmans, Clarence Streit (the American publicist and father of Atlantic federalism), Douglas Robinson (the young and successful secretary of the NATO Parliamentarians Conference), Willy Bretscher (an eminent journalist and editor of the Swiss newspaper *Neue Zürcher Zeitung)*, Robert Strausz-Hupé (professor at the University of Pennsylvania), and Italian industrial mogul Adriano Olivetti.

A young American diplomat, James R. Huntley, played a crucial role at this stage. A former Foreign Service officer in occupied Germany in 1952–55, he dealt with 're-education' and American cultural policy, and as such took care of exchange-of-persons programmes and then headed a successful American cultural centre. When he left Germany, he was an admirer of John J. McCloy and his Public Affairs officer, Shepard Stone, both of whom were convinced of the political importance of strong personal contacts between transatlantic elites, and who later worked for the Ford Foundation. In 1956, Huntley became a USIA officer in Washington, D.C., and at the end of 1957 he was about to become Deputy Public Affairs officer at the newly-created US Mission to the European Communities. From that experience he developed the conviction that an Atlantic Community, and not only a European one, was necessary to contain Germany; and that only a new, multinational elite could hold Europe and America together in the future. For him, building this elite was the task of an Atlantic Institute.[22] Huntley attended the Bruges Conference in a private and informal capacity. Stimulated by the constructive intellectual atmosphere of the Bruges discussions, he drafted a plan for an Atlantic Institute, which was adopted by the Bruges final report and, about a month later, by the NATO Parliamentarians Conference.[23]

In 1957, the Atlantic Institute, if still only a project, had become a coherent proposal resting on four principles: it was meant to give a cultural response to the challenge of communism and totalitarianism, to promote a sense of community and adequate leadership among Atlantic countries, to offer a clearing house for research on Atlantic issues, and to be 'a vehicle for private Atlantic-wide efforts to share social values and techniques, thus strengthening democratic institutions'.[24] At this stage, it was a conscious effort to mould an Atlantic elite, with values and world views close to the ones of the American elites of the time in the context of the Cold War.

THE CREATION OF THE ATLANTIC INSTITUTE

Between 1957 and 1959, the follow-up of the Bruges conference, the efforts of the Declaration of Atlantic Unity group and the continuous attention of the NATO Parliamentarians maintained a sustained interest in the Atlantic Institute project. The role here of Adolph W. Schmidt should be noted. The Vice-President of Mellon and Sons and an officer of the Mellon Foundation, he provided crucial financial support during this period. A member of Streit's Atlantic Union Committee, he had been interested in Atlantic questions for a long time, and became one of the main financial backers of the Atlantic Institute when it was created in 1961.

In June 1959 at the London Atlantic Congress, which had been actively supported by private Atlanticist bodies including Walden Moore's Declaration of Atlantic Unity group, the NATO Parliamentarians, and individuals like Hugh Moore, the tenth anniversary of the Atlantic Treaty was celebrated. It strongly recommended the creation of a Studies Centre for the Atlantic Community, a plan advocated in particular by Canadian diplomat L. Dana Wilgress (former Ambassador to NATO and chairman of the London Congress Atlantic Institute Subcommittee), Lucien Radoux (former chef de cabinet of Paul-Henri Spaak and author of a report based on the suggestions of the Bruges conference), and Paul van Zeeland (chairman of the Atlantic Economic Committee and a long-time supporter of such a proposal).[25] The Atlantic Congress was particularly important for the launching of the Atlantic Institute because it gathered people from various backgrounds behind the project.[26] The names of Eric Johnston, Walden Moore, Estes Kefauver (a Tennessee Representative and supporter of Streit in Congress), Mrs Oswald B. Lord (US representative to the United Nations), Father Jean Daniélou, and Léon Moulin (professor at the College of Europe), are particularly noteworthy here.

In October 1959, a Provisional Committee for the Atlantic Institute chaired by van Zeeland took the first concrete steps. In the Steering Committee of the Provisional Committee were Lucien Radoux, its Chairman, and James Huntley, its Secretary and Rapporteur, who took a one-year leave from the USIA to work on the Institute. About 300 interviews conducted mainly by Huntley confirmed the interest felt in many circles for the idea. Starting in April 1960, again with the active support and chairmanship of van Zeeland, contacts were taken to form a Board and raise funds. In addition to Huntley and van Zeeland, Adolph W. Schmidt, Adriano Olivetti, Kurt Birrenbach (a member of the Bundestag, linked with Thyssen), among others, were especially useful to gather private support in this phase. As a result, the first Board meeting was held on 12 December 1960 in Paris, and the Atlantic Institute was officially launched in January 1961 with van Zeeland as Chairman, and, as Vice-Chairmen, Kurt Birrenbach, the British diplomat Lord Gladwyn, the Norwegian Labour leader and representative Nils Langhelle and the French economist Jacques Rueff, then a Judge at the European Court of Justice.[27]

Support from private circles and business groups had been sufficient in Europe and the United States, but a strong official endorsement from the American government was still lacking, and the Institute was only provisionally set up in Milan under Professor Gerolamo Bassani, of the Italian Institute of International Politics. This official endorsement finally came in the spring of 1961. The interest of Dean Rusk and President Kennedy helped to convince Henry Cabot Lodge Jr. to become Director General, a position he officially accepted in November 1961, and the Institute definitively moved to Paris.[28] The Administration's sympathy and the interest of Lodge also helped to secure a $250,000 grant from the Ford Foundation in June 1961, announced the following September, and the work of the Institute could begin in a comprehensive manner.[29]

In the early years considered here, the Atlantic Institute was still a young body, hesitating between several roles and themes of research. In some respects, it was marked by its time and by a certain Cold War rhetoric, favored by Henry Cabot Lodge, as in one of its first pamphlets, *Free World's Aims for Humanity.* It also devoted ample study to the Atlantic partnership concept. The first main report of the Institute was entitled *Partnership for Progress*, with the research being directed by Pierre Uri, a distinguished economist and close collaborator of Jean Monnet. Finally, the links with the Third World and the collective contribution of Atlantic countries to international economic development was a third dimension explored in these years.[30] On the whole, even if it only really gained weight later in the 1960s and 1970s, the Atlantic Institute had the ambition to be a high-level, private and transatlantic think-tank, undertaking research but also formulating policy recommendations, collecting data and studies on Atlantic issues and convening international meeting with academics, economists and politicians from the Atlantic countries, more in the sense of the newly created OECD than of NATO – Switzerland and Sweden, for instance, were represented on the Board of the Institute. The underlying goal was to encourage the growth of a new generation of intellectuals and policy analysts working on Atlantic problems and thinking in Atlantic terms, as opposed to a national and restricted approach, therefore promoting harmonious and constructive Euro-American relations. As such, it was of course to come into conflict with French policy, and developed in the early 1960s as a kind of Atlantic outpost in Gaullist France.[31] It was also modeled after the American example of private, non-profit foundations that were almost unknown in continental Europe in the 1950s, and were considered by its founders as necessary for a dynamic, democratic and free society. On this level also it collided with the French tradition of state power and 'grandeur' on which de Gaulle drew heavily.

CONCLUSION

The similarities between the Atlantic Institute and Bilderberg are clearly evident, although both organizations were obviously of a different nature. Both relied on the role of elites, in private and official circles, to provide the essential fabric of international (transatlantic) relations and seek to organize an intimate and frequent contact between several sections of business, academic, and political milieux in Western Europe and North America. It is therefore not surprising that some personalities took an active interest in both groups. Paul van Zeeland is a striking example of this 'transatlantic leader' on which both Bilderberg and the Atlantic Institute relied. He was involved in the genesis and development of the two organizations from the very beginning. Among the financial backers of the Atlantic Institute, Adriano Olivetti and Fritz Berg, of the German Employers Association, and Eric Johnston, of the Motion Picture Association of America, were long-time participants of the Bilderberg group in that decade. Finally, it is no coincidence that the Ford Foundation, whose orientation in European affairs was largely influenced by Shepard Stone during this period, found both groups worthy of support and provided several grants for them.

Originally, Bilderberg and the Atlantic Institute were born from different networks. The first one originated as a European idea that rapidly attracted American elites. It benefited from the bonds created in the intelligence and resistance circles during the Second World War, drew on high-level personalities, and received official blessing from the start. The second one came from marginal, Atlantic circles and developed in the context of the cultural diplomacy of the United States. On the whole it gathered less prestigious and often younger personalities (with some notable exceptions) and had more difficulties in attracting official support. But in neither case do we find a systematic organization of a Cold War waged by covert means through these two private institutions. We see rather a more nuanced picture of multiple initiatives, rooted in the same conception of culture as a crucial tool in transatlantic relations, people who often had a similar experience of the war, of the occupation in Germany or of the Marshall Plan. They were convinced that the close interaction of European and American elites was a key to a stable, Atlantic region.

The recent analysis of Volker R. Berghahn, through the case of Shepard Stone, provides an extremely enlightening perspective on these two Atlantic groups.[32] Both were considered valuable by Americans at the time because they provided a way to influence the European vision of American culture, society and policy. As important as solidarity against Soviet ideological propaganda was, after the mid-1950s the fight against a traditional European anti-Americanism became the main priority. It is what the Bilderberg group and the Atlantic Institute, through regular intellectual exchange, sought to oppose by promoting an 'Atlantic spirit' and by debating polemical subjects in order to help promote a common understanding. This is exactly parallel to what Volker Berghahn describes about the Congress for Cultural Freedom, the Ford Foundation European Program, or more widely among governmental, philanthropic, business and intelligence circles in the 1950s. In addition, the Atlantic Institute and the Bilderberg group show a complex combination of private initiatives and official encouragement through which a shared experience in the war or the immediate after-war years was more important than distinctions between State and private groups.

Finally, in addition to the Americans, one has to stress the importance of Belgium and the Netherlands in these networks. Beyond economic interests, the Atlantic Community was often seen as a means to preserve a liberal-democratic tradition not sufficiently rooted in Germany, Italy or France. Also interesting is the responsiveness of Italian and German business leaders to these two initiatives, in which they could be full members of the new transatlantic networks of the 1950s, as well as the continuous interest of participants from Nordic countries, Switzerland and Austria. The British were important, but more cautious towards the less informal approach of the Atlantic Institute. But in these two groups, the French were rather isolated, except at the very beginning between 1952 and 1956.

NOTES

1. This is probably due to the destruction of most of the archives of the Institute in a bombing of its premises in Paris in 1984, and its closure in 1988 after difficult financial problems.
2. J. Pomian (ed.), *Joseph Retinger: Memoirs of an Eminence Grise* (London: Sussex UP 1972).
3. Retinger, 'Le Groupe de Bilderberg' p.3, Mollet Papers, Office Universitaire de Recherche Socialiste, Paris (OURS), AGM 143; 'Minutes of Meeting held in Paris on September 25th', 1952, Ibid.
4. Pomian (ed.) *Joseph Retinger,* pp.98–108; Th. Grosbois, 'L'action de Jozef Retinger en faveur de l'idée européenne 1940–46', *European Review of History* 6/1 (1999) pp.59–82.
5. On the League see M. Dumoulin and A.-M. Dutrieue, *La Ligue Européenne de Coopération Economique: un groupe d'étude et de pression dans la construction européenne* (Berne: Lang 1993).
6. V. Aubourg, 'Guy Mollet et le groupe de Bilderberg: le parcours original d'un 'Européen', 1952–1963', *Histoire(s) Socialiste(s)* 1 (November 1999) pp.14–33.
7. R.J. Aldrich, 'OSS, CIA and European Unity: the American Committee on United Europe, 1948–1960', *Diplomacy & Statecraft* 8/1 (March 1997) pp.184–227.
8. 'Commentaires du secrétaire général après réunion du Bureau Exécutif du 2 décembre 1951', December 1951, Retinger Papers, Polish Library, London (PL), Box VII/1 p.7.
9. Diary 1952, Retinger Papers, PL, Box XXIX; Retinger to Prince Bernhard, n.d., Ibid., Box VII/6.
10. C.D. Jackson to A. Whitman, 19 Nov. 1954, C.D. Jackson Papers (CDJ), Eisenhower Presidential Library, KS (DDEL), Box 35 Bernhard (2).
11. J. A. Bill, *George Ball. Behind the Scenes in Foreign Policy* (New Haven, CT/London: Yale UP 1997) pp.53–6.
12. A more detailed analysis is given in the Ph.D. dissertation of the author, defended in 2002.
13. Jackson to Bernhard, 25 April 1961, CDJ Papers, DDEL, Box 36, Bilderberg 1961 (1).
14. Ibid.(emphasis in original).
15. Shepard Stone, 13 Oct. 1957, Ford Foundation Archives (FFA), Grant Files, PA 5600341.
16. Interview with Dr. E. van der Beugel, 18 July 2001, The Hague.
17. Jackson to van der Beugel, 14 May 1964, CDJ Papers, DDEL, Box 109, Van der Beugel.
18. See e.g. H. Moore, 'Atlantic Service Bureau', 27 May 1953, Hugh Moore Fund Collection, Mudd Library, Princeton University, NJ, Box 6 (the box number refers to the old collection arrangement).
19. Report of the Second International Study Conference on the Atlantic Community, Copenhagen, 30 Aug.–5 Sept.1953, Box 24, Flynt Papers, Truman Presidential Library, Independence, MO, p.15.
20. *The Spirit of the Atlantic Alliance* (Paris: Atlantic Treaty Association 1956) p.11.
21. *La Coopération non militaire au sein de l'OTAN* (Paris: OTAN 1956) p.15.
22. Interview with James R. Huntley, 26 Aug. 2000 and 11 Feb. 2001, Sequim (WA).
23. Proceedings of the Bruges Conference in *Les Cahiers de Bruges* 1957 III-IV, esp. pp.157–8; NATO Parliamentarians' Conference, *Resolutions and Reports,* London, Nov. 1957, p.7.
24. NPC Memorandum on the Atlantic Institute, n.d. [probably 1958], p.3, Huntley Papers, Hoover Institution Archives, Box 1.
25. *Atlantic Congress Report*, 5–10 June 1959 (International Secretariat of the NATO Parliamentarians' Conference: London) p.58.
26. V. Aubourg, 'The Atlantic Congress of 1959: An Ambiguous Celebration of the Atlantic Community' in G. Schmidt (ed.), *A History of NATO–The First Fifty Years* (Houndmills/New York: Palgrave 2001) vol.2 pp.341–57.
27. Minutes of Meeting, Board of Governors of the Atlantic Institute, 12 Dec. 1960, Archives of the Atlantic Council of the United States, Hoover Institution Archives, Stanford, CA, Box 312/10.
28. Memo of conversation with Secretary of State Dean Rusk, 8 April 1961, Henry Cabot Lodge II Papers, Massachussetts Historical Society, Boston, MA, Box 127; see also letter from Dean Rusk to William C. Foster, Chairman of the US Committee for the Atlantic Institute,

23 March 1961, Ibid., Box 125.

29. Docket excerpt, Board of Trustees Meeting, 22–23 June 1961, 'Strengthening the Atlantic Community through the Atlantic Institute', and memorandum by Stone to Records Center on a visit by Cabot Lodge, 9 Aug. 1961, both in FFA, PA 6100335.
30. *The Free World's Aims for Humanity* (Boulogne/Seine: Atlantic Institute 1963); P. Uri, *Partnership for Progress, a Program for Transatlantic Action* (New York: Harper and Row 1963); K. Birrenbach, *The Future of the Atlantic Community* (New York/London: Praeger 1963).
31. Interviews with James R. Huntley, 14-15 Feb. 2001, Sequim (WA) and Andrew J. Pierre, 21 August 2000, Washington, DC.
32. V. R. Berghahn, *America and the Intellectual Cold Wars in Europe* (Princeton/Oxford: Princeton UP 2001).

PART III

Target Groups: Youth and Women

7

Putting Culture into the Cold War: The Cultural Relations Department (CRD) and British Covert Information Warfare

RICHARD J. ALDRICH

British wartime diplomats have sometimes been identified as taking an optimistic view of likely Soviet post-war behaviour in the international system.[1] Many, like Christopher Warner, Head of the Northern Department, clung to what some have called the 'co-operation thesis' and resisted pessimistic forecasts which often emanated from the British military – notably Field Marshal Sir Alan Brooke. But not all the wartime diplomats in the Foreign Office were determined to turn a Nelsonian eye to the activities of the Soviets in pursuit of 'co-operation'. In late 1943 the Foreign Office had created a small section to give political direction to the British Council and to manage the political and policy aspects of the growing scale of organized international intellectual, cultural, societal and artistic contacts, with a view to promoting Allied goodwill. By early 1945 this had been renamed the Cultural Relations Department or CRD and was being energetically directed by William Montagu-Pollock. Quickly this new department realised that international organizations represented a substantial area of Soviet manipulation and many so-called 'international' organizations, which claimed to be representative of world opinion, were in fact mere fronts that took their orders from Moscow.

Almost by accident, CRD had become a small British front-line unit in a clandestine struggle to prevent Moscow's domination of the world of international movements, federations and assemblies – what would later be called 'the battle of the festivals'. By November 1945 Archibald Clark-Kerr, the British Ambassador in Moscow, was urging London to take more action to stem the Soviet practice of obtaining control of international labour, youth, welfare and other organizations 'for the purpose of using them as instruments of Soviet foreign policy'. He predicted 'similar attacks' on women's and student organizations, as well as humanitarian and cultural organizations, and wanted British counter-measures stepped up. Clark Kerr wrote again on 15 December 1945 warning specifically about the Soviet search for an 'instrument for influencing international youth'.[2] On 21 December 1945 British diplomats in Copenhagen wrote to Montagu-Pollock in much the same spirit, warning that the collapse of Germany and France had left 'a vacuum which, particularly among the younger students, was only too likely to be filled by Russia'.[3]

Even before the end of the war, CRD in London were already hard at work on this problem, during something of an interregnum in British propaganda activities. The wartime Special Operations Executive (SOE) and Political Warfare Executive (PWE) had been largely wound down in 1945 and would not be replaced until the advent of the more widely known Information Research Department (IRD), created with the agreement of a reluctant British Cabinet in 1948. Interpretations of post-war British covert propaganda have focused on the birth of IRD and upon a Whitehall battle to resurrect agencies developed *for war* – namely SOE and PWE.[4] While the wartime heritage was certainly immensely important, there were other fascinating but neglected influences. CRD grew out of a different heritage – the British Council and agencies developed for cultural propaganda in *peacetime* – harking back to the interwar period. In 1945 CRD was at the cutting edge of Britain's information Cold War, focused upon the twin issues of culture and organized youth and working closely with MI5 and to a lesser extent the Secret Intelligence Service (SIS).[5] While cultural propaganda enjoyed a somewhat insubstantial existence, which some have likened to the Cheshire Cat, during the early Cold War it proved capable of showing its claws.[6]

It was in the immediate post-war period that some of the future trademarks of British Cold War propaganda, including intervention in British domestic organizations, were established. In mid-1948 British information warfare chiefs in London, together with SIS, met with the Head of the CIA, Rear Admiral Roscoe C. Hillenkoetter, and outlined Britain's political warfare programme. The Americans were particularly impressed by Britain's efforts in the area of 'grey propaganda' – efforts that were not publicly acknowledged, but were sufficiently low-risk to involve many government departments together with their friendly contacts in journalism, trade unions and so forth. Hillenkoetter carried his briefing papers back to Washington where George Kennan remarked that they represented a sophisticated and mature programme, somewhat ahead of anything the USA had to offer. On the face of it this is surprising, given that IRD had only been in existence a matter of months. It is less surprising when we understand that additional engines including CRD were allowing Britain to forge ahead in information warfare during the late 1940s.[7]

Arguably CRD represents the first British post-war effort to experiment with creating anti-communist front organizations, or what might more accurately be called 'state-private networks'.[8] These early efforts delivered some hard lessons that had strong commonality with the early American experiences in an area eventually taken over by Tom Braden and CIA's International Organizations Division. These included an early appreciation of the weakness and irresolution of genuinely free and independent organizations in the face of activities by better organized communist-controlled groups. They also discovered the difficulties of weaning such groups off their addiction to state funding. Like IRD and CIA, CRD found that its work in the area of counter-communism was conducted in a global arena without clear boundaries, rather than an international arena clearly separated into domestic and foreign constituencies. Thus, efforts with 'state-private networks' could require them to reach backwards into their own societies and thus to conduct growing intervention in domestic as well as foreign affairs.[9] These networks are also notable for the prominent role played by women in a manner that is unusual in the landscape of the early Cold War. This may reflect the way in which non-governmental organizations seemed to offer women greater opportunities to take a leading role in policy formation, or that Whitehall perceived areas such as cultural, student and youth affairs as an appropriate terrain for women.

THE FORMATION OF WFDY

British cultural diplomacy emerged in the 1930s as a result of two initiatives. As Michael Lee has shown, these were the British Council working to increase the numbers of overseas students attending British universities for commercial reasons, and broader efforts via the BBC to counter the efforts of the Italian government to undermine Britain's position in the Middle East through Radio Bari.[10] The creation of the CRD itself was a reflection of Whitehall's wartime growth and considerable bureaucratic replication. The Foreign Office began the war with seven departments and ended the war with more than twenty. Across Whitehall many new organizations were set up, taking the state into areas of public life upon which it had hitherto had little influence. CRD reflected efforts to manage growing initiatives in an area which increasingly involved symbolic public gestures of solidarity or allusion to common ideals. By 1945, CRD was conceived of as an organization which, together with the British Council, would manage the growing world of international associations, movements, conferences and exhibitions and other public efforts in the realm of international understanding. It was also required to deal with the cultural aspects of the re-occupation of the European continent and the questions arising out of the creation of the UNESCO organization. CRD had begun life in 1943 as the 'British Council Section of the Foreign Office', giving more political direction to pre-existing British Council work, and soon began to resist Soviet efforts to manipulate the world of international organizations.[11] By early 1945 – with its new name of CRD – it was taking the lead in attempting to persuade the International Federation of Journalists to set up their headquarters in London.[12]

The bulk of CRD work remained associated with that of giving 'political guidance' to the British Council in a number of areas ranging from UNESCO to overseas links with British learned societies. This reflected the fact that the greater part of the British Council's work was done on the Foreign Office vote. But in 1945 CRD's more specialized work in the area of international women's and youth organizations was regarded as being of growing importance because of the danger posed by communist infiltration of such movements. CRD's youth activities were given the highest priority by William Montagu-Pollock, the Head of the Department which worked closely with MI5 and later the Foreign Office Russia Committee. Within CRD, day-to-day youth matters were the responsibility of desk officers like Monica Powell.[13]

In 1945 CRD was particularly irked by the fact that the new Prime Minister, Clement Attlee, had decided to allow a communist-dominated World Youth Congress to take place in London in November that year. Attlee's decision reflected his wish – like that of many wartime diplomats – to give the Soviets the benefit of the doubt and also reflected his commitment to an internationalist perspective that shared much with the late Franklin D. Roosevelt and placed a strong emphasis on the United Nations.[14] But the World Youth Congress in London had concluded its business by setting up the World Federation of Democratic Youth (WFDY), one of the leading Soviet-owned international organizations of the post-war period. CRD and the Home Office had opposed the hosting of the Congress, arguing for a ban on the grounds that it was being manipulated by Moscow in a cynical way. But they then found that the State Department was 'actively supporting the preparatory work' for the Congress, partly because it had the blessing of an unsuspecting Eleanor Roosevelt. The Foreign Secretary, Ernest Bevin, smelt a rat and thought it safer to decline when invited to address the main rally at the Albert Hall.[15]

Attlee's new Cabinet had decided to allow the Congress to go ahead in London despite warnings about the strong communist elements behind it. The Cabinet argued that 'the more foreigners allowed to visit this country and breathe the air of intellectual freedom in which we live the better', insisting that this would contrast well with the Soviet policy of 'black out' already visible in Eastern Europe. Sir Stafford Cripps, the Chancellor of the

FIGURE 1
VENONA MATERIAL ON MGB WORK AT THE LONDON CONGRESS OF 1945

TOP SECRET

USSR

Ref. No: S/NBF/T76 (of 29/3/1951)

Issued: 31/12/1956

Copy No: 202

4th RE-ISSUE

MGB ARRANGEMENTS FOR COVERING SOVIET AND OTHER DELEGATIONS TO INTERNATIONAL YOUTH CONGRESS IN GREAT BRITAIN (1945)

From: MOSCOW

To: LONDON

No: 70 16 Sept. 45

To IGOR. [i]

In October 1945 an International Youth Congress is taking place in the "ISLAND[OSTROV]"[ii]. Our delegation consists of six parts - Central, Ukrainian, Belorussian and Baltic Countries[iii] - in all sixty persons. Included in the delegation [1 group missing] four of our colleagues - senior member of the group MON[0% IN][iv]

[21 groups unrecoverable]

On 15th September our representatives, numbering eight persons, are leaving for the "ISLAND" for work on the Preparatory Committee [B% of the Congress]. It is with this group that MONIN is leaving. Our colleagues have been briefed on [1 group garbled] looking after the delegation and will, [0% under the auspices] of the Central part, work completely under the direction of "PLATO[PLATON]"[v]. The Chairman of the whole delegation, MIKhAJLOV,[vi] the First Secretary of the Central Committee of the All-Union Communist LENIN League of Youth [TsK VLKSM], is also leaving with the first group. According to MIKhAJLOV's information the delegations of a number of countries - ITALY U.S.A., SPAIN and others, include illegal members of "FRATERNALs[BRATSKIE]",[vii

Distribution

[Continued overleaf]

FIGURE 1 (CONT.)
VENONA MATERIAL ON MGB WORK AT THE LONDON CONGRESS OF 1945

TOP SECRET

- 2 - S/NBF/T76

with whom [0% our] delegation has it in view to arrange clandestine contact. Therefore it is essential for you through "SERGEJ",[viii] who is also a member of the delegation, to begin studying the personnel of the foreign delegations, in the first place members of the "FRATERNAL" and people who sympathise with us.

[31 groups unrecovered]

No. 6729
[0% 14th September] VIKTOR[ix]

Comments: [i] Unidentified cover-name.

[ii] GREAT BRITAIN.

[iii] Presumably a portmanteau way of describing the Esthonian, Latvian and Lithuanian parts of the Soviet delegation.

[iv] Valentin MONIN represented the Soviet Teachers' Union at the World Youth Conference in LONDON in October 1945.

[v] Unidentified cover-name.

[vi] Nikolaj MIKHAJLOV, one of the controlling figures of the "World Federation of Democratic Youth", attended the World Youth Conference as a Soviet delegate.

[vii] Communist Parties.

[viii] Also mentioned in MOSCOW's External Serial No. 41 of 17th September 1945 (S/NBF/T29), as well as in the opening ("To SERGEJ, IGOR'..") of another (unpublished) message of the 16th.

[ix] Lt.-Gen. P.M. FITIN.

Exchequer, and his wife, Lady Isobel Cripps, who had long-established interest in youth movements, were especially active in assisting the Congress and thereafter in setting up a funding organization, the International Youth Trust, which supported the activities of the British Committee of WFDY.

The attitude of Attlee and his Cabinet proved to be naive. The considerable facilities afforded in London for the Congress gave the appearance of official British blessing and many British youth organizations attended only to discover that 'effective control of the proceedings was already in communist hands'. A 'vast' delegation of Soviet youth, with an average age of forty, had arrived a month before the conference to make preparations. By controlling the agendas, framing the motions and 'shouting the others down' they had 'swept the board'. Motions had been passed asserting that conditions in Belsen were nothing compared to those in colonial West Africa and that monstrous British colonialists 'cut off the thumbs of Bombay cotton-workers to avoid Indian competition' with British home cotton production. To add insult to injury, two of the three Balkan delegations proved to be armed with briefcases full of counterfeit sterling currency.[16]

Signals intelligence material in the form of Venona traffic from 1945 reveals a little of the Soviet effort devoted to this conference. On 10 September 1945, Lt. General Pavolov Fitin, Head of INU, the Foreign Intelligence Department of the MGB, sent a telegram to the London station regarding this conference. Although sections of the message have not been broken, it appears that four of the delegates from the Soviet Union were MGB officers with orders to co-ordinate efforts with sympathetic delegates from other countries. This Venona material was not available to CRD, partly because of its very limited circulation, and also because inroads into this traffic were painfully slow.[17] Notwithstanding this, CRD had seen enough at the Westminster Congress to know they had been outsmarted by Moscow. They were determined to prevent a repetition and if possible pay the Soviets back with the same coin. Non-communist youth organizations in Britain – presided over by their umbrella organization, the National Council for Social Service (NCSS) – were now keen to resist obvious communist encroachment and CRD was determined to give them every encouragement.

CRD RESPONDS

William Montagu-Pollock, Head of CRD, was the leading figure in a counter-campaign against WFDY. The first step was to look closely at the British figures who had taken a leading role in the Westminster Congress and who were now constituted as the British section of the WFDY. In March

1946 he warned his colleagues that the communist grip on the British section of the WFDY was 'so strong' that it was past saving. Attempting to dissuade these individuals from participation seemed pointless. What CRD needed to do was 'to set up a rival political organization' so it could intervene in this important field. This analysis in March 1946 led to Britain's first post-war experiment in the world of what has been called 'state-private networks' and the launch of the first covertly-run British front organization, the World Assembly of Youth.[18]

CRD teamed up with incensed members of non-communist British youth groups. The key non-official figure was Elizabeth Welton, (sometimes known as Violet Welton) the Secretary of the Standing Conference of National Voluntary Youth Organizations. She offered to help set up a secret group that would work against the communists. She was also in close touch with similar-minded groups in Belgium, France, the Netherlands and the USA. She reported that other private anti-communist groups were being set up in Denmark, Sweden and Switzerland. In the late spring of 1946 she prepared to depart on a tour of Holland, Belgium and France to cement relations with these groups, especially the Union Patriotique des Organisations de la Jeunesse in Paris. But she also confessed to some trepidation. Her European collaborators had warned her that life was dangerous for the opponents of organized communism on the continent. Recently there had been 'two cases of sudden death by poisoning and a mysterious disappearance of anti-communist organizers' in Europe, and everyone was on their guard. Welton was rightly cautious, for by 1948 it was rumoured that as many as 15 individuals involved in youth work in Denmark had been 'liquidated' by their communist opponents.[19] CRD noted that Elizabeth Welton's connection with the authorities was to be 'kept dark' but that she would be given some training and preparation before departing. 'Mr Hollis of M.I.5. is expected to brief her', they noted, in order to give her the benefit of Whitehall's intelligence on European youth movements and the issue of 'who is a communist and who is not'. Roger Hollis, who had superintended MI5's F Division (surveillance of political parties), had just taken over the supervision of C Division (security).[20]

Whitehall was interested in student politics as well as youth affairs and was especially anxious about communist inroads into the National Union of Students in Britain. Accordingly, CRD teamed up with MI5 and SIS to observe these activities. At a remarkably early stage in the Cold War they decided to take measures, again by trying to create their own counter-groups. Britain's National Union of Students (NUS) played into the hands of CRD because they were short of money. Hoping to attend an international student festival in Prague in August 1946, they approached the Foreign Office in May to request a government grant to cover the costs of their travel. While CRD privately noted that they were not going to 'finance this clandestine agency of communism', they nevertheless encouraged further meetings with student leaders to track their activities.[21]

CRD worried that this student festival would result in the setting up of a Soviet-controlled International Students Federation 'in which the communists will hold all the strings', a repeat of what had happened with youth organizations in London the previous year which led to the creation of WFDY. So their first aim was to 'discourage the NUS' from taking part, despite knowing that it would be difficult since 'three near-communists' were on the NUS Executive Committee and it had been effectively communist-controlled since 1940. CRD's decision was to warn the NUS off in the first instance, but if the 'worst comes to the worst', and the NUS attended the Conference, CRD resolved to 'take fairly rigorous action'. They would have to get clearance at ministerial level, but in the worsening international climate of May 1946 they had 'no doubt that it would be forthcoming'.[22] Together with MI5, they busied themselves checking the background of the NUS delegation. MI5 asserted that a number of the delegation, including Carmel Brickman, were members of the Communist Party, and claimed that A.T. James, the President of the NUS 'had a record of close association with communist activities'.[23] It had been communists on the NUS Executive who had helped to set up the World Youth Congress in London in November 1945.[24]

SIS took over the business of monitoring youthful British communists from MI5 once such individuals left Britain and reached the continent. In the summer of 1946, the new 'R5' Requirements section of SIS, which dealt with world communism, tracked the efforts of British communists, who had been denied visas by the Foreign Office, to reach a meeting of the WFDY in Vienna. Special attention was paid to Kutty Hookham, Joint Secretary of the WFDY and also active on its British Committee. Hookham, something of an old stager in the world of international organizations, was one of the few British nationals to elude Foreign Office visa restrictions. SIS explained that she had achieved this by first visiting the headquarters of the new WFDY in Paris, then going on to Moscow, and then travelling from Moscow to Vienna. She was then due to travel back to Paris for another WFDY meeting. The Soviets were able to watch British efforts to impede the progress of British WFDY delegates with some clarity, for the SIS officer liaising with CRD on this matter was none other than Kim Philby, Head of R5.[25]

By July 1946, CRD were ready for action on three fronts. Firstly, to try and create an element more resistant to communism within the NUS. Secondly, to try and prevent a British delegation going to the International Student Congress in Prague, and thirdly to set up rival conferences, even rival non-communist youth and student organizations. CRD hoped that their groups would constitute 'a standing perpetual challenge to gang-rule wherever it becomes manifest – whether by Nazi parties or Soviet parties, or by Zionist movements.' CRD urged that if they mobilized properly they could also arrange a great deal of open criticism in the Prague meeting, adding 'we should show these communist tricksters what world opinion ...thinks of them'.

But there was a great deal of work to be done. In the summer of 1946 the apparatus that CRD needed for countering organized communism at the international level was not yet there. This was the fault of those who had hastily dismantled Britain's propaganda machinery after the war. Rather unfairly, CRD rounded on the overt information services that remained, namely their colleagues in the British Council. The British Council, it complained, was busy promoting British culture in a superficial way without proclaiming core British political and social values, and it accused them of 'frivolities with ballet girls and second-rate painters.' In July 1946, CRD was one of the loudest voices in Whitehall urging action 'at a high-level' on political warfare against Moscow. Propaganda had to be 'overhauled' and 'strengthened'.[26]

In tackling the NUS they were initially baffled by the lack of a way in. CRD's objective was 'the creation of a body of opinion to balance the extremists' within the NUS.[27] CRD took a close interest in NUS but the nature of the action taken remains unclear. Sir Patrick Nichols, British Ambassador in Prague, watched preparations for the International Student Congress there. Nichols thought it would be difficult to block communist students attending, so instead the tactic should be to somehow get more non-communist students onto the British delegation to balance the communist elements. 'In other words', he said, 'we have to choose between infiltration and boycott'. He favoured infiltration as the way forward. Nichols also warned that the British delegates selected for Prague included the familiar Kutty Hookham, whom he called 'an ardent communist'.[28]

By January 1947, CRD's longer-term project, a rival youth conference in London designed to produce an alternative world youth movement to challenge WFDY, was under way. Elizabeth Welton, together with George Haynes, Secretary of the National Council of Social Service, an umbrella organization of British youth groups, were leading the effort. They had held informal discussions with similar elements in the USA, France, Belgium and Holland who 'very much hoped' that Britain would take the lead in this struggle. These individuals requested a 'special' grant to help finance the operation. CRD took the point but were worried that Labour backbenchers would become suspicious and might realise that it was as 'an open attack on WFDY'. It was important to disguise the nature of the 'international aspect of British youth work' and they warned that the grant application would have to be 'carefully wrapped up'.[29]

As CRD reached the jumping-off point in terms of covert activities, Hector McNeil, the Foreign Office Minister of State with responsibility for the intelligence services, thought it might be wise to seek greater support amongst senior Cabinet ministers for the growing campaign against WFDY. On 19 February 1947 he met with James Chuter-Ede, Home Secretary, and Stafford Cripps, the Chancellor of the Exchequer to show them a range of materials indicating the extent of Moscow's influence. 'I had a very bad time', reported McNeil, 'neither of them are prepared to accept the evidence of MI5'. Cripps was especially hostile as he was personally and closely involved in supporting the activities of both WFDY and the NUS. Gladwyn Jebb, a senior official in the Foreign Office who had taken over the running of the Russia Committee, was outraged at the treatment of his own minister:

> To anyone who does not wilfully blind himself, it must be obvious that WFDY is inspired and controlled by Moscow ... It seems to me grotesque that this bogus body, whose meetings appear to be dominated by elderly Russian Major-Generals, should pose as the only representative of 'democratic youth' everywhere.[30]

But in 1947 both Stafford Cripps and Lady Isobel Cripps were still adamant that these organizations were free and independent.

CREATING WAY

By January 1948, CRD's main project, an International Youth Congress in London, was tottering forward, but it was a weakling compared to the vigorous and well-organized WFDY events supported by Moscow. CRD staff attended the meetings of Britain's National Council for Social Services, who were charged with organizing the International Youth Congress and who were being funded with small grants from the Ministry of Education. But CRD were dismayed by the indecisiveness of the worthy individuals who staffed it. They came away 'depressed and despairing' for these figures were 'so afraid' of doing anything that might provoke an attack by the better-organized WFDY. It was clear that genuinely independent bodies were not going to lead the way of their own accord, so CRD would have to step up their own intervention and get things going. 'It is essential that we act quickly and boldly now', they concluded. There were further meetings between Montagu-Pollock of CRD and Elizabeth Welton, the toughest and most reliable individual within the British non-communist youth movements. Welton was not only someone who was incensed by communist infiltration of British youth movements, since a colleague has also recalled how she was someone who simply enjoyed cloak and dagger work for its own sake. She was ideal for the tasks that CRD wished to set her. Officials now began to approach a range of British youth organizations privately and 'indirectly' to persuade them to quit WFDY and to join the rival CRD-sponsored International Youth Conference.[31]

In the event, the International Youth Conference – held at Church House in Westminster, London, in August 1948 – proved a mammoth success. CRD measured its success by the extent to which it was attacked in the Soviet press. The experience also confirmed CRD in its tactics of creating new rival bodies rather than attempting to prise existing groups away from WFDY. Recent confrontations between various left and right youth organizations in Europe seemed to show CRD that 'any kind of "Trojan Horse" tactics are useless' and that competing bodies built afresh were more promising. Although NUS had in fact broken away from communist control by mid-1948 and left the WFDY later that year, the approach of building organizations anew remained CRD's chosen forward path. The International Youth Conference gave birth to 'WAY' or the World Assembly of Youth, Britain's first covertly orchestrated international organization. Elizabeth Welton became the Secretary of the British National Committee of WAY. In the same year Britain also set up a proper covert political warfare section, the Information Research Department. But for the previous three years it had been CRD and Montagu-Pollock – one of Britain's least known Cold War warriors – who filled the gap.[32]

In 1948 one of CRD's abiding anxieties in creating WAY was to avoid a situation in which there were rival British and American competitors to the communist WFDY. In theory this was not a problem, for the covert action arm of the CIA – known as OPC – was not really under way until mid-1948. But in practice, all sorts of privateer operations were being run by American private organizations, often with the encouragement of the State Department, the US Army and others. Thus in March 1948, to their dismay, CRD uncovered what appeared to be moves afoot in the USA to create a rival body to the WFDY led by Sturgeon M. Keeney. Keeney was now in Europe and although not an American government official was working out of the American embassy in Paris. CRD had asked their representatives at the British Embassy in Washington to investigate who was 'backing' Keeney. He proved to be a recent graduate of Harvard and son of an American official who was living in Rome, but who was 'not attached to the U.S. Embassy there'. Having attended the WFDY Prague meeting of 1947 he had decided to try and set up a counter-group with the encouragement of Robert Smith, Vice-President of the American National Student Association. Keeney was also the National Student Association representative in the National Commission on UNESCO. In 1948 CRD were making active efforts to contact him in order to engage him in the activities of WAY.[33]

Central to the successful creation of WAY were the efforts of Bevin and his officials to persuade the Chancellor of the Exchequer, Sir Stafford Cripps, of the communist nature of its WFDY opponents. Ironically, Cripps had not only been the most active Cabinet Minster in backing the formation of WFDY in 1945, but in 1948 was also the gatekeeper for the additional funds that Bevin needed to support the new British venture, WAY. However, as CRD officials warned Bevin in April 1948: 'Although the evidence supplied by MI5 and others was to us incontrovertible, Sir Stafford has never been convinced and [has] prevented unanimity in the Cabinet Committee which was set up to discuss this question in 1946'.[34]

In April 1948 Bevin and CRD set out to educate Stafford Cripps. Simultaneously they were working on Lady Isobel Cripps, another leading labour light and key figure in the world of youth movements, to persuade her of the communist nature of WFDY. Initially this involved sending George Haynes, the General Secretary of NCSS, to the USA to lobby the State Department and also Eleanor Roosevelt. Eleanor Roosevelt was then prevailed upon to approach Lady Cripps about the problems of communist penetration.[35] Bevin had several personal meetings with Lady Cripps, parading various witnesses to prove his point. This included a former Secretary General of WFDY, Sven Beyer-Pedersen, who had been expelled for not being sufficiently communist, and who was keen to tell all. Beyer-Pedersen was a crucial witness. In March 1948, CRD officials had debriefed him with George Haynes and Elizabeth Welton in attendance. His account 'coincided with various top secret reports on the organization' that they had already received, but had added material on personalities and, most importantly, was full of drama and had the ring of conviction.[36] Bevin argued that WFDY was now 'entirely run by communists' and set out the NCSS plans for a new and 'genuinely democratic' international youth organization called WAY. He was careful to stress that he had the support of both Hugh Dalton and Morgan Phillips who were 'very concerned' about this issue. Bevin warned that it would be 'fatal' to get out of step with an emerging Labour Party hard line on the WFDY. Lady Cripps took the point and now began working with Eleanor Roosevelt against the organization that they had previously supported. Doubts had probably been forming in her own mind since the stridently communist WFDY Congress in Prague in 1947.[37] In May 1948, Sir Stafford Cripps resigned from the International Youth Council (the headquarters of the British Committee of the WFDY) and later dissolved the International Youth Trust which he had helped to create and which largely financed the International Youth Council.[38]

In 1948 CRD hoped that funds for WAY could be made available discreetly through the Ministry of Education, but initially they encountered 'difficulties with their grant regulations' which did not permit them to fund overseas activities. The Ministry of Education was already subsidising the 1948 International Youth Conference itself through a grant to NCSS. George Haynes of NCSS had told the Foreign Office that if the 1948 International Youth Conference was to produce a permanent body to oppose WFDY – as they had hoped – they would need about £9,000-£10,000. Christopher Warner – who had transformed himself from an apologist for the Soviet Union in early 1945 into one of its most active critics by 1948 – was determined that they should find the money.[39] In the event it fell to Bevin to persuade Stafford Cripps to come up with the finance. Bevin exhorted Cripps about the importance of setting up 'permanent machinery' and asked him for an initial outlay of £5,000, expecting the rest to come from the USA and other sources. Bevin also asked for advice from Cripps 'as to the channel through which financial assistance should be forthcoming', explaining that there were likely to be objections to the political nature of this grant if it came directly from the Foreign Office. On 3 September 1948, Cripps authorised British government funds for WAY's permanent machinery and secured the agreement of George Tomlinson, Secretary of State for Education, that it would be funnelled through his department.[40] CRD had held talks with the Ministry of Education in the summer of 1948 and had stressed that the latter had a 'particular skill for giving support, without doing so conspicuously'. Ministry of Education officials did not take this as a compliment and were uncomfortable about being used for overseas activities which were outside their remit simply because this provided a discreet channel.[41] Stafford Cripps himself had been placed under considerable pressure by his fellow Cabinet ministers, but exactly how far Cripps had really abandoned his far-left associates remains in question. As late as 27 July 1948 the redoubtable Kutty Hookham of WFDY wrote to Cripps thanking him for intervening in Whitehall to secure visas for the latest travels of members of the International Youth Trust.[42]

Throughout this period CRD worked very closely with MI5 through its Foreign Office link man, A.S. Halford. CRD would often refer obliquely to MI5 as 'Mr Halford's friends'.[43] Roger Hollis, Director of MI5's C Division, remained the principal contact for Halford, and what CRD primarily wanted was name-traces to be conducted in the MI5 registry. On 24 June 1948 Hollis wrote to Halford conveying information about several trace requests on British citizens who had been involved in a recent International Student Service Conference in Rangoon. These included: Dr Kennett, John Spencer, Douglas Aitken, Nancy Richardon (NUS), and Christopher Seton-Watson.[44] Indeed, by 1948 British officials were working with MI5 on a global basis against WFDY. In July 1948 CRD were offered copies of a mass of material sent from the WFDY to the Democratic Peoples Youth League in Burma

FIGURE 2
LITERATURE PRODUCED BY THE WORLD FEDERATION OF DEMOCRATIC YOUTH

YOUTH FIGHTS COLONIALISM

MONTHLY BULLETIN PUBLISHED BY

"BUREAU OF YOUTH FIGHTING AGAINST COLONIALISM" OF

WORLD FEDERATION OF DEMOCRATIC YOUTH

which had been obtained from the Burmese Special Branch by the local MI5 Security Liaison Office at the Rangoon Embassy.[45]

CRD AND THE PROBLEM OF SLENDER MEANS

Front organizations are not cheap to run. Artists, intellectuals and writers often could not be easily co-ordinated by anything except largesse and some proved truculent when this was not available. Accordingly, money was soon an issue for the foot soldiers of CRD and IRD in London. This was certainly the case with the WAY which had competed successfully with the Soviet youth front, the WFDY. British government stringency in the early 1950s forced Whitehall to make hard choices and CRD found it hard to defend their project. To their dismay, because American financial support seemed to be forthcoming for WAY, the leaders of this favourite project gradually moved over to working more closely with Washington.

Problems began to loom as early as November 1950. CRD noted that WAY officials were 'touchy' about the money issue. Previously London had given 'considerable financial support both to the international headquarters of the World Association of Youth and to the British National Committee'. IRD and CRD had hoped that this was merely pump-priming money, since the original intention was that WAY should eventually 'stand on its own feet' and be maintained by voluntary subscription from its component organizations. Just like the CIA's Free Europe Committee in Washington, which was also originally intended to become free-standing and self-financing, WAY remained stubbornly dependent on government subventions. But unlike its American equivalents, WAY's impoverished parent could not afford to continue generous subsidies. In what CRD called 'our present financial straits' they began to cast around for possible additional subsidies from NATO.[46]

On 26 November 1951 John Nicholls, who superintended all the Foreign Office information departments, convened a meeting to consider the future of British clandestine policy in the area of youth movements. It was attended by figures from CRD, IRD and also the Information Policy Department. They agreed that one of their main aims was to provide the youth of Western Europe as a whole with an antidote to communism. They also resolved to make 'special efforts' in the area of German youth and colonial youth. WAY remained the crucial vehicle for these British projects. But obtaining hoped-for additional allied financial support for WAY was tricky, since both the continental European and American governments were avidly pro-federalist, which London did not like. Optimistically, London hoped to obtain allied funding for WAY, but at the same time to use WAY within European youth programmes to apply a brake to federalist tendencies.

In 1952 they urged 'a maximum British participation' in European youth activities, but 'aimed at opposing Federal Europe propaganda'. They also worried about the fact that the French and the Americans were now backing a youth programme which the European Movement was preparing for next year. WAY was working on this project together with the European Movement and International Union of Socialist Youth and a joint secretariat had been set up in Brussels. The WAY representatives on this Brussels Secretariat were the old CRD-sponsored stagers, including Elizabeth Welton, who had previously been Secretary of the British National Committee of WAY, together with Guthrie Moir and Robert Leaper, two of the more 'energetic' members of this Committee. But given the federalist complexion of the wider programme, should their task in Brussels be supporting, reporting or undermining? British officials were perplexed and had to seek 'higher guidance of HMG's attitude to the European Movement'.[47] WAY was consistently used to try and blunt the strong federalist tendencies of American- and French-backed outfits, including the European Movement itself. By January 1955, Lord Hope, Under-Secretary of State at the Foreign Office, was backing WAY in its efforts to secure Consultative Status from the Council of Europe, in direct competition with the European Movement's European Youth Campaign. CRD complained of the 'federalist bias' of the European Youth Campaign which was 'maintained by American funds'. CRD therefore had little doubt about who was really behind the Campaign's lavish funding.[48]

CRD and IRD could never obtain enough money from the Treasury for WAY to maintain smooth relations with their protegés, even though strenuous efforts were made. Between 1952 and 1954 both Anthony Eden and Selwyn Lloyd made repeated efforts to resist Treasury cuts in the subsidy to WAY.[49] In January 1954, Anthony Eden as Foreign Secretary 'made a personal intervention' to try and lever more money from the Treasury to support this project. Eden was joined in this enterprise by the Colonial Office and the Commonwealth Relations Office. But the Chancellor of the Exchequer, Rab Butler, refused to continue the subsidies, which had nevertheless been quite small. Since the launch of WAY in London in 1948, its international organization had received only £700 a year and its British National Committee, the real engine room of WAY activity, £2,000 per year. There had also been further *ad hoc* subsidies to ensure the effective attendance of British delegations at international conferences. British leadership of WAY, an international body with a membership of 60 countries, was a stunning achievement and it had been secured at a bargain price. Guthrie Moir, now the International President of WAY and with whom CRD had 'very close relations', contacted Eden regularly pleading its case. The Second General Assembly of WAY was planned for Singapore in September 1954. The venue had been 'chosen with the encouragement of the Foreign Office' but there was now no money to send a British delegation. This was doubly embarrassing since many other Western European governments now gave subventions to the International Secretariat of WAY and its various national committees 'most generously'.[50]

In May 1954 Ian Page, the British President of WAY, tried scare tactics. Despairing of his sponsors in IRD and CRD, he wrote to the Treasury directly asking for £7,000, enclosing material generated by his communist rivals. The Treasury were indeed 'shaken' and had to concede that their communist competitors 'looked pretty devilish'. But in July, Rab Butler continued to refuse funds. American funding from the Ford or Carnegie Foundations remained a possibility, but this was a sore point for those in Whitehall looking after colonial affairs, no less than European affairs, who saw the Americans as rivals. Oliver Lyttelton, the Colonial Secretary, warned Eden on 25 June 1954: 'I do not think either of us would want to see the controlling interest in this organization passing ... to the United States'.[51]

By July 1954 relations between CRD and Guthrie Moir were reaching a breakdown. The end of CRD-directed money had prompted the Carnegie Commonwealth endowment to withdraw their sponsorship of Singapore, leaving WAY with a $50,000 shortfall. Moir had become 'very bad tempered' and had begun to leak material to the press about 'inter-departmental struggles' in Whitehall. Eventually in desperation, CRD and IRD turned to 'sources not under Treasury control' to carry the Singapore Conference forward and to get a British delegation there. In practice this meant $20,000 from the Singapore Government together with a private subvention from Shell-Mex. The Singapore Government offered its own estimate that without WAY at least one third of its member organizations would join the Moscow-directed front, the WFDY.[52]

The issue of longer term funding beyond the 1954 conference remained. Guthrie Moir and his team, who controlled the International Secretariat of WAY, now threatened resignation unless secret British subventions continued. Ivone Kirkpatrick suggested a grant of £5,000 for 1955/6, about a third of all the Foreign Office's meagre allocation for developing 'multilateral co-operation'. This was largely used to pay off previous debts and WAY pointed out that by late 1954 the British delegation was the only delegation in the world that was likely to default on its subscriptions for 1953 and 1954. In February 1955 the Treasury relented. Although the circumstances were somewhat different, the grumpy relations between senior WAY figures and their British sponsors nevertheless bear comparison with the unhappy relations between Jay Lovestone's AFL and its CIA partners during the same period.[53]

Notwithstanding this, by the mid-1950s support for WAY's International Secretariat was already passing to American organizations with strong government connections, including the Asia Foundation (previously the Committee for a Free Asia), although it is likely that few if any of the WAY leadership were aware of the original source of some of the subventions. When the Singapore Youth Council was chosen to host the next WAY conference in August 1954, it was primarily the Committee for Free Asia, under the local representative Robert Sheeks, who provided the money. Indeed, even before the arrival of WAY it was the Americans who were supporting much of the non-government anti-communist youth work, including sponsoring the launch of a Chinese edition of the Singapore Youth Council's 'Youth World' magazine.[54]

By 1955 the International Secretariat of WAY was becoming a largely American-funded body, receiving subsidies from a range of groups. This began to reflect itself in the leadership. By 1955 the Vice President of WAY was a young American sociology student called Immanuel Wallerstein, who subsequently went on to become a highly influential International Relations theorist.[55] Britain's Guthrie Moir has explained that the big change began when they obtained $70,000 from the Ford Foundation for a General Assembly meeting in Ithaca, New York. This had led to the setting up of the Foundation for Youth and Student Affairs in New York shortly after. This American funding body had consistently 'invested large sums in WAY' including $114,000 for the Singapore conference of 1954. The Asia Foundation also put up $50,000 in travel grants towards delegates from Asian countries 'which were carefully selected by us in the light of the current political climate'. The Foundation for Youth and Student Affairs in New York was currently providing $48,000 per annum for WAY's International Secretariat in Paris, including a translation service for its magazine, WAY Forum. John Rennie, the Head of IRD, continued to press for money in 1955, arguing that Britain 'cannot effectively influence the organization and its activities ... without contributing to its funds', but the inescapable truth was that London had already lost the race for control of WAY as a whole.[56] However it should be stressed that influence in the councils of WAY was hardly a mechanistic result of funding, and many of its international delegates had tired of the strong British presence that had evinced itself during WAY's first five years. Some were keen to encourage a greater variety in WAY's leadership to confirm its genuinely international identity. The French were also keen to resist what they regarded as Anglo-Saxon domination.[57]

During the early 1960s cultural propaganda enjoyed a resurgence. Events in Hungary in 1956 had confirmed the collapse of more aggressive strategies denoted by political warfare and subversion. Moreover the growth of Arab nationalism in the late 1950s had also prompted London to place more emphasis on cultural propaganda.[58] During the early 1960s CRD was run by Robin Cecil, who had served as personal assistant to Sir Stewart Menzies, the Chief of SIS, both during and immediately after the war. Cecil was active on behalf of WAY and managed to increase Whitehall support, but this was now focused specifically on the British National Committee of that organization, rather than the international secretariat of WAY. During the early 1960s government subventions to the British National Committee of WAY rose to about £5,000 per year, partly as a result of favourable representations of their role to a 1960 working party on youth activities in the New Commonwealth.[59] CRD's avowed purpose was now sustaining the British National Council of WAY as a group that would 'counter the appeal of the communist youth organizations'. Whitehall remained almost the sole source of income for the British National Committee, although not for WAY as a whole. In 1965, when the Treasury attempted to shave its budget marginally, George Thompson, the Minister of State at the Foreign Office, made the usual protests. He stressed their concern about the 'important field of international youth work' and the potential of this organization as 'a valuable instrument of Her Majesty's Government'. He warned that 'it will fail to fulfil this purpose if we keep it at a bare subsistence level.[60] But at the end of the 1960s the British National Committee remained a Cinderella organization compared with the other national committees of an international organization that CRD had effectively created. Officials lamented that the British National Committee 'has always been dependent upon a Government subsidy' and had never developed a diversified funding base. As a result it was in debt and its HQ was 'in a dingy area' next to Euston station. In 1969 it was still receiving £5,000 a year from Whitehall, compared to the Dutch National Committee which received £15,000 from its government and the German National Committee which similarly received £75,000. Nevertheless, it remained active and played a significant role in helping to deal with 3,000 young Czechs stranded in Britain during the 1968 invasion. In 1969 the Treasury kept the subsidy going because they feared that if the British National Committee disappeared then its place would be taken by the Youth Action Council, 'a recently formed organization with communist connections'.[61]

CONCLUSION

CRD and its persistent creation – WAY – present us with an interesting phenomenon. They point us towards a more balanced vision of the heritage of British information warfare, alluding to both peacetime/cultural as well as wartime influences and precursors. British information warfare in the early 1950s was presided over by a troika of CRD, IRD and the Information Policy Department (IPD), which were at the same time being assisted by a host of other organizations. By the late 1950s, with ideas of 'liberation' proving to be increasingly démodé, political and psychological warfare were on the wane, while cultural warfare and 'soft liberation' enjoyed a resurgence. Although CRD enjoyed less of the limelight than its more famous IRD partner, it nevertheless outlived it, continuing its work well beyond the dissolution of IRD by David Owen in 1977. The Cultural Relations Department is still going strong despite much re-shuffling of Foreign Office organization since 1989. WAY also continues its activities, albeit in a much altered form and primarily directed from Malaysia.

Both WAY and WFDY are interesting as rare examples of a Cold War apparatus that was made by women as much as men. Despite the efforts of Cold War historians to refresh their agendas in recent years, the landscape of this conflict remains remarkably devoid of women, with the notable exception of women's organizations and their engagement with the Cold War.[62] Kutty Hookham was probably the most energetic British figure behind the creation of WFDY and Elizabeth Welton was certainly a dynamic figure behind the creation of WAY. Both Hookham and Welton relished the shadowy nature of some of their work, so much so that Welton was often criticized by her colleagues for her excessive enthusiasm for 'cloak and dagger stuff'. Helen Dale was Secretary-General of WAY in the mid-1950s, while Sonia Richardson and Ruth Schachter were also influential at this time. In terms of patronage, the work of Lady Isobel Cripps and Eleanor Roosevelt was clearly important. Meanwhile the desk officer in CRD with primary responsibility for this area was Monica Powell.[63]

Neither Britain nor the United States can claim to have invented the style of covert cultural and political warfare that resulted in the proliferation of 'state-private networks' during the Cold War. This accolade probably belongs to Willi Münzenberg, the mastermind behind much Soviet-inspired united front activity in inter-war Europe.[64] How far the British and the Americans in the late 1940s were deliberately emulating his tactics is hard to judge. What is clear is that the Soviet cultural apparatus was a matter of continual fascination to CRD by the late 1940s. Their attitude was not always one of admiration and they considered many aspects of the Soviet cultural apparatus to be somewhat baroque. In 1946 CRD officials noted that among Moscow's 50 theatres there numbered 'The Theatre of the Ministry of Internal Security' run by the MGB itself. Unfortunately they seemed to lack information about what sorts of shows were running at this unique venue.[65]

The persistence of CRD, drawing a line of continuity from the 1930s onwards into the twenty-first century, raises some interesting questions about culture, propaganda and front organizations. Most obviously, one is inclined to ask, 'where are they now'? Over the last decade, historians have made some notable discoveries about the extent to which many 'free and independent' international movements were enmeshed in 'state-private networks' during the Cold War. These networks were often clandestine or semi-clandestine and characterized by a complex partnership – albeit sometimes volatile – rather than by simple state manipulation. Surveying the scene for the 1950s, it now seems that many independent international organizations and groups enjoyed substantial state support and some, like WAY, were state creations. Conversely, some commentators working in the area of international relations have made a great deal of the period after 1945 as one characterized by the rise of Non-Governmental Organizations (NGOs) and global networks, even speaking of these things as pointing towards the eventual 'death of the state'. These assertions sit a little awkwardly with what we know now about NGOs in the period 1919–1960. In turn, they might prompt us to wonder what the real character of NGOs was in the later phases of the Cold War and beyond? The answer is likely to remain a matter of speculation for some time.

But now and then we catch a glimpse. In early 1986, George Soros set up the American-based 'Foundation for Chinese Reform and Opening' designed to accelerate the reform process in mainland China. Some would argue that the transnational activities of groups and foundations like this encouraged the reform movements and student societies that found themselves in Tiananmen Square in 1989. Beijing perceived these international foundations that were encouraging reform as vehicles that were being deliberately deployed by Western states to undermine political stability in China. In 1989 the Chinese Ministry of State Security thought it knew what was going on. Unusually, some of the Chinese internal government papers documenting the events of 1989 have now been published and in a report to Party Central of 1 June 1989, written days before the fighting began, the Ministry of State Security alleged that 'four members of the foundation's advisory committee had CIA connections'.

Who can say whether this is the truth, or the paranoid vision of one of the last significant authoritarian states? But one suspects that in another 30 years' time we will conclude that the influence of states and government officials has not always been on the wane in the face of NGOs or global forces, and that instead the officials found creative ways to bring the state back in.[66]

NOTES

1. J. Lewis, *Changing Direction: British Military Planning for Post-War Strategic Defence, 1942–7* (London and Portland, OR: Frank Cass 2003); M. Folly, *Churchill, Whitehall and the Soviet Union* (London: Macmillan 2000). Lewis is strongly critical of what he considers to be a diplomatic myopia, while Folly develops the idea of a 'co-operation thesis' amongst some Foreign Office officials.
2. Clerk-Kerr to London, 26 Nov. 1946, N16816/989/38, FO 371/47935; Clerk-Kerr to London, 15 December 1945, LC6031/1406/452, FO 924/206. The path-breaking work in this area is J. Kotek, *Students and the Cold War* (London: Macmillan 1996) which focuses upon students. For a wide-ranging analysis of British cultural diplomacy and the British Council see J.M. Lee, 'British Cultural Diplomacy and the Cold War, 1945–61', *Diplomacy and Statecraft* 9/1 (March 1998) pp.112–34. This paper seeks to focus specifically on youth movements and CRD.
3. Randall to Montagu-Pollock, 21 Dec. 1945, LC 359/191/452, FO 924/449.
4. P. Taylor, *British Propaganda in the Twentieth Century: Selling Democracy* (Edinburgh UP 1999); P. Lashmar and J. Oliver, *Britain's Secret Propaganda War: The Foreign Office and the Cold War, 1948–1977* (London: Sutton 1998); R. Smith, 'A Climate of Opinion: British Officials and the Development of Soviet Policy, 1945–7', *International Affairs* 64/4 (1988) pp.635–47.
5. On IRD's early years see H. Wilford, 'The Information Research Department: Britain's Secret Cold War Weapon Revealed', *Review of International Studies* 24/3 (1998) pp.353–70; W.S. Lucas and C.J. Morris, 'A very British Crusade: the Information Research Department and the Beginning of the Cold War', in R.J. Aldrich (ed.), *British Intelligence, Strategy and the Cold War* (London: Routledge 1992) pp.85–111; P.M. Taylor, 'Puissance, propaganda et opinion publique: les services d'information britanniques et la guerre froide, 1945–57', *Relations internationales* 55 (1988) pp.377–94.
6. Lee, 'Cultural Diplomacy' (note 2) p.112.
7. R.J. Aldrich, *The Hidden Hand: Britain, America and Cold War Intelligence* (London: John Murray 2001) p.149.
8. The term is drawn from W.S. Lucas, *Freedom's War: The US Crusade Against the Soviet Union, 1945–56* (Manchester UP 2000).
9. W.D. Miscamble, *George Kennan and the Making of American Foreign Policy, 1947-1950* (Princeton: Princeton UP 1992) pp.203–5.
10. Lee, 'British Cultural Diplomacy' (note 2) pp.116–7.
11. Change of name of British Council Section to Cultural Relations Department, FO 366/1452.
12. Nash min., 22 March 1945, LC 1242/1242/452, FO 924/204.
13. Montagu-Pollock memo, 19 April 1947, 'Future of CRD', FO 924/594B.
14. R. Smith and J. Zametica, 'The Cold Warrior: Clement Attlee Reconsidered, 1944–1947', *International Affairs* 61/2 (1985) pp.237–52.
15. Owen to FO, 20 June. 1945, LC2454/1406/45, FO 924/205; Hookham to Bevin, 23 Oct. 1945, LC5033/1406/452, FO 924/206. Kotek, *Students*, 81.
16. Montagu-Pollock, min. 19 Feb. 1946, W6865/524/50, FO 371/54787; Aitken min., 23 April 1946, W6861/524/G, ibid.
17. Viktor to Igor, 14 Sept. 1945, issue 31 Dec. 1956 (previous issue 29 March 1951), HW 15/5.
18. Brimelow min., 10 March 1946, W6861/524/G, FO 371/54787. On state-private networks see Lucas, *Freedom's War.*
19. Cowell min., 4 June 1946, W6864/524/50, FO 371/54787. Kotek, *Students* (note 2), p.128. I am indebted to Ingeborg Philipsen for her observations on this matter.
20. Brimelow minute, 12 June 1946, ibid.
21. Cowell min, 6 June 1946, LC2675/21/452, FO 924/383.
22. Montagu-Pollock min., 27 May 1946, and Lambert min. 30 May 1946, 6784/524/50, FO 371/54787. See also Kotek, *Students* (note 2) p.39.
23. Cowell minute, 31 May 1946, 6784/524/50, FO 371/54787.
24. CRD memo, 'British Participation in an International Student Congress', 28 July 1946, W8195/524/50, FO 371/54788.

25. Kim Philby (R5A) to FO, CX.94999/96, 17 July 1946, W7377/524/50, FO 371/54787.
26. Cowell min., 5 July. 1946, LC3185/21/452, FO 924/384. See also Kotek, *Students* (note 2) pp.84–5.
27. Lambert min., 3 July 1946, W8195/524/50, FO 371/54788. Also Bowen min., 2 Aug. 1946, ibid.; CRD memo., 'British Participation in an International Student Congress', 28 July 1946, W8195/524/50, FO 371/54788.
28. Nichols to FO, 14 June 1946, ibid.
29. Hector McNeil min., 10 Jan. 1947, W8186/540/50, FO 371/54788. Also Haynes to Montagu-Pollock, 'Consultation between International Youth Organizations', 3 Dec. 1946, ibid.
30. Kotek, *Students*, pp.110–1.
31. Powell min., 2 Jan. 1948, LC20/20/452, FO 924/670; Mason min., 7 Jan. 1948, LC253/20/452, ibid.. On grants see Macdermot to COI, 24 Feb. 1948, LC804/20/452, FO 924/672. Two confidential interviews with former members of the World Association of Youth carried out in 1999.
32. Powell min., 16 Jan. 1948, LC159/20/452, FO 924/670; Minutes of the International Youth Conference chaired by Professor D. Hughes Parry, LC404/20/452, FO 924/670.
33. Powell min., 18 March 1948, LC1258/20/452G, FO 924/673: British Embassy Washington to CRD, 13 April 1948, LC1643/20/452G, FO 924/675.
34. Min. to Bevin, 9 April 1948, FO 924/674.
35. British Embassy Washington to FO, 13 April 1948, LC1643/20/452G, FO 924/675.
36. Powell min., 18 March 1948, LC1258/20/452G, FO 924/673.
37. Bevin to Isobel Cripps, 13 April 1948 and Isobel Cripps to Bevin 2 June 1948, XXX, FO 924/674.
38. MacDermot min., 18 May 1948, LC1238/20/452G, FO 924/673.
39. Warner to Williams (Min. of Ed.), 8 July 1948, LC 2428/20/452, FO 924/679.
40. Bevin to Cripps, 30 July 1948, LC 2816/20/452, FO 924/679, Cripps to Bevin, 3 Sept. 1948, LC 2816/20/4523, FO 924/679. See also T 220/1210 and 1211.
41. Ministry of Education minute, 26 June 1948, ED 124/137. See also Tomlinson to Isobel Cripps, 2 June 1948, ibid.
42. Hookham to Cripps, 27 July 1948, File 524, Cripps Papers, NC.
43. See for example Powell min., 18 March 1948, LC1258/20/452G, FO 924/673.
44. Hollis (Box 500) to Halford, 24 June 1948, LC2615/20/4526, FO 924/679.
45. Glass to Finch, 27 July 1948, LC23041/20/452, FO 924/680.
46. Mayall min., 22 Nov. 1950, L317/48, FO 924/871.
47. Mtg, 26 Nov. 1951, CRL20017/2, FO 924/919; mtg., 1 Dec. 1951, ibid.
48. Hope (FO) to Hollis (HoC), 27 Jan. 1955, CRL2006/6, FO 924/1100.
49. Eden to Chancellor Exchequer, 8 May 1952, T2220/1210; Selwyn Lloyd to R.A. Butler, 14 July 1954, T220/1211.
50. Moir to Eden, 10 Feb. 1954, CRL20014/4, FO 924/1039; Grant min., 1 March 1954, ibid.; Haigh min., 1 April 1954, L20012/17, ibid.
51. Page to R.A. Butler, 8 May 1954, L20014/27, FO 924/1039; Grant min., 19 May 1954, L20014/30, ibid; Lytelton to Eden, 25 June 1954, L20014/43, FO 924/1040.
52. de Zueleta min., 29 July 1954, L20014/55, FO 924/1040; Walsh min., 12 Aug. 1954, L20014/62, ibid; Nicholls (Singapore) to FO, 14 Aug. 1954, L20014/68, ibid; Haigh min., 16 Sept. 1954, CRL20004/70, FO 924/1041.
53. Page (WAY) to Haigh, 4 Dec. 1954, CRL20014/85, FO 924/1041; Haigh min., 13 Dec. 1954, ibid; Brooke to Hope, 1 February 1955, CRL20014/10, FO 924/1100. See also T 220/1211. On Lovestone and the CIA see the fascinating essay by Anthony Carew, 'The American Labor Movement in Fizzland: The Free Trade Union Committee and the CIA', *Labor History* 39/1 (1998) pp.25–42.
54. Blum (President CFA) to Staats (OCB), 22 April 1954, Box 86, OCB Records, DDEL.
55. FO 924/1101. Immanuel Wallerstein was Vice President of WAY from 1954 to 1958. Private correspondence 12 Nov. 2000.
56. Moir to Hope, 17 March 1955, CRL2004/25, FO 924/1101; Rennie min., 20 May 1955, FO 1110/756.
57. Private correspondence, 10 & 11 Oct. 2001.

58. Lee, 'British Cultural Diplomacy' (note 2), pp.112–13.
59. Noney memo, 'BNC of the WAY', 2-FD 376/22/01, 16 Nov. 1965, T377/1436.
60. Thomson to Diamond (T), 8 Nov. 1965, T317/1436. Also Williams (BNC WAY) to Cecil, 21 Oct. 1965, ibid. The story of the Commonwealth Youth Trust effort can be followed in CAB 21/3161, 5341 and 5489.
61. Treasury memo, 'The British National Committee', 27 May 1969, T317/1436.
62. For example H. Laville, 'The Committee of Correspondence – CIA Funding of Women's Groups 1952–1957', *Intelligence and National Security* 12/1 (Jan. 1997) pp.104–21.
63. Confidential interviews with three early British WAY members, May 2001.
64. Stephen Koch, *Double Lives: Willi Münzenberg and the Seduction of the Intellectuals* (London: HarperCollins 1997).
65. 'Some Notes on Cultural Activity in the Soviet Union', 21 Aug. 1946, LC 3981/838/452, FO 924/480.
66. 'Western Infiltration, Intervention and Subversion', Ministry of State Security report to Party Central, 1 June 1989, reproduced in Zhang Liang, *The Tiananmen Papers* (London: Little and Brown 2001).

8

From Stockholm to Leiden: The CIA's Role in the Formation of the International Student Conference

KAREN PAGET

In 1967, *Ramparts* magazine exposed the Central Intelligence Agency's covert activities with the National Student Association (NSA), 'precipitating one of the worst operational catastrophes in CIA history', according to the CIA's in-house historian, Michael Warner.[1] The exposé brought down dozens of similar covert operations in the private sector, representing 'a combined budget of millions of dollars.'[2] The multi-million dollar campaign, known inside the CIA as 'the Mighty Wurlitzer', had been launched during the Cold War to challenge Soviet propaganda and influence in sectors ranging from youth to labour, intellectuals, artists, academics, women, jurists, and journalists.

In the firestorm that followed the *Ramparts* revelations, NSA officials were among the few organizations named in the article to confirm the CIA relationship, although they refused to disclose any operating details. In Leiden, the Netherlands, the Coordinating Secretariat (COSEC) of the International Student Conference (ISC), also named in the article and in which NSA was a founding member, issued a categorical denial. Officials claimed they knew of 'no evidence to suggest that any of its funds have ever come from clandestine bodies, nor have any ISC funds been used at any time for purposes other than those determined democratically by its organs'.[3] However, the ensuing collapse in 1969 of the International Student Conference, and the Coordinating Secretariat, suggested otherwise.

Before the last decade, information about private sector operations tended to be written by CIA insiders; most famously, perhaps, by former OSS/CIA operative, Tom Braden, who responded to *Ramparts*' charges in a *Saturday Evening Post* article, 'I'm Glad the CIA was Immoral.'[4] Cord Meyer, who oversaw covert operations as Braden's successor in charge of the CIA's International Organizations Division, defended them in his 1980 memoir, *Facing Reality*.[5] Meyer and Braden blamed McCarthyism for creating a climate that prohibited open government funding of liberal organizations, and both claimed they facilitated, not dictated, organizational goals, implicitly analogizing their funding to traditional philanthropy.

The view that CIA funding did not compromise organizational integrity was reasserted in a 1997 meeting of NSA alumni that included former officers who also worked for the CIA. Don Hoffman, NSA President (1960), told his colleagues he 'took no action, no resolution, etc., where the agency influenced the outcome'.[6] His comments were greeted with a good deal of skepticism, and one unwitting vice president demanded to know why, then, it had been necessary to swear selected NSA officers to secrecy about the true source of the funds.

In the last few years, scholars have begun to document the history, scope, and significance of intelligence operations among private sector groups. Their scholarship has stimulated further debate over how much, if any, influence the CIA exercised over the recipient organizations. Frances Stonor Saunders, in her recent work on intellectuals in *The Cultural Cold War* argues that the CIA piper called the tune.[7] Anthony Carew demonstrates that American labour officials between 1948 and 1952 battled the CIA for control, a struggle exacerbated by class differences between the two sets of officials.[8] Richard Aldrich found that the agenda funded by the American Committee on United Europe, a CIA conduit, was set by 'competing groups of Europeans actively seeking discreet American support'.[9]

Scholarship on the scope of student operations has lagged behind other work. Joël Kotek, who recently researched the early formation of international youth and student organizations, did not identify any CIA support for the ISC/COSEC before 1952. He concluded that both ISC and its COSEC staff were formed by students who, in desperation and as a last resort, turned to the CIA for funds.[10]

No detailed research has been published on the nexus between NSA, the formation of the ISC, and the US government. In fact, three government agencies, the US Army, the State Department, and the CIA, through its covert arm the Office of Policy Coordination (OPC), all played important roles during the formative period (1949–52) of the International Student Conference (1950) and COSEC (1952). One factor that has helped to obscure the American government role in this period is the insistence by former CIA insiders that financial subsidies did not begin until 1952, well after the ISC was founded.

The exception to this insistence came recently from the CIA's own in-house historian, Michael Warner, who in 1996 identified an earlier date in an important, albeit brief, article, 'Sophisticated Spies: CIA's Links to

Liberal Anti-communists 1949–1967'.[11] Warner, writing from classified material, wrote that CIA interest in private sector groups arose during the Marshall Plan, and was modified by 'NSC 10/2, which created the CIA's Office of Policy Coordination (OPC) to hasten America's psychological counter-offensive against Moscow and its clients'.[12] Surprisingly, Warner used the word 'spies', suggesting that the CIA's role entailed more than handing out funds.

The work presented here builds on Warner's revelations, and concentrates on the 1949–52 period. This essay will document US government involvement in the period before the founding meeting of the ISC in Stockholm, Sweden, in 1950. In 1949 and 1950 US government interest was aimed largely at building a consensus among Western student leaders to challenge the monopoly of the Soviet-backed International Union of Students (IUS). In July 1950, six months prior to the Stockholm meeting, the CIA/OPC financed projects that were already looking ahead to the development of non-European allies in Asia, Latin America, Africa, and the Middle-East.[13]

In the second period, after the Stockholm meeting in December 1950 and before December 1951, the CIA took steps to revamp its largely ad hoc relationship with NSA. These steps included giving direct subsidies to NSA and upgrading its personnel. The more formal relationship with the CIA, with its secrecy requirements, resulted in many changes within NSA, and also complicated NSA's overt relationship with the State Department. During this period, the goals of the funding, in addition to strengthening NSA, included an expanded programme in Latin America and Southeast Asia, two places seen as good prospects for building alliances with non-communist student leaders.[14]

Finally, during the third period, from January 1952 to the establishment of COSEC in August 1952, the CIA established a philanthropic conduit that could more easily move funds to NSA and ISC, and inserted an American on the COSEC staff to represent combined NSA/CIA interests.

While the primary focus here is on detailing these events between 1949 to 1952, the essay contributes to two questions that dominate scholarly debate about private sector covert operations. Was McCarthyism the reason for government secrecy, as CIA insiders argue? Did the CIA act merely as a funding source, or did it exercise control?

In brief, the evidence during this period, when McCarthyism was at its apogee, suggests that domestic anti-communism is an inadequate explanation for why the US government relied on clandestine relationships. The principal charge against the International Union of Students was that, ipso facto, it could not be independent of Soviet foreign policy objectives while receiving Soviet funds. The International Student Conference staked its difference from the IUS on its independence and freedom from outside government influence. Had McCarthy never existed, it is hard to imagine that the State Department would have openly bankrolled NSA's international activities or funded the ISC/COSEC. Open government funding would have undermined claims of independence, especially if, as was the case, financial dependency was significant, reaching as high as 90 per cent of both organizations' budgets.[15]

To the *sine qua non* of independence must be added another factor which emerges repeatedly from the material presented here. American leadership had to be downplayed, not just because the US government's hand might be exposed, but because American students constantly encountered suspicion of American motives. Anti-Americanism, while fueled wherever possible by IUS propaganda, existed quite apart from Soviet agitprop.

With respect to CIA control or influence, the evidence suggests that the locus of decision-making in this period was exceedingly complicated. Both NSA and COSEC officials derived their authority from annual conventions during which members passed policies and mandates that bound their elected leadership. Most of the CIA private sector operations, whether with labour, youth, intellectuals, academics, or journalists, did not have to contend with such a direct relationship with democratic processes.[16] Developing reliable personnel in NSA's International Commission and on the COSEC staff, the key to a smooth relationship, required a good deal of strategic manoeuvring. The episodes reported here suggest as well that a careful distinction must be made between CIA objectives and its capacity to execute them.

THE ROAD TO STOCKHOLM

Obstacles

Planning for a rival organization actually began the moment IUS was founded, and continued in fits and starts against formidable obstacles between 1946 and 1949.[17] Those obstacles included a founding ethos among IUS members to work for peace and not to repeat the mistakes of an older generation that led to World War II. Large constituencies within European student unions, and in NSA, independent of their attitude toward the Soviet Union, did not want to see the student movement split in two or to mirror the emerging camps of the Cold War.

Another obstacle was financial. The IUS had significant resources, including a well-staffed Secretariat in Prague. It annually hosted delegates from more than 50 countries at conferences or festivals, published a widely-distributed World Student News, funded trips for foreign delegations to the Soviet Union, and sponsored a variety of relief and reconstruction projects.

In addition to monetary resources, the IUS had a strong base of support outside Europe. Any international organization that hoped to contest IUS dominance had to have support from student leaders in Asia, the Middle East, Africa, or Latin America. The IUS had an advantage among these students, since it unambivalently backed anti-colonial movements where emerging students' leaders could be found. By contrast, key members of a potential Western student bloc, including Britain, France, and the Netherlands, were colonial powers, making the formation of alliances with colonized students more difficult.

A final obstacle was logistical. Geographical distances made it especially difficult for Western student leaders even to discuss their views on the IUS. Travel was expensive; money was scarce. Ironically, the IUS meetings in Prague, or its quarterly executive council meetings, provided one of the few initial venues for Western leaders to compare notes. Another venue was the International Student Service (ISS) in Geneva, Switzerland, an organization which distributed relief funds raised by students, and hosted annual conferences.[18]

NSA's Role

NSA's role in planning for the Stockholm meeting has been difficult to document since some of the principal participants had a casual relationship with NSA. From the beginning of NSA's existence, its international activities moved along two separate but related tracks. Not one but two international offices operated out of Cambridge, Massachusetts, one on the Harvard campus and one near-by, while the main NSA staff resided in Madison, Wisconsin. This structural complexity is crucial for understanding how intelligence relationships with NSA developed and grew.[19] The reasons for this complex structure can be traced to NSA's founding period.

In preparation for a December 1946 organizational meeting in Chicago to discuss founding a US national student organization, a small group at Harvard University formed a secretariat called the Harvard International Activities Committee, or HIACOM. Its creator was Douglass Cater, who had returned to Harvard after serving in the Russian section of the Office of Strategic Services (Research and Analysis–Central Intelligence Section). Cater, a Slavic studies major, had been chosen in May 1946 by a special Harvard University committee to join the American delegation for the IUS founding meeting.[20] This secretariat, originally envisioned as a temporary committee, continued its international activities after NSA was founded and until COSEC was fully established.

In the fall of 1946, the HIACOM staff prepared delegate packets, drafted sample constitutional provisions and model resolutions, organized delegates throughout New England, and handled other logistics for the Chicago meeting. Between the successful Chicago meeting and NSA's Constitutional convention in September 1947, it launched international projects, including the Salzburg (Austria) Seminar, and published several issues of a Student International Activities Bulletin, all of which established the Harvard students as leaders in the international field.

After NSA created its own International Commission, HIACOM continued to function as a 'sub-commission, under mandate to NSA'.[21] At the insistence of NSA's first international vice president, Robert Smith, a Yale Navy veteran, who intended to start graduate studies at Harvard, the official NSA International office located in Cambridge rather than Madison.[22] The relationship between the two international offices varied, depending upon the political compatibility between HIACOM and NSA officials, which ranged from symbiotic to prickly. During NSA's first year, Smith worked easily with Cater, and with HIACOM's second Chair, Frank Fisher, another Navy veteran who had returned to Harvard.

From its inception, funding for HIACOM projects did not always appear on either the Harvard Student Council or NSA accounts, since both Cambridge offices worked closely with the New York-based World Student Service Federation (WSSF), the major fund raising organization for student relief activities in the United States. The WSSF sent most, but not all, of its funds to the International Student Service in Geneva. It often allocated funds for NSA activities, or acted as a fiscal sponsor. Prior to the first NSA meeting in Chicago, for example, the WSSF provided travel funds so that William (Bill) Ellis, another member of the American delegation to Prague, could make a 'generous visitation' of campuses to pitch the idea of a national student organization. After Chicago, it supported HIACOM's international activities bulletin, and received and disbursed funds for projects such as the Salzburg Seminar, one of the first projects in HIACOM's portfolio.[23] Shortly after Smith's election, the WSSF authorized funds to pay NSA's Robert Smith a salary as 'Public Relations Director', supplementing his NSA salary.[24]

HIACOM staff not only initiated many of NSA's international projects but continually surfaced talented and seasoned students to lead them. Reflecting the times, most of these students were World War II veterans, and many had wartime intelligence experience. In 1949, during NSA's second year of operation, HIACOM officials recommended to NSA staff that a Harvard law school student, Tom Farmer, then 25, was ideally suited to lead a major project in Germany. Farmer, who spoke fluent German, served as a World War II military intelligence officer attached to the War Department General Staff and had worked with the American Military Goverment in Germany. In the fall of 1948, he returned to Harvard from Oxford, England to finish his law degree. While at Harvard, he belonged to a military intelligence reserve unit in Boston.[25] While Farmer is vague on when his reserve status changed from inactive to active, 'around the Korean War', archival documents indicate an earlier date of January 1949. Farmer subsequently joined the CIA in January 1951, and became the students' case officer. According to Farmer, Dulles asked him to join the CIA shortly after he accepted the position as CIA Deputy Director in December, 1950.[26] Farmer today describes his role in creating ISC and COSEC as 'central'.

Tom Farmer and the German Project

In 1949, the American occupation authorities in Germany had good reason for taking the student world seriously. The US Army had responsibility for educating a new generation with democratic norms. Among the recommendations that had emerged from several commissioned reports were that 1) US officials needed to democratize access to German higher education; and 2) they needed to inculcate principles of self-government.[27] As the divisions between the Russians and the Allies grew deeper, turning Germany de facto into two countries, the battle for the hearts and minds of German students expanded beyond checking for resurgent Nazism to guarding against communist penetration.

The German project that HIACOM officials recommended Tom Farmer to lead was authorized by the US Army Special Staff and funded by the American Military Government in Germany. Its purpose, a comprehensive survey of student conditions in Germany, was to be carried out by leaders from the American, British and Swedish student unions in cooperation with the newly-founded German student union, Verband Deutscher Studentenschaften, whose founding had been assisted by Occupation authorities. Farmer today claims credit for the original idea. 'I cooked up the idea of having an international student group do a study and give it to the [German] High Commissioner'.[28]

In the summer of 1949, the British-Swedish-American team surveyed every aspect of German student life, including housing, tuition, dining halls, health services, social clubs, and self-help projects.[29] Farmer found a sympathetic partner in Olof Palme, the future Prime Minister of Sweden, who then chaired the International Commission of the Swedish Federation of Students.[30] Palme early on became convinced that the IUS could not be reformed from within, that it was too controlled by the communists. The February 1948 communist coup in Czechoslovakia reinforced his belief. Farmer also identifies the Czechoslovakian coup as 'the thing that really woke us up' to the IUS threat.[31]

When in late 1949 the survey report was completed, Farmer gave it to High Commissioner John J. McCloy, to whom he was close, and to McCloy's right-hand man Shepard Stone.[32] Farmer, McCloy and Stone then agreed on a second project, which Farmer turned into a formal proposal while staying at McCloy's home in Bad Nauheim. The heart of the proposal was a summer seminar focused on self-government, to be held in Germany for German students but also attended by American and European students. The German Seminar created a site where Western student leaders could meet, build trust, and discuss problems related to the Prague-based IUS without being seen as actively organizing against it.[33]

The appellation 'seminar' is misleading, since the project included a 'Continuations Committee' to provide continuity between summer sessions. Archival documents indicate that some thought was given to whether the Seminar should operate a greater variety of student projects, or whether its base was too small. Once a date was set to host a broader meeting in Stockholm, arguments over expanding the German Seminar receded in importance.[34]

The significance of McCloy and Stone's involvement will not be lost on students of either psychological warfare or covert action. Both were strong advocates, and funding for the German project came from the High Commissioner and the Rockefeller Foundation, which regularly co-ordinated with McCloy and Stone. The Rockefeller Foundation allocated $10,000 for the first seminar in the summer of 1950, while McCloy and Stone gave 30,000 Deutschmarks directly to the newly-established German student union.[35] (Not so coincidentally, scholars of CIA activities in the youth field should note a similar project called the German Leadership Program, which was begun in 1949 and was also funded by the American Military Goverment in Germany. The American partner was the New York-based Young Adult Council, which soon became the American affiliate of the pro-West World Assembly of Youth, another CIA-funded organization. Funds for the Young Adult Council similarly came from the Rockefeller Foundation, while US Army funds were spent in Germany.)[36]

Farmer is remarkably blunt about his use of NSA. 'They were very tangential', he explained, except for 'producing' Olof Palme. 'I really knew very little about the NSA. I mean I just knew that I needed some sort of legitimacy for this German project. I never thought beyond that'.[37]

Did Olof Palme know of Farmer's government connections? 'Olof and I worked together constantly, and the expression "U.S. Government" was never mentioned. There was no point to it. I knew that Olof would resent any implication. We were simply engaged in a project that we felt had benefit for development of the post-war world'. He tells an anecdote to make the point. Once, when he had to get a confidential message quickly to Palme, he went through the CIA station chief. The head of CIA in Stockholm knew Palme and told Farmer, 'yeah, we're going to recruit this guy'.

'How stupid can you be', Farmer said he responded. 'One, we have a level of co-operation that couldn't be better, and if you ever do this he is going to be so offended that he'll never talk to me again'. Farmer adds that he generally had to 'fight with the collection people who believed that what you had to have were controlled agents, and so forth and so on ... that everybody could be bought'.

Their relationship worked well, Farmer insists, because the two men shared 'a common view of the world between fortunately what the CIA was willing to do, and the prevailing student sentiments. He was a Swedish patriot, and I was an American patriot, and why get into this whole business about *who was running who.*'[38]

What worked less well as the German survey (1949) and Seminar (1950) unfolded was the relationship between HIACOM's Farmer and NSA's elected international vice presidents, Rob West (1948–49), and Erskine Childers (1949–50). The two younger men were initially enthusiastic but they soon raised questions about the project's proximity to the American government. When West complained, Farmer shot back 'I can understand your worries about us deteriorating into becoming mere employees of Harry S. Truman. But I think I can assure you that these worries are unjustified. Hell, we didn't even have to sign an anti-communist affidavit, which I guess, is the best assurance that we still are solidly entrenched in the lofty spheres of student-self-government'.[39] He labeled Childers' fears 'silly' that 'the Commission was working primarily for the Military gov't'.[40]

The Search for Allies

While relationships between British, American, and Swedish student leaders were being solidified through the German projects, the CIA funded expansive travel to identify non-European students who might be interested in a new formation. In July 1950, before a meeting of Western allies in Stockholm had been decided upon, a 13-member US team of students fanned out to survey student leaders in the British Isles, Scandinavia, Benelux, France, French North Africa, Germany, Switzerland, Austria, Yugoslavia, Italy, Greece, Turkey, the Near East, Nigeria and Central Africa, the West Indies, and Southeast Asia. Funds for this ambitious agenda came circuitously from CIA's covert arm, the Office of Policy Coordination.[41]

Since no funding conduits yet specialized in student activities, the CIA/OPC channeled $12,000 to NSA through two trusted individuals, a Chicago lawyer, and a Wilmington, Delaware industrialist.[42] CIA officials sent two NSA staff members on a fund-raising trip that only one knew was a charade.[43] Donors' names were kept confidential from most of NSA staff.

The funds came to the Madison office, not the NSA International Office in Cambridge where Erskine Childers resided, quite probably because Childers' politics were distrusted. Childers was not only skeptical of a rival organization, and advocated working with IUS on specific projects, but throughout his term he actively resisted the intrusion of the State Department, condemning especially the practice of having students file detailed reports on their contacts with other students.[44]

Not surprisingly, the person in the Madison office who co-ordinated the fund-raising had a HIACOM background. Frederick Delano Houghteling, a relative of President Franklin Delano Roosevelt, chaired HIACOM during the 1948–49 school term. In August 1949, Houghteling won election to NSA's domestic staff as Executive Secretary. From this position Houghteling managed the fund-raising charade and helped direct the team.[45]

Team members had to abide by pages of confidential instructions which were detailed, legalistic, and almost onerously bureaucratic.[46] They required members to keep 'a daily diary noting the places and persons visited', and to write 'weekly reports of your activities and your proposed itinerary for the week ahead to the Paris office of the Association'. Those traveling within Europe were instructed never to interview a foreign student leader alone.

At the end of the summer, members were instructed to attend a meeting of dissident Western unions but 'under *no* circumstances [was] NSA to take the initiative in calling such a meeting'. Invitations 'must be left up to the British or the Swedes who are co-sponsors of the [German] Seminar'. The warning was repeated: the NSA team must 'not be known as a sponsor or co-sponsor of such a meeting'. Finally, they were forbidden to use any 'money for the German Seminar'.[47]

Three team members, Frank Fisher, James Grant, and William Polk, all older HIACOM staff, were explicitly exempted from all prohibitions. Navy veteran Frank Fisher (24), then enrolled in Harvard Law School, and who had succeeded Douglass Cater as the chair of HIACOM (1947–48), traveled to Yugoslavia on one of the more sensitive assignments. The IUS expelled Yugoslav students when Tito broke with Stalin. Perhaps the Yugoslavs would be sympathetic to working with the West. Graduate student William Polk and law student James Grant, a 28-year-old military intelligence veteran, covered the Middle East and Southeast Asia respectively.[48]

A direction to team members to be scrupulously neutral with respect to a rival organization heightened the tension between NSA's President, Robert Kelly, and former vice president Rob West, who sometimes represented NSA overseas. West, like Childers, was suspected of favouring continued contact with IUS. Before the team departed, Kelly removed Rob West from the list of overseas representatives, complaining that all he did was 'snarl up our discussions so that little in the way of positive planning' could take place.[49] Several weeks into the International Team's trip, Kelly ordered Childers to leave Europe in time to attend the annual NSA Congress in Ann Arbor, Michigan, effectively removing him from the meeting of 'dissident' students.[50]

The dissident group managed to meet in Prague in late summer, using the IUS Congress as a venue. Palme flew in for the crucial meeting.[51] At this meeting, the group decided to call a follow-up session for December in Stockholm. While those who met in Prague could agree on very little, they affirmed two principles that should distinguish a Western alliance from the IUS: It should be non-political, and it should focus on student concerns. The lack of consensus resulted in two conditions specific to Stockholm: they pledged not to create a formal organization, nor to discuss politics.

Preparation for Stockholm

On 6 November 1950, HIACOM members Frank Fisher, Jim Grant and William Polk announced a new project, the International Student Information Service (ISIS), funded by an unnamed 'private donor'.[52] The Information Service, run by HIACOM for overseas distribution, would collect information from American campuses that described how American students 'have solved such problems as housing and self-help'.[53] Descriptions of American self-help strategies would fill an important gap abroad, since 'at present, the only people making an appeal for students' favor in the world are the Russians'.

The Infomation Service had two other purposes. It provided a vehicle for contact with foreign student leaders between personal visits, and it enabled NSA leaders to arrive in Stockholm with an example of a student-run programme.[54] Polk credited the original idea to a grassroots meeting of New England students, but archival records indicate it originated at Berlin airport in discussions with US government officials.[55]

The Stockholm meeting introduced a new element. Since the meeting would consist of formal delegations, no-one from HIACOM could represent NSA. In October, NSA's newly-elected international vice president, Herbert Eisenberg, who had just finished his undergraduate degree, had been on the job less than two months. He soon complained that 'no one on the present National Staff' had the 'full story' on the negotiations for Stockholm. He vaguely understood that his assignment in Stockholm was to win for NSA the lead role in administering student-run practical projects, as exemplified by the Information Service.[56] He also learned that someone had committed NSA to explore financial support for additional projects. As the Stockholm date drew near, another World War II veteran with intelligence experience, Arnold Weiss, arrived on the scene to help prepare Eisenberg for the meeting.[57]

STOCKHOLM

First International Student Conference

Negotiations for the Stockholm meeting had been difficult. The preamble to the invitation had required over ten hours to draft, and Palme had given up all hope of creating a staffed organization. The conference delegates were in an interesting position, since the only way to attract a significant turn-out had been to agree that a rival organization *would not* be formed. Somehow, they needed to knit themselves into a tighter alliance under these adverse conditions.

By the time Eisenberg reached Stockholm, he carried a draft programme for expanding bilateral activities, the Student Mutual Assistance Program (SMAP), which he intended to introduce at the conference. He arrived in Stockholm upset that NSA's new President, Allard Lowenstein, had decided also to attend, reducing Eisenberg's role to that of 'technical expert'.[58] He and Lowenstein differed sharply on their approach to a rival organization. Lowenstein favored it, while Eisenberg backed a 'go slow' approach.

To Eisenberg's dismay, when Lowenstein took the podium, he gave a rousing anti-communist speech. He called directly for a rival organization, and belittled the practical projects approach. Already known for his rhetorical abilities, he declared: 'When the communists say they want peace we know too well what peace they want.... We will not be contributing to the attainment of peace ... if in our deliberations we confine ourselves ... to increased student exchange or better travel programs, in a world pushed to the brink...by the willful scheming of evil men bent on world domination for one nation'.[59] As a result of not confronting the IUS, Lowenstein continued, 'we are...four years behind', especially 'in those areas of the earth when communication is harder, democracy newer, and governments poorer, and where, with foresight and cunning, the IUS has laid a pattern to twist and undermine the legitimate aspirations of people long craving freedom'.[60]

The delegates voted to 'regret' Lowenstein's speech, a step just shy of a censure vote. The speech jeopardized Eisenberg's assignment to win the SMAP leadership, which in turn threatened the rationale for HIACOM/NSA's continued sponsorship of the Information Service. Lowenstein spoke from US Senate notepaper, further inflaming the delegates, who charged NSA 'was becoming the mouthpiece of the State Department'.[61]

Fortunately for Eisenberg, the British delegate stepped in before the conference ended, and saved NSA's leadership role in SMAP. The meeting ended with a general commitment to work together. To signal they had not created an organization, the delegates resolved that future meetings must be determined each year by majority vote.

Despite a largely successful conference, the American Embassy official closest to student affairs, Robert Donhauser, turned in a critical report on NSA's leaders. Whatever brilliance Lowenstein had as a speaker, and Donhauser conceded him that, was offset by his 'immaturity' and his 'abrasiveness'.[62] Palme and other Swedish student leaders (Jarl Tranaeus and Bertil Ostergren), in regular touch with Donhauser, told him that Lowenstein had 'blighted all chances for the US delegation to assume a leadership position at the conference'.[63] Donhauser judged Eisenberg to be 'also young' and inadequate for the programme ahead. His most effusive praise was for ex-NSA vice president Robert Smith (1947–48), who attended as an observer, and for the British delegation. He credited Smith more than the British with saving NSA's role in the Student Mutual Assistance Program.

Donhauser's conclusions had long-term significance for NSA. 'It is not felt that the present leaders of NSA are of sufficient caliber to carry through their part of the program with regard to its planning and implementation to the most advantageous extent.' He recommended that, given 'the importance of international student activities', more 'outstanding graduate students be found to run NSA's international program, permitting more continuity and leadership, more maturity and more experience both at home and abroad'.[64]

Stockholm Aftermath

Any plan to upgrade the calibre of NSA elected personnel, as suggested by Donhauser, necessarily had to wait until August 1951 when NSA held its annual Congress. Funding was another matter. Within weeks of the Stockholm meeting, CIA officials discussed directly funding NSA. A declassified CIA memo, dated 13 February 1951, summarizes a conversation between Deputy Director Allen Dulles and Harvard Government Professor William Y. Elliott, then a paid consultant to the CIA who recruited graduate students for psychological warfare work.[65]

According to the memo, someone unnamed (Lowenstein?) had rejected CIA funding: 'The National Student Association is not receptive to accepting government subsidy, because it considers that such a course of action would run contrary to its basic principle of independent thought and action and would in a sense reduce it to the position of being a tool of its government'. As a result, any 'such relation as is maintained is an extremely delicate one'. Dulles and Elliott discussed the Lowenstein-Eisenberg feud, 'personal differences currently rife in its high command', and noted that the National Executive Committee, NSA's oversight board, backed Lowenstein's position.

Dulles and Elliott concluded that a direct subsidy was not 'feasible, practicable, or desirable'. What to do? Move cautiously. Continue to fund 'individual projects...through the penetration which we have made into the National Association [line and half blacked out]', being careful not 'to arouse the suspicion...that the government is at all interested'.[66]

THE ROAD TO EDINBURGH

Camouflaging Government Interest

Throughout the spring of 1951, at a time when Eisenberg and domestic NSA officials complained bitterly about the lack of funding, projects aimed at Latin America, Asia, and the Middle East began to sprout under HIACOM's auspices.[67] Funding for these projects moved through a variety of conduits, succesfully disguising the US government's hand, as Dulles recommended. The strategies differed by region, but the goals remained identical: to identify student leaders sympathetic to the West or who might bolt from the IUS.

Latin America offered a potentially rich cache of delegates if student unions could be persuaded to support a new organization. An attempt to create a Pan-American union, a regional bloc consisting of Canada, the United States, and Central and South America, had been underway for some time.[68] In Brazil, as elsewhere, fierce battles between IUS loyalists and more conservative, often Catholic, student leaders raged within well-established student unions, slowing progress toward a regional bloc. Helen Jean Rogers, a former NSA official, and one of the few women to work with the HIACOM men, took the lead on Latin American strategy. Rogers claimed that financing for Latin American activities came from Mr. Braniff at Braniff Airlines, because she had the idea to contact him and request free transportation.[69]

Rogers clung to that story the rest of her life, but the best evidence that it is a fabrication comes from archival letters she left behind. In a confidential letter to Herb Eisenberg, the day before Rogers left for Brazil, she told him that when queried by an NSA staff member, she 'only vaguely referred to the Braniff-John Simons matter, not knowing how much information you had transmitted and not wanting to cause any friction'.[70] John Simons, another NSA founding father, had discreetly offered Rogers and Eisenberg funding. Simons' history with NSA dates from December 1946, when he was Treasurer of NSA's organizing committee. Before long, Simons would staff a new CIA funding conduit. Eisenberg, who admits he was approached by Simons, maintained a respectful silence until after Helen Jean Roger's death.

In contrast with the Latin American planning and funding, the evidence that the CIA planned the strategy for Southeast Asia is clear and unequivocal. According to the Dulles/Elliott memo, the Southeast Asia programme was 'prepared jointly by this office and the Far East division', then submitted for funding to the Rockefeller Foundation.[71] The Southeast Asia programme focused on Indonesia, which had the only really significant (non-communist) student union in Southeast Asia. The plan, patterned after the German project, called for a regional survey of student leaders in Asia in order to identify additional non-communist leaders, followed by a Southeast

Asian seminar.[72] The package that went to the Rockefeller Foundation also contained funding requests for the Middle East, Latin America, and a second year of funding for the German Seminar, although these regions were not specifically mentioned in the Dulles/Elliott discussion. It suggests that John Simons might have joined CIA/OPC by 1950.

The HIACOM person responsible for planning Southeast Asia strategy after his trip to the region was Jim Grant, another veteran intelligence officer. Grant did not wait for Rockefeller Foundation approval to move the strategy ahead. While Lowenstein and Eisenberg were still in Sweden, six weeks prior to the Dulles/Elliot discussion about the Rockefeller package, Grant requested from the two NSA leaders the 'authority to carry out the recommendations outlined in my summer report, including authority to raise the necessary funds'.[73] He also told them he had identified a qualified project director. After Eisenberg returned from Stockholm, Grant recommended that Mel Conant, a Masters student in Far Eastern Studies and the son of Harvard President James B. Conant, make a follow-up trip to Southeast Asia as soon as possible. Eisenberg endorsed the suggestion.

In late February, when the Rockefeller Foundation held up funding for Southeast Asia because officials had reservations about American dominance in the planning, Grant scrambled to explain to Lowenstein how they could proceed anyway. Grant wrote to Lowenstein on 7 March 1951, telling him that he 'finally wrangled a private contribution from a Harvard lawyer in the Washington area which should take care of Mel Conant's trip'.[74] When the funds arrived, HIACOM's Frank Fisher notified both Eisenberg and the Madison staff that since Conant's 'ticket must be purchased tomorrow or the next day we have had to have the check sent here. The ticket costs $2,200 and Conant will take a good bit of money with him. The rest we will keep here under the student council's financial control and send you the accounts just as soon as you are ready to receive them'.[75] The money never appeared in NSA accounts, and the private donor was never identified in NSA reports. In one financial report prepared by HIACOM for NSA, the amount listed for Conant was under-reported and listed as $500. Other HIACOM documents suggest it was more in the neighborhood of $5,000.[76]

In a reprise of the German Seminar strategy, Grant turned to the Scandinavians to offset the 'appearance of unilateralism' in running the Indonesian Seminar. Not all the colonial students liked 'the neutrals', Grant opined, 'but I would suggest that they are more popular than the Americans and the Germans alone'.[77] Grant understood that Rockefeller funding for Southeast Asia had not been denied categorically, but simply delayed, although this was not the impression in NSA's international office. The Rockefeller Foundation also granted funds for the second summer of the

German seminar, but they were sent, as before, to the World Student Service Fund, and did not appear in NSA accounts.[78]

New NSA leadership

NSA President Lowenstein knew about the Rockefeller omnibus package, and had signed off on HIACOM's strategy to seek funds, but his peripheral involvement must have galled him. In August 1951, at his out-going Congress, he made a last ditch effort to gain control over the international operation.[79] He and Eisenberg had bitter fights during his term. He had tried, for example, to elevate the NSA President as 'first among equals', rather than abiding by a more egalitarian division of labour among the elected officers. He had tried to consolidate the domestic and international offices into one location, and forced Eisenberg to spend time in the Madison office.

This time, Lowenstein's rhetorical skills failed him. The delegates to the annual Congress rejected his proposal to consolidate the offices. Lowenstein's many biographers believe that he was just too smart not to have suspected what was happening.[80] His behavior also squares with a comment he allegedly made to Roger Morris, a National Security Council official who served in the Nixon White House, that he was 'complicit' in the CIA's funding of NSA.[81] Accusations that Lowenstein created the CIA tie, given the dominance of HIACOM, seem highly improbable.[82]

HIACOM proved its utility once more by providing an entry point for Eisenberg's successor, someone who fitted to a tee Donhauser's recommended change in NSA personnel, someone who could never be called 'abrasive' or 'immature'. With no constituency, and no history with NSA except for a sudden appearance in spring 1951 on HIACOM's staff, a man named Avrea Ingram won the International Affairs Vice Presidency. Lowenstein later told his friend, David Harris, that it was the 'most curious' election he had ever witnessed, and that the 'one thing he knew for sure' was that Ingram could not possibly have been 'the spontaneous choice of the congress voters'.[83]

Ingram was identified as a graduate student in international affairs at Harvard University. Ingram's secretary in the NSA office, Kitty Fischer, in an interview years later, exclaimed, 'oh, Avrea wasn't a student', although Harvard records identify him as receiving a Master of Arts degree in 1953.[84] The *Harvard Crimson*, which regularly put NSA and HIACOM news on its front page, and especially heralded the achievements of any Harvard student, ignored Ingram's election.[85] It is conceivable, but speculative, that Ingram, then 24 years old, was recruited to run for NSA office via Navy ROTC, the Navy's reserve officer training corps programme. Before area studies programmes produced a pool of international experts, the CIA actively recruited among ROTC veterans. Ingram's Navy affiliation became known after his death.[86] Not long after his election, Ingram asked the Secretary of the Navy to assign another Georgia Tech (Ingram's undergraduate college) NROTC student to an NSA project in Atlanta, a request the Navy denied to Ingram's clear surprise.[87]

However Ingram was recruited, he immediately began to hint to the newly-elected NSA President Bill Dentzer that their funding problems were over. On 20 September, he informed Dentzer that he was investigating 'a long-term, revenue-producing project that could *eliminate* NSA financial problems in the future'.[88] In early October, Ingram told an NSA advisor that he had all the money he needed to operate a programme in Latin America.[89] Soon after he told someone else he had the money to cover his salary and the administrative/travel costs of the International Commission.[90] To an old friend from Georgia Tech, Ingram confided that he had found an 'angel'.[91]

Secret Funding for NSA

The total funding was far too significant to by-pass NSA's newly-elected President, William (Bill) Dentzer. Ingram helped bring Dentzer into a secret relationship with the US government without apparently disclosing the CIA's role. In mid-October, Ingram and Dentzer met with the Psychological Strategy Board, a new entity in the US executive apparatus charged with coordinating the government's psychological warfare activities against communism.[92]

On 10 November 1951, Dentzer sent the Board's Assistant Director John Sherman a synopsis of NSA's international programme and formally requested $75,000.[93] In the proposal Dentzer pitched the international programme in vivid anti-communist language, and demonstrated how the multiple programmes for Latin America, the Middle East, and Southeast Asia fitted together: 'In reality they are one package, each program a part of a total picture'.

Dentzer detailed NSA's strategy to create a 'truly representative' international organization of students: '1) Sending representatives to investigate student conditions in an area for the purpose of making contacts and analyses; 2) Following these contacts with information bulletins, assistance, and seminars which are run under the auspices of an indigenous group; and 3) Working for more broadly representative student conferences aimed at increased practical cooperation between student unions outside of and opposed to the partisan political activities of the IUS'.[94]

In an interview Tom Farmer looked puzzled when asked about Dentzer's approach to the Psychological Strategy Board, since the board had no funds of its own to allocate, then said simply 'it was in our chain of command'.[95] A hand-written notation on one of the NSA/Psychological Strategy Board documents contains the telephone extension of Col. Milton Buffington of the

CIA, the official who earlier recorded the conversation between Deputy Director Dulles and Professor Elliott.[96] Dentzer left the follow-up to Ingram.

Dentzer emphatically denies knowing during his year as President that the ultimate source of the funds was CIA.[97] His denial rests on a distinction between secret US government funds and secret CIA funds. He was instrumental in soliciting secret US government funds, and in keeping this knowledge from his NSA colleagues, its Executive Committee, and the NSA Congress. Dentzer also may have been vetted by the US Government prior to his election. A friend of Dentzer's in the summer of 1951, a few months before his election, wished him 'a successful summer with the State Department'.[98]

The new funds increased Ingram's and Dentzer's preoccupation with internal secrecy. On one occasion, Dentzer told Ingram that he 'nearly died' when he saw a draft article for NSA news in which the author referred (correctly) to the origin of the International Student Information Service as having begun in Berlin.[99] In another letter, he commiserates how careful he and Ingram must be, now that they are in a 'cloak and dagger stage of really super-secret work'.[100] Fund-raising proposals drafted in the NSA Cambridge office had to follow new procedures. For example, three copies of the Latin America proposal were numbered and labeled, 'Top Secret, Top Secret', and sent only to Ingram, Dentzer, and Helen Jean Rogers. The distribution list of the version for the second level, labeled only 'Top Secret', included two copies each for NSA and the State Department. Potential donors and NSA's Executive Committee, which oversaw NSA's finances on behalf of its membership, received a specially prepared 'Confidential' version.[101]

The new relationship complicated NSA's overt relations with the Department of State, since NSA occasionally received small grants for individual student exchange programmes or foreign student hospitality. Not many State Department employees were privy to the secret funding.[102] An early example of this intricacy occurred on 20 October 1951, when Ingram told HIACOM's new chairman, Carl Sapers, to go ahead and prepare a student exchange programme for the Department of State, since 'they are put more or less in the position of accepting our proposals if we can give them convincing enough arguments'.[103]

As planning intensified for the 2nd International Student Conference in Edinburgh, scheduled for January 1952, Ingram spent considerable time in Washington, DC and New York working out details for the new funds. He ecstatically reported to Dentzer that John Simons had authorized an air ticket for the President of the Indonesian PPMI to come to Edinburgh. 'Really, it is one of those breaks one dreams about. Now I will be able to discuss the Seminar with the person who may well be running it...'.[104] The practice of authorizing tickets with an airline is one reason that total funding for the Edinburgh meeting (and other events) cannot be fully determined.

When Dentzer and Ingram headed to Edinburgh, funding was no longer a problem. They went armed with proven success in running practical programmes. They were ready to push for a Secretariat.

ESTABLISHING COSEC

Ingram and Dentzer arrived in Scotland to find a Castle specially illuminated in honor of the student conference. But all the floodlights in the world couldn't eliminate their chilly reception. Outside the castle, pro-IUS students picketed the meeting, accusing the delegates of dividing the student movement.[105] Inside the conference, Ingram later reported, the NSA delegation was 'looked at askance on arrival, many people being dubious about their motives, so both NSA representatives decided to move with extreme caution, not to speak in debate unless something of real importance was at stake, and generally be more self-effacing than was natural to them'.[106]

Yet, once again, NSA emerged with everything they wanted, including the authorization to form a Secretariat, the leadership of SMAP (practical programmes), and the joint responsibility with the Swiss to find a location for the following year's conference. Ingram acknowledged that this success occurred without 'having to intervene', since the delegates from Sweden and England 'kept things moving in the direction NSA wished'.[107]

This time the proposal to establish a Coordinating Secretariat (COSEC) engendered no controversy, although delegates argued over how powerful it should be. Ten delegations, including NSA, voted for a loose structure, while eight voted for stronger central powers.[108] The United States easily secured a position as one of six national unions, along with England, France, Holland, and Sweden, on the Supervisory Committee which would oversee the Coordinating Secretariat. One slot was reserved for a future representative of Latin America. NSA cast the deciding vote (8–7, 3 abstentions) to locate COSEC in Leiden rather than Paris, even though Ingram recognized that 'the Dutch colonial policy might have made them a poor choice, from the viewpoint of Southeast Asian countries'. But he judged it a minor problem, describing how the ex-president of PPMI [the Indonesian student union] 'talked gaily of shooting Dutch planters before breakfast, and felt it was merely a joke to be laughed over with the Dutch now – which he did'.[109]

While the Edinburgh conference ended with 'peace and love', Ingram noted signs of future trouble. Only two of the expected six Brazilians arrived and on major questions they voted with the French, not the United States. The Yugoslav delegate sided with the French and not the United States on the question of stronger central authority for COSEC. The Israeli delegate attacked the German delegation, and 'kept asking what the VDS

[German student union] was doing to fight the resurgence of Nazism and anti-semitism among German students.'[110]

Attendance by non-European students was still scant. But any attempt to go further, Ingram told the the US Information Service in Edinburgh, 'would have, in effect, thrown students in these areas [Near East and Southeast Asia] into the arms of the International Union of Students, with all that implies'.[111] American officials did not have to rely on Ingram's observations alone. John Simons openly attended the Edinburgh meeting as an observer, and seems by this time to have been operating as the director of the Simon's Fund, a philanthropic institution which had assisted with the Edinburgh meeting.[112]

The sudden financial largesse did not go unnoticed by IUS. Its news bulletin identified one purpose of the money, 'to organize South America into the Western bloc'.[113] The newsletter (accurately) reported that the few third world students who attended the Edinburgh conference came mostly from colleges and universities in Europe, and represented no organization in their home countries.

Closer to home, on 20 March 1952, Fred Jarvis, Deputy President of the British National Union of Students, by letter warned Bill Dentzer that NSA was being discredited by IUS over 'outside sources' of funding 'used to further US foreign policy'.[114] In reply, Dentzer told Jarvis with blatant dishonesty, 'I can assure you that we have never yet received one cent from any agency or person in any way connected with the US government. I only agree wholeheartedly that the IUS propaganda makes it that much more imperative that we tell all students the facts of what we are doing.'[115]

Leadership

Had NSA's enemies (or friends) seen the cable traffic that spring between the American Embassy in Stockholm and the State Department in Washington DC, the Coordinating Secretariat might have been still-born. The Americans had decided they wanted Olof Palme to take the Permanent Secretary position in COSEC, but were having trouble convincing him to apply. The delegates in Edinburgh had established a deadline of 1 May 1952 for applications. The new five-member Supervision Commission (still without Latin American representation), would make the final selection.

On 29 April 1952, two days before the 1 May deadline, Secretary of State Dean Acheson sent a 'secret security information' cable to the American Embassy in Stockholm, asking for their assistance. Palme's reluctance had been interpreted as career-related. The State Department understood he planned to accept a position with the Swedish Foreign Office, and thought perhaps he feared making 'a bad impression with the SWED GOVT' if he abandoned his duties as President of the Swedish Federation of Students. Acheson reminded Embassy officials that the Edinburgh meeting had been 'a major step forward in propaganda battle against INTERNATL Union of Students (IUS), one of the most important worldwide COMMIE front ORGS', and that Palme's leadership was 'an essential element in success new Secretariat'.[116]

While Palme was respected for his dedication and past achievements, the fact that he was from Sweden made him especially attractive. 'DEPT feels that since Secretariat's primary function is influence student groups in areas which now or recently under colonial rule, a SCAN student leader wld be best person lead Leiden Secretariat successfully'.[117]

France and Britain had colonies. The Dutch had been appeased, by having the Secretariat on their soil. (They could not be a contender, since delegates also passed a resolution prohibiting a national from any country which housed the Secretariat from also holding the Permanent Secretary position.) America lacked colonies, but NSA officials judged that widespread anti-Americanism gave them little chance of capturing the chief staff position. Dentzer, who considered applying, later complained to a British colleague that he 'could not apply for the position of Permanent Secretary for a reason that does not apply to hardly any other national union of students – that reason being that I am from the national union of students of the United States'. Dentzer blamed the hostile atmosphere on the 'actions of many of my country-men, often in bad faith and at other times in sincere though grossly misguided thought, [which] have made it difficult for many of us to be accepted on the same basis as those from other parts of the world'.[118]

Despite Britain's status as a colonial power, US officials considered as a fall-back candidate Stanley Jenkins, who earlier risked his Presidency in November 1950 to get the British National Union of Students to attend the Stockholm meeting, but acknowledged he had major liabilities. Not only did he represent a colonial power but, according to the State Department, he had 'for a YR been employed in Colonial office'. Acheson directed Embassy officials therefore to approach the Swedish Foreign Office, since the Department's information was that the 'relationship between SFS and SWED GOV'T very close', and that 'Palme has been reporting for some YRS to SWED FONOFF on activities of IUS'.[119]

The Swedish Foreign Office agreed to approach Palme.[120] When Foreign Office officials reported Palme declined to apply, American Embassy officials approached Palme directly. Their efforts also failed. On 23 May 1952, more than three weeks after the official deadline for nominations, the State Department again requested that the 'EMB again approach FONOFF to encourage Palme take nomination'. Donhauser, having returned from Stockholm to Washington DC, and who cleared the memo, urged Embassy officials to spell out in greater detail the advantages for the Swedish Foreign office, including the 'possibilities of the position as source of intelligence for FONOFF'.[121]

Finally, in the face of Palme's refusal, a deal was worked out.[122] Jarl Tranaeus, President of the Swedish Federation of Students prior to Palme, agreed to take the position temporarily. Tranaeus also had strong ties with the US Embassy, had been a member of the German Seminar, and, according to Palme, was 'in the picture'.[123] Despite strong reservations by Ingram against a British student holding the key position, Tranaeus agreed to relinquish the position in November to John M. Thompson, Jenkins' successor as President of the British National Union of Students.[124]

American Staff

Anti-American sentiment might make it difficult, but the CIA appears to have been reluctant to fund COSEC without a reliable American on the Leiden staff. Sometime in the spring of 1951, before COSEC opened its doors, Ingram, Simons and Dentzer began to plan strategy for landing Dentzer a position in the Secretariat. Ingram worried that getting Dentzer a staff position would not be easy 'without arousing suspicions of our motives or without appearing to be using our contribution as a lever'.[125] Finally, they concocted a cover story. At the next meeting of the Supervision Commission, Ingram would announce that Dentzer had been awarded a 'floating fellowship', possibly from Princeton University. He could locate in Leiden and say he was doing 'independent study'. Once in Leiden, Ingram told Dentzer, you could 'devote 50% of your time to COSEC work if the part-time staff position had been approved'.[126] The advantage of this strategy was that it sought a solution within the scope of the existing budget.

Dentzer, who outlined his qualifications, and a full page of arguments for Ingram to use, joked about the relationship between his presence and US money. In an otherwise serious letter, he wrote, 'You could tell them that I am 99 44/100 per cent pure, that more doctors like me better than any other brand, that I'm free from nicotine and harmful throat cough.... But, that wouldn't do, just as it wouldn't do to tell them that if I go over, American $$$$$$$'s will follow and that if I don't, they won't'.[127] On the second page, he listed six arguments. Point Five: 'The money argument. You know what cannot be said about the fact that Americans will not be able to contribute unless someone they know is there'.[128]

On 10 June 1952, the five-member Supervision Commission convened in Paris. The minutes, conveniently written by Ingram, indicate that the strategy was followed. He reported that all members of the Commission had 'unanimously accepted this generous offer' of assistance. Dentzer would be paid 1500 guilders for nine months as an 'assistant to the Permanent Secretary'.[129] Ingram later bragged to Dentzer how he engineered this feat.

'I told them simply that we considered ourselves (COSEC) to be on trial for the first year–we would be judged on the amount and quality of the work done between now and the next [ISC] Conference. We had seen the extent of the work, how could one man do it?'.[130]

The manoeuvre which seemed so successful in June suddenly threatened to unravel in July. When John M. Thompson, the British Supervision Committee member expected to succeed Tranaeus, returned home, he found his colleagues furious over the decision to hire Dentzer. Thompson's executive council objected that 'just because someone is available doesn't mean we should hire him'. Thompson was forced to notify Ingram that the British 'wish to press for a reversal of the decision to make an appointment of an Assistant at this stage'.[131]

Both Ingram and Dentzer wrote extensive letters back. Ingram took the high ground, insisting that 'all was in order', since the salary had been previously authorized, and Dentzer was chosen for his qualifications. Dentzer's salary amount and 'how Mr. Dentzer was able to arrange his personal affairs are of secondary importance'.[132] Ingram must have rejoiced that he had found a strategy that fitted within the authorized budget. He told Thompson that he would not vote for a reversal.

Dentzer's letter to Thompson alternates between contrition and defiance. He expanded on Ingram's letter for three pages, restating all the 'facts', but offered to resign if they thought it necessary, although it would mean 'a great deal of change in personal plans and real disappointment'.[133]

Thompson backed off. The French delegate decided to support Dentzer, as did the Swedes and the Dutch. That left only the British to object. Finally, Thompson wrote to Palme that they would go with the majority.[134] The Dentzer plan stayed in effect.

New Funds

On 1 August 1952, after some delay, COSEC officially opened its doors. A few weeks earlier, a CIA conduit posing as a New York-based philanthropy, the Foundation for Youth and Student Affairs (FYSA) had been incorporated. It, too, began operating on 1 August. On 6 August 1952 John Simons wrote a witty congratulatory letter to Jarl Tranaeus: 'According to Avrea Ingram congratulations for you are in order on your appointment as Permanent Secretary of the Coordinating Secretariat, etc., from now until some mysterious date this winter'.[135]

On 8 September 1952, Ingram notified Tranaeus that 'funds were now available' for NSA's 'full contribution'.[136] Ingram told Tranaeus that future financial support from FYSA might be available for a number of projects, including a Spanish translation of the Edinburgh conference, travel grants to the 3rd International Student Conference, and a student publication aimed at Latin America.[137]

From that time forward, FYSA funded most of the NSA's International Commission work and the International Student Conference/COSEC. The foundation paid NSA's dues. It funded the Supervision Commission meetings. It authorized an initial budget of $28,500 for the 3rd International Student Conference in Copenhagen.[138] FYSA financed foreign students to visit NSA's annual Congresses.

Money bred success. Success increased funding. In February 1953, John Thompson, who had assumed Jarl Tranaeus's position as expected, told Simons 'that the attendance was so broad and representative [in Copenhagen] is due to the fact that the Secretariat was in a position to award travel grants to many of the representatives; this fact being due in turn, of course, to the grant from the foundation'.[139] By 1954 FYSA had increased its support for the 4th annual conference in Istanbul, Turkey to $66,823.80, so that each attending organization could send two delegates.[140] The funding meant that most delegates who attended the International Student Conference meetings had their way paid by the US government, and over time, the competition for these free tickets created many episodes of political intrigue.

In September 1953, after Ingram's (unprecedented) second term as NSA vice president finished, he joined the COSEC staff. Before leaving for Leiden, Ingram established a summer seminar as a vehicle to bring a steady flow of vetted students into NSA's international work. Promising students were evaluated by the seminar staff, including some students previously recruited by the CIA, while background and security investigations were completed.[141] Not only was the ISC/COSEC up and running, but NSA had been stabilized.

CONCLUSION

While the focus here is on the 1949–52 period, and not on the entire life-span of the CIA relationship with NSA and ISC/COSEC, some observations may be offered. Nothing in this period suggests that domestic McCarthyism drove the US government's decision to work covertly, as suggested by CIA insiders.[142] Rather, suspicion of American motives required HIACOM and NSA leaders constantly to downplay their role by putting others, often Sweden or Britain, in the lead. This was the case during both phases of the German project. It lay behind the instructions to the NSA International Team members not to call or to sponsor the meeting of dissident unions. When Lowenstein's speech inflamed the delegates in Stockholm, suspicions of US government involvement nearly cost NSA its leadership role. The fear of 'unilateralism' slowed the development of the Southeast Asian strategy. As late as the Edinburgh meeting in 1952, Americans obtained their objectives, as Ingram noted, mainly through the actions of British and Swedish delegates.

Keeping a distance from the US government involved more than the risk that its financial hand might be exposed. Distance was important to establish NSA's independence from American foreign policy. Cord Meyer backhandedly acknowledged this in his memoir when he wrote: 'the open receipt of government funds would have damaged the reputation for independence that the NSA had found valuable in dealing with foreign students'.[143]

Meyer emphasizes reputation or the appearance of independence. The unnamed NSA official in the Dulles/Elliott memorandum objected on principle that CIA funding 'would run contrary to its basic principle of independent thought and action'.[144] Whether strategic (Meyer) or principled (NSA official), the choice of covert means to implement a moral claim to independence built in a time-bomb that, once detonated, was guaranteed to discredit both.

As we shift the focus to ask questions about control and influence, the picture becomes quite complicated. Did the CIA piper call the tune? Or did it simply enable students to achieve their own stated goals?

Meyer, Farmer and other CIA officials have emphasized that the relationship worked best when they and the students shared the same goals. But, even in these early years, finding compatible students required careful recruitment, bringing in students who could be trusted, such as Dentzer or Ingram, and excluding skeptical students, such as Erskine Childers. The CIA's Michael Warner again has been one of the few CIA officials to acknowledge this screening: 'CIA tacitly judged the merits of the political opinions held by American college students; only certain students and causes were worthy of taxpayer-funded subsidies'.[145]

What is misleading about the philanthropic analogy is that it presupposes a clear boundary between the recipient organization and the CIA that did not always exist, such as when a previously-recruited student was maneuvered into an elected or appointed position. Other aspects of the relationship surely blunt the comparison with philanthropy: Security oaths, which the CIA administered under the US Espionage Act to ensure secrecy, were backed up by prison terms of up to twenty years, and CIA case officers required detailed reports on foreign student contacts. As the relationship developed, both students and case officers used code names to communicate. These requirements, present but perhaps not onerous in the formative years, became substantially greater as the operation expanded.

When CIA officials argue they exercised no control, they may mean they never *felt* in control. Lowenstein nearly set back two years of work. Eisenberg almost lost his bid for the Student Mutual Assistance Program, a loss which would have deprived NSA/HIACOM of a rationale for its future work. Palme refused to be seduced by either status or other blandishments into becoming COSEC's leader. Ingram objected to a colonial power, Britain, holding the Permanent Secretary slot but his objections were overridden, most likely by officials more powerful than John Simons, and quite possibly by negotiations *between* British and US intelligence. Dentzer's positioning for the COSEC staff almost backfired. Who had the power to make decisions, and to make them stick, varied greatly throughout the life of the relationship. In this initial period, almost every contact between the CIA and the students necessarily had to be improvised, as circumstances unfolded.

In the earlier years, careful recruitment meant that most differences between the CIA and NSA or ISC officials tended to be tactical: the paymaster and his pipers largely played the same tune. Even then, whether the tune was played in key, or ever reached an intended ear, depended upon much more than the paymaster's intent.

NOTES

1. Michael Warner, 'Sophisticated Spies: CIA's Links to Liberal Anti-Communists 1949–1967', *International Journal of Intelligence and Counter Intelligence* 9/4 (Winter 1996/7) p.425. Warner is Deputy Chief of the History Staff of the Central Intelligence Agency.
2. Ibid. p.426.
3. Press release from files supplied by *Ramparts* Magazine researcher, Michael Ansara.
4. Tom Braden, 'I'm Glad the CIA is Immoral', *Saturday Evening Post*, 20 May 1967.
5. Cord Meyer, *Facing Reality: From World Federalism to the CIA* (New York: Harper & Row 1980).
6. Madison, Wisconsin. A group of 30–40 NSA alumni, largely from the 1947–60 era, discussed the CIA relationship for nearly three hours on 26 July 1997. Others knowledgeable about the CIA relationship who expressed views similar to Hoffman's included former NSA Presidents William Dentzer and Richard Murphy. The author attended this meeting.
7. Frances Stonor Saunders, *The Cultural Cold War* (New York: The New Press 1999).
8. Anthony Carew, 'The American Labor Movement in Fizzland', *Labor History* 39/1 (1998), and 'Anti-Communism and Anti-Colonialism in the 1950s', *International Review of Social History* 42 (1996).
9. Richard Aldrich, 'OSS, CIA and European Unity: The American Committee on Europe, 1948–60', *Diplomacy & Statecraft* 8/1 (March 1997) p.194.
10. Joël Kotek, *Students and the Cold War* (New York: St. Martin's Press 1996) pp.200–7. (English edition translated by Ralph Blumenau). Kotek dates the CIA's financial involvement from the summer of 1952, a year and a half after the first International Student Conference meeting in Stockholm in Dec. 1950. He describes the ISC in 1952 as 'close to bankruptcy', and argues that action by a CIA conduit saved the ISC and COSEC.
11. Warner, 'Sophisticated Spies' (note 1) p.425.
12. Ibid. p.428.
13. Sources include interviews with former OPC Deputy Director, Franklin Lindsay, former CIA case officer Tom Farmer, as well as archival documents cited later in the essay.
14. During his term of office (1947–48), NSA's first International vice president, Robert Smith, acknowledged the genesis of NSA's international projects. 'When NSA's Constitutional Convention ended ten months ago, a vast program of possible activities had been prepared for action in the international student field.' Smith also cited an unspecified financial

'legacy' from HIACOM to NSA for its international activities. See, Stanford University, Hoover Archives, NSA papers (henceforth cited as Hoover (NSA)), Box 66, IC Reports, December 1947.

15. While the funds were intended only for NSA's International Commission activities, in practice, funds were also spent on the domestic side.
16. For instance, in the related 'youth' field, the United States Youth Council, the American affiliate of the anti-communist World Assembly of Youth, was a leadership coalition, comprised of dozens of organizations. The American Federation of Labor maintained a special international department that was virtually autonomous, its decisions rubber-stamped by unions peripherally concerned with international affairs.
17. The history of these initial efforts is too complex to discuss fully in this piece. See, for example, the announcement in the *New York Times*, 29 Aug. 1946, that 'A special group has been formed to exchange information and be prepared to withdraw or protest if fears that communists intend to use the student union as a propaganda agency are realized. This group includes delegates from China, some of the United States delegation, and representatives from six other countries.' The following year, an NSA founder, William Bierenbaum, attended the World Youth Festival in Prague, met with the Prague underground, and indicated that planning for 'just such an agency (the International Student Conference, ISC) had already gone pretty far.' See memoir by William Bierenbaum, *Something for Everybody is Not Enough* (New York: Random House 1971).
18. In 1949, the ISS hosted its annual conference at Wells College, in Aurora, New York. Many delegates remained afterward to discuss the IUS situation. See Hoover (NSA), Box 33, 10 Aug. 1949, Confidential letter from Rob West to NSA President Ted Harris, reporting on the meeting. The meeting included representatives from Finland, Sweden, Denmark, Norway, England, France, Switzerland, India, and the US. For a time, the ISS was considered as a possible rival to IUS. In preparation for the 1949 NSA Congress, held after the Wells College meeting, University of North Carolina delegates were told that one of the 'grave and explosive issues' they could face was a 'proposal likely that the NSA affiliate with an organization known as the International Student Service, as a counter to the communist-run International Union of Students.' 10 Aug. 1949 memo in Lowenstein Papers, #4340, Series 2.6, Box 87 Southern Historical Collection, University of North Carolina Library, Chapel Hill.
19. The author is working on a book, covering the period 1945–67, which covers the activities of the two offices at Harvard in greater detail.
20. *Harvard Crimson*, 16 May 1946. Chair of the selection committee was Associate Dean Robert Watson. Students voted in principle to send a delegate to Prague but did not elect a specific person. On 25 May 1946, the *Harvard Crimson* identified Cater as the committee's selection. Cater's OSS credentials were public and considered an asset. See *Harvard Crimson*, 25 May 1946.
21. Hoover (NSA), Box 66, IC Reports, Dec. 1947.
22. This decision was taken casually. The first NSA President William Welsh remembers Robert Smith as 'adamant' about opening the office in Cambridge. Author interview with William Welsh, 22 Oct. 1991. After Smith reached Cambridge, in correspondence with others, he cited the importance of the Harvard Secretariat. See for example, Hoover (NSA), Box 280, Smith letter 1 Oct. 1947 to Jack Peter, General Secretary, International Student Service, 'the main reason for this is that Harvard students had done such a fine job last spring for the preparatory organization of the NSA.'
23. Hoover, Box 299 WSSF. See 2 Dec. 1946 letter from Wilmer Kitchen to HIACOM's Jonathan Silverstone regarding Bill Ellis's travel. Ellis, an African American, was a former Treasurer of the Harvard Student Council, and for a short time was an IUS Vice-President. See acknowledgement of funding support for the Bulletin in 21 May 1947 letter from William J. Richard, Jr. Sec. HIACOM to Wilmer Kitchen, Executive Secretary of WSSF. For financial support of other projects, see WSSF financial reports for 1947–48.
24. Hoover (NSA), Box 299, 1 Oct. 1947 Hoover #299 Appendix B of the WSSF Treasurer's report: 'Resolved EC 47-42: that the employment of Robert Smith as publicity director be approved for a period of a year effective as of October 1st at a salary shown in the proper

document of records, and that it be understood further that the proper budget adjustments be made to cover Mr. Smith's salary.' No amount is given.

25. Author interview with Tom Farmer, 19 April 1999. See also Hoover (NSA), Box 101. Farmer left behind a detailed resumé. He had interrogated top German military officers and diplomats; he also 'wrote Order of Battle and General intelligence reports; directed a team of Allied and German officers in a comprehensive study of Germany Army Training Methods'.
26. Author interview with Tom Farmer. See also Farmer's resumé, Hoover (NSA), Box 101. He wrote, 'I expect in the next few weeks to be commissioned a First Lieutenant in the active Military Intelligence Reserve'. The resumé is dated January 1949. Farmer dates his CIA service from Jan. 1951. He left in 1954.
27. Hoover (NSA), Box 101 German Project. The project proposal cited the Zook Report (1946) and the Holborn Report (1948). Hajo Holborn was a Yale historian and former OSS member. His graduate student assisted Farmer on the survey project. Box 101 contains extensive documentation on the German project.
28. Farmer interview. Archival detail suggests a more complicated history of the survey's origin, since the survey project was conceived and funded before the US Army turned over its occupation authority to John J. McCloy, who became the High Commissioner in July 1949.
29. Hoover (NSA), Box 101. Internal NSA documents identify the proposal as submitted to Mr. Paul Bodenman, of the Re-education Division of OMGUS, Washington, on 13 Jan. 1949. It was forwarded to Germany by the Civil Affairs Division chief, Brigadier General E. E. Hume, US Army, Special Staff.
30. See Kotek, *Students* (note 10) p.174 (English translation) for a description of Palme's attitudes.
31. Farmer interview.
32. In discussing this project with Frank Lindsay, Deputy Director (European) Office of Policy Coordination (1949–51), Lindsay remarked that Shepard Stone was 'a little Wisner.' Frank Wisner headed the OPC, and both Stone and Wisner had a facility for devising covert operations. Author interview with Franklin Lindsay, 26 Jan. 1999. See also Frances Stonor Saunders' description of Shepard Stone's role with the CIA-funded Congress for Cultural Freedom in *Cultural Cold War* (note 7) p.143.
33. The official title was the 'International Seminar on Student Self Government.' Harvard University Archives contain a complete copy of the final survey report. HUD 3688.251.90, as does Hoover (NSA), Box 101.
34. Hoover (NSA), Box 102 HIACOM, 10 Feb. 1951 Frank Fisher memo on Foreign Seminars. Fisher outlined the controversies, including the problem of 'looking too American', and whether the German Seminar should be a 'stepping stone to other desirable international student projects such as an international student newspaper.' Farmer's co-director, Robert Fischelis, had recommended that 'operational projects ... should be developed in other form, as is happening.' The word, 'Stockholm', is hand-written to the left of this sentence. Fisher stated that he agreed with Fischelis. See also Hoover (NSA), Box 294. Long after the Stockholm meeting, on 23 June 1952, HIACOM Chairman Carl Sapers wrote to the State Department that 'the German Seminar remains the single significant meeting place for the free exchange of ideas among student leaders of the Western world.'
35. See Hoover (NSA), Box 33, 18 May 1950 letter from Erskine Childers to staff.
36. University of Minnesota National Social Work Assembly collection, SW4.2, Series 3.5, Box 39, International Social Welfare Programs, 1946–1970. See 15 March 1949 Minutes. The German Leadership Project was discussed earlier, 7 June 1948. This file also contains a four-page history of the German project, written in 1950.The sponsor of the Young Adult Council was the National Social Work Assembly.
37. Farmer interview. Farmer also said that, once the German Seminar was underway, and despite his listing as co-Director, he had almost no direct contact with it.
38. Farmer interview.
39. Hoover (NSA), Box 101, 18 Aug. 1949 letter from Farmer to West. The context of these remarks is that Farmer opened a letter from West addressed to Palme, in which West spelled out his concerns.

40. Ibid. West had conveyed Childers' concerns as well as his own. Childers subsequently became critical of McCloy's hiring of Shepard Stone in the fall of 1949; he though that Stone's presence signified a policy shift toward 'mass public relations', which was 'totally out of place in the Germany of today, and terribly damaging if implemented.' See Hoover (NSA), Box 33, Report #1, 19 Oct. 1949, p.16.
41. Franklin Lindsay interview.
42. The author identified the two individuals from archival material as Laird Bell, Chicago, and Thomas E. Brittingham, Jr., Delaware. See Hoover (NSA), Box 127, International Team 1950 Correspondence. When some students did not submit their reports, the two donors wrote to the new NSA officers and requested an accounting. It is not clear whether this money was the first to come directly from the Office of Policy Coordination. Frank Lindsay remembers that OPC made money available to the students 'shortly after we were getting organized'; Lindsay interview, 26 Jan. 1999. Since OPC got organized in 1948, and this money came two years later, it may not have been the first. One can speculate that the CIA's Michael Warner used the 1949 date because OPC was involved in the German project, whose activities began in 1949. Tom Farmer identified the original money as Rockefeller, and 'a little bit of ...' and changed the subject. Farmer interview.
43. I am grateful to Craig Wilson, the unwitting NSA staff member who traveled on this fund-raising trip, for sharing his account with me. Both Bell and Brittingham sent the Madison office cheques for $6,000. Wilson had been sure the staffers had failed in their mission, since the donors seemed distinctly uninterested in NSA.
44. Hoover (NSA), Box 33, NSA Miscellaneous Correspondence, Report #1, 19 Oct.1949. Childers said he did not 'mind forwarding to State [Dept] official or printed literature', but 'was reluctant to the point of refusing to write my personal resumé of the events'. And, further, 'I will be adamant about expenditure of especial efforts to secure information for the State Department about suspect groups or radical elements in the student community.' In general, Childers feared becoming 'an extension division' for the State Department. p.15
45. While later NSA officers signed secrecy oaths under the US Espionage Act in posh hotels or safe houses, Houghteling signed his alongside a Wisconsin cornfield. Houghteling described the process to a NSA colleague in 1967 after the *Ramparts* story appeared. He told how two cars met on a country road outside Madison, Wisconsin. After a pre-arranged blink of the headlamps, two CIA representatives emerged from the other car. Houghteling signed a security oath under the US Espionage Act. Information supplied by Craig Wilson.
46. Hoover (NSA), Box 127 The four signatories to the Confidential Instructions were NSA's President, its two domestic vice-presidents, and Fred Houghteling. The international vice president, Erskine Childers, was not a signatory, even though he held the nominal title of Chairman of the International Team.
47. Ibid.
48. Grant, like Tom Farmer, had a military intelligence background, which was omitted from his NSA resumé. See Hoover (NSA), Box 66, SE Asia '50. Information on his intelligence background was taken from a life history published on the Internet after his death. See <www.ipa-france.net/pubs/inches/inch6_3grant>. Born in China, he served on Gen. Stilwell's staff during World War II, and accompanied Gen. Marshall on his famous peace mission to reconcile Mao Tse-Tung and Chiang Kai-shek's forces. In 1946, Grant served as the Special Representative for North China to the United Nations Relief and Reconstruction Agency (UNRRA), then worked as a regional representative in Northern China. After he returned to Harvard, he worked summers between law school terms as Special Assistant to the Chief of ECA Mission [the Marshall Plan] to China. Grant's father, John Grant, headed the Rockefeller Foundation office in Paris, where he worked closely with McCloy and Stone funding projects of mutual interest. William Polk is identified as having '15 years in South America including work in the student movement at the University of Chile', and a year and a half in the Middle East. In 1950, Polk was finishing a graduate degree at Harvard.
49. Hoover (NSA), Box 127, 3 July 1950 letter from Bob Kelly to staff.
50. Ibid., 4 Aug. 1950 letter from Bob Kelly to Erskine Childers. Kelly demanded 'written confirmation' of Childers' intent to be 'at Ann Arbor ... by August 8th.' It is clear from the two-page letter than Childers is very upset by the constraints placed on the International

Team, and on himself in particular, and had complained to Kelly.

51. Hoover (NSA), Box 127, International Team 1950 Correspondence, Rob West's daily journal records Palme's one-day visit. The entry was made on Sunday, 13 Aug. 1950. By inference, the meeting was held on the 12th.
52. *Harvard Crimson*, 7 Nov. 1950.
53. *Harvard Crimson*, 14 Nov. 1950.
54. Hoover (NSA), Box 1. Eisenberg acknowledged this significance in a 11 December 1950 letter to the Madison staff. He summarized his discussions with the Scandinavians at an International Student Service meeting prior to Stockholm. He thought that those students who wanted an immediate counter organization 'will hold off for a while if we can get some practical projects in operation.'
55. Hoover (NSA), Box 104 International News Center. In the spring of 1952, tensions arose between the new NSA President and a knowledgeable source who almost publicly identified the Berlin discussions. See proposal identifying relationship with State Department. See also 18 Feb. 1952, NSA President William Dentzer's notation on a letter from Leon Selig, and 8 March 1952, Ingram reprimand letter to Selig. 'Please be very careful in the future to disassociate ourselves completely from any State Department activity.'
56. Hoover, Box 27 NSA IC Correspondence letter from Herbert Eisenberg to Curtis Farrar on 31 Oct. 1950. In this letter, Eisenberg echoes former President Kelly's animosity toward Rob West, calling his continued presence at international meetings 'invidious', and telling Farrar that, if West appeared in Liverpool at a crucial British National Union of Students meeting prior to Stockholm, he had no standing with NSA. Farrar, another NSA founding father, represented NSA's interests in Liverpool.
57. Hoover (NSA), Box 66. A penciled note on a 27 Oct. 1950 letter, no signature, identifies Weiss as OSS [Office of Strategic Services], but the public record indicates that his experience was with the CIC [Counter Intelligence Corps] in Germany, where after the war he famously helped track down rumours of Hitler's continued existence.
58. Eisenberg discussed his annoyance with Lowenstein informally at the NSA Madison reunion in July 1997.
59. Hoover Archives, Box 1, International Student Conference. Copy of Lowenstein's speech as first printed, p.3.
60. Ibid. pp.3–4.
61. Hoover, Box 1, International Student Conference, 24 Dec. 1950 memo from Eisenberg to [NSA] Executive Committee, re 'Results of Conference. In brief, Effect of Lowenstein's Speech.' Lowenstein, who returned to the United States before Eisenberg, distributed his speech to the NSA's National Executive Committee, which voted to endorse it. Committee members greeted Eisenberg's report of the delegates' reaction with disbelief.
62. National Archives and Records Administration, RG 59, 800.4614.1-2251 Report on Stockholm, 22 Jan. 1951, Robert Donhauser to Secretary of State.
63. Ibid. Donhauser reported that the three Swedish leaders, 'have been cooperating in every way possible...' Donhauser also had a report from the British delegation.
64. Ibid.
65. 17 Feb. 1951, 'Memorandum for CSP: United States National Student Association' in Michael Warner (ed.) *The CIA under Harry Truman, CIA Cold War Records* (CIA History staff, Center for the Study in Intelligence) pp.383–4. The memo writer is Milton W. Buffington. Information on Elliot's CIA employment information may be found at Stanford University, Hoover Institute, William Y. Elliott collection, Box 110, CIA.
66. Ibid.
67. See for instance, Hoover (NSA), Box 294, 24 April 1951. Gloria Abiouness in the Youth Activities Branch of the State Department introduced herself by letter to Herbert Eisenberg, and chastised him for not keeping in better touch with the department. On 5 May 1951, Eisenberg responded churlishly that he had not been in touch 'because there is nothing to report.' See also Box 102, Aug. 1951 HIACOM report: 'The Cambridge subcommission has found it possible to raise substantial sums of money to assist the carrying out of NSA's program.'
68. Hoover (NSA), Box 177. Canada 1946–53. Ingram detailed the strategy to Sidney L. Wax,

his counterpart in the National Federation of Canadian University Students, and reviewed previous attempts at forming a regional union.

69. Her claims became the subject of much discussion among NSA alumni at the Madison reunion in July 1997, and afterwards.
70. Hoover (NSA), Box 171 Brazil '46-56', 15 July 1951, confidential letter from Helen Jean Rogers to Herbert Eisenberg.
71. Dulles/Elliott memo. 'There is pending before the Foundation a request by the National Student Association for financial assistance in the amount of $60,000 for the subsidization of projects for an International Student Information Service, and for regional university student seminars in Germany, Southeast Asia, and the Middle East.'
72. Jim Grant, the HIACOM member responsible for surveying Southeast Asian countries during summer 1950, had recommended that a project be considered similar to that of 'West Germany by the international group chaired by Tom Farmer'. See Hoover (NSA), Box 66, SE Asia Report '50 for a copy of his 128pp report.
73. Hoover (NSA), Box 102, HIACOM. 28 Dec. 1950, letter from Grant to Eisenberg and Lowenstein. He mentions that he had identified potential personnel, 'who are desirous of specializing on SEA who might be suitable for the job.' See also 16 Jan. 1951, Frank Fisher letter to Lowenstein, written after meeting in Cronin's bar with Lowenstein, restating HIACOM's authority to approach the Rockefeller Foundation with a package of programmes.
74. Ibid., 7 March 1951, Grant letter to Lowenstein.
75. Ibid., 11 March 1951, Fisher letter to Eisenberg, and Shirley Neizer, Lowenstein's secretary in Madison. Before Conant left for Southeast Asia, he was briefed by former OSS member Edmond Taylor, then director of a confidential study group at the Council on Foreign Relations co-ordinating private, often covert, efforts to strengthen democratic leadership abroad. Membership in this study group was an A list of OSS and military intelligence officers from WWII, including Allen Dulles. The study group was chaired by Whitney H. Shepardson. See Council on Foreign Relations Archives, Study Group 5152.
76. Hoover (NSA), Box 102 HIACOM. August 1951 report prepared by Carl Saper, 1951 Co-director of the German Seminar, and HIACOM member. Both versions are in the file.
77. Hoover (NSA), Box 102 HIACOM. 17 Feb. 1952 letter from Jim Grant to Allard Lowenstein.
78. Hoover (NSA), Box 125 German Seminar, July 1951 HIACOM report. See also, Box 102. 11 March 1951, Fisher letter to Eisenberg informing him that the WSSF had 'in the pinch received German funds.'
79. By this time, Lowenstein seemed aware that problems lay ahead. In a 5 July 1951 letter to James Conant, President of Harvard, Lowenstein made a distinction regarding State Department interest in NSA, which he approved, and said 'there are [other] government agencies that might prove damaging to have too close a connection between our program and theirs.' Cited in William H. Chafe's biography of Allard Lowenstein, *Never Stop Running: Allard Lowenstein and the Struggle to Save American Liberalism* (New York: Basic Books 1993) p.107. Chafe cites as his source the Allard K. Lowenstein papers, located in Chapel Hill, North Carolina.
80. See, for example, Chafe, *Never Stop Running* (note 79) p.106. '...it is beyond credibility that Lowenstein did not at last suspect the connection'. See also Richard Cummings, *The Pied Piper: Allard K. Lowenstein and the Liberal Dream* (New York: Grove Press 1985). Cummings thinks the evidence is stronger that Lowenstein developed his first CIA ties through NSA.
81. Internet Document, <www.Copi.com/articles>. NameBase Newslines, No. 15. Oct.–Dec. 1996. NSC official Morris and Congressman Lowenstein became friends when they worked in African-related matters in the 1960s.
82. See Hendrik Hertzberg, 'The Second Assassination of Allard Lowenstein', *New York Review of Books*, 10 Oct. 1985. Herztberg responded to Cummings' assertions of Lowenstein's CIA ties.
83. David Harris, *Dreams Die Hard* (New York: St. Martins, 1982). Harris and Lowenstein were friends at Stanford University in the 1960s. This remark was made to Harris, p.169
84. Author interview with Kitty Fischer McLean, 17 March 1999. At the time, Fischer was married to George Fischer, son of Louis Fischer, co-author, *The God that Failed* (New York:

Harper 1949), who had just returned from Munich with Harvard's Refugee Interview Project, funded by OPC and the Rockefeller Foundation. Degree information from telephone communication with Harvard University Archives.

85. The author examined all *Harvard Crimson* issues on microfiche for 1946–52.
86. See 'Mystery Death Hides CIA Ties', *Los Angeles Times*, 26 Feb. 1967. Ingram is pictured in his Navy uniform. He graduated in 1947 from Georgia Tech in Atlanta, Georgia at the age of 20. This report, ten years after Ingram was found dead in his New York hotel room, asserts that he studied at Harvard between 1949 and 1951. In 1957, Ingram returned from COSEC to work for the Foundation for Youth and Students, a CIA funding conduit.
87. Hoover (NSA), Box 104 INC Project, 4 Dec. 1951, Ingram request to the Secretary of the Navy. The request was denied on 20 Dec. 1951 by the Asst Chief of Naval Personnel, R.N. Smoot. Ingram wrote 'I am advised that the captain of a naval unit at Georgia Tech has requested that after his commission, Mr. Lewis Levenson be assigned to that unit. As you no doubt have been informed, the National Student Association has established in Atlanta an International News Center.' The INC intended to publish newspapers in Spanish, German, French, and Russian, and Ingram specifically mentions it was to combat the International Union of Students. Another principal, William Kennedy, belonged to Air ROTC.
88. Hoover (NSA), Box 67, 20 Sept. 1951, letter from Ingram to Dentzer.
89. Hoover (NSA), Box 74, 20 Oct. 1951, Ingram to Harold Taylor, President of Sarah Lawrence College, and an NSA advisor.
90. Hoover (NSA), Box 34, 7 Nov. 1951, Ingram to Herb Goldsmith on the NSA staff in Madison, Wisconsin.
91. Hoover (NSA), Box 104, 6 Nov. 1951, letter from Jim Grant of Georgia Tech (not Harvard's Jim Grant) to Ingram, congratulating him on 'finding his angel.'
92. NARA; Truman Library Psychological Strategy Board Files, 1951–53 (NSA). The three-page memo of that meeting, dated 19 October 1951, is still classified. The 13 Oct. 1951 Ingram letter to Gordon Gray, PSB director, requesting the meeting, has been declassified.
93. Ibid., declassified 10 Nov. 1951, William Dentzer letter and proposal to PSB's John Sherman.
94. Ibid. In the aftermath of the *Ramparts* disclosures, Dentzer registered outrage over accusations that he solicited CIA funds. He referred to this charge against him again during NSA alumni discussions in Madison, Wisconsin, July 1997.
95. Farmer interview.
96. Truman Library PSB files (NSA). Notation appears on Ingram's 13 Oct. 1951 letter to Gray.
97. See Kotek, *Students* (note 10) p.202 (English translation). Dentzer claims his knowledge of CIA funding began in Sept., 1952. Some years earlier, Dentzer reportly told Lowenstein biographer Richard Cummings, *The Pied Piper* (note 80) p.46. 'Oh, someone must have called up Allen Dulles and said "Give these people a few bucks".' At the NSA reunion, Dentzer explained the reason for his lack of knowledge was because the CIA worked through Ingram, again implying he had no awareness of covert funding.
98. Hoover (NSA), Box 294 Youth Leadership Training 1950. 8 June 1951 Sheldon Steinhauser (Ohio Ken. Reg. Office of the Anti-Def League of B'nai B'rith) letter to Dentzer, about keeping in touch, says 'Please be assured of my continued co-operation in your behalf and my best wishes for a successful summer with the State Department.'
99. Hoover (NSA), Box 104 INC Project. 18 Feb. 1951 notation on Leon Selig's letter, which Dentzer forwarded to Ingram, on the near debacle reads, 'Good Heavens, Av! For NSA News'.
100. Hoover (NSA), Box 29 IAC Correspondence. 6 April 1951 Dentzer letter to Ingram.
101. Hoover (NSA), Box 32, Helen Jean Roger's file. These levels are made most explicit in a 13 March 1952 Ingram memo from to Rogers (HIACOM) and Dentzer. See also, 25 May 1952 letter from Rogers to Ingram.
102. Discussion with Lewis Lapham, a former CIA career official who worked with Cord Meyer. Lapham told me that the CIA had their own people in State Department offices, but the position did not follow line authority. Author interview in New Brunswick, Maine, 22 Oct. 1991.

103. Hoover (NSA), Box 144, 20 Oct. 1951 Ingram letter to Carl Sapers, HIACOM. In later years, this dual relationship created much confusion, and, occasionally, deliberate mischief as NSA leaders learned to play State Department officials off against their CIA case officers.
104. Hoover (NSA), Box 104 INC, 19 Dec. 1951 Ingram letter to Dentzer 'I had to remain in Washington until Friday morning as John Simons wanted to take care of several of the details with the funds before I left.'
105. Hoover (NSA), Box 67. Reports from NSA field staff, 1951–53. Jan. 1952 Ingram Report to International Activities Control Board.
106. Ibid.
107. Ibid.
108. Ibid. For more detail, see also Box 36 Alexander Korns Confidential Senior Thesis: 'A History of the International Student Conference 1950–1960', prepared for Harvard University, 15 March 1962. Korns was later elected NSA international vice president in 1963–64. Two delegations abstained from voting.
109. Ibid.
110. Ibid.
111. Hoover (NSA), Box 294, US Government. 20 Jan. 1952, Ingram memo to USIS, cc to State Department.
112. Hoover (NSA), Box 37, IUS Correspondence General '46–'54. Simons transmitted an analysis over the phone to HIACOM's Frank Fisher, who made notes of the 22 Jan. 1952 conversation. Simons is already thinking about the next International Student Conference. Beirut has been mentioned as a possible site, and Simons told Fisher therefore 'somebody on the Secretariat should know something about the Middle East'. In fact, the next meeting would be held in Copenhagen, Denmark. Foreign students began to see Simons as a source of funding. See Hoover (NSA), Box 52, 30 Jan. 1952 Britain's Fred Jarvis letter to Bill Dentzer stating that he would like to come to the United States, and wondered 'if John Simons would consider me a worthy "project"!'
113. Hoover, Box 52, British-IUS Relations, IUS news clip.
114. Ibid., 20 March 1952 Jarvis (BNUS) letter to Dentzer.
115. Ibid., 25 March 1952 Dentzer letter to Jarvis.
116. US National Archives (NARA) Record Group 59 800.4614/4-2952. 29 April 1952 Acheson to Am Emb Stockholm.
117. Ibid.
118. Hoover (NSA), Box 12, COSEC Correspondence. 31 July 1952, letter from Dentzer to John Thompson and Fred Jarvis, British NUS.
119. NARA RG 59 800.4614/4-2952.
120. NARA RG 59 800.4624/5-752. 7 May 1952 Cable from Stockholm to Secretary of State, Secret Security Information. The Swedish Foreign Office was 'completely in accord with the effort'.
121. NARA, RG 59, 800.4614/5-1652. 23 May 1952 Cable from Acting Secretary of State David Bruce to Am Embassy Stockholm, Secret Security Information. The cablegram also indicates that with 'increasing amount of support for him in many areas, he WLD be almost certain to be elected if available.' [The NARA citation indicates that it was 5/16, but the actual date on the document is 23 May 1952.]
122. International Institute of Social History (IISH), Amsterdam, the Netherlands. International Student Conference, Box 1208, Sup Com material 1952-53. 8 Dec. 1952, Ingram letter to Thompson in which he reviewed these decisions.
123. Ibid. n.d., but in context July 1952, Confidential letter from Ingram to Palme.
124. Hoover (NSA), Box 14 COSEC, 26 November 1952, Ingram letter to Dentzer.
125. Hoover (NSA), Box 32, 30 June 1952 letter Dentzer to Rogers describing their strategy after the fact. See also Box 29 Correspondence IC. 17 Feb. 1951 and 27 March 1952, letters from Dentzer to Ingram regarding funding the Secretariat.
126. Hoover (NSA), Box 32, 30 June 1952, letter Dentzer to Rogers, describing their strategy after the fact.
127. Hoover (NSA), Box 29 IC Correspondence '50–'54, 26 May 1952, Dentzer letter to Ingram.

128. Ibid.
129. IISH Box 1223 Sup Com Mtgs '52-59. Minutes of 10 June 1952.
130. Hoover (NSA), Box 32, 30 June 1952, Dentzer letter to Rogers. Dentzer is reporting after the fact.
131. Hoover (NSA), Box 52 Reports, 15 July 1952, Thompson letter to Ingram.
132. Hoover (NSA), Box 52, 21 July 1952, Ingram letter to Thompson.
133. Hoover (NSA), Box 12 COSEC correspondence, 31 July 1952, Dentzer letter to John Thompson and Fred Jarvis.
134. Hoover (NSA) ,Box 52 British-IUS Relations. On 1 Aug. 1952, Thompson notified Palme of his decision, which appears to have been made before Dentzer's letter reached him. On 1 Aug. 1952, Dentzer wrote a letter of thanks to the French delegate on the Supervision Commission, suggesting this was worked out verbally, and the letters were perfunctory. Hoover (NSA), Box 23, COSEC '51-'53.
135. IISH Box 628 FYSA. Aug. 6, 1952, Simons letter to Tranaeus.
136. IISH Box 1208 Sup Com 1952-53, 8 Sept. 1952, Ingram letter to Tranaeus.
137. Ibid. See also Hoover (NSA), Box 104 INC. For details on the purpose of the Latin American publication: 'The end goal of this project is to erase antagonism, which has resulted specifically in Central and South America from such things as the American Army's occupation of Panama, and alleged industrial and business exploitation of the Latin Americas in certain areas'.
138. IISH Box 628 FYSA. 16 Dec.1952, Dentzer letter to FYSA indicates the request was cut to $23,124.62. On 12 Dec. 1952, Simons letter to Tranaeus references their telephone conversation and Pan Am contact. It is probable that some tickets were issued directly by Pan Am, and not run through the COSEC account in the Netherlands. See also IISH Box 1208 '52–'53 Sup Com for a challenge to the practice of travel grants. Fred Jarvis, BNUS President-elect, questioned the Secretariat's authority to apply for such large sums without the sanction of the Supervision Commission. Tranaeus replied to Jarvis on 20 Nov. 1952, citing an Edinburgh resolution that the Secretariat 'may seek and use finance from such sources as may from time to time become available, provided that such monies are given in support of the principles of co-operation.'
139. IISH, Box 269 FYSA, 23 Oct. 1953, letter from Thompson to FYSA, citing Feb. 1953 Report on Copenhagen.
140. IISH, Box 628 180/2, 31 Aug. 1954, COSEC audited statement See also Box 269, 23 October 1953, Thompson letter to FYSA. Relying on a single delegate to persuade his colleagues upon his return home to favour ISC had not proved effective.
141. The author's ex-husband was selected for this seminar in the summer of 1965, then offered a position on NSA's International Staff. After moving to Washington, DC, he was taken to a safe house and asked to sign a security oath, and told he was 'doing work of importance to the United States Government.' Not suspecting any intelligence involvement, he signed. Only then was he informed of the CIA relationship. Throughout that year, 1965–66, a handful of NSA officials, most prominently NSA President, Philip Sherburne, worked quietly to sever the relationship with the CIA, a year before the *Ramparts* investigation.
142. Thomas W. Braden's remark, 'In the 1950s, when the cold war was really hot, the idea that Congress would have approved many of our projects was about as likely as the John Birch Society's approving Medicare' is often quoted in this context. See *Saturday Evening Post*, 20 May 1967. More recently, Joel Kotek advances this argument. See Kotek, *Students* (note 10) (English version). On page 202, he writes 'Why was it not done openly by the State Department or the Department of Education? The answer is to be found in the domestic political situation.'
143. Meyer, *Facing Reality*, p.101.
144. Warner, *The CIA Under Harry Truman* (note 65) p.383.
145. Warner, 'Sophisticated Spies' (note 1) p.432.

9

Youth Organizations as a Battlefield in the Cold War

JOËL KOTEK

In 1967 the Californian magazine *Ramparts* published an article that had an explosive effect.[1] It revealed close and 'unnatural' links between the US National Student Association (NSA) and the CIA.[2] Many readers found it scandalous that the secret services of a democracy should, in their own country, be pulling the strings of a youth organization that was in theory free and independent. More revelations were to follow: it soon appeared that ever since 1952 the CIA had financed and was still financing, by way of a series of 'screen' foundations, the overwhelming majority of youth and student organizations, not only in the United States, but throughout the free world. Non-governmental organizations (NGOs) as respectable as the International Union of Socialist Youth (IUSY), Pax Romana and the International Student Conference (ISC-COSEC) had benefited, at some time or other in their history, from the generosity of the CIA. In some cases the funds allocated to them could amount to more than three quarters of their entire budget.

It appeared paradoxical that the American intelligence agencies should have financed organizations that often stood well on the left of the political spectrum. To explain it, it is not to Washington that we must look, but to Moscow, and more precisely to the Cominform. The reason for American involvement lies in the policy of systematic infiltration that the Soviet Union had initiated since 1919. Its constant aim, relentlessly pursued and never openly avowed, was to control Western civil society.[3] By 1950, the communists had succeeded in effectively controlling all the international mass organizations that had been set up after the Liberation, such as the World Federation of Trade Unions (WFTU), the World Peace Council, the International Organization of Journalists (IOJ) and the bodies that are of special interest to us here: the World Federation of Democratic Youth (WFDY) and the International Union of Students (IUS).

The Bolsheviks had been the first to conceive of youth as a politico-ideological weapon, and it was they who forged a new and remarkably efficient instrument: the front organization. What is a front organization? Since the 1920s, the communists had become aware that organizations that professed non-communist ideas could actually be more useful to the Party than those that were more or less openly pro-communist. So they created front organizations, which invariably proclaimed objectives (Peace, Democracy, Disarmament, and the economic, scientific, and cultural Progress of Humanity) with which all decent people would sympathize. Invariably, however, the real purpose was to safeguard the interests of the Soviet Union and to disarm its enemies. Youth organizations in particular would enable the communists to exploit groups whose idealism, ardour and lack of experience caused them to be particularly vulnerable to slogans that generally appealed to their generosity of spirit.[4]

After the Second World War, on the crest of this hard-fought common victory over fascism, it was much easier than it had been before the war for the Soviet Union to create vast international organizations, ostensibly dedicated to prevent any recurrence of fascism, but in fact manipulated to serve the post-war policies of the Soviet state. Through the WFDY and the IUS, the Soviets had a monopoly in international youth and student affairs.[5] The WFDY and the IUS were the only two international youth organizations to be recognized by the United Nations and its specialized agencies. Controlled as they were by the communists, this meant that from 1945 to 1950 the representation of young people at the international level was a Soviet monopoly; and it was exercised along Stalinist lines, attacking the Marshall Plan and the European movement, supporting Tito in the Trieste crisis, backing the North Koreans and so on. In February 1948 the IUS, based in Prague, went so far as to support the communist coup there, ignoring the opposition of the Czech student union and doing nothing to protest against the arrest of its leaders.

The WFDY and the IUS were therefore integral parts of the entire communist system. Indeed, in 1958, Alexander Shelepin became head of the KGB while still a Vice-President of the IUS. He could hardly have reached such heights without first having had a thorough experience of the politics of infiltration. The USSR certainly spared no expense in capturing the spirit of young people, especially those of the Third World. Who else could have invited more than a million young people from all over the world to the Third World Festival of Youth and Students in Berlin in 1951?

THE WESTERN COUNTER-OFFENSIVE

Eventually the United States and Great Britain countered these infiltrationist tactics. The Western counteroffensive began and was worked out in London. In 1948, Ernest Bevin and the Foreign Office created the World Assembly of Youth (WAY). In 1950, Stanley Jenkins, President of the British National Union of Students (NUS), together with Olof Palme, laid the foundation for the International Student Conference. The ISC was created in complete independence and without any outside help; but that meant it had – like WAY – chronic difficulties in making ends meet. Both bodies stood, from the beginning, on the edge of financial collapse. Before the 1950s, no Western government had a positive youth policy. When the British government finally began to develop one in 1950, it was so stretched economically that it did not have the resources to help the WAY, which it had been so instrumental in setting up. The other countries of Western Europe could not afford it either, much as they wanted the ISC or the WAY to pick up the communist challenge. The American government was equally unable to help, though for different reasons.

This article will examine how it came about that the CIA built up a network of secret financial channels and confidential contacts to help youth and student organizations; why it was given responsibility for the ISC and the WAY; and why these bodies were not financed openly by the State Department or by other Western governments. One key to understanding the American & CIA involvement is the 1951 Youth and Student World Festival.

THE BATTLE OVER THE BERLIN FESTIVAL

In August 1951, the communist World Federation of Democratic Youth and the International Union of Students organized the Third World Youth and Student Festival, the greatest post-war gathering of young people, involving nearly one and a half million participants in Berlin.

The Berlin Festival originated in a decision by the WFDY council in November 1950 in Vienna. Its Preparatory Committee was headed by Enrico Berlinguer,[6] who had just been elected WFDY President, the Czech Josza Grohman representing the IUS and Erich Honecker, leader of the Free German Youth (FDJ) movement.

The choice of Berlin was highly significant in the context of the Cold War. In Asia the flash-point was Korea, where the war had just begun; but in Europe it was Germany. The Berlin blockade had failed, and the Pleven Plan envisaged the integration of the German army into a West European framework.

The Berlin Festival aimed to mobilize young people to support communist policy in both arenas. The Cominform reminded participants that the Festival would take place 'while tens of thousands of young people were dying in Korea, in a war launched by rapacious imperialists'![7] The

WFDY brochure announced that the festival 'in Germany's capital city' would show that 'the Germans on both sides of the Elbe have the same aim: they intend to prevent the remilitarization of West Germany'. For East German politicians too the Festival was very important. Wilhelm Pieck, President of the GDR and of the Socialist Unity Party (SED), announced that he would open the Festival and anticipated that:

> these delegations will give the world and the German people living proof that the desire of millions of young people for peace is stronger than the diabolical plans of the imperialist warmongers to plunge humanity into a catastrophic new world war. These delegations will show that the youth of the world stands four-square in the camp of peace headed by the mighty Soviet Union.[8]

There followed a campaign to mobilize the world's Young Communists to swell the number of participants as much as possible. *Avant-Garde*, the weekly paper of the communist Union de la Jeunesse Républicaine de France (UJRF), proclaimed to its members that 'To go to the Festival is to help save the Peace'. But not only its members: the Festival was open to 'all those young people who wanted peace, whether they were religious or not, socialists, communists, or non-party…, workers, peasants, or students who love laughter and fraternal songs'.[9]

Only a few of the totality of young people who went to Berlin went out of political conviction: most went to enjoy themselves and to meet thousands of young people from other countries. But of course their very presence served the aims of Soviet propaganda. In theory the Festivals (such as Prague, 1947; Budapest 1949)[10] were non-political, and their programmes consisted essentially of cultural and social events. But in practice politics was ever-present, and as Western youth had become aware of their partisan character, non-communists had increasingly stayed away. Most of those who came from the West were therefore communists. The young people from Africa and Asia, on the other hand, had less experience of the communist movement, and they knew little of the history of the IUS and the WFDY. The visits of many of them were subsidized by a Solidarity Fund set up for this express purpose. At the Festivals they heard only the communist version of events: the allegation that the non-communists had abandoned them during their struggle against colonialism was hardly ever challenged. The success of the Soviets with the youth of Asia and Africa was incalculable. It is also hard to calculate the astronomical sums spent by the communist states. In addition to the subsidies, they provided special trains, free transport on buses, special editions of newspapers and magazines in up to eight languages, pamphlets, tracts, prospectuses and posters. The host cities also spent lavishly, since an essential aim of the festivals was to show life in communist countries in the best possible light. Each Festival had therefore seen the construction of new public buildings and a face-lift given to old ones.

PREPARATION IN BERLIN

East Berlin was far behind West Berlin in clearing up the effects of the war. This run-down city (or rather half-city) therefore faced a formidable challenge of logistics, finance and control as more than a million young people would have to be provided with transport, food and lodging. No efforts were spared to rise to the occasion.

At the beginning of February 1951 the site of the old Hohenzollern Palace was levelled to create a vast assembly area, which on May Day was given the name Marx-Engels Platz. Nearby, the Berlin Museum was partially restored and readied to receive an exhibition expected from the People's Republic of China. Some of the most famous monuments on Unter den Linden were renovated: the Arsenal Museum, the Brandenburg Gate, the central building of the Humboldt University and the war memorial. To give the city a prosperous air, several new and rather luxurious stores were opened in the main streets. So that all these works should be ready in time, the FDJ and the Young Pioneers instituted 'Socialist Sundays', when their members worked without a break on the construction or renovation of stadiums, swimming pools and camp sites.[11] Hotels, boarding houses and private homes were enlisted to provide beds or mattresses: 120,000 participants were accommodated in this way. These were mostly foreign visitors; most of the East German delegates were put up in huge tents. The 542 enormous kitchens that were set up to feed the delegates were scarcely adequate, as we shall see. Six thousand doctors, 20,000 nurses and 50,000 medical assistants were specially recruited. Public transport within Berlin was provided free. Thirty thousand guidebooks were printed in Leipzig.[12]

The cost of all this, according to official East German sources, was 160 million East German marks. At the official rate of exchange that was over $48 million (though only $8 million at black market rates). Some of that money came from 'spontaneous contributions', as workers and employees agreed to a deduction of between 1 and 3 per cent from their wages and salaries. Each ordinary policeman, for example, paid between 10 and 15 and each of their officers East German 25 marks. In addition a huge savings campaign was launched: savings banks, schools, cooperatives and so on issued special stamps, the proceeds from which were earmarked for travel subsidies, sports clothes and so on. As Henderson of the American High Commission in Germany (HICOG) noted, the tremendous cost of the festival bore heavily on the East German economy.

The organizers also had a political headache. How could they stop young people from crossing over into West Berlin and being exposed to ideological contamination? The authorities introduced a control of all vehicles passing to or from the Western sectors and these were searched for prohibited written materials. Three hundred and ten extra policemen were added to the usual force of 8,500, and a 920-strong youth battalion was recruited to reinforce the People's Militia.[13]

PREPARATION IN THE WEST

The Western governments were better prepared this time than they had been for the two previous Festivals.[14] There were no more divided counsels: the time of indecision was over. In West Germany Konrad Adenauer had the FDJ banned by his Council of Ministers (27 June 1951). Of course the whole communist world angrily denounced this 'fascist decree which is a straight imitation of Hitlerian methods'.[15] In Italy the Council of Ministers did its best to frustrate links with Berlin. 'In numerous international meetings Italian democracy is grossly attacked and injured', De Gasperi told the Senate on 31 July; and on 29 August the Italian authorities withdrew Enrico Berlinguer's passport.[16]

In Britain, Scotland Yard Special Branch was asked to check the identity of all British participants at the Festival. But the Foreign Office was more nervous about the Festival's intention than about gathering information on who planned to go there from Britain. It feared that the Festival might be a manoeuvre intended 'peacefully to reunite' the two parts of Berlin.[17] On 30 May Herbert Morrison, the Foreign Secretary, said in parliament that Great Britain would do all it could to help the government of the German Federal Republic and to thwart the communist plans:

> We have to consider the purpose of this Festival.... Its avowed aim is to support the campaign for peace on Soviet terms. I have therefore agreed to consultations between the three Western High Commissioners in Germany on ways and means of preventing this exploitation of young people to serve the aims of the Soviet Government.[18]

In May 1951, the Labour Party Executive declared that participation in the Festival was incompatible with party membership. This upset J. P. Morris, the President of the National Association of Labour Student Organizations, NALSO, who had planned to go to Berlin, together with two colleagues specially selected for their anti-communism. He enquired confidentially whether he would be risking his career in the Labour Party if he went.[19] In his reply, Gwylym Williams preferred to persuade rather than threaten: he pointed out that the two previous Festivals had shown how vain it was to imagine that any positive contribution would be possible.

Like Scotland Yard, the State Department arranged surveillance of American and indeed other participants in the Festival. For example a certain Jerome Waldo Goodman, editor of the *Harvard Crimson*, spontaneously offered his services to the State Department and insinuated himself into the American delegation to sound out its members. The 65 American delegates had taken the precaution of never addressing each other by their surnames, but Goodman still managed to collect a significant number of names from luggage labels and 'from a laundry list which he entered in a pocket German-English dictionary'.[20] This he did so assiduously that he soon came under suspicion, was subjected to a rather uncomfortable interrogation and was forced to flee during the night. The report he sent to the American authorities included 35 photographs and several biographical notes. He divided the delegates into two categories: the (naïve) sheep and the wolves. The latter included Halsted Holman, Frances Damon and Joy Silver: 'This young woman is a very dangerous, vicious, and unscrupulous communist'.

Lists of other 'subversives' poured in from all over the world. On 28 June the State Department received a list of eight South Australian participants from its consulate in Adelaide.[21] The biographical notes about them were often unflattering. The American embassy in Ceylon sent in the names of five local participants.[22]

The State Department did not share the anxiety of the Foreign Office that the Festival might escalate into a political crisis. If British policy was nervously defensive, for the Americans the Berlin Festival was to be a pilot project for a positive counter-offensive, closely co-ordinated by the State Department and the American High Commission in Germany. On 23 May Dean Acheson telegraphed McCloy, his High Commissioner in Frankfurt: 'Dept preparing global campaign to counteract and discredit communist World Youth Congress scheduled Berlin in Aug. Recognize HICOG and Allied planning well along … and appreciate you have situation well in hand so far as FDJ concerned'.[23]

In February 1950 the three Western High Commissioners, the West German government and the Berlin Senate set up an ad hoc committee known as the August Committee. Its main purpose was to prepare the best possible reception for the thousands of young people who were bound, despite all East German efforts to discourage them, to visit the Western sectors. Ernst Reuter, the Mayor of West Berlin, had already broadcast an invitation to the FDJ to visit his part of the city: 'We intend to show them that the difference between the system of totalitarian propaganda and the system of a free and peaceful life is manifested in the image of the city.'[24]

On 28 May 1951, McCloy set out a series of projects that the August Committee had concocted to provide a worthy welcome to the 200,000 East German visitors expected.[25] Positive measures included free entry to theatres and many cinemas; the publication of a special guidebook to West Berlin; a UNESCO exhibition on the Rights of Man; a pavilion devoted to the European Recovery Programme and another to the European Co-ordination Assembly; special broadcasts on Radio Free Europe; and the distribution of two million pamphlets and satirical booklets (for example *Wir brauchen keinen Marshall Plan*; *Berlin baut auf*; and one written by a former official of the Freie Deutsche Jugend, entitled *Feinde Deutscher Jugend*).[26]

Money was no object. On 9 July the American Political and Economic Projects Committee increased the HICOG contribution to the Western counter-offensive by at least DM 200,000: 'It was agreed that HICOG's contribution of any such sizeable amount should be handled very delicately vis-à-vis the British, French, and German authorities who are participating in the planning activities incidental to the WYF' [World Youth Festival].[27]

Measures that might be described as negative were designed to keep as many young Westerners as possible away from the festival: passports, visas and permits to cross the Federal Republic were refused. No special trains were to be laid on in West Germany, nor would a special train from Czechoslovakia be allowed through the American Zone. Accordingly, on 27 July Dean Acheson notified the main American embassies that 'Govts Western Europe generally willing do all possible obstruct travel' to Berlin. The Festival organizers nevertheless tried their luck. In the afternoon of 2 August the French authorities informed American officials in Vienna that a train carrying 650 Frenchmen was about to leave Innsbruck and would be crossing the American Zone of Germany via Passau, en route to Berlin. Vienna immediately telegraphed HICOG that the train should be stopped and the delegates sent back to the French Zone on the grounds that they had no transit permits.[28] That operation ended in failure because the special train went via Linz. But the Americans had better luck elsewhere that day. On the advice of the British authorities, they intercepted and turned back a British and a French train at Saalfelden. That operation involved a skirmish between American troops and the 2,000 young passengers, during which several of the latter were hurt. Communist propaganda made the most of that incident. On 15 August the *Daily Worker* carried a full page about it, with several photographs of blood-stained delegates and of American soldiers with fixed bayonets. A few weeks later the British Youth Festival Preparatory Committee published a pamphlet about the incident, which described the Americans as 'fascist brutes'.[29]

PROPAGANDA AND COUNTER-PROPAGANDA

From a numerical point of view, the Festival was an obvious success. It welcomed nearly one and a half million participants, according to a confidential East-German police report that reached the State Department: East Germans, 1,418,831; West Germans, 12,649; non-Germans, 22,158.[30] The non-Germans came from 104 countries and included 4,000 from France, 1,500 from Italy and 900 from Britain. The East German authorities had spared no effort to impress them, and they were obviously delighted with the trip to East Berlin.

The Festival opened on 5 August 1951 in the Walter Ulbricht Stadium. Foreign delegations paraded in national costume, there was a speech from President Pieck and doves were released. A cultural programme followed, consisting of a ballet depicting the Five Year Plan, folk dancing, and a gymnastic display by the People's Police and the Young Pioneers. During the Festival there were nearly 150 daily events, including various exhibitions (for example on the defensive armaments of the North Koreans), ballet, theatre, opera (by the Koreans) and symphony concerts. In artistic competitions 69 groups and 270 soloists from 32 countries took part. Concurrently with the Festival, the IUS staged the ninth University Summer Games, in which 2,000 athletes from 42 countries competed in 14 main sporting categories (sub-divided, it was solemnly reported, into 134 sub-categories). Even this large number of events was not enough for the mass of young East Germans: the visitors had priority for tickets, and as a result the allocation for the East Germans was severely limited.

The most impressive event of the Festival was without doubt the huge parade of the FDJ (Free German Youth) on the Marx-Engels Platz (12 August). For eight hours, in the presence of half a million spectators, one million young East Germans marched past the leaders of the GDR and 22,000 foreign delegates. At the head of the procession were the Young Pioneers, who carried little red flags and waved bunches of flowers above their heads. They were followed by a column of young people bearing an immense portrait of Stalin.[31] There followed giant photographs of Mao Tse Tung, Wilhelm Pieck, the leaders of the communist and Workers' Parties from the People's Democracies, and of 'other guides of the people who are committed to peace and who support the just cause of the German people in its struggle for a united and democratic Germany.'

A few things did go wrong, mainly on the supply side. A British observer reported that only one 'serious' mishap had befallen the foreign delegations. The tragi-comic incident is revealing of the Stalinist spirit: 'There was a minor mutiny among the Belgians, who objected to maggots in their sausages. One Ruckacki, responsible for the sausages, was arrested for sabotage.'[32]

Paradoxically, it was the young East Germans who caused the greatest trouble to the GDR authorities. Many of these left Berlin feeling that they had been tricked. They had been promised an unceasing programme of festivities, but tickets for them, as we have seen, were few and far between; and for most of their free time they wandered aimlessly around the town, often seriously hungry. The foreign visitors had been given priority for tickets, accommodation and food. For many young Germans the only sustenance consisted of some biscuits and a piece of sausage in the mornings. They were accommodated in enormous tents, or in barns where straw was sometimes their only bedding, while the foreign guests stayed in private homes and requisitioned schools, and were decently fed. Each day ever more young Germans went across to the Western sector, where hot meals, sandwiches, exhibitions, free concerts, film shows and helicopter trips awaited them.[33]

The Americans counted 1,004,206 crossings into West Berlin by East Germans. (The actual number of visitors was probably about half that figure, since the same person might cross several times.) More than one and a half million free meals were distributed: the American authorities provided 414,690 military portions (400 calories) to the value of DM 110,000;[34] the British 50 tons of food worth DM 60,000; private German firms another DM 60,000 worth – all on top of the DM 266,000 put up between them by the Allied Kommandatura, the Berlin Senate and the Federal Government. Thirteen hundred volunteers had been recruited to receive the visitors in the best possible conditions.

The most popular spot was RIAS (Radio in the American Sector), where John McCloy, the American High Commissioner, Kurt Schumacher and many other West German and American politicians received nearly 15,000 visitors; 3,235 people were approached either singly or in small groups by a team of political interviewers[35] and DM 5,000 worth of drinks and sandwiches were distributed there. Other statistics recorded by the Americans are equally impressive: more than two million pieces of literature were distributed; 150,000 young people visited the 'Europe Train', 42,000 the West Berlin 'Haus der Jugend', 70,800 the Marshall House, 180,000 the pavilion of the European Recovery Program, 47,000 (3,000 a day) the American Information Centre in the 'Amerika Haus', 155,055 attended theatrical performances, 724,500 went to the free film shows, and 29,000 attended performances at the Titania Palace.[36]

It must have been an eye-opening experience for the young East Germans. They had been used to near-empty shops. Now they saw the shop windows in West Berlin, but also briefly in East Berlin, filled with the most varied goods, but at prices they could not afford. One wonders what they thought when, at the end of the Festival, they had to return to the familiar conditions of scarcity.

HONECKER'S ATTACK ON WEST BERLIN

The exodus into enemy territory presented the East German government with a serious problem. Given the presence of tens of thousands of visitors from the West and of the foreign press, the authorities could not use highhanded measures to put a stop to it. Initially they confined themselves to spreading rumours: that the West Berlin police were jailing East Germans, that they were being given poisoned food, or even that the Foreign Legion was kidnapping young visitors to send them to fight in Indochina.[37] But these rumours took a long time to spread, so the authorities resorted to stronger measures. They posted reliable members of the FDJ in strategic places to dissuade, by all means short of force, those who wanted to cross over; but that did not work either. On the day of the great parade, the metro stations from which the West could be reached were closed; but even so more than 100,000 young people managed to spend the day 'on the other side'.

Finally, the FDJ leaders, headed by Honecker, used a stratagem that they hoped would enable them to demonstrate the brutalities of the West Berlin police. On 15 August 1951 several thousand members of the FDJ were taken by lorry to a spot close to the Western border:

> Between mid-day and 1300 Aug 15 FDJ chairman Erich Honecker broadcast rousing speech via loudspeakers to thousands of reliable, hard-core, FDJers assembled at 10 camps in Berlin Muggelsee, proclaiming militantly 'we are going to accept the invitation of Mayor Reuter to visit West Berlin'.... Immediately after Honecker's fighting talk, leaders of 50-man groups were drawn together for marching instructions ... Some 8.000 Muggelsee reliables ... moved in segments to Treptow ... They were instructed to assemble at Karl Marx Platz (Kreuzberg) in US sector at 1800 hours.[38]

Though it was supposedly peaceful, the demonstration degenerated immediately, just as its organizers had anticipated. A West German charge on horseback drove most of the group back towards the Soviet sector and by 18.30 all the rest had been pushed out. Some were wounded and there were 115 arrests, including that of an East German policeman. Seven of the West German police were wounded, one seriously. The FDJ got the demonstration of 'police brutality' they had wanted, and on 30 August Erich Honecker described the incident as 'a new stage in the revolutionary formation of German youth'.[39] Nonetheless the exodus to the West continued.

THE BALANCE SHEET

That half a million East Germans visited West Berlin must not delude us – after all, two thirds of the young East Germans stayed quietly on their own side. The Festival met all the objectives of its organizers, including the launch of two great new campaigns: one against German remilitarization, the other against the Schuman Plan. The presence of 22,000 foreigners from 104 countries was taken by the organizers as bestowing recognition and legitimacy on the East German government. At the seventh Council of the WFDY, held in East Berlin immediately after the Festival, Enrico Berlinguer could justifiably describe the Festival as 'the greatest enterprise the WFDY had undertaken since its inception'; and Mikhailov spoke of 'a great test for the young Partisans of Peace, passed triumphantly'.[40]

Western observers came to similar conclusions. McCloy thought that the many imperfections of the Festival did not detract from the communists' success. His report stated frankly that 'all of those failures were probably to some degree inevitable in view of the huge scale of the WYF. Completely satisfactory feeding and billeting for all the youth participating in rally probably could not (rpt not) have been achieved under any circumstances'.[41]

George A. Morgan, the director of HICOG, also thought the Festival a success for the communists,

> given the way the delegates reacted to the tide of anti-American sentiments, to the deification of Stalin, to the appeals to defend peace at no matter what price, and to the measures by which the Festival managed to give young people the necessary confidence, the practical and psychological preparation for revolutionary action under the aegis of the Soviet Union.... It appears that on the whole the communist hard core and fellow travellers ... were impressed with what they experienced and saw, particularly regarding the progress the GDR has apparently made in the way of reconstruction.... Defections from beyond the Iron Curtain were few and the contacts with the West and with circles not connected with the Festival were extremely limited.[42]

The communist victory did not necessarily mean a defeat for the West. On the contrary: for the West too the Festival was a success. General Lemuel Matthewson, commander of the American forces in Berlin, was not wrong when in his report he spoke of 'a well-earned propaganda victory'.[43] The lessons the American authorities drew from the Festival and from the counter-measures of the Allies are interesting in more than one respect: to them the Festival demonstrated the importance and effectiveness of psychological warfare and the possibility of matching the communists at their own game. As McCloy wrote: 'Unsuspected opportunities for Western psychological warfare have been revealed'.[44] This was the cue for the CIA to enter the picture.

THE GREAT AMERICAN COUNTER-OFFENSIVE

The Western governments were slowly moving from passive observation to active intervention in youth and student affairs. This change showed itself in the first instance over the choice of a permanent secretary for the International Student Conference. Who should be appointed to this strategic post? For the US National Student Association (NSA) and the State Department the answer was obvious. Dean Acheson thought that Olof Palme, then chairman of the international committee of the Swedish National Union of Students (SFS), would be the ideal person:

> Dept has learned a no. of past officers of USNSA ... have urged Mr Palme to accept position permanent sec Leyden Secretariat. Palme has replied he is unwilling due his duties within Swed resulting from Presidency of SFS and that he is planning accept position in Swed Fonserv some time in fall 1952. Dept feels that since Secretariat's primary function is influence student groups in areas which now or recently under colonial rule, Scan student leader wid be best person lead Leyden Secretariat successfully. In particular Dept feels election Olof Palme an essential element in success new Secretariat.[45]

In the eyes of the State Department, Palme was far preferable to Jenkins, former President of the British NUS, who was ruled out as coming from a colonial power, and who was in fact then working in the Colonial Office. Washington decided to communicate directly with the Swedish Foreign Office, with which 'the SFS was in constant touch', and to urge it to persuade Palme:

> Therefore request amb explain Swed Fonoff interest which USG has in success this important anti-commie development. Request that in your discretion you point out Fonoff fact that Leyden Secretariat will concern itself primarily with work with student groups in non-Eur areas and that, therefore Dept feels active participation Swed student groups in gen and Palme in particular wld be a very welcome development .... Sgd. Acheson.

In 1951, the two communist front organizations, the WFDY and the IUS, were at their strongest. When they were holding the gigantic Berlin Festival, they were able to finance a new Arab-language edition of *World Student News* and launch a great campaign against 'bacteriological warfare' in Korea.

On 8 May the Swedish Foreign Ministry assured Washington that it would do what it could;[46] but on 16 May it had to report that although Palme had been directly contacted, he had declined. On 23 May Washington urged its embassy to try once more, but it was all to no avail.[47] In the end, another Swede, Jarl Tranaeus, took the post of Permanent Secretary for a few months, to be followed in November 1952 by John Thompson.[48]

Yet the International Student Conference, like the World Assembly of Youth, was to find itself practically condemned to inaction for lack of adequate and consistent financial resources. They could not match the funds which communist governments made available to their youth and student movements. The success of the World Youth Festival in Berlin in 1951 threw this difference into sharp relief. Tom Braden, who was then a divisional director of the CIA, recalls: 'The CIA estimated at the time that the USSR spent $2,500,000,000 a year on the front organizations. The IUS had limitless funds at its disposal'.[49] The West simply had to meet this challenge. It could not allow the ISC and the WAY to collapse. If Western governments did not support their own youth movements financially, they would stand little chance of competing with those of the East.

Obviously, the European governments could not afford to finance them, and therefore the salvation of these bodies would depend on the involvement of the United States, the strongest and wealthiest country of the free world. On 3 April 1952 Avrea Ingram, the Harvard NSA international vice-president, wrote to Joseph Kolarek of the State Department for help in raising contributions from the relevant government agencies. One would have thought that the request would have borne fruit.[50] After the Berlin Festival, the State Department had already been urged by its own offices abroad to do something:

> In several overseas countries, our International Exchange offices have urged us to develop programmes to defend ... our ideas ... and to counteract the siren songs and sophisms of Soviet communism. As you know, in some parts of the world, students become prominent in government and in communal life immediately after the end of their studies. It is important that these future leaders should be friendly towards the United States. As you also know, in many countries youth as such is a political force of considerable importance and regularly ... exercises great influence in national development .... With the exception of trade unions and of intellectuals, no communist target groups have received as much assiduous attention from the Kominform as have students and youth.[51]

Yet it seemed that the State Department could not oblige, despite the obvious sympathy shown by its officials for the NSA's struggle. William

Dentzer, from Muskingum College, then President of the NSA, wrote: 'At the Department of State they just sigh and look depressed and say we're wonderful and isn't it too bad, but they just don't know.... I am inclined to think that something will happen, but when?'[52]

Bill Dentzer was right: something did begin to move. He was called to a mysterious meeting with a government agent who was accompanied by a former NSA leader, and who offered funding by the CIA. It was miraculous, unexpected and disturbing. Dentzer recalls:

> We were offered money for our international activities. I was quite shocked, and had a long and serious discussion about it with Avrea. It was a moral problem: no-one wants to lie. But it was clear to us that there was no alternative, since no other source of money was available to us. At the end of the day we would have accepted money from anyone to save the NSA and to defend our ideas. You must also remember that at the time the CIA did not have the same reputation that it has today.[53]

A secret agreement with his own government seemed a reasonable price to pay for the survival of an organization in which he believed profoundly. That is how the NSA – and through it, the ISC – came to accept money from the CIA. Nor did it take long for almost all the other Western youth organizations to become involved.

WHY THE CIA?

That the American government should subsidize most of the Western non-governmental organizations seemed understandable in the context of the Cold War. But the question remains: why was it not done openly by the State Department or the Department of Education? The answer is to be found in the domestic political situation. The State Department was paralysed by McCarthyism, then in full spate. At the very moment when Dentzer was appealing for money, Halsted Holman, the American Vice President of the communist IUS, was appearing before the Senate Un-American Activities Committee. It was McCarthyism that was scaring off public and private institutions from helping the NSA. Much as the government wanted to meet the communist challenge, in the present hysterical climate it dared not help bodies such as the NSA and the ISC, which generally defended liberal and progressive causes. Without being a left-wing organization, the NSA was radical enough to be a *bête noire* in many conservative American circles: it had supported the presidential candidature of Henry Wallace in 1948, opposed colonialism, supported civil rights and academic freedom, had many black and Jewish members, and had had an outspoken radical leader in

Allard Lowenstein. It had been the first student organization to oppose McCarthyism, and had been the only one to organize racially integrated meetings in the Southern states. The NSA (like the ISC and the WAY, which were also anti-colonialist) was therefore subject to the worst suspicions. In December 1952 Robert Munger, President of Students for America (previously the Union of National MacArthur Clubs), had accused the NSA of having a socialist, if not a communist, programme. He described the NSA as 'the most dangerous of all the pressure groups now working on the campuses', and he suspected that the purpose of the NSA's campaign for academic freedom was to protect communist teachers.[54]

Under such circumstances the State Department found it impossible to give any help in public. McCarthy had already accused Dean Acheson, 'the Red Dean', of deliberately having lost China to the communists. The State Department was at the time 'one of the weakest departments in Washington'.[55] McCarthy had practically condemned it to inaction. Congress was likewise under McCarthyite control. Tom Braden recalls: 'You can imagine how the Senate would have reacted to a proposal to include in the State Department Budget an item of $300,000 for the NSA'.[56] Private institutions were similarly intimidated. Cord Meyer, Braden's successor at the CIA's Department of International Organizations, recalls: 'At that time the climate for collecting private funds was hardly ideal for an organization which on almost every question took up a position on the left of the political spectrum. Private foundations were intimidated by the hysteria which Senator McCarthy had generated'.[57]

If, therefore, it was felt necessary to help the Western youth organizations in their competition with the communists, it would have to be done secretly; and only the CIA could do that. The CIA enabled the US administration to plan and carry out wide-ranging secret operations that were outside the control of Congress. We have seen that Congress would never have sanctioned help being given to bodies it considered left-wing; but Allen Dulles had come to the conclusion that the only way of effectively fighting the communists was by allying with the non-totalitarian left.[58] In 1947 he had already helped to finance the split in the French trade union movement when Léon Jouhaux had broken away from the CGT to form the rival CGT-Force Ouvrière; and in 1949 the CIA had helped the British and American trade unions to set up the International Confederation of Free Trade Unions (ICFTU) to counteract the influence of the Soviet-run World Federation of Trade Unions. A key adviser to Dulles, who played a significant role in shaping the strategy of the CIA, was Tom Braden, a former hero of the OSS. He recounts how, soon after the Korean War started,

> I was called to Washington by Allen Dulles who gave high priority to clandestine activities. The idea was to break the communist monopoly

> in specialized organizations. The young CIA held several trump cards: we had contacts with most of the trade union leaders and socialists in Europe and America.... We selected certain organizations which needed help to fight the communists. From the time I was appointed, I urged the creation of an International Organizations Division.... Up till then the CIA, like most of the Foreign Ministries, worked on a geographical basis: there was the European Division, the Belgian desk etc. But the communist front organizations knew no such limitations. You could not fight them through national branches.... For example, to support the Congress for Cultural Freedom, we had to work right across all the national desks. So we needed a central set-up to transcend all these national sections. Of course all the departmental chiefs opposed this idea. You can never underestimate the power of bureaucracy.... My proposal led to a terrible battle within the CIA, which lasted six months. At one point I even resigned; and that was perhaps what helped me to win the battle: Allen Dulles supported me against the bureaucracy.[59]

Once the IOD had been created, it could secretly finance those centre and left organizations that Congress distrusted so much. Tom Braden recalls:

> At the OSS we had had experience of Europe. We understood the political situation there. After the war, we knew we would have to work with the Left. Today that has all been forgotten: even the present CIA personnel don't understand it.... Why was the non-communist left so important? It's because there weren't many bankers, lawyers or stock exchange speculators among the patriots and democrats. I had been in the French maquis ... and we had learnt in the war that it was the left which rose against the occupation, not the bourgeoisie, which supported Pétain.[60]

So the CIA worked with the former Trotskyist Mel Lasky at the Congress for Cultural Freedom, and with Jay Lovestone at the AFL/CIO (Lovestone had once been General Secretary of the American Communist Party, but was converted to passionate anti-communism by the Stalinist terror campaign). Such a relationship would have terrified American conservatives. McCarthy was suspicious, and he tried to attack the CIA through Tom Braden; but Dulles appealed to Eisenhower, and the President managed to call McCarthy off.

After the Korean War the budget and staff of the OPC increased considerably. Between 1949 and 1952 its annual grant grew from $4.7 million to $82 million; its staff from 302 in seven stations to 2,812 (plus 3,142 paid contacts abroad) in 47 stations.[61] As the years went by the CIA was increasingly entrusted with special operations, because the State and

Defense Departments would not or could not carry them out publicly. As we have seen, it was unthinkable for the government to give help openly to the Western international youth and student organizations. There was of course nothing progressive in the nature of the CIA. Its attitude was wholly pragmatic. Whilst the OPC (its division for clandestine operations) supported the non-totalitarian left, the OSO (its espionage division) made as much use as possible of the expertise of former Nazis such as Klaus Barbie. Organizations that were helped by the CIA usually received their funds through 'screen' foundations. Tom Braden recalls:

> We had many foundations! We never used the large and genuine American foundations like the Rockefeller, Ford or Carnegie, except once in the case of the Ford Foundation. We preferred to use Mid-West bankers or industrialists. We would give them $20 million with which they would set up a foundation which would then offer its services to one or other of the specialised organizations.

In these organizations the CIA had 'agents'. They were not usually agents in a strict sense, but were individuals who knew what the arrangements with the CIA were. In most cases it was an official who had already been elected: the President or the International Vice-President. But occasionally it was a real undercover agent from the CIA. Tom Braden again:

> These could not only propose anti-communist programmes to the official leaders, but they could also suggest ways of overcoming the inevitable budgetary problems. 'Why not try to secure funds from such-and-such an American foundation?'. Of course they knew in advance that these creations of the CIA would respond generously to any request for funds.[62]

This, then, was the mechanism that was put into operation for the International Student Conference.

THE FOUNDATION FOR YOUTH AND STUDENT AFFAIRS (FYSA) SAVES THE ISC AND WAY

In 1952, a former NSA leader who had been involved in the negotiations leading up to the Stockholm Conference was working in the CIA. He was well placed to alert the CIA to the needs of the NSA. And so it was that Bill Dentzer was approached: 'I was taken to meet CIA officials through the mediation of a former NSA leader. They offered to finance our international activities. I accepted. The other leaders of the NSA knew nothing about it. Nor did my predecessor as President, Allard Lowenstein.'[63]

The CIA did not finance the NSA directly. As usual, funds were channelled through an apparently respectable and private foundation: the

Foundation for Youth and Student Affairs, or FYSA, which was registered in New York on 25 June 1952. Its Executive Director was a former State Department official, David Davis. John Simons was at his side for specifically student affairs. They worked together with a group of men who carried considerable financial weight. The FYSA President was the great industrialist, M. Houghton Jr, Director of Steuben/Corning Glass and President of the Museum of Modern Art (MoMA) in New York. Henry J. Clay was Treasurer and Secretary, and the Executive Committee was completed by J. Garvan Cavanagh of the Cavanagh Division, Michael Ross, director of the International Affairs Department of the Congress of Industrial Organizations (CIO), and Kenneth Holland, President of the Institute of International Education.

Everything now moved very rapidly. Funds from the FYSA transformed the NSA into an organization fully up to its new mission. It received money for its overseas programmes abroad: help for colonial national unions, seminars abroad, student exchange, participation in international events and so on. Its deficits at home were also covered. In 1952, just before the creation of the FYSA, the NSA had a tiny annual budget of $27,822. In 1955-56 it would be $106,933, of which $92,719 (or 86 per cent) came from the CIA. The FYSA had given birth to a real superpower among student unions, capable of rivalling the IUS. The NSA could therefore save the ISC/COSEC, and indeed was able to dominate it. Nothing could now stop the ISC from becoming politicized. We can see from an internal report how pleased the CIA was:

> The ISC/COSEC ... represents the first stage towards a world federation capable of competing with the communist IUS, as its annual meeting at Copenhagen on 12 January (1953), in which 37 national unions of students. [demonstrated] The decisions taken at Copenhagen authorize the organization to carry on a large-scale programme of publications and to implement, through its Secretariat, a student aid programme across the world. The main objective of the organization is to have the non-communist national unions leave the IUS, and to weaken and isolate the communists. The ISC is controlled through one of our agents in a key position, through two leaders of the NSA, and through a foundation financed by the CIA which enables us to control its finances.[64]

CONCLUSION

So it came about that from 1952 onwards large sums of money went to organizations that were for the most part progressive and were actually independent, so much so that towards the end of the 1960s they did not hesitate to criticize the foreign policy of the United States. The situation was not, however, as paradoxical as it seems: we must remember that the chief objective of the intervention was not to control or interfere in the internal affairs of these organizations, but to break the communist monopoly.

CIA funds notwithstanding, the WAY and the ISC would never be able to compete with the resources of the WFDY and the IUS. One set of statistics is enough to show this disparity of means: they relate to the first eight World Youth Festivals, and are enough to indicate the formidable financial and organizational strength available to the Soviet mass movements:

Place	Year	No. of foreign participants	No. of countries represented
Prague	1947	17 000	71
Budapest	1949	10 370	90
East Berlin	1951	24 000	104
Bucharest	1953	29 000	111
Warsaw	1955	30 000	114
Moscow	1957	34 000	131
Vienna	1959	18 000	133
Helsinki	1962	10 800	137

Source: Joël Kotek, *Students and the Cold War* (London: Macmillan 1996) p.212.

What exactly these festivals cost has never been officially published, but estimates do exist: $1 million for Prague, $50 million for East Berlin, $100 million (some 5 per cent of Poland's annual expenditure) for Warsaw. The International Confederation of Free Trade Unions calculated that if the sums spent on the Festival had been used for productive ends, the average wages of Polish workers could have been increased during 1955 by about 6 per cent. The CIA estimated that the Moscow festival had cost the incredible sum of $200 million.

Even if this figure was based on the official rather than the unofficial exchange rate between the rouble and the dollar, one still has to ask whether this was not a colossal waste of money and whether it is not indeed one explanation for the bankruptcy of the Soviet system.

NOTES

1. This article consists of excerpts from my book *Students and the Cold War* (London: Macmillan/New York: St. Martin's Press 1996).
2. Sol Stern, 'A Short Account of International Student Politics & the Cold War with Particular Reference to the NSA, CIA, Etc', *Ramparts* 5/9 (March 1967) pp.29–38.
3. The Soviet Union had always been first in the field of infiltration. In this contest, the advantage naturally goes to those whose determination and ability to seize the favourable moment rest on a long-term plan. In this respect Leninist doctrine and practice had a head start over Western pragmatism.
4. Such manipulation of youth is of course not unique to communist movements: fascism and Nazism did the same. But it is the communists who have done most to develop this particular twentieth century form of political corruption: the calculated exploitation of idealism.
5. On the surface the WFDY, which was created in London in November 1945, was pluralist and non-political. Eight ministers of His Majesty's Government, and indeed the King himself, appeared to vouch for this. The list of the delegations who took part in London seemed to bear further witness to the representative nature of the organization. If its officials were to be believed, only 3.2 per cent of the delegates were 'communists', fewer than the estimated 3.6 per cent who represented Jewish bodies. In fact the WFDY was not born *ex nihilo*, nor out of the delirious enthusiasm of hundreds of anti-fascist delegates, as the propaganda proclaimed. The evidence shows that it was deliberately planned by the Kremlin; that its covert agents had a majority on the organizing committee, whilst others were strategically positioned in more than 13 of the Western delegations. They therefore controlled the course of the conference. The initiative had come from Moscow, and from the beginning Moscow controlled all the levers of power through the election of communists to the executive and the secretariat: three of the four secretary-generals were crypto-communists. The same happened a year later in Prague, where the International Union of Students was created. There, too, the apparently pluralist nature of the meeting did not prevent two crypto-communists being elected to the posts of President and Secretary-General.
6. He became later the charismatic leader of the Italian Communist Party.
7. *Appointment in Berlin*, the glossy brochure prepared for the Festival, with many photographs (Berlin 1950) p.5.
8. Ibid. p.8.
9. *Avant-Garde*, 7–13 March 1951. For the impressive campaign in Italy, see Vincent R. Tortora, *Communist Close-Up* (New York: Exposition Press 1952).
10. The idea of a festival had been born at the London World Youth Conference in 1945. It seems that the Chinese delegation had suggested that the WFDY should also organize cultural activities. It was an attractive notion to bring together one summer the greatest possible number of young people from around the world for a festival of song, dance, sport and drama. Previously planned in Denmark, Jan Masaryk agreed that the Festival would take place in Prague, on condition that it would be strictly non-political. Of course, the festival was very political and above all a tremendous success. All reports bear witness to this: those from the communist bloc as well as many from Western embassies (no fewer than four from the American Embassy in Prague). It was understandable: the Festival brought together 20,000 young people and twice that number of Czechs; and all that just two years after the bloodiest of conflicts. And the programme was exceptional: 75 sports events in which 1,337 athletes from 27 countries took part; 279 concerts of classical and folk music performed by 96 groups and 3,459 artists; a daily festival journal printed in four languages and so on. Thousands of young people enthusiastically streamed out of Prague as they were taken to see sites such as the martyred village of Lidice, the student house in Warsaw, a canal in Bulgaria, the Youth Railway in Yugoslavia, which grew by 20 km during the festival towards its target of 227 km, and so on. During that summer, Prague became for young idealists the crossroads of the world.

    The American diplomats were fully aware of this triumph. Laurence Steinhardt reported the great success of the Festival, both quantitatively and qualitatively, 'in spite of obvious leftist orientation'. And it was a success for the Soviets. Lewand (cultural attaché at the American embassy in Prague) and Steinhardt could only deplore that, in propaganda terms, the Festival was a total fiasco for the United States. Lewand wrote that 'this was obvious right from the opening parade, in which the procession of large and spectacular East European contingents in folk costume or uniform contrasted with the sloppy appearance of around 50 Americans.' The same was true of the cultural presentations by the Americans. Steinhardt reported that, in the absence of any official support, these were particularly mediocre, especially when compared with those of the Soviet Union. A Canadian observer reported that the Soviet Union's participants won all along the line, as much by the sheer quality of their performances – 'they had brought the best musicians of their country' – as by the veneration of which they were the object. Even when occasionally their performances were not very good, they were received with boundless enthusiasm: 'Here was something as dangerous as the hysterical wave of red-baiting which has swept over our continent.'

11. Howard Jones, Acting Director, Berlin Element, HICOG, to Washington, NARA 800.4614/4-2051.
12. Henderson, HICOG Berlin to Washington, NARA 800.4614/7-2351.
13. Howard Jones, letter see note 10. Ninety per cent of the American documentation of the Festival comes from NARA. Many of the relevant documents are also printed in *Foreign Relations of the United States* (herafter FRUS) 1951,vol. 3 (Washington DC: Government Printing Office 1981), pp.1330–60, 1775–9, 2005–23.
14. On the 1947 Prague WYF, the severest criticism of the State Department came from the press. On 9 Sept. the *New York Herald Tribune* said it considered the Festival had shown up the absurdity of the excessively cautious policy of the State Department. The Festival had been a tremendous laboratory into which America could have injected the germs of democracy. The refusal of the State Department to involve itself had thrown away that chance. This was hard on the State Department, which had initially been willing to help its young people, but had been prevented from doing so by the forerunners of McCarthyism. In the context of the anti-communist psychosis, involvement in the Festival, even if for the purpose of sabotaging Soviet plans as American embassy had suggested, would have wrecked the chances of the Mundt Act going through Congress; and that Act would make funds available for other international cultural exchanges.
15. *Avant-Garde*, 4–10 July 1951.
16. Telegram 3177 from Rome to Washington, 7 Aug. 1951, NARA 800.4614/8-651 and Dunn (Rome) to Washington, 29 Aug. 1951, NARA 800.4614/8-2951.
17. The East Berlin Student and Youth Festival, June 1950, FO 975/51, p.8.
18. Ibid., p.10.
19. Morris to Gwylym Williams, Transport House, 29 May 1951, Labour Party Archives, GS/NALSO/40.
20. M. Buckingham, American Consulate, Berlin, to Washington, 17 Aug. 1951, NARA 800.4614/8-1751.
21. 'Robert Downing Potter ... an atheist who frequently meets members of the atheist society.... He has openly told his grandparents and a neighbour that he was a communist and that in a war he would fight with the USSR against Australia and her allies' (John F. O'Grady, Consul at Adelaide, to the State Department, 28 June 1951. NARA 800.4614/2551).
22. J. B. Ketcham (Colombo), 1 Aug. 1951, NARA 398.461-BE/8-151.
23. *FRUS*, 1951 volume 3, p.2004.
24. 'Two Weeks in August: East German Youth Strays West. Background', Office of Public Affairs, Department of State, Sept. 1951, p.9.
25. NARA 800.4614/5-2851.
26. Charles S. Lewis (HICOG, Frankfurt) to Washington, Telegram 476, 14 Aug. 1951.
27. HICOG, Frankfurt, 10 July 1951, NARA 800.4614/7-1051.
28. Telegram No. 488, 3 Aug. 1951, Donnelly (Vienna) to Washington.
29. *The Innsbruck Story* (London 1951).
30. Telegram, Cunningham (HICOG, Frankfurt) 22 Oct., NARA 800.4614/10-2551. Also Dunn (Rome) to Washington, 29 Aug. 1951, NARA 800.4614/8-2951.
31. 'The square witnessed an immense ovation to honour the guide of all progressive humanity,

the best friend of youth.... The message of greetings from German youth to Comrade Stalin carried 4,145,839 signatures', *Avant-Garde*, 17 Aug. 1951, p.3.

32. James C. Flint, President of the August Committee, who noted this incident in a 16-page report by one of the British participants, NARA 800.4614/10-2251.
33. The American National Archives hold about a dozen reports from HICOG, Berlin on its 'Efforts to counter Soviet intentions at the World Youth Festival in Berlin, August 5 to 19, 1951', NARA 800.4614/10-2251.
34. HICOG Report, 23 Aug. 1951, NARA 800.4614/8-2351 and McCloy's report in *FRUS*, 1951, vol. 3, p.1334 and 2005.
35. 11 page report by Gordon A. Ewing, director of RIAS.
36. Anti-communist non-HICOG information materials distributed in West Berlin during the WYF, telegram 661 from HICOG, Frankfurt to Washington, 27 Sept. 1951. NARA 800.4614/9-2751. See also the humorous pamphlet *Was Bringt Dir der Schuman Plan*, of which the West German Government had printed 300,000 copies. The Amerika Haus showed 205 films, organized a series of lectures on Europe and the United States, distributed 11,250 papers and magazines and 45,420 brochures. The Americans had invited Jesse Owens and the Harlem Globe Trotters, who played before 65,000 spectators, at that time the largest number of spectators that had ever watched a basketball game.
37. Flint's report, see note 31.
38. Telegram No. 256, Berlin to Washington, 16 Aug. 1951, NARA 800.4614/8-1651.
39. Telegram No. 252, Jones to Washington, 16 Aug. 1951, NARA 800.4614/8-1651 and telegram No. 1785, HICOG, Berlin, to Washington, 12 Sept. 1951, NARA 800.4614/9-1251.
40. 'The result of the third World Festival of Youth and Students for Peace and the Tasks for the Strengthening of the Unity of Youth in the Fight for Peace', report presented by Enrico Berlinguer, President of the WFDY, in Documents and Declaration of the 7th Annual Council Meeting of the WFDY, 21–24 Aug. 1951 (Budapest, 1952).
41. McCloy (Frankfurt) to Washington, 19 Aug. 1951, NARA 800.4614/8-1951.
42. Note 176 from George A. Morgan, director HICOG (Eastern Element, Berlin) to Washington, 12 Sept. 1951, NARA 800.4614/9-1251.
43. Berlin, 19 Aug., ibid.
44. McCloy to Washington, see note 41.
45. 2 May 1952, signed by Dean Acheson, Secretary of State since 1949, NARA 800.4614/4-2952.
46. Telegram (signed Woodward) Secret Security Information, copy to the CIA, NARA 800.4614/5-752.
47. 'The Embassy could discreetly put to the Swedish Foreign Ministry the advantages that such a position might have for Sweden: prestige, and the possibility of a source of information for the Ministry.' telegram (signed Woodward) copy to the CIA, NARA 800.4614/5-1652.
48. Bill Dentzer became Assistant Permanent Secretary in Sept. 1952.
49. Interview with Tom Braden, Washington DC, 16 Dec. 1988.
50. Ingram to Kolarek (Office of East European Affairs), NARA 800.46/4-352.
51. 13 June 1951, confidential letter from Francis J. Colligan, head of the International Exchange of Persons Division (IEP) to Kenneth Holland (Institute of International Education), NARA 800.4614/6-1351.
52. 25 May 1952, Dentzer to Ingram, NSA Archives, Box 72 (Hoover Library, Stanford University).
53. Interview with William Dentzer, New York, 22 Dec. 1988.
54. 'NSA: an insidious political pressure group', *American Student*, 1/10 (Dec. 1952) p.1.
55. John Ranelagh, *The Agency. The Rise and Decline of the CIA* (London: Sceptre Pocket Books 1987).
56. Interview.
57. Interview with Cord Meyer, Washington, 18 Dec. 1988. See also his book *Facing Reality: From World Federalism to the CIA* (New York: Harper & Row 1983) p.101.
58. Allen Dulles had been a brilliant intelligence officer in the Swiss outpost of the Office of Strategic Service (OSS). After the war he worked as a consultant to the various American intelligence organs before becoming Assistant Director of the CIA in Aug. 1951.

59. Tom Braden had been an isolationist until the German attack on Poland. In 1940, aged 20, he enlisted in the British Army. He fought with the 8th Army in North Africa and Italy. Then he joined the OSS. He was parachuted behind the French and Italian lines, with the mission to finance trade union movements in their resistance to the Nazis. After the war he used both his experience of organizing clandestine operations and the contacts he had established with the trade unions: 'The control of trade unions was always a high priority for the communists. It was one of the activities on which they spent the most money. This was, for instance, the case in France. We responded with the Force Ouvrière. It was the same in Italy' (interview by Joël Kotek).
60. Interview by Joël Kotek.
61. Gregory Treverton, *Covert Action: The Limits of Intervention in the Post-War World* (New York: Basic Books 1987) p.40.
62. Interview by Joël Kotek. In the case of the Congress for Cultural Freedom, the money, to the tune of $800,000 to $900,000 a year, came from the Hoblitzelle Foundation of Dallas. The money financed its publications in various languages: *Encounter* in English, *Monat* in German, and so on (Ranelagh, *The Agency*, note 55, p.246).
63. Interview with Dentzer (New York).
64. Internal CIA document communicated orally to the author by Tom Braden. See also Le Monde du travail, CISL, Brussels, July 1957.

10

The Memorial Day Statement: Women's Organizations in the 'Peace Offensive'

HELEN LAVILLE

Women have had a long tradition of using their supposed greater interest in peace as the basis for their claim to an increased political role, expressing the belief that their 'natural' desire, if matched with political power and influence, would inevitably result in a more peaceful world. American suffragist Alice Stone Blackwell argued before World War I, 'Let us do our utmost to hasten the day when the wishes of mothers shall have their due weight in public affairs, knowing that by doing so we will hasten the day when wars shall be no more'.[1]

The experience of World War II aroused many women across the world to a new-found sense of activism. Scarred and weary from the suffering of the war, and deeply concerned about the frightening destructive potential of the new atomic age, many women claimed that conditions demanded that they take an active role in fighting for peace. Susan B. Riley, President of the American Association of University Women, instructed her members in 1947 on 'The Art of Survival':

> In the long evolution of society, generic Man has represented the forces of destruction, generic women of conservation. Women have more power than they have dreamed of. If their latent strength was once aroused and organized they could accomplish miracles. They could even stop war ... If women care passionately enough to consider the whole world their home and if women of all nations and races would unite and say, 'No more talk of World War III. Find another way to settle your differences. But we will have no more talk of war. For in this Atomic Era we must live in peace if we would live at all'.[2]

Lena Phillips, President of the International Federation of Business and Professional Women's Clubs (IFBPWC) also drew upon essentialist descriptions of the connection between women and peace in her keynote address to the Fourth International Congress of the IFBPWC in Paris in July 1947:

> I wish ... that women could sit at these diplomatic tables where the fate and future of the world is being decided; women who think more in terms ofs human beings and less in terms of material things; women so long trained in protecting the weak and curbing the unruly; women who know the way to fight an idea is not through war. I wish that more women sat at those international conference tables because women are perhaps more socially conscious about many of the things that count for the most now. They are close to the Church and therefore have more faith in God and in good. They would be less bound by protocol; they have much more experience in difficult situations and therefore might display more flexibility and ingenuity. They have had long experience in selflessness.[3]

International women's organizations recognized that the desire for peace could allow women to transcend their national differences. In 1946, the International Alliance of Women (IAW) held a conference at South Korkright, New York, calling for women from all over the world to unite in the cause of peace. Mildred Adams, who narrated the event, stressed that while the women who attended might be divided by national, political and cultural differences,

> one thing they knew, all of them, and that was that the world must not again be put to the consuming cruelty of another war such as the one they had survived. How this could be prevented they did not know, but they felt that driving need to take counsel and find out.... If their children and their children's children were to live they must somehow live in peace or put humanity itself in peril.[4]

Even in the immediate post-war months, however, some women expressed reservations about basing their activism and constructing their political identity upon the cause of peace. Behind this concern lay the fear that, unless 'peace' was tied to concrete and achievable aims, it would inevitably remain a lofty ideal, impossible to work for in a practical sense. *The Journal of the AAUW* worried, 'The peace, too, has to be won; and this is far more difficult because there is no longer the singleness of purpose and the obvious goal that we have in time of war.'[5] An editorial entitled 'Wanted: Adult Citizens' in *Action*, the journal of the League of Women Voters, explained that women needed a sophisticated understanding of world affairs if they were to be responsible citizens:

> We need a general goal upon which we can agree — one which is more explicit that simply 'peace'. For example, is our goal a co-operative international framework in which individual nations may develop politically, economically, culturally, as they see fit, provided their policies are peaceful? Is it our goal to strengthen the non-communist world? Is the second goal an alternative if the first fails? By having the second as an alternative do we make the failure of the first more likely?[6]

The editorial of the League expressed the concern that women's commitment to peace constituted a vague and intangible ideal rather than a mandate for a specific political programme or course of action. This concern has been a recurrent one for many women. Feminist theorist Mary Deitz, in her critique of Jean Bethke Elshtain's work, has argued that vague expressions of women's essentialist commitment to peace based on factors such as their role as mothers, does not offer a viable basis for political identity. Deitz explains, 'A movement or a political consciousness committed simply to caring for "vulnerable human existence" … offers no standards … when it comes to judging between political alternatives or establishing political values.'[7] Women's commitment to peace may serve to create and justify their activism, but it does not inherently *direct* that activity in any specific direction.

THE MEMORIAL DAY STATEMENT

Instead, in their desire for peace, women's activism could be directed, or rather misdirected, towards what might strike American observers as unfortunate paths and policies. In particular, it could be recognised and exploited by the Soviet Union through its 'Peace Offensive'. The March 1949 conference of the National Committee of Arts, Sciences and Professions at the Waldorf-Astoria Hotel in New York City had sparked an immediate response from the US Government, with the State Department and the House on Un-American Activities Committee denouncing the Soviet 'peace offensive' as a propaganda trick.[8] The Stockholm petition launched at the meeting of the World Peace Council in March 1950 was further evidence to the US government of a concerted propaganda campaign in the name of 'peace'. In July 1950 the House Un-American Activities Committee responded, condemning the 'peace campaign and its manifestation in the form of petitions' which were designed to 'confuse and divide the American people'.[9]

Organizations identified by the US government as tools of the Soviet 'peace offensive' made the maternal interest of women in peace a vital part of their campaign. The report of the World Assembly for Peace, held in Helsinki in June 1955, pronounced:

> There is no doubt that mothers will everywhere prove among the most active workers for peace, with the object of changing the present ruinous atmosphere of fear and uncertainty into an atmosphere of confidence and security. Maternal love is undoubtedly one of the most powerful forces for peace represented at the Helsinki Assembly... Many women who have never before dared to take part in the fight for peace, who previously hid themselves behind the old argument that they did not wish to be political, today understand that they must act in order to protect their children from death and from all the physical and moral suffering which follows wars.[10]

Soviet-sponsored women's organizations, led by the Women's International Democratic Federation (WIDF), played a significant part in the Soviet peace offensive. The 1949 Session of the Council of the WIDF in Moscow wrote a gushing letter to 'Joseph Vissarionovich Stalin', thanking him for his sincere personal work for peace. The Executive Committee of the WIDF used the occasion of their conference in Bucharest in July 1952 to advertise the forthcoming Congress of People for Peace to be held in Vienna, resolving, 'The War in Korea must be ended! Re-born German and Japanese militarism must be stopped!'[11] The Federation's booklet in 1953, 'The Child needs Peace as the Flower needs Sunlight', took the form of a 'round-up' of nations across the globe, detailing the effect of militarism and war on them. According to the booklet, Soviet-satellite nations in Eastern Europe such as Poland, having suffered appallingly from the devastation of World War II, had become determined advocates of peace. The booklet made copious reference to the WIDF-sponsored report 'Korea: We Accuse' published in 1951.

'Korea: We Accuse', written in spring 1951 by a 17-woman commission under the sponsorship of the WIDF, claimed to have uncovered evidence of various atrocities and abuses by the US forces in Korea. The report caused immediate concern within the US government. Mary Cannon, Chief of the International Division of the Women's Bureau at the Department of Labor, wrote to Marion Sanders and Herbert McGushin of the State Department enclosing a copy of the report with a cover letter explaining, 'The United States Women's Bureau is concerned that such a distorted picture of America's character is being circulated to women's organizations and leaders throughout the world ... This kind of propaganda will probably be an effective weapon in gaining support among women for the communist "peace offensive".'[12] The State Department passed the report to Doris Cochrane of the Division of Public Liaison, who wrote to Mr Fierst, head of the United Nations Association:

> Do you think it would be helpful for some women's organizations to issue comments on the WIDF report? It is possible that one or more of the other organizations which has consultative status with the Economic and Social Commission might be interested in preparing statements on the WIDF report — or that the American Secretary of one of these international organizations might take the initiative.[13]

The American response to 'Korea: We Accuse' came, not from any agency of the US Government, but from a coalition of American women's organizations. This was coordinated by Rose Parsons, president of Women United for United Nations (WUUN), a clearing house for more than 30 American women's associations interested in the work of the United Nations. Working with leaders of prominent women's voluntary associations, Parsons drafted what became known as the 'Memorial Day Statement'.

The Statement, signed by the leaders of ten women's organizations including the American Association of University Women, the League of Women Voters, the Young Women's Christian Association and the National Council of Negro Women, was a vital document in the history of women's involvement in peace campaigns. Formally presented to the US Ambassador to the United Nations on Memorial Day 1951, the Statement was also distributed to US information services abroad through the State Department and broadcast on Radio Free Asia and Radio Free Europe. Whilst not undermining or negating women's special interest in peace, the Statement sought to redefine and limit that interest in order to avoid its open-ended potential.

The strategy of US women's organizations reflected that of their government, who recognized the need to articulate and define a position of peace rather than to allow the accusations of the Soviet Union to go unanswered. Francis Russell, Director of the Office of Public Affairs, enthused to Assistant Secretary of State Edward Barrett in February 1951, 'The communist "Crusade for Peace" represents an opportunity for the State Department and for private citizens to point out the kind of peace for which we stand, i.e. a peace with freedom, liberty and justice.'[14]

The 'private citizens' represented by the signatories of the Memorial Day Statement made this 'American' definition of peace explicit: 'The women of the United States have long worked for peace. They know that peace to endure must be accompanied by freedom and justice and founded on law and order. They know that law, to be respected, must be based on spiritual and moral values.'

The Statement explicitly linked the cause of peace with the cause of democracy and freedom and implicitly attacked the Soviet-sponsored peace campaign, 'because it seems to use that peace, without justice and without freedom, is being promoted in an effort to undermine the unity of the free world, it seems wise at this moment for our organizations to reaffirm our desire for a just and lasting peace, and for the preservation of human values everywhere.' The Statement expressed the commitment of US women's organizations to the United Nations as the best hope for a peaceful world.[15]

FELLOW TRAVELLERS: 'WOMAN' AND BERLIN

The Statement quickly assumed the status of a position paper which not only countered Soviet accusations but also limited calls, campaigns and demonstrations for peace which, whilst not in themselves Soviet-sponsored or directed, risked the appearance of lending moral or ideological support to the Soviet peace offensive. There were the Soviet-sponsored organizations, such as the WIDF, who knowingly and cynically used the issue of peace in a propaganda campaign against the United States, but there was also the more complex group called 'fellow travellers'. This group consisted of women who were genuinely and sincerely committed to the cause of peace but whose enthusiasm might be directed and manipulated by the Soviets.

In their attempt to discredit the efforts of Soviet-sponsored organizations to claim peace and associate the United States with 'war-mongering', American women recognized that they had to tread very carefully. The genuine interest of women in peace could neither be under-estimated nor lightly dismissed. The Stockholm Peace Pledge, despite attempts to discredit it by the US government, gained some 1,350,000 signatories in the United States alone, and within five months of its launch had received some 273,470,566 signatures world-wide. A memorandum from Mrs. John Lee of the League of Women Voters to her State and Local presidents urged members not to be drawn into what she called 'a misleading peace campaign', but acknowledged that the appeal of the campaign was based upon genuine and heartfelt sentiments: 'There is no reason to believe that League members themselves will subscribe to the propaganda underlying the Peace petition, but the campaign for signatures may become active in your community and many people sincerely wishing to do something personally to bring about peace, may sign or be drawn into the effort.'[16]

The World Organization of Mothers of All Nations (WOMAN) was typical of the 'fellow-travellers' in the peace offensive. Founded by journalist Dorothy Thompson, WOMAN was established as a response to the enthusiasm for Thompson's articulations of women's interest in peace. Writing in *The Ladies Home Journal* in 1946, Thompson addressed herself to the 'Gentlemen of the United Nations'. Thompson wrote evocatively of women's maternal influence over men, explaining that women represented 'the greatest international in the world. We speak a common language from

Chungking to Moscow, and from Berlin to New York.... I am pushed forward by the host of mothers, for whom you first groped in the dark.'[17] Thompson explained to the statesmen of the world the various ways in which women had served them and the sacrifices they had made:

> Housekeeper, homemaker, wife, mother. You, gentlemen, have often called us the pillars and preservers of civilizations. You have pinned golden stars upon our bosoms and laid Purple Hearts in our hands. You have asked us to give our sons, our children 'to save the world'. You have asked us to endure the crucifixion of our sons, that the sins of nations might be wiped out and all people everywhere live out their lives in freedom from want and fear. We have given you our sons. Some are dead and some are blind, and some gibber behind bars, and some walk without feet and hands, and each of those is as precious to us as all the world we gave them to you to save.[18]

Thompson concluded that women were unprepared to tolerate the sacrifice of their children forever. She warned, 'You must lay aside your guns. You cannot talk to the mothers with bombing planes and atomic bombs. You must come into the room of your mother unarmed.'[19]

Thompson's article was met with an enthusiastic, often impassioned response. The journalist claimed she received 2,700 letters from American women, with a further 4,200 letters in response to her second article 'If No-one Else, We the Mothers'. One letter in particular caught Thompson's eye, 'You have no right to write as you do, to move us all as you do, unless you do more than write articles.'[20] Suitably chastised, Thompson set to work transforming her vision into a programme for action, composing a letter to all her correspondents:

> I cannot erase from my mind the conviction that in all countries, of whatever political and economic composition, the mothers – and the maternal instinct – are working, hitherto silently, for the total abolition of war and violence as instruments for the furthering of national aims or theoretical ideas, and that among women there is an enormous and as yet untapped power, that can be released to dispel the present nightmare, which neither the political leaders, the theoretical ideologists, nor even the scientists have been able to do.[21]

Failings of political leaders aside, it is hard to picture what new skills Thompson imagined she could bring to the task of harnessing the maternal instinct in a meaningful campaign. Famously dismissive of women's organizations and unwilling to offer any real commitment of time to her new organization, Thompson seemed to feel the power of her inspiring words was sufficient as her contribution to her cause, publishing 'A Woman's

Manifesto' in *The Ladies Home Journal* as a rallying call for women to join her organization. Perhaps as a result of the lack of leadership from Thompson, WOMAN, launched in November 1947, initially failed to arouse much interest. Operating with a small membership of 665 individuals with a further 105 clubs offering support, WOMAN seemed destined to remain a small, ineffective, if well-intentioned organization that would wither away with the fading enthusiasm of its members and leaders. In 1951, however, the original director of WOMAN, Jane Hayford, was joined by a new and enthusiastic executive director, Mary Hughes, and WOMAN began to develop more ambitious plans. Hayford, Hughes, and Thompson met to discuss a suggestion from Ilse Bentler, Chairman of the California State Division of WOMAN, that the organization arrange a pilgrimage to Berlin, an idea supported by German representatives of WOMAN.

Tentative plans for the pilgrimage were sketched by Thompson, who envisaged the contributions of the playwright Carl Zuckmayer, a personal friend and professional producer, to 'put on this Congress with all the fanfare of parades, music, speeches'.[22] Thompson, at the request of Hayford, wrote a letter to peace organizations explaining the objectives of the Berlin Congress.[23] She invited influential women to join the Board of Directors of WOMAN, 'at least for one momentous year':[24]

> It is my profound conviction that the present foreign policies of the Great Powers, including the United States, are heading the peoples of the world, with or without a general war, toward a disaster unparalleled since the dark age following the fall of Rome; that these policies – based ironically enough on universal appeals to Peace, Progress, Liberation and Democracy, and upheld, where they are upheld, largely through the appeal of such words – are totally unrepresentative of the world's peoples, who are listening in despair for the voice that does not speak.[25]

Thompson argued that the voice had an obligation born of 'the function of nurturing and conserving human life'. She recognised the symbolic importance of Berlin as 'the spot where the two conflicting powers met each other, in most dangerous tension – the ruined, battle-scarred city of Berlin'. Inviting women from both sides of the Curtain to be present at the climax of the pilgrimage, Thompson assured, 'I do not imagine anything loud, coarse, agitatory, or demonstrative in the usual sense – for its purpose will be to create a new platform altogether, in a new atmosphere and mood.'[26]

Washington Post journalist Malvina Lindsay noted approvingly that WOMAN was 'a group of American Women of intellectual standing and unquestioned patriotism'. Lindsay entertained high hopes that WOMAN could rise above the 'red-tagging' of peace activists:

> Originating in the United States, it should help to counter the communist chant about American warmongers. If, as planned, the world flight of its leaders ends in a Congress of Women in Berlin at which sincere and feasible disarmament proposals are made, a big step will be taken at a strategic spot towards grabbing the peace offensive.[27]

However, given American anxieties about Soviet attempts to target women with the 'peace campaign', Thompson's plan aroused some skepticism. Thompson's optimism that an emotive demonstration would be able to distinguish itself from Soviet-sponsored activities was not shared by everyone, including her friend Carl Zuckmayer. Since Thompson planned to make one of Zuckmayer's plays central to the pilgrimage, it was disheartening to discover that he was less than enthusiastic. Whilst Zuckmayer wrote in admiration of Thompson's 'imaginative [*sic*] and honesty and deep appreciation for truth and right … [and] your passionate will to act and not only to talk for the good cause', he doubted the wisdom of the Berlin scheme.[28] Zuckmayer feared that 'any group-statement in public would rather contribute and add to the general confusion in our world instead of light it up'. He warned Thompson, 'the policy of the East … is a cold, icy-cold, calculated and enormously shrewd cunning, a way of turning everything to their advantage', and worried that a group of Americans criticizing all governments could be represented as a group of Americans criticizing their own government:

> You are certainly right when you say that there is no government in the world which really represents the people. But there are governments which represent it even less than the others altogether … I'm afraid we cannot deal with them by the true and honest means of 'going there and speaking it out' – without weakening our own position.

The location of the proposed pageant in Berlin was particularly controversial. The Soviet Union had already sponsored peace rallies of women and students in Berlin, and many within both the US government and mainstream women's organizations feared that it would be impossible for a European to make any meaningful distinction between the Soviet-sponsored rallies and the 'independent' activities of WOMAN. Moreover, the German Branch of WOMAN had not endeared itself to the Women's Affairs Section in West Germany. In May 1949 two staffers in the Section, Joy Evans and Elizabeth Holt, expressed concern that

> '[WOMAN's] programme puts little emphasis on civic education for women … It is unconstructive in that it draws the attention of women

> away from their role as responsible citizens with specific tasks in their community ... Its principal dangers is that it can become a peace movement which through an emotional appeal leads women aside from the serious task of being informed citizens.'[29]

Concern about the intent and potential effect of any women's demonstration in Berlin was also raised by Gabrielle Strecker, a leader of German women's organizations who had been the first German to visit the United States under the Exchange of Persons Programme. Strecker warned Rose Parsons in October 1951 about WOMAN:

> It is exactly the least of all we need, it is exactly the unrealistic type of organization which we must get rid of. It will offer large possibilities for communist infiltration. The types of women who run WOMAN are apt to spoil sound activities of good organizations and will bring mischief and confusion in the German women's movement.[30]

Strecker was exasperated about the emotional nature of WOMAN's programme, recounting to Parsons an encounter with Monckenberg-Kolmar, Chair of the Hamburg branch of WOMAN, during a meeting of women's organizations in Bavaria. Strecker complained that her speeches and those of the wife of the US High Commissioner, Mrs John McCloy, warning of 'the communist danger ... [and] the big fallacies of peace slogans', were constantly interrupted and angrily denounced by Monckenberg-Kolmar. Strecker reflected, 'A mass of ignorant un-political women in the hands of such dangerous demagogues! It's terrible!'[31]

The concern of the Women's Affairs Section in West Germany was matched by that of the State Department. On 2 September 1951 Chester Williams, a member of the United States delegation to the United Nations, wrote to the State Department with his worry that '[Hughes] and Dorothy Thompson have now launched themselves upon an enterprise which could produce very disruptive and confusing results'. Williams concluded that, whilst Hughes' plan did not have the backing of the leaders of 'the large women's organizations... she may have considerable influence with a coterie of prominent women who appreciate being in the limelight of international society in the company of queens and lady bountifuls'. He believed that 'it would be impossible to guide this group of women into safe and useful channels', but he was wary of expressing outright opposition since 'it would be most difficult, if not impossible, to discourage them from going ahead with their idea'. He suggested that Doris Cochrane of the Public Liaison Office of the State Department 'discuss the matter with responsible women leaders' and find ways of 'bringing the influence of the non-governmental organizations to bear on WOMAN and discourage the scheme'. Ultimately it would be this governmental influence of the 'responsible' women's organizations which put a decisive end to the 'Pilgrimage to Berlin'.

As with the initial issue of the Memorial Day Statement, the response of the 'official' US women's organizations was co-ordinated by Rose Parsons. On 26 November 1951, Rose Parsons wrote to Gabrielle Strecker to explain what she and others were doing to obstruct WOMAN. Referring to WOMAN as a 'movement that has almost a psychopathic feeling about it', Parsons described Hayford as 'a very neurotic and excitable person…apt to go off the handle'.[32] Parsons also referred to the co-operation between herself and the government, describing a visit paid by Hayford, Parsons, and an unnamed woman to the State Department. Parsons reported that the Department representative was 'of course…very disturbed about this pilgrimage to Berlin'. However, 'he felt it would be wrong for the State Department to discourage this cock-eyed plan, so he told [Hayford] the great expense it would be, and how it had to be planned down to every detail etc.' After the meeting, the representative told Parsons that 'he thought it was up to the women's organizations to discourage this rather than the State Department'.[33]

Given the organizational chaos and personal disagreements that were rapidly distinguishing the activities of WOMAN in the United States, Parsons had little trouble 'discouraging' the pilgrimage. Parsons airily reminded her friend and political ally Eleanor Roosevelt: 'Several of us were successful in getting the Board of Directors to resign, and put quite a crimp in the idea of her pilgrimage to Berlin…. We were in close touch with the NGOs in Paris at that time and what you too were trying to do to discourage D. Thompson.'[34] When Ruth Woodsmall, the head of the Women's Affairs Branch in West Germany expressed her extreme concern at the confusion in the mind of German women, who had been told that thousands of American women belonged to WOMAN:

> The NGO's [*sic*] showed Miss Woodsmall a copy of a statement that 10 women's National organizations had presented to Mr Austin last year on Memorial Day…. Miss Woodsmall was thrilled to see this and said that it would be a great help to her if there could be more of this kind of thing from the representative US women's organizations. It would help her in the building of constructive and positive attitudes among German women.[35]

ELEANOR ROOSEVELT

The Memorial Day Statement was accordingly re-published, together with an exchange of letters between Eleanor Roosevelt and Anna Lord Strauss. The organizations offered the statement as both a response and an alternative to Thompson's manifesto:

> In view of the recent publication of a full-page advertisement in the *New York Times* and elsewhere of a 'Woman's Manifesto' under the auspices of Dorothy Thompson's group known as WOMAN.... We believe it is appropriate to bring to your attention the carefully drafted statement in support of the United Nations, officially presented on Memorial Day 1951 to Ambassador Austin by ten of the most influential women's organizations in the United States.[36]

This was a statement on behalf of 'a combined membership of more than 26,000,000' who had 'co-operated with each other many times to support genuine efforts to bring the nations of the world together to secure peace and to promote freedom among all nations'. In implicit contrast to WOMAN, the organizations that signed the statement described themselves as democratic and representative: 'Each of our organizations arrives at its policies separately through democratic procedure. Each woman in her organization can have a part in electing the leaders ... Each member can have a voice in influencing positions on questions of national and international policy.'[37]

Unsurprisingly, Roosevelt's reply supported the Statement. In a strong allusion to WOMAN and its possible effect, Mrs Roosevelt warned: 'At a time when Soviet-inspired and directed "peace-movements" are seeking to infiltrate and maneuver women's groups in various parts of the world, and especially in Germany, it is essential for all women's organizations to be on guard and to be precise in the positions they take in order to avoid being used in behalf of false peace propaganda.'[38] Peace had to be constructed to negate Soviet claims to that word:

> Support of aggression by the Soviets in Korea and in their imposition of communist minority domination on Eastern Germany, the Baltic states, Poland, Czechoslovakia, Bulgaria, Hungary, Rumania and Albania should convince all of us that their use of the word 'peace' has nothing in common with our aspirations and struggles for a real peace with freedom and justice under the United Nations Charter.[39]

Roosevelt then turned to Thompson. Whilst 'presuming' that Thompson had 'no intention of promoting Soviet objectives', Roosevelt nevertheless accused her of 'reflecting' the approach of communist-front organizations. Roosevelt sternly rebuked: 'It shocks me to think that any American women would bracket our country with the Soviet Union in the light of their record.' In contrast, the former First Lady congratulated the organizations

FIGURE 1

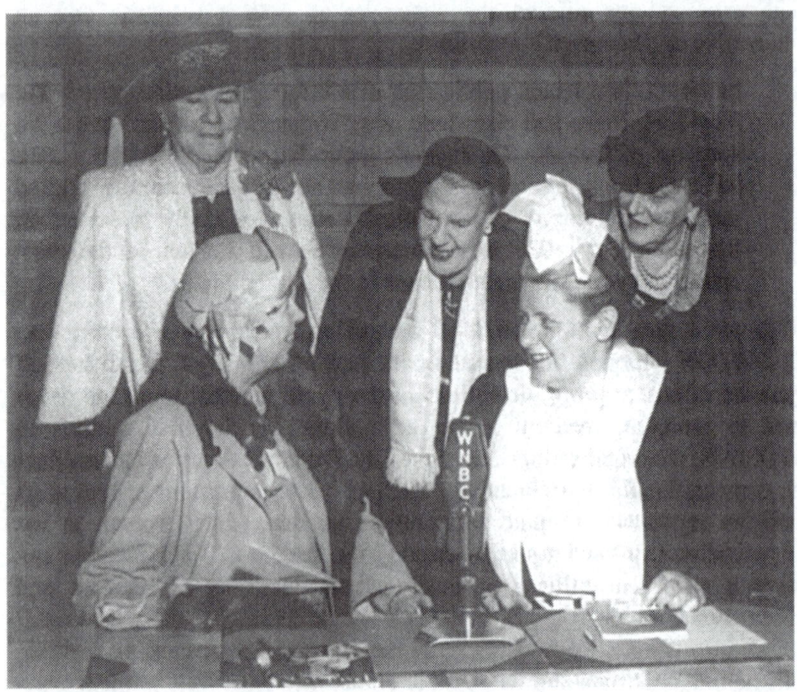

Eleanor Roosevelt and Dorothy Thompson (both seated) on 10 March 1950 at the UN temporary headquarters at Lake Success, NY. She and a group of influential women, including Dorothy Thompson, Emily Post, and Clare Booth Luce were interviewed by Mary Margaret McBride.
Franklin D. Roosevelt Library, Hyde Park, NY

that were signatories of a statement 'which can reassure women in other parts of the world that this ill-considered expression of WOMAN is not really representative of any substantial group'.[40] It was these organizations, wrote Roosevelt, which were the true voice of American women, bearing 'a heavy responsibility to inform their sisters around the world on where American women really stand in the common pursuit of peace'.[41]

According to Roosevelt and her allies, WOMAN, in contrast to representative bodies 'proven' by reference to their democratic methods, could not claim to speak for a constituency. Anna Lord Strauss reiterated the point in her response to the Memorial Day Statement:

> One of the significant points made by the group of women's organizations in this statement is contained in the description of how these organizations truly represent large membership who participate in the formation of policy. This statement, unlike the 'Woman's

> Manifesto', was drafted by the responsible, elected heads of established women's organizations in consultation with each other and reflects the official policies adopted in national conventions. These policies and opinions reflect discussion in local and state bodies in which the membership as a whole participates. They are not the mere literary expression of a small group of individual women, presuming to speak for a great body of American women.... The cause of peace can be harmed by well-intentioned people who release statements with the intention of getting them accepted abroad as the considered expression of the great body of American women.[42]

Roosevelt sent Thompson the text of these letters and the Memorial Day Statement, explaining: 'The Representatives of a number of important women's organizations who are here at the General Assembly as observers have disowned the approach you are making through WOMAN.'[43] This sparked a bitter correspondence. Thompson resented Mrs Roosevelt's insinuation that her actions risked confirming her as a misguided 'fellow-traveller':

> I deeply regret that in your reply to the memorandum apropos the Women's Manifesto, signed by ten American women's organizations, in liaison with the U.N., you found it proper to 'presume' that 'Miss Thompson has no intention of promoting Soviet objectives'. I think, Mrs Roosevelt, that you need not 'presume' it, but that you absolutely know it.[44]

Thompson then challenged Roosevelt by outlining the central dilemma posed to Americans advocating peace:

> If all popular peace demonstrations are to be confined to communist or communist-inspired groups, we are handing them the greatest weapon of psychological strategy that exists, and one which cannot be answered by the mere official accusation that they are 'fraudulent'. In all countries which I have recently visited, in Europe and the Middle East, I found many persons, positively anti-communist, who had signed the Stockholm Manifesto simply because they wanted to go on record for peace and no one else had offered them a chance.[45]

Thompson's analysis of the Memorial Day Statement was incisive. The linkage of 'peace' with other issues such as the 'Freedom and Justice' and 'Law and Order' proposed in the Statement was deeply problematic:

> Philosophical considerations are involved – considerations of whose concepts of freedom, order and justice, and what moral and spiritual values. Even within the western world there is no unanimity regarding

> those, and the achievement of such objectives is inconceivable without the overthrow of the communist and many other regimes, which cannot be imagined without war.

Like Roosevelt, Thompson saw the role of the United States in the Cold War as confronting the Soviet Union in a battle of ideals: 'The notion of a world with one concept of freedom, justice, order, law and spiritual and moral values is, in fact, the communist concept, nor do I anticipate success from trying to rival it with our own concept of the same values, but that we will do better to limit our aims and leave universal salvation to the millennium.'[46] Yet her point that 'spiritual and moral values cannot be divorced from cultural and religious and historic experience' was a fundamental criticism of American responses to the peace offensive. American propaganda had diluted the meaning of and commitment to peace until it was not only weakened but also actually inverted into a commitment to military preparedness.

Thompson's solution, through the founding of WOMAN, was not an attempt to end the Cold War hostility between the United States and the Soviet Union. Such a detente was not realistic. Instead, Thompson attempted to separate support for peace and disarmament from any political position in the Cold War. WOMAN merely urged disarmament so that the consequences of inevitable disputes would not be so devastating:

> Total disarmament would not remove communism from the world, nor even through total disarmament would a millennium of freedom, justice, law, order, and universal spiritual and moral values be established. Envy, hate, greed, and exploitation would not therewithin be removed. There would still be disagreeable neighbors. The spirit of the Sermon on the Mount would not reign even by establishing one prohibition of the decalogue. There would still be a struggle of classes and ideology. All that would be removed would be the possibility of governments launching vast organized masses of men and weapons at other vast organized masses of men and weapons, whether in the name of liberty or of equality, or for any other ideal.[47]

Whatever their merits, Thompson's arguments against the Memorial Day Statement had become peripheral since she realised that the Berlin Pilgrimage could not succeed. The organizational difficulties of WOMAN and opposition of the 'official' American women's organizations were insurmountable obstacles. In January 1952, Thompson wrote to Vilma Monckenberg-Kolmar, head of the Hamburg division of WOMAN:

> The attitude of the Occupation Authorities and women's groups represented by Mrs Roosevelt makes it all but certain that our

> demonstration would play into communist hands. For it could not escape being known that we held the demonstration counter to American policy and desire, without even benevolent neutrality, and this fact, by itself, would give the communist peace groups every opportunity to attack the USA.[48]

CONCLUSION

E. P. Thompson has suggested that as a result of the Soviet peace offensive, the causes of 'peace' and 'freedom' broke apart, with the Soviet Union claiming 'peace' and the United States 'freedom'.[49] This division is simplistic. While the United States did construct itself as an advocate for freedom, it did not want to abandon its claims to be the champion of peace. To do so would invite hostility from the rest of the world, already fearful about the extent of US military power.

Initial responses from the US government to the peace offensive indicated their willingness to abandon their claim to the cause, assuming that advocates of peace were either Soviet-sponsored or Soviet sympathizers. The Council of the WIDF, meeting in Moscow in November 1949, complained:

> The governments of capitalist countries are banning all assemblies of the defenders of peace. They raise all manner of obstacles in the matter of issuing visas and passports for travel to international congresses and subject the partisans of peace to humiliating interrogations, going even so far as to try, for instance, in the United States of America, to force honest people to sign revolting papers branding the champions of peace as foreign agents. In these countries mothers who fight for peace are persecuted, baited and imprisoned.[50]

The WIDF's claims were not mere propaganda. In March 1950 the United States refused entry to twelve people, including Pablo Picasso and the Dean of Canterbury, acting for the World Congress of Partisans for Peace. The US occupation authorities in West Germany arrested Lily Waechter, a German woman who had been invited by the WIDF to speak at the World Peace Congress in London in 1951. Waechter had been a representative on the WIDF commission that had visited Korea and was scheduled to address the Congress in London on the topic.

This 'red-tagging' of peace advocates undoubtedly had a devastating effect on 'genuine', non-Soviet campaigners, as Thompson has noted.[51] However, the US government came to recognize that this tactic had its drawbacks. Persecution of those working for such a moral cause of peace was a public relations failure, as the riots and protests that greeted the arrest of Lily Waechter demonstrated. It was particularly difficult to justify the prosecution of women, or worse, mothers for expressing their commitment to saving the lives of their children and the children of the world. As historian Harriet Hyman Alonso has argued, the maternal claim gave women 'a unique position that men cannot share and therefore cannot really argue against'.[52]

So, instead of simply repudiating the cause of peace, the US government sought to define it (and thus limit it), as they 'proved' that their policies and not those of the Soviets worked towards the goal of a peaceful world. President Dwight Eisenhower led this strategy of defining peace positively, with the 'Chance for Peace' speech and 'Atoms for Peace' campaign of 1953. Eisenhower developed his personal definition of peace through his autobiography, the second volume of which is entitled *Waging Peace*, and his speeches, a collection of which was entitled, *Peace with Justice*.

In its effort for a positive definition of peace, the US government was joined enthusiastically by private organizations such as the signatories of the Memorial Day Statement. The Statement re-affirmed American women's gendered commitment to peace but defined this peace in a way which could oppose and thwart the aims of the Soviet peace offensive. The interest of 'mainstream' American women's organizations did not propel them towards immediate disarmament, a withdrawal from Korea, or a de-militarized Germany. They became less partisans for peace and more advocates of a partisan peace, one which demanded such corollaries as freedom and democracy.

NOTES

1. Quoted in Nancy E. McGlen and Meredith Reid Sarkees, *Women in Foreign Policy: The Insiders* (New York: Routledge 1993) p.4.
2. *Journal of the AAUW* 40/2 (Winter 1947) p.69.
3. Lena M. Phillips Papers, Schlesinger Library, Radcliffe College, Cambridge, Massachusetts, box 6, Phillips speech to the 4th International Congress of the International Federation of Business and Professional Women's Clubs, Paris, 19–25 July 1947.
4. Mildred Adams, *The World We Live In, The World We Want* (Hartford, CT: Stone Brook Press 1947) p.14.
5. Mabel Newcomber, 'A Signpost towards International Co-operation: Significance of the Bretton Woods Conference', *Journal of the AAUW* 38/1 (Fall 1944) p.20.
6. 'Wanted, Adult Citizens', *Action. Journal of the National League of Women Voters* (May 1947) p.25.
7. Mary G. Dietz, 'Citizenship with a Feminist Face: The Problem with Maternal Thinking', *Political Theory* 13/1 (Feb. 1985) p.30.
8. The Waldorf Conference, while the most notorious, was not the only peace conference. It was preceded by the World Congress of Intellectuals for Peace in Wroclaw, Poland in Aug. 1948 and was followed by the World Peace Congress in Paris in April 1949 and the Stockholm Peace Congress in March 1950.
9. Gerald Horne, *Black and Red: W.E.B. Dubois and the Afro-American Response to the Cold War 1944–1963* (State Univ. of New York Press 1986) p.132.

10. *Report of the World Assembly for Peace*, Helsinki, 22–29 June 1955 (Stockholm: Secretariat of the World Council of Peace).
11. Message and Resolutions adopted by the Executive Committee, WIDF, Bucharest, 1952, Pamphlet Collection, The Women's Library, London.
12. US National Archives, Records of the Women's Bureau, Office of the Director, General Correspondence Files, 1948–1953, box 25, Cannon to Sanders and McGushin, not dated.
13. US National Archives, Washington DC, Records of the Department of State, Miscellaneous Records of the Bureau of Public Affairs 1944–1962, letter, Cochrane to Fierst, July 1951.
14. US National Archives, Records of the Department of State, Miscellaneous Records of the Bureau of Public Affairs 1944–1962, box 126, letter, Russell to Barrett, 28 Feb. 1951.
15. Memorial Day Statement, Dorothy Thompson Papers, Syracuse University Library, Department of Special Collections, series 1, box 31. The other signatories were the American Nurses Association, the General Federation of Women's Clubs, the National Association of Women Lawyers, the National Council of Catholic Women, the National Council of Jewish Women and the United Church Women of the National Council of Churches of Christ in America.
16. League of Women Voters papers, Library of Congress, Washington, DC, box 744, letter, Lee to Local and State League Presidents, undated.
17. Dorothy Thompson Papers, series 5, box 4, manuscript, 'A Woman Says, "You must come into the room of your mother unarmed"', *Ladies Home Journal*, February 1946.
18. Ibid.
19. Ibid.
20. Dorothy Thompson papers, series 1, box 31. Citizen's Committee for United Nations Reform Bulletin, November 1947, 1:4.
21. Dorothy Thompson papers, series 1, box 31, form letter, not dated.
22. Dorothy Thompson papers, series 1, box 31, letter, Hayford to Monckenberg-Kolmar, 29 May 1951.
23. Dorothy Thompson Papers, series 1, box 31, letter, Hayford to Thompson, 29 May 1951.
24. Dorothy Thompson Papers, series 1, box 31, form letter from Dorothy Thompson, not dated.
25. Women United for the United Nations Papers, Schlesinger Library, Radcliffe College, Cambridge, Massachusetts, file 22, letter, Thompson to Parsons et al, 9 July 1951.
26. Ibid.
27. Malvina Lindsay, 'Dramatizing Peace Aims', *Washington Post*, 10 June 1951.
28. Dorothy Thompson Papers, series 1, box 31, letter, Zuckmayer to Thompson, 10 Aug. 1951.
29. Dorothy Thompson Papers, series 1, box 31, memo, Evans and Holt to Ruth Woodsmall, 26 May 1949.
30. Women United for the United Nations Papers, file 22, letter, Strecker to Parsons, 16 Oct. 1951.
31. Ibid.
32. Women United for United Nations Papers, file 22, letter, Parsons to Strecker, 26 Nov. 1951.
33. Ibid.
34. Franklin D. Roosevelt Presidential Library, Hyde Park, New York, Eleanor Roosevelt Papers, box 3267, letter from Rose Parsons to Eleanor Roosevelt (not dated).
35. Ibid.
36. Dorothy Thompson Papers, series 1, box 31, Memorial Day Statement, 1951.
37. Dorothy Thompson Papers, series 1, box 31 Eleanor Roosevelt's reply to 'Women's Manifesto', 21 Dec. 1951.
38. Ibid.
39. Ibid.
40. Ibid.
41. Ibid.
42. Dorothy Thompson Papers, series 1, box 31, Anna Lord Strauss's reply to 'Women's Manifesto', 17 Dec. 1951.
43. Dorothy Thompson Papers, series 1, box 25, letter, Eleanor Roosevelt to Thompson, 21 Dec. 1951.
44. Dorothy Thompson Papers, series 2, box 25, letter, Thompson to Eleanor Roosevelt, 7 Jan. 1952.

45. Ibid.
46. Ibid.
47. Ibid.
48. Dorothy Thompson Papers, series 2, box 4, letter, Thompson to Monckenberg-Kolmar, 7 Jan. 1952.
49. E.P. Thompson, *Beyond the Cold War* (London: Merlin Press 1982).
50. Report of the Executive Committee, WIDF, Moscow, Nov. 1949, The Pamphlet Collection, The Women's Library, London.
51. Ibid.
52. Harriet Hyman Alonso, *Peace as a Women's Issue*: *A History of the U.S. Movement for World Peace and Women's Rights* (Syracuse UP 1993).

PART IV

Target Areas

11

The Cold War Culture of the French and Italian Communist Parties

MARC LAZAR

My subject calls for some preliminary remarks.[1] By 'Cold War culture', I refer to an intense moment that exaggerated certain aspects of the political culture of the French and Italian communist parties. Of course, the idea of political culture raises an impressive array of conceptual or methodological problems and objections.[2] In the hope of escaping 'culturalist' or 'systemic' definitions, I prefer to take an anthropological approach to culture, considering it a way of life, a 'grammar of communication', a 'symbolic process of social interaction' or 'a complex body of norms, symbols, myths and images that penetrate the inner self of the individual, structure instincts and orient emotions', to use the definitions of Clifford Geertz, Pitirim Sorokin or Edgar Morin.[3] In this perspective, a culture is not innate, essential or timeless, but rather is repeatedly subject to re-composition and transaction, and is marked both by permanence and change.[4] The same thing applies to political culture, which, by extension, represents an ensemble of ideas, values, symbols and beliefs and a diverse multitude of rules and practices. The combination of these elements gives meaning to reality, sets down rules of the game, shapes political behavior and helps inculcate social norms.[5]

Though difficult to apply at the level of a whole society, the notion of political culture becomes much more relevant when applied to a party. According to Jean-François Sirinelli and Eric Vigne, it consists of 'a sort of code and a series of referents, formalized within a party or more broadly spread among a political family or a political tradition'.[6] Political culture finds expression in propaganda, rituals and symbols;[7] it conveys those values that are so meaningful to and deeply rooted in their adherents as to have become invisible and unconscious.[8] Finally, it can, in certain cases, bring about a real political sub-culture: a specific form of political behavior of militants and sympathizers manifested by voting stability, participation in a number of networks across a specific territory, perpetuation of community relations and reinforcement of the feelings of belonging to and identification with the party.[9] However, not all parties are equal in this respect. Their goals, founding principles, organizational structures, means of making and implementing policy, as well as the nature of their militants and key figures all differ considerably, differences which spill over into their cultures. Thus, in mass parties of a totalitarian bent, to take Maurice Duverger's distinction which is particularly relevant when speaking of communist parties during the Cold War, political culture is first and foremost defined by the importance of ideology.[10]

For reasons of space, I will thus concentrate on the study of ideology, the backbone of communist culture, and on propaganda, its means of distribution. I will deliberately leave aside the positions of the two communist parties in the domain of culture and their cultural production.

Political ideology, particularly in communist parties, cannot be summed up, as sociologist Raymond Boudon suggests, as a simple 'doctrine based on scientific argumentation'.[11] It also offers a vision of the world, a perception of current and future society, and constitutes 'a collective scheme of interpretation'[12] with which to construct representations of the past, present and future in a coherent, simplified and schematic way. It serves as a kind of collective semantics for the members of these parties; it helps to shape their identity and gives a general meaning to their individual commitments by declaring 'the sense, the real-life sense of collective life which makes a truth out of common action and gives reason and intelligibility to each practice'.[13]

Consequently, the analysis of ideology must take place on at least three levels. It must attempt to uncover the ideology's internal structure, its doctrinal foundation, which, though laid out in a precise fashion, is susceptible to change over time. It must also comprehend the functions an ideology performs for its believers, its effects on these believers or on their adversaries, and the social uses to which those whom it addresses put it. Finally, such an analysis can try to identify the broader context, for an ideology exists rarely in isolation; on the contrary, it is in constant confrontation with other ideologies, sometimes to the point of forming an entire system of interaction in which each ideology feeds on its opposite, or responds to that which it perceives to be its enemy.

As for propaganda, it was of capital importance for first the Bolsheviks and then for communist parties of the German social-democratic party model. As time went by, they introduced substantial innovations and modernized the concept. Thus Lenin, in *What is to be Done?* (1902), his highly influential work dedicated to the problems of organization and agitation, took on and adapted Plekhanov's ideas of 1891 (a time when the

Russian social-democratic party was greatly interested in these questions). 'The propagandist offers a mass of ideas to one or a few individuals,' wrote Plekhanov. 'The agitator presents one single idea, or a few ideas, to a whole mass of people'. Lenin held that the mission of the propagandist and of propaganda was to intensify class-consciousness. Propaganda should endlessly 'organize political revelations', link an event to a larger phenomenon or, as Hannah Arendt noted later in her classic work *The Origins of Totalitarianism*, debunk mysteries and suggest that there is no such thing as chance or accidental reality, but that, on the contrary, everything can be explained.[14] Propaganda thus is closely linked to ideology and culture: as real know-how serving so-called knowledge, it is the keen knife-edge and the medium of culture and ideology.

These preliminary reflections serve to orientate my remarks, which will focus on the culture, as reflected in ideology and propaganda, of the two most powerful Western communist parties, the French and Italian, between 1947 and 1953, the hottest phase of the Cold War. This period of radical, virulent, sometimes violent confrontation of communist and anti-communist propaganda and ideologies left little room for intermediate positions (such as, for example, those of the neutralists). The resulting polarization offers many advantages for the observer: the sheer excess it engendered stripped the underlying ideology, in this case communism, down to the essentials.

The principal intent of my contribution is to underline the points in common of communist ideology in France and Italy, as it was understood at the leadership level of the PCF and the PCI. But I will also spell out, more briefly, the differences between them, and then note some of the effects, receptions and usages of this ideology and this propaganda. Given the space at my disposal, I will focus my study on the French Communist Party (PCF), and use the Italian Communist Party (PCI) only as its comparative counterpart.

COMMON CHARACTERISTICS

During these 'cold years', communist ideology was devoid of everything that disguised, in other periods, its raw message: it corresponded perfectly to Alain Besançon's model of 'confrontation communism', or 'hard communism', to use the expression of Martin Malia. It gave pre-eminence to Marxist-Leninist doctrine, which at Stalin's initiative had become, by the end of the 1920s and beginning of the 1930s, a state ideology and the common tongue of first the Communist International and then the Cominform, created in 1947.[15] It was codified according to certain schematic principles, including the basic affirmation that the history of humanity is the history of the class struggle. Thus the world is built around an irreducible antagonism. On one side, capitalism and imperialism (the roots of all evil, and in particular of war and poverty), private property and man's exploitation of man provoke alienation, with the state, and even democracy, if it in fact exists, as mere superstructures at the service of the ruling class. On the other side is communism, synonymous with happiness, peace and prosperity: the collectivization of the means of production will assure the well-being of humankind and, once over the necessary stage of the dictatorship of the proletariat, a superior form of political organization, respecting all liberties, will come to pass. This doctrine called for a systematic defence of the USSR and, after 1945, of the entire socialist camp. It established the primacy of the working class in current and future society, which determined political strategy and spawned a veritable mythology. It made the party sacred, governed by democratic centralism. And it claimed to be both wholly new and a synthesis of pre-existing ideological currents, such as those of the utopians.[16] But without doubt its most salient characteristic in this period is what Raymond Aron described at the time: 'communism is defined less by the acceptance of Marxist theories (historical materialism, dialectic, class struggle, the crisis of capitalism etc.) than by the recognition of the USSR as the first socialist state, and of the communist party, in each country, as the sole depository of the historical mission earlier attributed to the proletariat'.[17]

Communist propaganda on both sides of the Alps focused on several points: anti-imperialism; anti-capitalism; the denunciation of parties and peoples considered, in France and in Italy, to be lackeys of the United States; defence of 'national independence' threatened by American imperialism; the combat against the threats of war imputed to the United States and the struggle for peace incarnated by the USSR (see the two comparable formulas, that of the Bureau Politique (BP) of the PCF of 30 September 1948, which would become a slogan: 'The people of France will not, will never, wage war on the Soviet Union', and that proclaimed by Palmiro Togliatti in March 1949 in the Italian parliament: 'Against the Soviet Union war will not be waged, because the people will stop you from doing so'); the unconditional defence of socialism; the strict condemnation of all 'Titoist', 'Trotskyist' or 'opportunist' deviation; approval of repression and terror used against 'enemies of the people'; praise for the accomplishments of the USSR and other socialist states and, finally, repeated homage to their leaders, primarily Stalin, who was the object of a veritable cult that reached its peak in 1949 on his seventieth birthday, celebrated by communists world-wide.

It is not possible to examine the above list in any detail; its contents have, in any event, inspired a number of studies in both France and Italy. I will instead take a single – French – example to illustrate the virulence of communist propaganda (which, it is true, found its counterpart in the opposing camp) and, drawing on the recently opened PCF archives, will describe the manner in which the PCF leadership developed its propaganda themes.

The example I have chosen (from among thousands of other potential examples) concerns the manner in which French communists denounced American domination. The PCF did not hesitate to compare the United States to the Nazi regime, citing in support its ideology (racism), its internal repression of opponents and the influence it exercised over Europe as a whole. The journalist Pierre Courtade made it his specialty, decrying, in *L'Humanité* 'the concentration camp of Marshallized Europe', where the ideas of General Marshall seemed to come straight from 'a document discovered in the ruins of the Berlin chancellery, or in the cellars of the Eagle's Nest at Berchtesgaden'.[18] The establishment of American bases on French soil was depicted by communist propaganda as a second invasion, and a second foreign occupation.

PCF archives show the care taken by the party leadership in shaping these arguments. The impact of the 30 September 1948 declaration by the BP of the PCF – 'the French people will not, will never, wage war on the Soviet Union' – was closely monitored. The secretariat, on 4 October, 'noted the profound repercussions' of the declaration and decided to 'recommend [its] study to all party cells'; however, on 22 November, doubtless worried by the excessive use made of it by certain sectors of the party, the same secretariat specified that care must be taken such that this phrase 'not be used out of context'. The BP also examined the impact of its statement and spelled out its deeper meaning in its session of 20 January 1949: 'Solemnly affirm in speeches that communists do not consider the USSR to be a foreign power like any other, and that every progressive man has two homelands: his own and the USSR'. This internal documentation further reveals the jubilation felt by many leaders when the time came to do battle. Jacques Duclos, who had been sharply called to order during the constituent meeting of the Cominform in September 1947 in Poland, exclaimed a month later, during the Central Committee meeting of 29–30 October 1947 that triggered the PCF's real entry into the Cold War: 'this formula of the American party [i.e. the socialist party], I'm sure it will be very successful in France (they were furious when we shoved it down their throats today during a session of the Parlement)'. The rapid adoption of expressions from the East in the language of French communists was also very noticeable. Waldeck Rochet, who was in charge of peasant affairs already before the Cold War, had tried to reconcile communist and republican traditions in French rural areas. Also at the Central Committee of October 1947 he declared that the PCF must bring together 'peasant workers, that is, small and medium-sized agriculturalists, farmers, tenant farmers and agricultural workers' against the 'rich peasants and the kulaks'.[19]

All propaganda techniques were mobilized, including theatre, radio and cinema. But the communist parties were a little lacking in these areas. Cinema, above all, was their Achilles' heel; they produced their own propaganda films, to be screened during meetings, and encouraged the production of fiction films as an alternative to American cinema, which they denounced and tried to boycott, but they were largely unsuccessful against the tide of Hollywood films that swept across French and Italian screens and were received with much popular enthusiasm. Quite apart from the extraordinary diversity of the forms of propaganda (tracts, posters, newspapers, brochures, meetings, demonstrations, strikes, petitions, etc.), two characteristics particularly mark this period.

The first was the intense mobilization of the whole of the communist system of action, both the party as an organization, with its apparatus but also with its elected representatives, as well as the municipalities, unions and every kind of association imaginable. The effect was such that, just as Lenin would have wanted, even the smallest individual event (for example, a specific problem of housing or salary raises) was set against a much broader political backdrop (most frequently, the struggle against American imperialism and for the defence of national independence and peace, exaltation of the USSR and reminders of the benefits brought by communist parties).

The second aspect is the intensity of militant life in those Cold War years. The party demanded a total commitment and a strong receptiveness, which were transformed into unbridled activism as a result of what Daniel Gaxie has called the 'over-regenerative effect' typical of a total institution.[20] In effect, 'a mass organization built on militancy can only subsist if it functions continually at something close to its peak rhythm. To accept a slowing-down of militancy interrupts the satisfaction that can be gleaned from it and risks losing members over the long run'.[21] To maintain this rhythm, communists struck out ever harder at their adversaries, thus maintaining a polarization, both to strengthen among their believers the feeling of belonging to a camp, and to put them in the situation of having either to undergo a psychologically humiliating retreat or to reinforce their identification with the cause.[22] Total commitment surpasses all limits: it invades private life, which in turn practically ceases to exist or becomes completely politicized.

DIFFERENCES

Though there were strong similarities between the two communist parties, especially in this period, it is also true that there were certain notable differences. The score might have been the same, but the PCF played it *allegro vivace*, while the PCI preferred *allegro moderato*.

First, with respect to the ideology of the two communist parties: the PCF's was monochrome, entirely modeled after the Soviet example even when it strove to incorporate certain French ideological trends (Guesdism, or a certain republican, national and Jacobin concept), and was accompanied by the discrediting and permanent stigmatization (through abuse, insults and threats) of all opposing ideologies. For its part, the PCI's ideology, though subject to the Cominform line, had its own particularities: reference to Stalin was somewhat less obsessive than in France; confrontation with liberal and Croceian thought, though hard-line in form and content, continued without, however, systematically turning to denigration; Gramsci's works began to be published, though in a truncated form and only by transforming their author into 'an inoffensive icon' (to use Paolo Alatri's phrase); after a hardening of relations with intellectuals, marked by the exclusion of Elio Vittorini, a slight softening of the cultural line began in 1950–51.

Above all, it was the concept of the ideological combat to be fought (and its corresponding propaganda) that differed. The PCI sought to avoid being ghettoized. This constant worry became a strategic priority for Palmiro Togliatti who, as PCI archives show, imposed it on his comrades starting in November 1947 and for the whole of that period. It can be seen in the analytical nuance, the refusal of certain simplifications, the art of tactical maneuvering, the efforts to make contact, including with opposing forces, all illustrated in Togliatti's statement to the Central Committee of 11 and 13 November 1947: 'When one starts to say everyone is gray, one no longer practices politics, one is blind, and walks in darkness'. The PCI certainly benefited from the support of Pietro Nenni's Socialist Party, which became an 'appendix party' (to use the expression of the Italian historian Pasquale Amato). It was also open to contact with Catholics, though not without an ulterior motive (up until 1949 the PCI cherished the hope that the Christian Democrats would reject the Atlantic Pact) and not without difficulty, just as it also kept contacts with neutralists (whom the PCF condemned).

The PCF was in a more difficult situation. It could only count on progressives, of secular, republican, radical, socialist or Christian origin, which included several famous personalities (Pierre Cot, Emmanuel d'Astier de la Vigerie, Gilbert de Chambrun, l'Abbé Boulier, Henri Denis etc.), but hardly any 'troops'. However, the PCF could also on occasion display real tactical ability. Thus it ably worked together with the Gaullists to demolish the European Defence Community. Its campaigns for the defence of national independence (much more vigorous than those of the PCI), notably in cultural matters, its attacks against Coca-Cola or the 'American occupation' – 'Are we being coca-colonized?' asked *L'Humanité* on 8 November 1949)[23] – found a reasonable echo in those sectors of French public opinion traditionally open to anti-Americanism.[24] In contrast, the anti-Americanism of communists in Italy was more political than cultural given the great popular attraction for the American way of life, customs and civilization, due in large part to the intense fascination with American cinema.[25] In the same way, the PCF's denunciation of German rearmament found a certain success beyond its own membership; the issue, for obvious reasons, was of little interest to the PCI. Finally, the PCF, like its Italian counterpart, reached out to Christians, notably concerning the evocative theme of peace. The Stockholm Appeal offered the chance to work closely with these groups: it garnered from nine and a half to 14 million French signatures and more than 16 million Italian signatures, often from people very far removed from communism.[26] However, these undeniable successes of the PCF were limited by its doctrinal intransigence and its political rigidity, both of which kept it in an isolation which was, in fact, to the liking of a large number of its leaders and militants, whereas the PCI, for its part, continually sought to consolidate its links to non-communist groups, particularly Catholics.

RECEPTION AND PRACTICE

For the most active militants and sympathizers, communist ideology and propaganda formed an orderly whole that gave coherence and sense to their lives. The all-encompassing binary perception of reality (following the principle of good guys and bad guys, 'us' and 'them') had its drawbacks (it required permanent mobilization), but also proved to be very reassuring. It has, in fact, inspired recently in France (and in Italy) an impressive wave of accounts, essays, autobiographies, novels, films and plays: depending on the author, the tone is variously acerbic, amused, ironic, mocking or nostalgic when depicting this period of firmly anchored certitudes, often associated with the youth of those who evoke it.

Thus it is that this ideology and propaganda characterize those who identify themselves with them. All the opinion polls undertaken in France in the 1950s by IFOP make this clear. To take a single example: in August 1950, 52 per cent of French respondents overall claimed that, in the case of conflict between the US and the USSR, their sympathies would lie with the United States, versus 17 per cent who favored the USSR. But 84 per cent of communists lined up on the side of the USSR, while supporters of centrist and right-wing parties expressed the same level of support for the United States. For their part, socialist voters were 58 per cent in favor of the United States, 2 per cent for the USSR and the rest undecided.[27] This anti-American, pro-Soviet bias of the communist electorate was evident with respect to all questions of international policy (Marshall Plan, Atlantic Pact, Korean War, etc.). Given its strong working-class roots, this characteristic was thus not only political but social, one of the original aspects of communism in France.

All the polls from that period reveal that workers were quite distinct from other social categories in their clear distrust of (not to say hostility towards) the United States, and by their relatively (compared to other socio-professional categories) pro-Soviet feeling. However, this latter sentiment remained very moderate: in truth, the USSR never really inspired overwhelming enthusiasm among them. Thus, in October 1947, 47 per cent of workers expressed confidence in the United States (versus 60 per cent of salaried workers and civil servants, 64 of farmers, 72 per cent of business people and 73 per cent of professional classes) and 18 per cent in the USSR (versus 8 per cent of salaried workers, civil servants and farmers and 4 per cent of business people and professionals).[28] The same phenomenon was apparent in Italy where, according to a Doxa poll of December 1955, communist workers were the only group to believe that the USSR was the country in which workers were happiest, and even then only by a slim majority.[29] Communist workers were undoubtedly pro-Soviet by conviction but also sought to provoke those they considered to be their enemies: the 'bourgeois', the 'bosses', and the 'social traitors'. Some managed, like the intellectuals, to turn a completely blind eye to Soviet reality, but others used the USSR to their own ends in their daily struggles. Thus steelworkers of Italian origin in the Lorraine, very much under communist influence, decided in March 1953 to respond to the call of the PCF for a work stoppage and a moment of contemplation on the day of the funeral of the master of the Kremlin, as a sign of mourning. But on their own initiative, and against the advice of the PCF, they did the same on two other occasions, for the deaths of Fausto Coppi and Humphrey Bogart.[30]

This gives rise to consideration of the social uses of communist ideology and propaganda. In this respect, one can perhaps propose a double hypothesis. On one hand, the sharp edge of communist ideology and propaganda both reflected and reinforced strong social conflicts, particularly in industries and, in Italy, in both factories and the countryside. The tendency of a certain number of working-class groups to resort to conflict and confrontation was thereby encouraged, and even legitimized. From this stemmed threats to the 'bourgeois' and the 'fat cats' and the use of Stalin as bogeyman (or *Baffone*, the Italian term). The link between ideology and the social condition was thus very close, acting as a sort of cement, which explains to a degree the strength and the duration of communist commitment in certain working-class circles. On the other hand, the spread of the themes of communist ideology and propaganda did run into serious obstacles and could not overcome certain limitations. First, it must be forcefully repeated, in France (as in Italy, and in the rest of Western Europe) it was anti-communism, in all its variants on the left and on the right, both spiritual and moral, which was the majority view – except among intellectuals, which may explain the considerable errors of appreciation of those historians who insist that communism had the upper hand. In addition, even communist sympathizers, and particularly workers, kept a critical mind and did not passively absorb the communist party line. Rather, they displayed a real selective capacity, notably concerning the USSR and the USA. If we believe the polls, as cited above, the USSR was never a model or example for them. And workers, including communists, overwhelmingly preferred American to Soviet films. In 1950, an observer of the Centre National de la Cinématographie stated that 'in working-class suburbs, despite the well-known opinions of the majority of the population, attendance at American films increases every year. The same trend exists in the East [and] in the Lille region. ... The Marseilles region is also witnessing an ever-clearer preference for American films'. In 1954, according to research by the Dourdin institute, 25 per cent of the workers questioned preferred American films (versus 15 per cent and 14 per cent among the middle and upper-middle classes).[31] Moreover, this trend did not merely represent cinematographic success; much of the American way of life and 'civilization' shown in these films also seemed to hold a strong attraction for French workers. In general, American propaganda addressed the individual and seemed more welcoming and human, while Soviet and communist propaganda, aimed at the masses, was more austere and impersonal.

A product of an international confrontation, the Cold War had a considerable impact in France and Italy, being relayed domestically by two powerful communist parties and amplifying already-existing conflicts in each of these societies. In France, as in Italy, the confrontation was violent, and developed into a kind of 'war culture' (Stéphane Audoin-Rouzeau, Annette Becker).[32] It permitted polemical and political passions to be unleashed against that essential (according to Carl Schmitt) political category, the 'enemy', which was to be scorned, criticized and detested. Yet, despite its intensity and continual stoking, this confrontation was always mastered and controlled on both sides by communists and anti-communists alike.

NOTES

1. A first version of this text was published in French: Marc Lazar, 'Idéologie et propagande des partis communistes français et italien durant la guerre froide' in Jean Delmas, Jean Kessler (eds.), *Renseignement et propagande pendant la guerre froide (1947–1953)* (Brussels: Complexe 1999) pp.183–94. This is a considerably modified and updated version of that text.
2. On these questions, see (in French) notably: Bertrand Badie, *Culture et politique* (Paris: Economica 1993); Philippe d'Iribarne, 'Des cultures politiques' in Philippe d'Iribarne (ed.), *Culture et mondialisation* (Paris: Seuil 1998) pp.277–98; Jacques Lagroye, *Sociologie politique* (Paris: Dalloz-Presses de la FNS 1997) pp.172–3 and pp.372–83; Yves Schemeil, 'Les cultures politiques' in Madeleine Gravitz et Jean Leca (eds.), *Traité de science politique* (Paris: PUF 1985) vol. 3 pp.237–307. In my analysis, I do not presume to provide a formal definition of political culture, but rather to propose an operational definition.
3. Respectively: Clifford Geertz, *The Interpretations of Culture* (New York Basic Books 1973), Pitirim A. Sorokin, *Social and Cultural Dynamics* (New York-Cincinnati: American Book Co. 1937–41) quoted in Bernard Valade, 'Culture' in Raymond Boudon (ed.), *Traité de sociologie* (Paris: PUF 1992) p.487, and Edgar Morin, *L'esprit du temps* (Paris: Grasset 1962) p.12.
4. See Jean-François Bayart, *L'illusion identitaire* (Paris: Fayard 1996).
5. See (in French) Philippe Braud, *Sociologie politique* (Paris: Montchrestien 1992) particularly p.163; Jacques Lagroye, ibid; Serge Berstein (ed.), *Les cultures politiques en France* (Paris: Seuil 1999); Daniel Cefaï (ed.), *Cultures politiques* (Paris: PUF 2001); Jean-François Sirinelli and Eric Vigne, 'Des cultures politiques', in Jean-François Sirinelli (ed.), *Histoire des droites en France* (Paris: Gallimard 1992) Vol.2, pp.I–XI. Denis Constant-Martin, in 'La découverte des cultures politiques. Esquisse d'une approche comparatiste à partir des expériences africaines' *Les Cahiers du CERI* 2 (1992), accords a prime role to political affectivity in political culture.
6. Sirinelli and Vigne, 'Des cultures politiques' (note 5) pp.iii–iv.
7. See the clarification by Serge Berstein, 'Rites et rituels politiques' in Jean-François Sirinelli (ed.), *Dictionnaire historique de la vie politique française au XXe siècle* (Paris: PUF 1995) pp.929–32 and David Kertzer, *Ritual, Politics and Power* (New Haven: Yale UP 1988).
8. For other organizations, though the remark applies to the French Communist Party, the sociologist Edgar Schein, in *Organizational Culture and Leadership* (London: Sage 1986) calls 'basic underlying assumptions', those values which have become invisible, unconscious and taken for granted by those who have totally assimilated them.
9. Subculture analysis is particularly developed in Italy, with respect to the red subcultures in Central Italy and the white subculture of the North-East of the peninsula. Out of the extensive bibliography one can refer, for that which concerns Italian communism, to Marc Lazar, *Maisons rouges. Histoire des partis communistes français et italien de la Libération à nos jours* (Paris: Aubier 1992). See also, for comparative comments on Europe, Percy Allum, *State and Society in Western Europe* (Cambridge: Polity Press 1995) pp.147–52 and the theoretical propositions of Alessandro Pizzorno, *Le radici della politica assoluta* (Milan: Feltrinelli 1993).
10. Maurice Duverger, *Les partis politiques* (Paris: Seuil 1981) p.572.
11. Raymond Boudon, *L'idéologie* (Paris: Fayard 1986) p.52.
12. Pierre Ansart, *Les idéologies politiques* (Paris: PUF 1974) p.10.
13. Ibid. p.15.
14. Hannah Arendt, *The Origins of Totalitarianism* (New York: Harcourt Brace Jovanovich 1973).
15. See Dominique Colas, *Le léninisme. Philosophie et sociologie politiques du léninisme* (Paris: PUF 1982) and Georges Labica, *Le marxisme-léninisme* (Paris: Bruno Huisman 1984).
16. See, for example, on this theme, Alain Besançon, *Les origines intellectuelles du léninisme* (Paris: Calmann-Lévy 1977) and the articles by Yolène Dilas-Rocherieux, 'Le système associatif 1840–1850' *Communisme* 28 (1991) pp.49–68 and 'Communisme et socialisme: questions de définition', *Communisme* 45–6 (1996) pp.115–24.

17. Raymond Aron, Postscript, *Le Dieu des ténèbres*, by Arthur Koestler, Ignazio Silone, Richard Wright, André Gide, Louis Fischer, Stephen Spender (introduction by Richard Crossman) (Paris: Calmann-Lévy 1950) p.291.
18. Articles published in *L'Humanité* of 22 June 1948 and 19 Oct. 1948, quoted by Philippe Roger in *Rêves et cauchemars américains. Les Etats-Unis au miroir de l'opinion publique française (1945–1953)* (Villeneuve d'Ascq: Presses Universitaires Septentrion 1996) pp.247–8.
19. All these quotations come from the Archives of the Secretariat, the Political Office and the Central Committee of the French Communist Party, Place du Colonel Fabien, Paris.
20. Daniel Gaxie, 'Economie des partis et rétribution du militantisme', *Revue française de science politique* 1 (Feb. 1977) pp.123–54. The concept of a total institution is taken from Erving Goffman, *Asylums* (New York: Doubleday 1961). See the pages that Jeanine Verdès-Leroux dedicates to the application of this concept to the PCF in *Au service du Parti* (Paris: Fayard-Minuit 1983) pp.109–56 and the remarks of Marie-Claire Lavabre, Marc Lazar 'Au service du Parti', *Communisme* 5 (1984) pp.138–42 and of Claude Pennetier, Bernard Pudal 'Ecrire son autobiographie (les autobiographies d'institution, 1931–1939)', *Genèses* 23 (juin 1996) pp.53–75.
21. Gaxie, 'Economie des partis' (note 20) p.149.
22. See Eric Hirsch, 'Sacrifice for the Cause: Group Processes, Recruitment and Commitment in a Student Social Movement', *American Sociological Review* 55 (1988) pp. 243–54.
23. Quoted by Richard Kuisel, 'Coca-Cola au pays des buveurs de vin', *L'Histoire* 94 (Nov. 1986) p.25. See also Kuisel, *Seducing the French: The Dilemma of Americanization* (Berkeley-Los Angeles: Univ. of California Press 1993).
24. Jean-Baptiste Duroselle, *La France et les Etats-Unis des origines à nos jours* (Paris: Seuil 1976).
25. See for example G.P. Brunetta and David Ellwood (eds.), *Hollywood in Europa 1945–1960* (Florence: Ponte alle Grazie 1991); Pier Paolo D'Attorre (ed.), *Nemici per la pelle. Sogno americano e mito sovietico nell'Italia contemporanea* (Milan: Franco Angeli 1991) et Stephen Gundle, *I comunisti italiani tra Hollywood e Mosca* (Florence: Giunti 1995).
26. For France, 14 million is the official number put forward by the PCF, while the figure of 9.5 million is taken from an internal document of the organizational secretary of the PCF, August Lecoeur. See Olivier Lecour Grandmaison, 'Le Mouvement de la Paix pendant la guerre froide: le cas français' *Communisme* 18–19 (1988) p.128. For Italy, see Giovanni Gozzini, Renzo Martinelli, *Storia del Partito comunista italiano. Dall'attentato a Togliatti all'VIII congresso* (Turin: Einaudi 1988) p.174.
27. Roger, *Rêves et cauchemars américains* (note 18) p.132.
28. Ibid. p.151.
29. Doxa poll conducted among 149 workers with communist sympathies and 210 non-communist workers. The poll shows that 38 per cent of communist workers thought workers were happiest in the United States (as opposed to 71 per cent of non-communist workers), while 37 per cent designated the USSR (versus 1 per cent of non-communist workers). Quoted by Gozzini and Martinelli, *Storia del Partito comunista italiano* (note 26) p.461, note 40.
30. Fabrice Montebello, 'Joseph Staline et Humphrey Bogart: l'homme des ouvriers. Essai sur la construction sociale de la figure du 'héros' en milieu ouvrier', *Politix* 24 (1993) pp.115–33.
31. Fabrice Montebello, *Spectacle cinématographique et classe ouvrière. Longwy: 1944–1950* (history thesis, Université de Lyon 2 1997) p.532.
32. Stéphane Audoin-Rouzeau, Annette Becker, 'Violence et consentement: la 'culture de guerre' du premier conflit mondial' in Jean-Pierre Rioux and Jean-François Sirinelli (eds.), *Pour une histoire culturelle* (Paris: Seuil 1997) pp.251–71 and *14–18. Retrouver la guerre* (Paris: Gallimard 2000).

12

The Propaganda of the Marshall Plan in Italy in a Cold War Context

DAVID W. ELLWOOD

In 1990, at a post-Cold War conference held to discuss the impact of American culture in all its forms in the ideologically radicalized Italy of the 1950s, the veteran left-wing intellectual Enzo Forcella proclaimed: 'The American myths kept their promises and won through!'[1] Forcella was referring specifically to the images purveyed by the documentaries of the American way of life which accompanied the Marshall Plan, particularly those showing workers arriving at factories at the wheels of their own cars, an unthinkable notion in the Italy of 1949.[2]

We now know that European audiences always adopted whatever America was offering as far as this corresponded to their needs and no further, and that the cinema was one of the key sites of this filtering and appropriation process. The mechanisms at work are well illustrated by a long and interesting analysis of European attitudes to America supplied to the US intelligence services by an anonymous Italian observer, just after that country's elections of June 1953: '95% of all Europeans – friends and enemies of America – judge American society by what they see at the cinema', declared the source. From Hollywood's products many had taken away a dreadful impression of the country, of its crime and corruption, and of the venality and brutality of its ruling groups in particular. But the medium

> ... was useful above all in reinforcing the European admiration for the American standard of living, for American technique... Undoubtedly film has given the US a propaganda triumph, to the extent that it has reminded Europeans of their traditionally optimistic vision of the 'American paradise'.[3]

Whatever the pattern of adoption and rejection, Forcella's opinion confirms the essential role played by the cinema in all its forms as a transmitter of the American inspiration and example during Italy's parallel experience of modernization and Cold War. It is clearly impossible to separate out the long-term functions of Hollywood from the concentrated drive of the mass of documentaries which accompanied the Marshall Plan. But we can suggest that if the message of the Marshall films expressed an invitation to follow the American example all the way, the feature films on the same programme demonstrated, for better or for worse, where the road might lead. Alternatively, we might hypothesise that whilst the concept of productivity-based growth came to furnish the key modernizing concept on the supply side of the market transformations under way in the 1950s and 1960s, a force like the cinema worked on the demand side of the same social and economic changes, accelerating and channelling the evolutions of mentality and behaviour.

PROSPERITY AND DEMOCRACY

It was a Marshall Planner, Harlan Cleveland, who invented the notion of the 'revolution of rising expectations', a metaphor for the qualitative change in the dynamics of modernization which had happened at that post-Great War cross-roads, where mass production for mass consumption on the Fordist model had encountered the new mass communication media, and the newest versions of mass democracy.[4] It was the task of Marshall Plan propaganda to guide this revolution in countries like Italy, awakening elites and masses alike to the universal significance of the connection Americans made between prosperity and democracy. America's historical success in running democratic capitalism was to be transformed into a recipe for the rest. The key question in Italy, according to the *New York Times* correspondent in Rome, Michael L. Hoffmann, writing in June 1949, was not the defeat of communism. It was instead whether the country could develop its own authentic, viable form of capitalism. A real capitalistic mentality, unafraid of risks, enthusiastically in favour of individual initiative, was 'as rare in Italy as a communist on Wall St.', according to Hoffmann's sources. The market was divided horizontally, a huge gap separating the luxury level from that of the workers and peasants:

> Italian industrialists have never shown much interest in the job of adapting their products to the mass market, with the result that the scale of their operations remains small and their costs high. The idea of persuading the low income consumer to feel the need for something he's never had, using advertising, and then to give it to him at a price he can afford, could be the Marshall Plan's biggest contribution to Italy – if it gets anywhere.

Italian conservatives were far too inclined to use force to hold communism down, Hoffmann insisted, instead of trying the remedy of mass consumption and mass production. Italian industrialists rigged what feeble market there was and encouraged the unemployed to emigrate. If this mentality could be changed, Marshall Plan administrators expected other obstacles such as high interest rates and the obsession with frugality to disappear as a consequence, Michael Hoffmann reported.[5] The Marshall Plan administrator, Paul Hoffman, was more blunt: '(The Europeans) learned that [the USA] the land of full shelves and bulging shops, made possible by high productivity and good wages, and that its prosperity may be emulated elsewhere by those who will work towards it'.[6]

So the Marshall Plan in a country like Italy was never just an abstract affair of economic numbers to do with loans, grants, investment, production, productivity etc, even if these were its key operating tools. Nor was it merely another weapon in America's Cold War anti-communist crusade, though all concerned were well aware that the Italian communists, operating as an 'indigenous group', had an immense psychological and political advantage over the trans-Atlantic superpower. Hence the ERP effort aimed to get as close as possible to the people it was benefitting, at all levels of society, and particularly in the relations between the citizen and the state. The challenge was to channel attitudes, mentalities, and expectations in the direction Americans understood as an ever-greater prosperity for an ever-greater majority. 'You Too Can Be Like Us': that was the message accompanying the Plan in Italy, the largest of its kind in any European country. And cinema was its preferred medium of communication.[7]

'What the European worker wants first of all', wrote one of the directors of the ERP field headquarters in Paris, was 'a promise of a larger stake in his country's economy – enough income to enjoy better food, a new suit, a picnic or the movies, less cramped living quarters, a chance to retire when he is old'.[8] Beyond anti-communism, beyond the figures on production and trade, beyond even the vision of a new era of European co-operation, this was the promise of the Marshall Plan in its heyday and it was the task of the propaganda effort to bring that promise home to Europeans everywhere.

But there was deep, structural diffidence about all this in every quarter in Italy, and it is worth noting that the Marshall Plan is not celebrated every ten years in this country as it is in nations like Austria and Germany, according to Hans-Jürgen Schröder in his new study of ERP propaganda in those countries.[9] After 20 years of Fascist propaganda, followed by that of the Nazi-Fascists and the Allies during the war, then the tremendous ideological confrontation of the April 1948 elections – with the propaganda of both sides heavily subsidized by their super-power sponsors[10] – it was not surprising that the *general population* gave little credit to 'information' bombardments coming from any new quarter. It is now very hard for us to

FIGURE 1

The Productivity Clock from a Marshall Plan exhibit. It shows how little time an American worker needs to buy the various products.

National Archives, Record Group 286, European Recovery Program, Photographic Archive

FIGURE 2

'Constructing Prosperity' – a mobile Marshall Plan exhibit in Italy

National Archives, Record Group 286, European Recovery Program, Photographic Archive

reconstruct the cognitive, imaginative dissonance involved in moving from 'Believe, Obey, Fight' to 'Prosperity Means Liberty' in a mere five years.

ITALIAN RELUCTANCE

Let us now consider the other major sources of doubt and resistance. Within *the government*, the Christian Democrat De Gasperi made no secret of how alien and bewildering the entire 'Piano Marshall' idea was to him, and there began an enormous effort up and down the state structure to contain its effects, politically and especially economically, as new studies have been showing. Mario del Pero writes: '... [the government] opted for an ambiguous economic policy where anti-inflationary monetary policies ... combined with the protection of several sectors of the Italian economy, and the preservation of part of the corporatist structure inherited from the Fascist era'.[11]

There was a nationalistic streak at work here, and as the leading diplomat and historian Sergio Romano has argued, it led to an intense effort to 'defend our economic sovereignty and pay the price of the loss of our military sovereignty'. After being forced to abandon notions of neutralism in the face of the Atlantic choice, De Gasperi and his ministers then seized on European integration as a face-saving alternative – an 'alibi', Romano calls it – covering the price to be paid for the salvation of the governing group's very restricted idea of Italy's economic future.[12]

This effort was reinforced by another source of resistance to the message of the Marshall Plan: *the industrialists*. The ERP men found an unlikely adversary in the head of the principal industrialists association (Confindustria), the formidable and influential figure of Angelo Costa. Exasperated by the ceaseless preaching and pressuring of the Marshall Planners, which increased visibly after the Korean outbreak, Costa accused them of understanding little or nothing of the context in which they were operating. The Genovese shipping magnate explained that to begin with, unlike those of the American constitution, the institutions of the Italian State did not rest on a firm foundation of historical legitimacy; instead the laws of Rome were regarded as a form of legalized robbery, and as such were systematically evaded. As for the economic planning demanded by the ERP, with targets for investments, GNP, imports etc., this could only cause damage and anyway the country had already recovered from the war without such measures being necessary.

Costa was implicitly opposed to the spread of large-scale industry and urbanization, and now expressed all his scepticism concerning the culture of productivity and high wages. No matter how cheap synthetic fibres became, he insisted, Italian women would always prefer clothes made in the home with natural materials; tinned food might be sold very cheaply, but Italian traditions of cooking would always be preferred. Small firms and traditional artisan skills would be central to Italy's future just as they had been in the past. As for the concept of productivity, it ignored the basic difference betwen Italy and America: there capital was cheap, labour dear; at home the situation was the opposite.[13]

Costa was a practicing Catholic and the *Church of Rome* provided yet another source of difficulty. The Vatican was quite clear that militant communism in all its forms was enemy number 1, and had demonstrated its fervour in this belief with its all-out effort in the 1948 elections and with an Anathema pronounced against Marxist-inspired political parties and their members in 1949. Yet the Vatican refused to embrace America in an unrestricted alliance against the forces of evil. Diplomatic efforts to set in motion a sort of Holy War were checked for various reasons (including Congress's refusal to include Spain in the ERP).[14] More serious were the doubts about US values and life-styles, doubts which had emerged at the end of the nineteenth century but which now took on a more urgent form. Like many conservative thinkers in the 1930s, Pius XII was inclined to see common defects in Soviet communism and Americanism: an obsession with material output, technical progress and consumption, a standard of life defined economically. But only in America were individualism and secularization so openly proclaimed and encouraged, only there was licentiousness commercialized and godlessness so flaunted. That was why the mass media held such awful responsibilities, as the Pope had reminded a group of Hollywood producers in 1946.[15]

The Vatican made its own efforts to come to terms with the revolution of rising expectations – Pius XII was the first to use openly the word 'progress' – and had no reservations about the benefits of American aid in all its forms. But at the same time as the Marshall Plan propaganda was purveying a vision of life which was economic, private, consumerist, limitless and available for emulation, the Vatican and Christian Democrat politicians were encouraging the emergence of a strong state which was socially-oriented, collective and welfarist. The Marshall Plan eventually found itself obliged to make a serious effort to adapt to this reality.[16]

COMMUNIST OPPOSITION

Where then did all this leave the formal opposition, the supreme adversary, the mass *Italian Communist Party* (PCI)? With the benefit of hindsight, and much detailed analysis, we now know that these years saw the birth of a complex live-and-let-live deal between the Christan Democrats and the Communists, a long-term arrangement which succeeded – just – in stabilizing Italian democracy over the entire Cold War period. The workings of this bargain defied the logic of the Cold War in both its Soviet and American versions, and recently revealed documentation shows just how exasperated the Americans became as a result of it. But the ERP started just after the frantic 1948 elections and the insurrectionary outbreak which followed the attempt on party leader Togliatti's life. At that precarious time the two parties were still groping painfully towards this form of peaceful co-existence, and its successful outcome was far from certain.[17]

After being thrown out of the government in 1947 and heavily defeated in the elections, the PCI was caught between different pressures. Its uncontestable, uncontested obedience to the new Soviet line laid down at the birth of the Cominform did not only mean that total opposition to the ERP was obligatory. At the famous meeting in Poland, the French and Italian parties had been heavily criticized both for their belief in the importance of traditional institutional politics, and their failures on this front. This meant that the PCI was neither willing nor able to use Parliamentary mechanisms to organize an effective critique of the government's approach to the Marshall Plan, nor be part of any Parliament-run control system for its application. Opposition to the Plan would instead be largely extra-parliamentary, in the streets, in the factories, in the front organizations and media the Party controlled. But at the base of the party quite other priorities ruled. These were years of extreme hardship, suffering, deprivation and a ruthless shaking out of labour by the *padroni* in the outdated and overburdened industrial structures left over from Fascism. Power had shifted decisively to them with the election results and no holds were barred. So the pressure on the PCI leadership for mass action came as much from below, from the near 2.5 million members the party counted in these years.[18]

Seen from this perspective, the ERP offer looked extremely embarrassing to the party. Here was a scheme which, whatever its strings, promised immediate relief on a mass scale, a promise of industrial revival, and a long-term future of inclusion in a prosperous international community. The Soviets had nothing of the sort to offer and in the elections had shown how little it really cared for Italy and the PCI – for instance by refusing to surrender Trieste, renegotiate the 1946 Peace Treaty or aid the country's admission to the UN. In this situation it was an uphill struggle for the party to proclaim convincingly that the whole ERP scheme was a plot to colonize Europe, escalate the Cold War and transform the national economy into a market for rapacious American corporations and Wall Street. The party was forced onto the defensive, and its own propaganda strategy reflects this. There was an endless and ever more intense denunciation of the Plan in the party's press, meetings and demonstrations, with the message varying in form and content only according to the location and the level of education of the audience. But this was a losing battle. The Marshall Plan delivered the goods, and deployed an ever-wider range of communication methods to inform, educate, and convince its beneficiaries. The Party failed to learn the importance of mass audio-visual media from its defeat in the 1948 elections, and had no useful response to the double onslaught of Hollywood and the USIS/ERP film programme.[19]

SOURCES OF TENSION

Three new areas of tension between American intentions and Italian priorities opened up in these years and they also need to be considered in any discussion of context. The first was in Emilia Romagna, where a new model of communist-run development began to emerge painfully after years of great hardship and class war. As I have shown elsewhere, the Marshall plan did what it could in the region, but it was irrelevant for the conditions of the time and no match for the new kind of co-operative culture which was beginning to emerge there. Centred on Bologna, a new model of organization from below developed which took older strands of collective action and adapted them for the new circumstances.[20] Yet the first post-war Mayor of Bologna, a historic figure of Italian communism over many years, welcomed the Marshall Plan, a fact noted and recorded with pleasure in a made-for-America ERP documentary film of the time.[21] He told a visiting ERP delegation at one point that if the PCI had been running the Marshall Plan, it would have worked much better. In the light of Bologna's eventual emergence as a model city for the PCI, at the heart of a model region, this was not an idle boast.

Second, aside from this, there was certainly an objective congruence between the Marshall Plan's economic methods and what one PCI-related part of the left was proposing, the CGIL, the biggest trade union. As is well-known, the ERP as a whole attached crucial importance to changing the balance of power, structures and attitudes in the world of organized labour. Here information activities were only part of a vast operation (both overt and covert) directly aided by the American trade unions, which actively sought to organize non-communist trade unions where hardly any existed before. But the immediate aim was to provide work, to revive industrial activity, promote development and new aspirations for unionist and worker alike. Experience and extensive opinion polling had brought a significant shift in the outlook of ERP strategists, to the point that they felt obliged to realize... 'the underlying concern of the majority of Europeans today is security...(meaning) employment, health and old-age benefits ... (or further), that a man's life, when begun, contains the reasonable assurance and expectation of a rational progress toward a reasonable conclusion'.[22]

To the ERP challenge, the CGIL responded with its own 'Plan for Work', a series of large-scale initiatives paralleling the government's public works and housing schemes, but also calling for nationalizations and land development plans. CGIL leaders openly referred to the model of the New Deal, but this did not make them any more attractive to ruthless Cold Warriors like Irving Brown of the AFL. For a series of reasons which Federico Romero and others have demonstrated, the CGIL plan never took off, and the left trade unions as a whole were weakened by this period of intense Cold War confrontation. In any event, the great persuasion effort to capture the hearts and minds of the working and peasant classes must also be scripted into any discussion of Cold War culture in these years.[23]

Finally, there was the 'Peace' campaign launched by the Left after the birth of NATO in 1949. According to Simona Colarizi, a full-scale 'war psychosis' developed in the country between 1948 and 1951, a fear of war which was simultaneously genuine and manipulated by all parties for their own ends. The Left bloc had set up an even more intense assault on NATO than that already seen on the Marshall Plan, and the two were presented together as one grand imperialist design, with the military alliance simply a means to drag Italy into America's wars. The outbreak of hostilities in Korea, a faraway country of which no-one knew anything, and the immediate general mobilization in Europe, seemed to confirm the worst fears and there was a vast upsurge in anti-war feeling within public opinion. This was of course intensely encouraged by Soviet policy, and the PCI mobilized with youth fronts, the 'Partisans for Peace' organization, neighbourhood and factory peace committees, and numberless petitions against re-armament and nuclear arms. Opinion polls and police reports of the time all show that diffidence towards American aims, and fears that Italy was little more than a pawn in the East-West struggle, were by no means limited to the militant left.[24]

ERP'S RESPONSE

To avoid direct confrontation with the massive waves of communist propaganda directed against the Plan was a basic principle of ERP information policy in Italy. So, according to a 1949 document, 'when the communists said the Marshall Plan was a plan of war, the Mission never said it was not a plan of war but over and over again, in thousands of inhabited centres, with every medium at its disposal, the Mission put across the slogan – "ERP means peace and work".'[25] America's response to the Korean war could not have been more unfortunate from this point of view. However, the ECA men on the ground in Europe quickly decided that there was no conflict between the need for an increased focus on defence and the

ERP objectives: it was just a matter of bending the existing policy goals to the new requirements. As the concept of 'Mutual Security' began to develop, so did the appropriate propaganda policy. Expenditure for the persuasion effort across the participating nations passed from roughly $1m to almost $6m per annum; in Italy alone almost $1m was being spent annually by the end of 1950.[26]

No effort was spared when it came to defending re-armament. An October 1951 telegram from Rome to Washington illustrated the activities under way at that time aimed at re-orientating the 'information' campaign. New truck convoys had been organized to carry the story of NATO up and down the country. They offered two colour documentaries and two in black and white, on subjects such as the reconstruction of Italy's armed forces, including illustrations of the new motorized units, the renovated Alpine divisions, and the rebuilt Navy and Air Force. Meanwhile on the radio 12 weekly documentaries offered more on the same subjects, with special programmes for all branches of the armed services. For background use additional films were being prepared: '...color documentary *A Ship is Born* and *Naples' Other Face* (steel); in production *Nossa* (zinc for defense); *Cornigliano* (steel for defense)'.[27]

The impact and reception at all the various local levels of this new turn in the propaganda war remain to be studied.[28] In the longer term the episode needs to be inserted into the tortuous history of Italian pacifism, that amorphous but strong body of feeling which surfaces every time public opinion is called upon to make a decision about peace and war. Six million signatures were gathered in a petition organized by the Left against Italian participation in NATO, a step which even the conservative governments of the time hesitated to make, hoping vainly to find a middle way between the blocs. But a much broader appeal launched in Stockholm in 1949 against nuclear armaments gathered *16 million* signatories in the country. Italian defence spending was always rather less than those of comparable countries, and relied much more on the efforts NATO in general. and the US in particular were likely to make in the event of war. Even the outbreak of the Korean war did not change this pattern.[29]

At the same time it should be remembered that the shift to Mutual Security and the construction of a multi-national NATO gradually brought to an end the sort of unilateral mass persuasion campaign which accompanied the Marshall Plan in its hey-day.[30] Henceforth the emphasis in Washington was on building an elite body of opinion which would unite like-minded thinkers from all the member nations around a common body of Western ideals. These would then be projected, in translation, into many different contexts by well-known opinion makers and public figures. This was one of the effective ways to foster a belief in 'Atlanticism' and a sense of shared values between Europe and America.[31]

Nevertheless, Italy remained a society – like the others in Western Europe – which was free to resist the projection of American power in all its forms, to take what it wanted from the American model and to organize its own means for reconciling what America was offering with its own traditions, customs and priorities. After the onslaught of Hollywood and the ERP/MSA campaigns, Italian cinema itself became one of the most effective mechanisms for this purpose, and the celebrated *commedia all'italiana* showed it off with pride. The evolution of the Italian communists, oscillating between Moscow and Hollywood as Steven Gundle has written, shows that they too recognized the force of the same logic.[32]

NOTES

1. This article should be read in conjunction with David W. Ellwood, 'Italian modernisation and the propaganda of the Marshall Plan', in Luciano Cheles and Luciano Sponza (eds.), *The Art of Persuasion: Political Communication in Italy from 1945 to the 1990s* (Manchester UP 2001), which offers a more detailed look at the propaganda strategy in its own terms.
2. Proceedings of the conference of Bologna, Jan. 1990 in P.P. D'Attorre (ed.), *Nemici per la pelle. Sogno americano e mito sovietico nell'Italia contemporanea* (Milan: F. Angeli 1991); Forcella's intervention is conserved on audio tape at the Istituto Gramsci, Bologna.
3. Report 'European Attitudes Toward the U.S.', sent 10 June 1953, in National Archives (henceforth NA), Record Group (RG) 469, ECA Mission to Italy, Office of Director, Subject Files (Central Files) 1948–57, 'Public Relations' sub-file.
4. Cf. David W. Ellwood, *Rebuilding Europe: Western Europe, America and Postwar Reconstruction* (London: Longmans 1992) Chapter 12.
5. *New York Times*, 3 June 1949.
6. Paul G. Hoffmann, *Peace Can be Won* (New York: Doubleday 1951) p.53.
7. Cf. Ellwood, 'The Impact of the Marshall Plan on Italy, the Impact of Italy on the Marshall Plan', in R. Kroes, R.W. Rydell and D.F.J. Boscher (eds.), *Cultural Transmissions and Receptions: American Mass Culture in Europe* (Amsterdam: VU UP 1993) pp.100–24.
8. Memo from Henry S. Reuss to A. Friendly, 25 Feb. 1949, in NA, RG 286, OSR Information Division, Office of Director, 'Publicity and Information 1949' sub-file.
9. H-J. Schröder, 'Marshall Plan Propaganda in Austria and Western Germany', in G. Bischof, A. Pelinka, D. Stiefel (eds.) *The Marshall Plan in Austria*, Contemporary Austrian Studies Vol.8 (New Brunswick & London: Transaction Publishers 2000).
10. Cf. David W. Ellwood, 'The 1948 Elections in Italy: A Cold War Propaganda Battle', *Historical Journal of Film, Radio & Television* 1 (1993).
11. M. Del Pero, ' Containing Containment: Re-thinking Italy's experience during the Cold War', unpublished paper, ICAS, New York University, 2001.
12. S. Romano, 'Comments' in Ellwood (ed.), *The Marshall Plan Forty Years After* (Bologna: Johns Hopkins University, SAIS Bologna Center 1989) p.104.
13. Ellwood, *Rebuilding Europe* (note 4) p.196.
14. E. Di Nolfo, *Vaticano e Stati Uniti 1939–1952. Dalle Carte di Myron C. Taylor* (Milan: F. Angeli 1978) pp.552–73.
15. On the Vatican and the West, P. Scoppola, *La repubblica dei partiti: Profilo storico della democrazia in Italia 1945–1990* (Bologna: Il Mulino 1991) p.155; on Papal audience of Hollywood producers' group, David W. Ellwood, 'Il Rapporto Harmon (Rapporto di un gruppo di dirigenti dell'industria cinematografica americana, 1945)', in *Mezzosecolo 3* (Turin: Guanda 1982).
16. Document cited in Ellwood, *Rebuilding Europe* (note 4) pp.165–6.
17. Cf. Scoppola, *La repubblica*, Pt. IV,V, S. Lanaro, *Storia dell'Italia repubblicana* (Padua: Marsilio 1992) Pt.I.

18. G. Gozzini and R. Martinelli, *Storia del partito comunista italiano. Dall'attentato a Togliatti all'VIII congresso* (Turin: Einaudi 1998).
19. Cf. Ellwood, 'The 1948 Elections in Italy' (note 10).
20. Ellwood, 'The limits of Americanisation and the emergence of an alternative model: The Marshall Plan in Emilia Romagna', in M. Kipping and O. Bjarnar (eds.), *The Americanisation of European Business* (London: Routledge 1998).
21. Ibid.; ERP film is 'Talking to the Italians', n.d. but presumably early 1950, located in NA, RG 301, no.301.3808.
22. Cited in Ellwood, *Rebuilding Europe* (note 4) p.165.
23. F. Romero, *Gli Stati Uniti e il sindacalismo europeo 1944–1951* (Roma: edizioni lavoro 1989) Chapters 6 and 7; the covert dimension is now well covered; cf. R.J. Aldrich, *The Hidden Hand: Britain, America and Cold War Secret Intelligence* (London: John Murray 2001) pp.458–9.
24. S. Colarizi, 'La Seconda guerra mondiale e la Repubblica', in G. Galasso (ed.), *Storia d'Italia dall'Unit alla fine della prima repubblica* (Milan: Tea 1996) pp.652–57; Del Pero, *Containing Containment.*
25. 'Notes dictated by Berding for use in Congressional presentation', 16 Jan. 1950, in NA, RG 286, OSR Information Division, Information Subject Files, 'Previous Testimony' sub-file; (Andrew Berding, a former AP correspondent in Rome, was the first head of the Rome ERP Mission's Information Division).
26. *Ninth Report to Congress of the Economic Co-Operation Administration*, quarter ending 30 June 1950, dated 17 Nov. 1950, p.39; ECA, *Overseas Information Program of the ECA*, Second Year, 1950, p.45.
27. Telegram ECA Rome to ECA Washington, 9 Oct. 1951, in NA, RG 469, Director of Administration, Administrative Services Divn., Communication & Records Unit, Geographic Files 1948–53, 'Italy – P.R.1950' sub-file.
28. Cf. Ellwood, 'Italian modernisation', pp.39–44.
29. L. Sebesta, *L'Europa indifesa. Sistema di scurezza e caso italiano 1948–1955* (Florence: Ponte alle Grazie 1991) Chapter 4.
30. Richard Aldrich has shown how the mass persuasion effort now went underground, concentrating on the generation of support for European integration; Aldrich, *Hidden Hand* (note 23) Chapter 16.
31. See other contributions in this collection.
32. S. Gundle, *Between Hollywood and Moscow: The Italian Communists and the Challenge of Mass Culture, 1943–1991* (Durham, NC: Duke UP 2000).

13

Out of Tune: The Congress for Cultural Freedom in Denmark 1953–1960

INGEBORG PHILIPSEN

The Congress for Cultural Freedom (CCF) was an international anti-communist organization established in 1950 to counter the success of the Soviet-sponsored peace campaign among European intellectuals.[1] The Congress represented a moderate anti-communism, appealing to the intelligentsia of the 'non-communist left' and developing a (high) cultural agenda to solidify the image of western societies as representing freedom and democracy. The CCF arranged conferences, seminars and art festivals, and published several literary magazines. In 1966 it was revealed in an article in the *New York Times* that the Congress and its magazine *Encounter* were financed by the CIA, a revelation that has since caused this notorious publication to be seen by many critics as no more than a reactionary anti-communist organization playing the tune the American government wanted to hear.[2] Up to now most literature about the CCF has focused on its broad history, stressing the overall positions of the organization and the CIA's role.[3] Yet one cannot say that the CCF was an organization characterized by internal unity. From the start there were disagreements among the intellectuals about its aims and purposes. Different interests were also at work inside the CIA itself.[4] CIA agent Michael Josselson headed the Congress Secretariat in Paris but ended up disagreeing with his Agency superiors.[5] The lack of concord within the CCF is clearly demonstrated by the relationship between the national committees and the Secretariat, with the Secretariat struggling to keep the national committees in line with the overall agenda of the organization. In order to enhance understanding of the CCF and its role in European cultural life during the Cold War, more in-depth studies are now needed of how it worked in various countries.[6]

In the early months of 1948 the international situation, particularly in the wake of the communist coup in Prague in February, was causing considerable fear and uncertainty throughout Western Europe. In Denmark this was demonstrated by the 'Easter Crisis of 1948', when rumours about imminent Soviet moves against Denmark were triggered by alarming diplomatic and personal reports coming from the Danish embassy in Washington. Although it was soon realized that the threat had been exaggerated, the situation caused the Danish government to adopt measures intended to increase preparedness both domestically and internationally. The situation also caused a good deal of uncertainty in Danish society. Dramatic rumours circulated about how the communists were hiding large stocks of weapons and that the Danish Communist Party was plotting a coup. At one point, members of the former wartime resistance assembled in 'Dyrehaven', a park area north of Copenhagen, believing that this site was the target for an imminent Soviet airborne invasion. During this period, the Danish social democratic government tried to negotiate a Nordic Alliance with Sweden and Norway in place of the proposed Atlantic Treaty with the United States. However, this attempt failed, and the Danish government reluctantly decided to sign the Atlantic Treaty in 1949, thereby breaking with a long-standing neutralist stance in foreign policy. Support for the Atlantic Treaty was lukewarm in both government and society at large because it was feared that such a treaty would encourage rather than discourage aggressive Soviet behaviour towards Denmark. Therefore the Danish government, although now belonging to the Western Alliance, made it a point not to act in ways that might provoke a Soviet response.[7]

THE FIRM

The initiative to form a national committee of the CCF in Denmark was not taken by the Congress Secretariat in Paris as was the case in other countries. Behind the founding of the Danish committee was a former resistance leader, Arne Sejr.[8] When Sejr got involved in the resistance during the German occupation of Denmark between 1940 and 1945 he was only 18 years old. When the war ended, Sejr tried to return to his studies, but the transition from wartime to peacetime proved too difficult. He was soon operating underground again, this time organizing for the struggle against communism. Sejr became head of a secret anti-communist organization, a kind of private intelligence service called the Firm ('Firmaet'). Who took the initiative to set up the Firm, and what its activities precisely were, still remains unclear.[9] However, the establishment of the Firm is generally reckoned to have taken place in the aftermath of the coup in Prague in 1948, and Sejr is known to have formed a 'stay-behind' network consisting of former members of the resistance movement later that same year. Sejr's anti-communist activities certainly began soon after the war's end. Personal contacts with several important figures in the government helped his cause.

At one point the social democrat H. C. Hansen, later Prime Minister, encouraged Sejr to set up a group to manage anti-communist psychological warfare in Denmark. Finally the Firm co-operated with sections of the Danish Military Intelligence Service.[10] Sejr had already worked during the war with members of the Danish Intelligence Service stationed in Stockholm. Among them were Poul Adam Mørch, later Deputy Commissioner ('sous-chef') of the Danish Military Intelligence Service, and Svend Truelsen, later Treasurer in the Danish Society for Freedom and Culture. Sejr would maintain his contacts with Mørch, and kept him informed about the activities of the Society for Freedom and Culture in later years.[11] Wilhelm Christmas-Møller, historian and former employee of the Danish Intelligence Service, has described the establishment of the Firm as part of an agreement between Danish and American military intelligence to set up 'stay-behind' and intelligence-gathering networks in Denmark. Negotiations started in November 1946 but no settlement was reached until the beginning of the 1950s.[12] In 1952 the Firm got involved in illegal bugging, when by chance they got access to an apartment next to the home of the Vice-Chairman of the Danish Communist Party, Alfred Jensen. The intelligence gained from the bugging operation was most likely passed on to Mørch and the CIA, who provided the equipment used for the bugging.[13]

Yet the results of the operation were not very important until 1957–58, when the Communist Party was in a crisis due to serious internal disagreements over the 1956 Hungarian revolution and the Soviet invasion. Information from the bugging was leaked to the press and used in anonymous letters sent to Communist Party members, thereby causing a great deal of paranoia and mistrust and adding to tensions that caused a split in the party in 1958.[14] Aside from such activities, the Firm also worked through 'open' organizations such as Atlantsammenslutningen (Atlantic Association), the Society for Freedom and Culture, and its follow-up Frihed og Folkestyre (Freedom and Democracy).

THE CCF IN DENMARK

In 1951 Sejr came into contact with the CCF through Michael Goodwin from the British Society for Cultural Freedom. At this time Sejr had already begun to plan a propaganda organization called Intellectual Liberty and Human Rights, intended to have a structure very similar to that of the CCF. However, the plan was also to have a network of confidential agents inside various cultural and intellectual circles all over the country. According to Sejr's correspondence, a promise of the necessary money for this work was obtained from 'official authorities' in Denmark.[15] However, when he heard of the existence of the Congress for Cultural Freedom, he set out to build a

FIGURE 1

Arne Sejr

Polfoto, Copenhagen, Denmark

Scandinavian section of the Congress instead. The CCF was planning a Scandinavian Conference for March 1952, arranged by communist-turned-social democrat Ture Nerman.[16] Sejr intervened in the planning by sending Nerman detailed suggestions about how to form a Scandinavian section of the CCF. He strongly advised that the effort in Scandinavia should be a wholly Scandinavian initiative 'both with regard to efficiency and mentality'. Furthermore the Scandinavian Committee should be on equal footing with and not subordinate to the 'French Committee', presumably meaning the Paris Secretariat. In his letter to Nerman he emphasised the importance of attracting the right kind of people: 'it must be the most distinguished people in the highest intellectual positions … no need to start with ten chance intellectuals out of which one or two has a name', he wrote to Nerman.[17] Sejr listed possible Danish candidates, all with impressive academic credentials, for the proposed Scandinavian Committee. In this respect Sejr was not in line with the other Scandinavian representatives. Nerman and his magazine *Trotts Allt!* were rooted in the Swedish labour movement and he had just asked Haakon Lie, the Norwegian union leader and the Congress's contact in Norway, to involve more union personnel. 'I presume we agree that this should not turn into a bourgeois affair', he told Lie.[18] Like Irving Brown, Haakon Lie had wanted to see the CCF turn into a mass movement building on already-existing connections within the unions. Yet Lie would also oppose the formation of a Scandinavian branch of the Congress, and opposed any move to establish a CCF network in Norway itself.[19]

The Stockholm Conference proved to be a fiasco, mainly because of the attitude of the Swedish delegates. Many of them were elderly people from the temperance and peace movements, and they did not abstain from expressing neutralist sentiments that presented the American and Soviet systems as being equally objectionable.[20] These circumstances prevented the creation of a united Scandinavian CCF. Instead, Sejr and his friends from the Danish resistance movement formed the Society for Freedom and Culture (SFC) in January 1953. However, he did not announce this development publicly, since he wanted the existence of the new organization to remain secret. In his briefings to the CCF headquarters in Paris, Sejr also requested that news about the Danish Society be kept confidential until Sejr himself decided otherwise. He also requested that the Danish Society be autonomous in relation to the Congress. Sejr even stressed that he had chosen a name which did not – at least in his opinion – place the Society too close to the CCF in the minds of Danish intellectuals.[21]

Did the secret atmosphere surrounding the founding of the Danish Society cause any astonishment or reaction from Paris? Not that we know of. The fact that the Danish 'official authorities' were involved in an organization which was – at least officially – supposed to be unaffiliated was not commented upon either. Josselson seems to have agreed with all of Sejr's proposals.[22] He sent the Congress' statutes to SFC secretary Jens Buhl, 'so that if your Society desire [sic] to affiliate with us it can do so in the proper manner'.[23] Whether the Danish Society actually did officially affiliate to the Congress at this point is not clear. But Sejr considered the right of autonomy very important.[24] The smooth relationship between the Danish Society and the Secretariat might also have to do with the fact that Sejr and the other Danish delegates at the Stockholm Conference in 1952 had made 'a very good impression' on the Congress' representative, Willy Brandt.[25]

In his letters Sejr refers to 'the special situation in Denmark' to explain why he had to keep the founding of the SFC secret, but it is not exactly clear what he was referring to. Electoral support for the Danish Communist Party (DKP) was insignificant (only 4.3 per cent) in 1953 when the Society was established. Denmark had signed the Atlantic Treaty in 1949 but neutralism and anti-Americanism was still widespread, especially in intellectual circles.[26] Exposés of McCarthyism and 'book burnings' in the US embassy in Copenhagen in 1953 made this even worse. The popular wish to avoid

'American conditions' of anti-communist paranoia in Denmark was leading to a situation where critics of the communists or the Soviet Union were being labelled as 'McCarthyist'. In reports from the US National Security Council in 1953, Denmark was pinpointed as one of the Western European countries where the reputation of the United States 'was disturbingly unsatisfactory', a classification Denmark had in common only with Italy and France. The Danes were on the alert with regard to aggressive anti-communist propaganda from the US, so much so that the US Information and Education Program recommended using only 'factual' and 'non-propagandist material'.[27] In other words, there seemed to be a lot to do for the Society for Freedom and Culture in the 1950s in order to counter the scepticism and neutralism that was prevalent across the country.

The executive committee of the Society consisted of eleven esteemed gentlemen, many of them Sejr's friends from the non-communist section of the wartime resistance. Politically they belonged to the social democratic or conservative parties. It is not known exactly how many of the members knew about the Firm, but those definitely 'witting' were the Secretary, Jens Buhl, the Chairman Erik Husfeldt, the Treasurer Svend Truelsen and one other member, the journalist Karl Bjarnhof from the Danish National Radio. Sejr had himself chosen as Press Secretary. The executive committee had several contacts with important cultural institutions such as the Royal Theatre, the Royal Music Conservatory and Danish National Radio. Still, they did not hold the central positions in cultural life that Sejr had envisioned, and were thus not considered to be *intellectuals* or important opinion-makers. According to Henning Fonsmark, editor of the magazine *Perspektiv*, who mixed in the Society's circles, the executive committee consisted of 'a circle of well-meaning men who were appalled that the partition of Europe was not taken more seriously'. They were capable men in other respects, but in the cultural field some of them were 'quite primitive and their discussions were not conducted at any high level'. When Prime Minister H. C. Hansen visited the Society one evening, he announced afterwards that he 'was not impressed by the level of the discussion.'[28]

The Society had no ordinary open membership. It arranged so-called 'Cultural Evenings' where the executive committee and a few selected guests discussed the conditions of Liberty and Democracy with an invited speaker. But except for the 'Cultural Evenings' and the publishing of a few pamphlets, the Society was not very active. Because Sejr feared infiltration and had a *penchant* for secrecy, only the initiated were invited to the meetings, so the Society ended up preaching to the converted. However, Sejr himself remained very active. He contacted friends in the Congress – among others Irving Brown – in order to collect information and documentation on the USSR, such as accounts of forced labour, humiliating

FIGURE 2

Jørgen Schleimann, 1967.

Polfoto, Copenhagen, Denmark

divorce decrees, and the penal code for juveniles.[29] The collected material was used in articles with titles like 'World Revolution or Co-existence' and 'The Communists and the Peace' which were accumulated in a so-called 'Library' and made available to the press, politicians, union leaders, youth organization leaders and military institutions.[30]

Although the Secretariat desisted from criticizing the SFC during the first years, members of the SFC did not hold back criticism when they disagreed with decisions made in Paris. When in 1954 the Society discovered that the Danish composer Niels Viggo Bentzon had been invited to a festival in Nice, Jens Buhl was very upset and wrote to Josselson: 'Niels Viggo Bentzon is ... rather closely in contact with people whose political and cultural aims are no doubt far from yours.' According to Buhl, the office in Paris had made the same mistake when the Icelandic author Halldor Laxness was invited to the Festival of the Twentieth Century in Paris in 1952. 'These mistakes are causing us great troubles as well in our common work as in obtaining sufficient support from the Danish authorities [sic]', wrote Buhl.[31] The Secretariat had already apologised for this mistake and gave reassurances that it would not happen again.[32] As a result, the Society's candidate (and member of the SFC Executive committee), composer Knud-Aage Riisager, was invited to the CCF's music festival in Nice in 1954.

THE ARRIVAL OF JORGEN SCHLEIMANN

In 1954 a young librarian and journalist Jørgen Schleimann contacted the SFC. In contrast to many individuals in the CCF, Schleimann did not have a background in the resistance or the Communist Party. Instead, he was one of the many Danes who were disappointed with their government's 'dishonourable' surrender to the German troops in April 1940. For some this disappointment made them more sympathetic towards the occupying power. Thus Schleimann (born 1929) became a devotee of Hitler in his early youth, which did not falter until Hitler's death in 1945. After that Schleimann dissociated himself from his past, but this experience with Nazism was important for his post-war devotion to the anti-totalitarian cause. In 1954 his attention was drawn to the persons and the activities of the international organization of the CCF. But he also made contact with the SFC and its Secretary Jens Buhl. His presence at the Society is shown in letters sent by Buhl to the Paris Secretariat. In 1955 Buhl starts asking for information about the 'libraries opened to the public in connection with the Freedom Houses', stating that 'every activity in this respect is of the greatest importance to the general (adult) education.'[33] The impulse to ask for information about the libraries probably came from Schleimann, who was a trained librarian. All through his career in the CCF Schleimann paid great attention to the role of libraries. In 1955 Schleimann joined the Social Democratic Party despite his predominant interest in cultural matters, a subject not very high on the party's agenda. Yet he was never a party man and in the long run he fell out with both the party leadership and the Prime Minister H. C. Hansen.[34]

In 1955 Schleimann participated in a CCF conference in Gothenburg. Like the conference in Stockholm in 1952, the Gothenburg event was a fiasco as most of the time was spent finding a common definition of 'intellectual' and agreeing upon the purpose of the CCF.[35] But the Gothenburg gathering, in combination with the Milan 'Future of Freedom' conference held the same year, seem to have given the Society the opportunity to widen its contacts by inviting a number of authors, literary editors and journalists to participate. This little circle – only about eight to ten persons remained – was to be known as 'friends of the Society'. Most of them were associated with conservative papers and magazines, and it was these 'friends' who came to give public voice to the anti-totalitarian messages in Denmark. What exactly caused this broadening of scope in the Society's activities is difficult to explain because of the lack of internal sources from the Society – no archive is known to exist. But the initiative behind the changes does not seem to have originated in Paris. In 1954, in an article about the CCF, Schleimann criticised the Society for being too cautious. There is some indication that some members of the Danish executive committee agreed and wanted the Society to be more active. In 1955 Sejr tried to deal with this problem by forming a new propaganda organization in connection with the Firm under the name *Frihed og Folkestyre* (Freedom and Democracy).[36] Sejr moved some of his 'psychological warfare' activities to this new propaganda organization, while efforts were made to raise the profile of the Society in Danish cultural-intellectual circles. Sejr still considered himself to be in charge of the Society's activities.

More important changes followed in 1956. First, the Society began co-operating with *Perspektiv – a magazine for politics, science and culture*, published by another of Sejr's former friends in the resistance movement, Hans Reitzel. *Perspektiv* was a well-established magazine and had done well on the Danish and Scandinavian market since its foundation in 1953. Its content was wide-ranging, but it followed a clear anti-neutralist line concerning the cultural situation in the Soviet Union. *Perspektiv* gave the Society the cultural and ideological base it needed. The editor of *Perspektiv*, Henning Fonsmark, was interested in co-operating with the Society primarily because it made it possible for him to publish articles from the Congress's international magazines, and the money available from the Society reduced the publication's retail price. On top of this, Fonsmark took an interest in the cause and soon he was an important member of the inner circle of the SFC.

Second, in the summer of 1956 Jørgen Schleimann received a NATO scholarship to study 'Communism and the Intellectuals' in France. He looked up Michael Josselson at the Congress's headquarters in Paris, but, despite the fact that the SFC had helped him get the NATO scholarship, Schleimann was not 'their man' at the CCF. In his first report for the Congress he described the Danish committee as 'some sort of an exclusive political-cultural circle with no strong intentions of letting new people in'. Yet the mistrust was not mutual. The secretary Jens Buhl wrote to Josselson that 'Mr. Schleimann is one of our nearest friends' and that Josselson could 'consider Mr. Schleimann as a contact to the Danish Society except for major questions'.[37] Accordingly Schleimann was much more positive in his next report, 'The Congress in the North'. Schleimann thought that the SFC reflected the various cultural and political views within Denmark. What the Society needed was 'a better financial foundation' and 'ways and means for extending its activities'. In accordance with Sejr's wish to keep the work in Denmark under national control, the Danish Society had taken the categorical decision only to accept economic contributions from Danish sources. Therefore Schleimann suggested that the Congress pay 'well-known intellectual personalities' to give lectures in Denmark. The reasoning seems to have been that this would influence the activities and the development of the Society in a favourable way. Schleimann's vision for the Congress's work in Scandinavia and elsewhere (he included the Netherlands in his analysis) was that these small countries could be portrayed as good examples of successful democracies to the new states in Africa, South-America and Asia.[38] Michael Josselson seems to have accepted these arguments and for the next ten years Schleimann strove to fulfil his vision.

Schleimann's plan worked. Sejr liked the idea of having the Congress pay for prominent lectures in Denmark. The first visitor was the black American novelist Richard Wright. The visit made headlines and soon others followed: Czeslaw Milosz, Vladimir Dedijer and the Hungarian George Faludy, editor of the *Hungarian Literary Gazette in Exile*, were among the visitors.[39] Czeslaw Milosz was a cultural attaché in Paris and Washington until he defected in 1951 and was enthusiastically accepted into the ranks of the CCF. In December 1953 the SFC published his pamphlet 'La grande tentation' in Danish.[40] The visit of Vladimir Dedijer attracted special attention in the Danish press, since he was Tito's biographer. Dedijer belonged to the moderate opposition inside the Communist Party in Yugoslavia and had supported the former Foreign Vice-Minister Milovan Djilas in his confrontation with Tito. Dedijer had been imprisoned by Tito as a result.

Soon Sejr asked for economic subsidies for other activities as well. Hence the principle of economic independence from the international organization was starting to dissolve. Nonetheless Sejr tried to maintain the image of the Society's status as independent and equal. Sejr saw himself and the Danish Society as the centre of CCF activity in Northern Europe. Without asking the Paris Secretariat he tried to set up committees in Norway and Finland. In October 1956 he did inform the Secretariat in Paris that he was going to establish a committee in Norway. In Paris a young American novelist John S. Hunt had replaced Josselson for the daily work of the CCF headquarters. Hunt, like Josselson, was recruited by the CIA.[41] Hunt hesitatingly – and only after consultation with Schleimann – accepted that Sejr should continue his work in Norway. But he insisted that Sejr should inform the office before similar steps were taken in the future, since Paris had the Hungarian Lazlo Hamorí working on the same project.[42] In his letter Sejr indicated that the Norwegian committee was almost ready to be announced. Yet when Jens Buhl and Henning Fonsmark visited Norway in March 1957, they had talks with Haakon Lie and discovered that the plan had not been a success: 'Mr. Lie ... told us, that he considered a work in connection with the Congress completely unnecessary in Norway. According to Mr. Lie this was due partly to the fact that there is no political problem of any importance at all among the Norwegian intellectuals, and partly to the fact that other organizations, especially one called *Folk og Forsvar* (People and Defence), was doing fairly well the job that had to be the main task of a Norwegian committee.' A Norwegian committee was never formed.[43] But Sejr was obviously trying to impress the Paris office and his letters were full of descriptions of actions conducted to control various Danish and international student organizations. According to Sejr, *his* man had prevented the attempt of the communist-controlled International Union of Students to infiltrate its western adversary, the International Student Conference. He had also placed *his* people in every Teacher Training College in Denmark.[44] In 1956 Sejr wanted to establish a so-called 'Liaison Bureau to co-ordinate some of the international activities of the different organizations in order to exchange experiences and to discuss international operations'. Michael Josselson was invited to a meeting in Denmark, which in line with Sejr's propensity for secrecy, was going to be 'confidential, private and informal and only announced to the participating persons'. This time Josselson refused to participate. 'Such activities were not the Congress' field', Hunt answered, but stressed that he did not mean 'to imply any limitation of the activities of the National Committees'.[45]

In the summer of 1957 Schleimann came back to Denmark as a correspondent for *Der Monat* and the *New Leader*, but also as an unofficial representative of the Congress in Scandinavia with a mission to reform its activities in the region.[46] The stay at the Paris Secretariat had given Schleimann some insights into the problems of the organization. In a letter to Josselson just after his return he wrote:

> I arrived at Paris a year ago with a certain amount of friendly scepticism. I felt that the Congress ought to go back to the Berlin 1950 formula... I was able to see, that it was time for me to change my views a little bit. The Congress was no conformity, indeed, and the relations between persons and views were more complicated than I had imagined.[47]

In Denmark the CCF was still seen as 'a hard-boiled anti-communist product of the Cold War' and so Schleimann set out to change its image. Schleimann's main strategy was to prevent it from being associated with the 'wrong people' on the right-wing of Scandinavian politics.[48] He wanted to attract more left-wing/social democratic intellectuals and here his contacts with prominent CCF intellectuals helped him. When Sidney Hook visited Schleimann in Denmark in August 1957, Schleimann invited three left-wing intellectuals to the SFC's 'cultural evening' and reception for Hook. This was done without the knowledge of the Society's Executive. According to Schleimann it caused some astonishment among the Executive members, yet they all accepted in the end that it was a good idea.[49] Statements and campaigns were now made in the name of the CCF and not in co-operation with the Danish Society, since it was now the CCF which did not wish to be associated with the SFC. Yet at the same time Schleimann's influence in the Society grew as it became more dependent on its contact with the Congress. In Paris Hunt was pleased. Only two months after Schleimann's return, he wrote to Schleimann: 'I'm glad to note that "thaw" seems to have set in with regard to your committee. Your liberalizing influence seems to have worked wonders.'[50]

However, with Schleimann acting as the Congress representative in Denmark, Sejr's position was threatened. Sejr strove to give the impression that he was 'running the business', but in Paris they were not impressed by his activities. Hunt wanted to turn the SFC away from political propaganda and more towards the cultural field, and he made it clear that the CCF wanted a new line in exchange for the money that was now coming from Paris. In November 1957 Hunt conducted a meeting in Copenhagen with the Danish Society and delegates from the Swedish and Icelandic committees.[51] The purpose of the meeting was to bring the activities of the committees into line with the overall purpose of the CCF.[52] But in connection with the meeting, a disagreement between Sejr and the CCF, represented by Schleimann and Hunt, apparently broke out and Sejr was put in his place. Afterwards Hunt wrote to Sejr: 'My concern is simply that your committee be as representative as possible of the aims and activities of the Congress, since your group bears our name and shares our principles.'[53] In case Sejr did not get the message from Hunt, Michael Josselson made it quite clear in a letter following the meeting in Copenhagen:

> I am sure that you do not think of yourself as some kind of special Northern representative of ours delegated to set up committees in various countries neighbouring to Denmark, but I wanted to call this to your attention, so that there would be no doubt in your mind about the fact that we cannot accept committees set up in our name, without detailed consultation between the people involved and ourselves.[54]

This effectively nullified the autonomy and equality that Sejr had demanded all along. Hunt had had enough of the Society for Freedom and Culture and Arne Sejr, and wanted Schleimann to stay out of trouble: 'It is my fervent hope that you will stay out of difficulties with that group, which difficulties only bring headaches to everyone concerned [*sic*], and get on with the task of building a community around our magazines.' Schleimann focused on the well-stocked system of public libraries in Scandinavia which he considered were an important link for influencing the intellectuals there. He worked hard to get the magazines into the reading-rooms of the public libraries. In 1957 the CCF magazines were not found in any of the Danish libraries, but with the help of friends of the Society he arranged for the magazines to be reviewed in the Danish newspapers, thereby making them more publicly known. But Schleimann did not stay away from the SFC. Soon after the Scandinavian meeting, he was a elected member of its executive committee (on the recommendation of Jens Buhl) and a council of five persons was elected to 'guide the secretaries in their work'. It was also decided to accept financial funding from foreign sources. One would think that Sejr wanted out after this, but he did not. Apparently he accepted the new cultural line in the Society. But by 1958 the funding of *Perspektiv* was more or less the only activity the Society had, and in the spring of 1959 Sejr ran into financial problems.[55] Urged by Schleimann, the CCF agreed to take over the contract with *Perspektiv* and in 1960 the CCF's name replaced that of the SFC in the colophon of *Perspektiv*. Despite the demise of the SFC, Sejr continued producing anti-communist propaganda via the organization 'Freedom and Democracy' until it lost its popular and financial support in the late 1960s. It appears from one of Sejr's reports to Mørch from the late 1960s that he claimed to control the Conservative Students, the Liberal Students, the Conservative Party's Youth Organization, the Liberal Party's Youth Organization and the Danish national committee of YMCA.[56]

In 1960 the CCF opened a Scandinavian office in Copenhagen headed by Schleimann. He successfully continued his work for the CCF, making contacts with opinion-makers all over Scandinavia. He succeeded in extending the network of the Forum Service, the CCF's news service in Scandinavia. In his effort to fulfil his vision of the Scandinavian countries as models of living democracies to the new states, he arranged several Afro-Scandinavian conferences and seminars. In 1962 the CCF gave up the idea of having national committees, and chose to work with personal contacts instead.[57] At that point Schleimann had already built up a large personal network in Scandinavia behind the back of the national committees. When the exposure of the connection with the CIA appeared in 1967, Schleimann stood up to defend the organization, but the Scandinavian office was closed down in the same year. Later, in 1976, when Sejr's activities in connection with the Firm were revealed, the SFC was mentioned as one of the organizations that Sejr had controlled, and many of the people who had been in contact with him felt compromised. Yet one must stress that the engagement of the 'friends' of the SFC had not been defined by a rigid anti-communism. They had given voice to the opinion that freedom of expression also included so-called 'pornographic' (communist or fascist) literature, since it was their opinion that bad literature was a case for the reviewers, not the police.

The establishment of the Society for Freedom and Culture was an all-Danish initiative. Until the late 1950s the CCF accepted that the Danish section was playing out of tune, but in the end working with a man like Sejr became too troublesome for the CCF and they decided to put an end to his influence. Yet this does not necessarily support the picture of the CCF as one big propaganda machine controlling everything. The Secretariat in Paris had many difficulties controlling the national committees. In Denmark and Sweden the message of the CCF had attracted people ill-suited for the job – yet in the case of the Swedes the problems were of a different kind than in Denmark. In Norway, Haakon Lie wanted to keep the battle with the communists to himself. Like Sejr, he wanted to keep control. And how much did the CCF Secretariat know exactly about what was going on in the national committees, if the national representatives did not tell them? The inability to understand the language must have caused some trouble. The Congress was able to take control of the work in Denmark mainly because of Schleimann's knowledge about the situation in Denmark and his engagement with the basic principles of its work. Like most of the friends of the SFC, he was drawn towards the CCF because he felt that the anti-totalitarian message needed to be presented. He was the ideal representative and an important link for the CCF in Scandinavia. Yet even Schleimann came to disturb the peace inside the Paris HQ, because of his harsh criticism of the UN for its treatment of Patrice Lumumba in Congo in 1960–61. Neither the national committees nor the individual members were easy to manage. They played out of tune, they played a different tune – or they refused to play at all.

NOTES

1. This article is based on research done for my master's thesis 'Selskabet for frihed og kultur 1950–60. Arne Sejr og dansk kulturliv under den kolde krig', at the University of Copenhagen, Department of History, July 2001. Archival material comes mainly from the following: the International Association of Cultural Freedom Papers, series II, at the University of Chicago Library; and Svenska Kommiteen för Kulturens Frihets arkiv, Arbetarrörelsens Bibiliotek och Arkiv (ARAB), Stockholm. I would like to thank Poul Villaume, Regin Schmidt, Rasmus Mariager, Hans Hertel, (University of Copenhagen), Klaus Petersen (University of Southern Denmark), Niels Barfoed, Sarah von Essen and ARAB in Stockholm for helping me in my work.
2 See the *New York Times*, 26 April 1966.
3. Peter Coleman, *The Liberal Conspiracy: The Congress for Cultural Freedom and the Struggle for the Mind of Postwar Europe* (London and New York: Collier Macmillan 1989); Frances Stonor Saunders, *Who Paid the Piper? The CIA and the Cultural Cold War* (London: Granta Books 1999).
4. About the differences of opinion in the CCF and the CIA see Giles Scott-Smith, 'The Masterpieces of the Twentieth Century Festival and the Congress for Cultural Freedom:

Origins and Consolidation 1947–52', *Intelligence and National Security* 15/1 (Spring 2000) p.134; Saunders, *Who Paid the Piper* ?(note 3) p.97–9; Coleman, *The Liberal Conspiracy* (note 3) p.47.

5. Saunders (note 3) p.108.
6. One important example of an in-depth country-study of the CCF is Michael Hochgeschwender, *Freiheit in der Offensive? Der Kongress für kulturelle Freiheit und die Deutschen* (München: R. Oldenburg Verlag 1998).
7. Poul Villaume, *Allieret med forbehold. Danmark, NATO og den kolde krig. En studie i dansk sikkerhedspolitik* 1949-1961 (Copenhagen: Eirene 1995) p.99ff.
8. At the CCF's initial conference in Berlin in 1950, Denmark was represented by the social democrat and former resistance movement leader, Frode Jakobsen. He was a devotee of the CCF until the revelations of CIA funding in 1966–67. Yet Frode Jakobsen did not, as far as is known, take any initiative to form a Danish national committee of the CCF.
9. In Denmark access to official archives is restricted because of an exceptionally strict information law. The Danish Police Intelligence Services' activities during the Cold War are currently under investigation by a commission set up by the Danish Government. This investigation is expected to finish its work in 2004.
10. Ulrik Høy in Weekend Avisen 'Fup eller Fakta?' 9 Nov. 2001. Copy of letter Arne Sejr to Ole Trock-Jansen, 14 May 1991, Frode Jakobsen private archive, Danish National Archive, Copenhagen.
11. Wilhelm Christmas-Møller, *Obersten og Kommandøren: efterretningstjeneste, sikkerhedspolitik og Socialdemokrati 1945–1955* (Copenhagen: Gyldendal 1995) p.182.
12. Ibid. pp.96–116 and 161–83. The negotiations between the Danish and the American intelligence services caused strife when it turned out that the Americans thought that they were entitled to set up groups in Denmark behind the back of the Danish service. According to Christmas-Møller, Mørch began negotiations with the American Office of Strategic Services (OSS) in Nov. 1946. (p.98) It should be noted that OSS had been officially disbanded by that date, so it is unclear who is meant here. The agreement between CIA and the Danish Military Intelligence Service was not settled until around 1951. In his presentation of the case, Christmas-Møller repeatedly refers to OSS when referring to the partner in the negotiations. Presumably this indicates that the Danish service did not know exactly whom it was negotiating with. Quotations given in Christmas-Møller's book indicate that they were not sure to whom they should address themselves (p.107). Christmas-Møller mentions this possibility, yet the OSS/CIA point is not clarified in the book.
13. 'Danmark i den kolde krig', television programme about the Cold War in Denmark, DR2, 2002.
14. The Danish Communist Party (DKP) officially supported the Soviet Union's reaction to the Hungarian crisis, but DKP's Chairman, Aksel Larsen, was troubled. He tried to reform the Party from within. But in Oct. 1958 Larsen was expelled from the Party and formed a new socialist party independent of Moscow, which attracted a large group of former communist intellectuals. Kurt Jacobsen, *Aksel Larsen. En politisk biograf* (Copenhagen: Vindrose 1993). Until 1962, the tapping of the Vice-Chairman of DKP was not known by Mørch's chief in the Danish Military Intelligence Service, Hans Mathiesen Lunding. When he found out that Mørch had been working behind his back, he was furious.
15. Sejr to Hamorí, copy sent to Nerman, 29 Feb. 1952, Svenska Kommittén för kulturens Frihet arkiv, vol.1, ARAB, Stockholm.
16. Ture Nerman was the author of several historical books about the Swedish labour movement and the editor of the anti-fascist and anti-communist magazine *Trotts Allt* (1939–54).
17. Sejr to Nerman, 5 March 1952, Svenska Kommittén för kulturens Frihet arkiv, vol.1, ARAB Stockholm.
18. 'Och så behöver vi speciellt folk från arbetarrörelsen, jeg antar att vi är ense om att det hela inte får bli en borgerlig historia'. Nerman to Lie, 26 Feb. 1952, Svenska Kommittén för kulturens Frihet arkiv, vol.1.
19. On relations between the Congress and Haakon Lie see: Matthias Hannemann, 'Kulturkrieg in Norwegen?' *Nordeuropa Forum, Zeitschrift für Politik, Wirtschaft und Kultur* (2/1999).

20. Willy Brandt, 'Bereich für die deutsche Executive über die Stockholmer Konference am 29. und 30. März 1952. (Vertreulich)' NL Willy Brand, Mappe 1829, AdsD/ Bon.
21. Sejr to M. de Dadelsen, Centre Européen de la Culture, 6 Feb. 1953. CCF Papers, box 87.
22. In a memo from the CCF's General Secretary to the president and members of the CCF executive from 31 March the Society is mentioned as: 'un comité autonome pour la liberté et la culture vient de se former au Danemark', quoted in Matthias Hannemann p.33, note 33.
23. Josselson to Sejr, 16 Feb. 1953, CCF Papers, box 87.
24. Not until 1957 did the Paris Secretariat take the initiative to get the national committees in Scandinavia in line.
25. Willy Brandt, 'Bereich für die deutsche Executive über die Stockholmer Konference am 29. und 30. März 1952. (Vertreulich)' NL Willy Brand, Mappe 1829, AdsD/ Bon.
26. In his book, *The Students and the Cold War* (London: Macmillan 1996) Joël Kotek mentions that 15 Danish anti-communists were reportedly 'liquidated' within a month in 1948 by their communist opponents (p.147). This is repeated by Richard J. Aldrich in *The Hidden Hand: Britain, America and Cold War Secret Intelligence* (London: John Murray 2001) p.124. There is no indication that this report has any background in reality and should be interpreted in connection with the panic atmosphere in 1948.
27. Poul Villaume, *Allieret med forbehold. Danmark, NATO og den kolde krig. En studie i dansk sikkerhedspolitik 1949–1961* (Copenhagen: Eirene 1995) p.791.
28. Interview with Henning Fonsmark, 30 March 2000.
29. Sejr even stressed that the documents were to be sent to a post-office box without the receiver's name on the envelope.
30. Ole Stæhr to Irwing Brown, 11 November 1953, Irving Brown files, 1943-89, box 13 (CCF), George Meany Memorial Archives, Silver Spring, Maryland. Manuscript of speech by Erik Husfeldt in connection with the visit of Colonel Deakan in 1955, Erik Husfeldt private archive, box 2, The Danish National Archive, Copenhagen.
31. Buhl to Josselson, 30 Jan. 1954, CCF Papers, box 87.
32. Bondy to Sejr, 28 April 1952, CCF Papers, box 87.
33. Buhl to Nabokov, 4 Aug. 1955, CCF Papers, box 87.
34. In 1957 Jørgen Schleimann was appointed General Secretary of the Danish Atlantic Association, while at the same time officially representing the CCF in Denmark. But he soon withdrew from his post in the Atlantic Association, presumably because he felt deceived by the former general secretary of the Association, a fellow social democrat, who had some shady financial practices within the Association without Schleimann's knowledge. Schleimann's refusal to accept this irregularitiy and his resignation embittered his relationship with the Social Democratic Party leadership, especially H.C. Hansen. In letters to Irving Brown, with whom Schleimann kept contact, mainly to apply for money for his projects, Schleimann informed Brown that: 'I fear that H.C. [Hansen] has been picked up by some international neutralist (and even more) circles to perform the future role of a Scandinavian Nehru. And what is worse, they might get away with it because of his extreme vanity.' Schleimann to Irving Brown, 30 Dec. 1957, Irving Brown Papers, George Meany Memorial Archives, Silver Spring. Schleimann's accusations were absurd as H.C. Hansen was one of the foremost anti-communist politicians in Denmark.
35. *Kulturkontakt* 5 (1955) p.9-37.
36. According to an article about Arne Sejr and the Firm in *Information*, 7–8 Feb. 1976, the organization *Freedom and Democracy* was established after disagreements inside the executive committee concerning how the Society for Freedom and Culture react to McCarthyism.
37. Buhl to Josselson, 26 July 1956, CCF Papers box 88.
38. 'The Congress in the North', report by Schleimann to Hunt, 10 October 1956, CCF Papers, box 285. Just before Schleimann came to Paris he had visited Iceland. Also he had personal contacts in the Netherlands through the editor of the newspaper *Het Parool*, Sal Tas, and the editor of the magazine *Tirade*, Mr van Oorschot. Hunt to Schleimann, 2 Dec. 1957, Schleimann to Hunt, 20 Dec. 1957, CCF Papers, box 288.
39. The visitors often went on to Sweden and in some cases Norway and Finland after Denmark.
40. Buhl to Josselson, 17 Dec. 1953, CCF Papers, box 87.

41. Saunders (note 3) p.241. Hunt, who was formally appointed to the Congress Secretariat around Feb. 1956, has said about the first two years that he was 'behaving like a cleaning boy, never saying anything, just watching and learning' (ibid. p.343). This picture of Hunt's role in the Secretariat does not fit with the impression one gets from the correspondence of Schleimann and Hunt during 1956–58. Here Hunt is always full of enterprise.
42. Sejr to Hunt, 10 Oct. 1956; Letter Hunt to Sejr, 22 Nov. 1956, CCF Papers, box 88.
43. Buhl to Hunt, 14 March 1957, CCF Papers, box 88.
44. Sejr to Hunt, 18 Oct. 1956, CCF Papers, box 88.
45. Sejr to Hunt 29 Oct. 1956, Hunt to Sejr 22 Nov. 1956, CCF Papers, box 88.
46. Schleimann had already shown his abilities in this respect when he helped Hunt reorganize the Swedish Committee in 1957. In a letter Hunt told Sejr: 'I would like to take this opportunity to tell you how helpful Schleimann was, especially in Sweden. The situation would have been much more difficult to observe and evaluate without his contacts, his advice and his enthusiasm for getting at the truth.' Hunt to Sejr, 6 March 1957, CCF Papers, box 88. In 1955 the philosopher Ingemar Hedenius had taken over the post as president of the Swedish committee. Ture Nerman was going to replace the secretary, the Hungarian Lazlo Hamorí, but in connection with the visit of Schleimann and Hunt in March 1957 this job was given to the journalist and novelist Birgitta Steenberg. Hunt thought it was important that this post was held by a Swede (but presumably he did not want Ture Nerman). See also Nils Runeby, 'Die Halbjungfrauen der Demokratie. Zur Geschichte des "Schwedischen Komitees für Kulturelle Freiheit" 1950–1960', in Helmut Müssener (ed.) *Aspekte des Kulturausstausches zwischen Schweden und dem deutschsprachigen Mitteleuropa nach 1945* (Stockholm 1981).
47. Schleiman to Josselson July 15 1957, CCF Papers, box 285.
48. This was the case with the Danish author Kelvin Lindemann, who was representing Denmark at the PEN conference in Tokyo in 1957. Schleimann informed Hunt that 'Mr. Lindemann is a strong anti-communist, whose democratic attitude there is no reason to doubt. But due to the fact that he is generally considered in this country a very right-wing, conservative and reactionary personality, probably one of the most right-wing people we can present, and you have to bear in mind that our Danish conservatives are less extreme that the normal continental type, but due to this fact we never tried to draw him close to our Danish Congress group.... We have felt that he should never in the public mind be linked too closely to the our activities.' Schleimann to Hunt, 25 Aug. 1957, CCF Papers, box 285.
49. The left-wing intellectuals at the meeting were Peter P Rohde, editor of the cultural magazine *Vindrosen*, his well-known wife Ina Rohde, and foreign policy editor of the Danish paper *Information*, Erling Bjøl. Schleimann to Hunt, 24 Aug. 1957, CCF Papers, box 285.
50. Schleimann to Hunt, 15 Oct. 1957, Hunt to Schleimann, 23 Oct. 1957, CCF Papers, box 285.
51. The Icelandic Committee was formed in March 1957 under the name 'Frälls Menning'.
52. The invitations send out by the Danish Society for Freedom and Culture said that the purpose of the meeting was to 'discuss the Nordic problems in connection with the establishment and organizing of the work in line with the CCF's work in other countries'. Delegates from Denmark, Sweden, Iceland, Norway and Finland were invited to the meeting, yet the delegates from Norway and Finland never showed up. Buhl to Steenberg, 4 Oct. 1957. Svenska Kommittén för kulturens Frihet arkiv, vol.2, ARAB, Stockholm.
53. Hunt to Sejr, 2 Dec. 1957, CCF Papers, box 88.
54. Josselson to Sejr, 2 Dec. 1957, CCF Papers, box 88.
55. Sejr to Schleimann, 22 Dec. 1959 CCF Papers, box 88.
56. Christmas-Møller, *Obersten og Kommandøren* (note 11) p.169.
57. *Til medlemmarna av Svenska Kommitteen för Kulturens frihet*: in translation the Swedish text reads: 'To members of Svenska Kommitteen för Kulturens frihet. In consequence of a letter from the international office in Paris [the committee] has to make an important decision. In the letter we are informed that the Congress has reorganized its activities so that it does not co-operate with national committees any more, but only through personal contacts in the different countries.' In the letter the Congress also forbids the use of the Congress name. 29 May 1962, Ture Nerman's private archive, Vol.1, ARAB, Stockholm.

14

The Absent Dutch: Dutch Intellectuals and the Congress for Cultural Freedom

TITY DE VRIES

During the last week of June 1950, a day after the start of the Korean War on 25 June, a sizeable group of anti-Soviet writers and intellectuals from all over the world assembled in Berlin for the founding conference of the Congress for Cultural Freedom (CCF):

> For the first time since the rise of the dictators in our day, the liberty-loving writers, artists, [and] scientists of the free world met together in an expression of their devotion to the ideal of democracy.… It was the initial attempt of the intelligentsia of the civilized world – poets and scientists, philosophers and journalists, socialists and conservatives, churchmen and trade-unionists, painters and publishers – to join together freely, to discuss, to criticize, to formulate an independent program for the defense of their common democratic ideal.[1]

During the 1950s and early 1960s the CCF was one of the main international organizations for Western intellectuals who were concerned about the communist threat to the freedom of intellectual and cultural life. 'Culture can exist only in freedom and that freedom can lead to cultural progress', said the 'Manifesto of Intellectual Liberty' which was read during the closing session of the founding conference.[2]

The CCF was considered 'the cultural counterpart of NATO'. Every year the members convened in pleasant European cities like Milan or Paris, or less pleasant cities like Hamburg or Berlin. Famous names attended these conferences: Arthur Koestler, Raymond Aron, Nicola Chiaromonte, Hannah Arendt, and Daniel Bell. At the Future of Freedom conference in Milan in 1955, Edward Shils declared the beginning of the end of ideology for the first time. In the 1950s the CCF's activities were highly politicized, while art and intellectual life became more important later. In its policy, the CCF linked the defence of modernist culture with the politics of anti-communism. Periodicals like *Encounter*, *Preuves*, *Tempo Presente* and the Austrian *Forum* were sponsored by or closely associated with the CCF.

The conferences, periodicals, festivals and other activities made the CCF a centre for prominent Western anti-communist intellectuals with either a social democratic or a more conservative background. Together, its members created a network of people with an anti-communist stand and a willingness to contribute to the freedom of the Western world in common, but in other respects they were often very different in outlook and opinion. Still, in anti-communist Western intellectual circles, membership of the CCF or participation in its activities was considered essential. No doubt the financial generosity of the CCF contributed to this status.[3]

CCF headquarters were located in Paris. In 1960 national branches of the organization could be found in 35 countries, of which ten were European. Athens, Berlin, Cologne, Copenhagen, Geneva, Hamburg, London, Manchester, Paris, Reykjavik, Rome, Uppsala and Vienna all had CCF offices. In other words, almost every Western European capital, with at least one striking exception: Amsterdam.[4] Checking the lists of participants of CCF conferences discloses a similar tendency. During the first ten years of the CCF, only five Dutch intellectuals visited the conferences.[5] In other words: the Dutch were almost completely absent in this core organization of anti-communist and freedom-loving intellectuals. Considering the fierce anti-communist Dutch politics of the 1950s and the prominent Dutch role in the founding and development of NATO, this is rather surprising.

Till the end of the 1960s the Netherlands can be characterized as one of the most loyal and pro-American allies of NATO. There were exceptions to this loyalty, due to decolonization troubles, but generally, and particularly after the Prague coup in 1948, the main Dutch political parties and associated organizations like labour unions shared a consensus on the necessity to combat communism, in the international arena as well as within Dutch society.[6]

As did its counterparts elsewhere in the Western world, the Dutch Communist Party (CPN) had a hard time during the 1950s. Party members or affiliated organizations like the communist daily newspaper were harassed, in parliament the communist representatives were isolated, and at universities reputedly communist intellectuals or fellow travellers were excluded from professorships. Very often anti-communist activities were initiated by the social democrats of the Labour Party.

Considering this anti-communist climate of opinion one would expect Dutch intellectuals to have participated eagerly in the CCF. After all, Dutch policy and public opinion towards communism were not very different from the British or Danish.

In the historiography of the Cold War, in particular the cultural Cold War, the CCF is presented as one of the main platforms of intellectual support for the anti-communist cause. Its activities stimulated the international exchange of opinions between prominent writers and intellectuals, and it has been recognized as providing an important contribution to the formation of a Western intellectual community. CCF historians have tended to focus on the organization itself, the CIA sponsorship, and the contributions of famous intellectuals and their differences in political opinions.[7] The image of the CCF in these publications focuses on the British, American and French perspectives, and on the broad consensus on the necessity to defend the freedom of culture. How the CCF related to the different national cultural and intellectual traditions of the smaller Western European nations has hardly been an object of study so far. This paper on the absence of Dutch participation in the CCF presents a case for this new perspective, shedding a different light on the diversity of Western cultural anti-communism and showing that national *cultural* contexts could be decisive for the success of an international organization like the CCF.

FAILED EFFORTS

It was not out of lack of interest from the CCF that a Dutch branch of the Congress never succeeded. During the early 1950s CCF secretaries François Bondy and Michael Josselson made several efforts to establish a national office in the Netherlands, asking the assistance of leading, fiercely anti-communist Labour Party members. From December 1950 on, Alfred Mozer, the foreign affairs specialist of the Labour party, and CCF secretary Bondy corresponded for more than six months on possible candidates for a Dutch CCF committee, but with no results. A year later, in September 1952, the next CCF secretary Josselson tried again, with two editors connected to The Hague newspaper *Het Vaderland*, which had published an article on 'the friends of freedom', referring to the CCF Berlin conference in 1950.[8] Josselson gave them directions about the profile of this possible Dutch CCF group: '... it should be avoided giving this group a label of being too conservative or reactionary. The aim of our organization, after all, is to try to convince those who are wavering and who are the prey of communist or other totalitarian propaganda. It is therefore essential, for example, that this group includes liberals and socialists, regardless of whether or not they have party affiliations. It is furthermore important that the group includes some academicians, both university professors and students.'[9] Again, this contact led to no results. Later, Josselson corresponded with the journalist Sal Tas, who contributed some articles on Indonesia to the CCF periodicals *Forum Service* and *Preuves*.

FIGURE 1

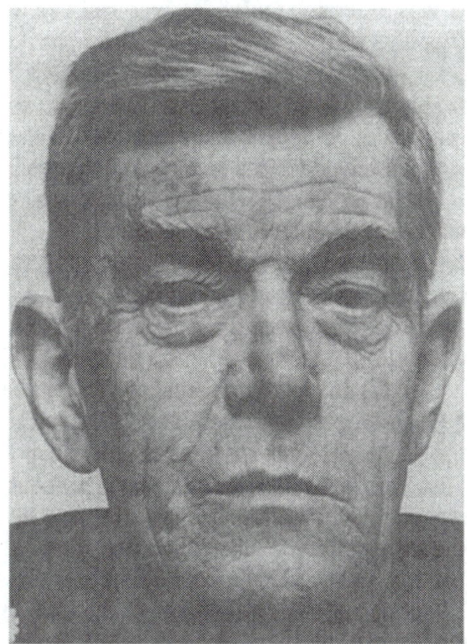

Alfred Mozer
A. Mozer, 'Gastarbeider' in Europa *(Zutphen: De Walburgpers 1980). Cover.*

FIGURE 2

Sal Tas
Sal Tas, Wat mij betreft *(Baarn: Ten Have 1970). Cover.*

Both Alfred Mozer and Sal Tas fitted very well into the CCF profile. Originally, Mozer was a German journalist, who had fled to the Netherlands in the 1930s. After the war he was employed by the Labour Party and belonged to the vanguard of the European Federalist Movement.[10] He participated prominently in the extensive European social democratic network, and in particular co-operated several times with the SPD. Within the Labour Party he was considered a hawk – Dutch membership of NATO was for him, as for other leading Labour politicians, essential for the Netherlands to survive as an autonomous nation.[11]

Mozer's political opinions, his position among the sub-elite of Dutch social democrats, his international contacts and his easy way of communicating with different sorts of people (in this he was rather un-Dutch) made him an ideal candidate to set up a Dutch CCF committee.

So was Sal Tas. Like many CCF intellectuals, Tas had been a communist in the 1920s and 30s, but became an anti-communist social democrat in the second half of the 1930s and can be considered as a pre-eminent Dutch renegade. After the war he was a foreign correspondent with the social democratic newspaper *Het Parool*, and was influential in forming the hawkish anti-communist profile of this paper. Tas travelled a lot, and lived for long periods of time in Paris. There in 1949 he met the American writer James T. Farrell, later one of the co-founders of the CCF. Farrell was Tas's introduction to the international intellectual world.[12] He started to write for the AFL/CIO and *The New Leader*, and for the CCF-related periodicals *Preuves*, *Der Monat* and *Encounter*. Later, in 1957, he was the intermediary between the CCF and a new Dutch literary periodical, *Tirade*, which resulted in the publication of articles from *Preuves* and *Der Monat* in *Tirade*. In fact, Sal Tas would have been the most suitable person to initiate the Dutch CCF committee, if he had not had one large handicap: he was not accepted by the established intellectual elite of the Netherlands – he simply did not fit in. As a journalist he had a sharp pen and was admired in that respect, but his efforts to be more than a journalist by writing essayistic articles and books were a failure, and gave him no recognition as an intellectual. This rather isolated position (and his long stays in Paris) prevented him from becoming the vanguard for a Dutch branch of the Congress.

A EUROPEAN FEDERALIST AND A CONOISSEUR OF MODERN ART

Although the efforts to establish a Dutch CCF branch failed, a few Dutch intellectuals did participate in conferences and activities of the Congress during the 1950s. The first was Professor Henry Brugmans. He was one of the 118 people present at the founding Berlin conference of the CCF in June 1950, which made him a member of the General Assembly.[13]

FIGURE 3

Prof. dr. H. Brugmans
H. Brugmans, Levend in Europa. Ontmoetingen en herinneringen *(Alphen a/d Rijn: Sijthoff 1980). Cover.*

Brugmans fitted partly into the standard profile of the CCF intellectuals. As a young man he had belonged to the radical left, but he became a social democrat in the 1930s. During the war he was a close friend and advisor of the first Dutch post-war prime minister, Schermerhorn. Very soon after the war, Brugmans started to support the European Federalist Movement and in 1946 he became the chairman of this organization. Four years later he was appointed director of the College of Europe in Bruges, Belgium, an institute for future European civil servants. As a consequence of this appointment, he moved to Belgium where he remained for the rest of his life.

In the late 1940s and early 1950s Brugmans travelled at least three times to the United States.[14] During these visits he developed very outspoken ideas on the position and role of Europe between the superpowers: Europe should keep its independence and not become a part of an Atlantic bloc or federation.[15] An Atlantic federation would mean an inferior role for Europe, while in his opinion Europe and its diversity was too unique to be blended with the US. Instead, he pleaded in favor of a European federation, which could operate as the countervailing power to American and Soviet superpower politics.[16] The Western world was to be divided into equal regional federations, with no hierarchy or American leadership. At the same time European culture, which was tired and in decline after the disastrous experiences of the twentieth century, should renew itself in a European cultural renaissance.[17]

This last topic, the renewal of European culture, was also the focus of his lecture at the 1950 CCF conference in Berlin. In this speech he predicted the decline of the Soviet Union *and* of the Western world: 'And as the real drama is really this, the "defence" ... of what is known as the "Occident", or "Christianity" or "Democracy" can only be effective through a true revolutionary spirit, that is to say, with the idea that liberty must always conquer in order to live.'[18] According to Brugmans the West had lost its freedom to an overdose of centralization, monopolization and technocracy: '... it is not physical force which strangles liberty, it is fear, laziness of mind, the prejudices which are no longer criticized.'[19] The only solution to this was 'die Heilung durch den Geist', the liberation of the mind by the mind. Opinions like these make Brugmans similar in stance to the European cultural critics in the tradition of historian Johan Huizinga and the philosophers Ortega y Gasset, Georges Duhamel and Oswald Spengler, although Brugmans was not as pessimistic on the future of European culture as some of them. The outlook of this lecture was distinctly different from the fierce anti-Soviet and anti-neutralist tone of some of the other Berlin speakers.

Brugmans was more like a European citizen than a Dutch intellectual. For him the CCF was mainly an important lobby platform for the European Federalists. He did agree with the basic goals and ideology of the Congress, but his opinions on the West and his rather moderate anti-communism set him apart from more hard-line CCF members like James Burnham or Arthur Koestler. Due to his positions as chairman of the European Federalist Movement and director of the College of Europe, the CCF considered him to be one of the leading intellectual and academic figures of a future united Europe.[20] In 1955 Brugmans was again invited to the CCF conference in Milan, where he participated in the General Assembly, but there was still no longer-lasting affiliation with the CCF as a result.[21]

The profile of the second Dutchman with some affiliations with the CCF is much the same, although Abraham Hammacher operated in a world very different from that of Brugmans, the art world. Hammacher began his career as an art critic, and was appointed deputy-director of the Kröller Möller museum in 1947. Under his leadership the museum developed into one of the most famous Dutch museums on modern art, with an internationally praised sculpture garden. From the end of the 1940s Hammacher travelled many times to the United States in search of works of art, in order to study American sculptors and their work, and to make arrangements for exhibitions like the large Van Gogh exhibition in the New York Metropolitan Museum of Art in 1949. He became acquainted with art critics Meyer Shapiro and Dora Ashton and Museum of Modern Art director Alfred Barr, and very soon he was considered to be an international authority on modern art in the Netherlands alongside the other major Dutch museum directors Willem Sandberg and Eddy de Wilde.[22] He wrote internationally acclaimed studies on sculptors like Lipchitz, Zadkine and Marini Marino. In Dutch he published the first overview of Dutch modern art in the twentieth century in 1955.[23] And above all, his efforts made Vincent van Gogh even more internationally famous than he already was.

FIGURE 4

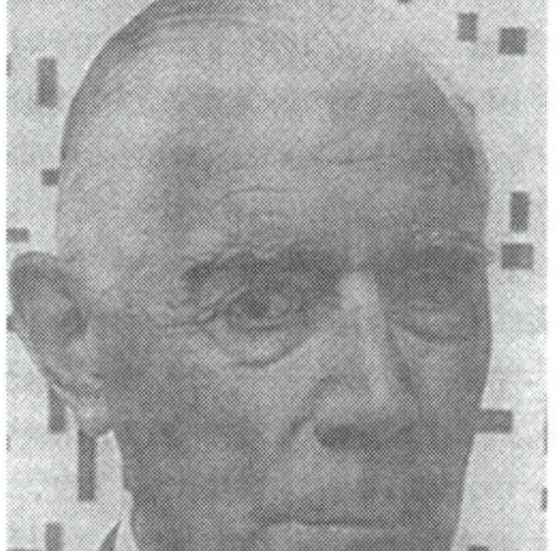

A.M.Hammacher in 1962
Private Collection R. Hammacher-van den Brande, Brussels

Hammacher did attend the CCF conference in Berlin in 1960, although why is rather obscure. Five years earlier the Kröller Möller Museum had lent some works to a CCF exhibition in Rome. Since there is no documentation on Hammacher's post-war political opinions (and it is doubtful if he had any), Hammacher's connections with the CCF seem to have been based mainly on his status and relations in the international art world, his cooperation with American museum directors and his admiration of American modern art. From the perspective of the CCF, Hammacher must have seemed an excellent intermediary between the European art world, which was partly ignorant and partly disparaging of American modern art, and the fast-developing modern art world of the United States. The interest of the CCF in such an apolitical person like Hammacher is also a clear sign that at the end of the fifties the Congress had changed its focus from hard-boiled anti-communism to more cultural topics. For Hammacher himself the CCF was probably another of his many opportunities to expand his international contacts.

Operating on the Dutch margin of the CCF, these four men – Brugmans, Mozer, Tas, and Hammacher – were in a way very much alike: in their internationalism, and in being 'men of the deed', instead of reflective desk-writers. They aimed at policy-making, publishing newspaper articles, developing a European federalist union or organizing exhibitions on modern art. And in more ways than one, they were, in fact, very un-Dutch representatives of the Netherlands. With their international, often European orientation, and the frequency of their longer or shorter stays outside the Netherlands, they were not firmly embedded in wider Dutch intellectual or cultural circles, but belonged to very specific groups which made them rather isolated in their home country – or even , in the case of Brugmans and Tas, outsiders. The CCF failed to see this. When the Paris headquarters started its search for Dutch intellectuals who might take the lead in setting up a Dutch branch, Bondy and Josselson obviously chose those people whose publications were written in a language they could read, and whose names circulated in European or transatlantic networks. They did not take into consideration that these might not be the right persons to serve as mediators between the established groups of Dutch writers and other intellectuals, and the CCF.

A SEPARATION OF POLITICS AND LITERATURE

However, the main explanation for the Dutch lack of interest in the CCF has to be found in Dutch society itself, and its intellectual and cultural traditions and climate of opinion. Unlike other Western European countries, post-war Dutch writers and artists hardly had a deeply-rooted tradition of political engagement.[24] Dutch literary works dealt mostly with personal experiences, with romantic individualism, or with issues of personal responsibilities and ethics, and not with political or social problems and issues. In general, Dutch writers showed no sense of political or social responsibility in their work, particularly not in the 1940s and 50s.[25] Political engagement was the domain of academics, journalists and politicians. As a consequence Dutch politics and literature were separated, with only a few people making cross-overs.

This observation is confirmed by the reaction of Dutch writers to the first CCF conference in Berlin, 1950. The literary journal *Critisch Bulletin* (*Critical Bulletin*) dedicated one issue to the Berlin conference by printing some of the speeches, and asked ten Dutch writers to give their opinion on engaged literature. Most were left-wing, and there seemed to be a broad consensus among them.[26] Almost all considered it wrong to dedicate their literary work to a political cause – the only choice you can make as a writer is a choice for humanity. None of these ten writers applauded the Berlin initiative, finding the conference speeches far too politicized.

While very few Dutch writers showed political interest in their work, Dutch political intellectuals lacked cultural interest. Considering this division in intellectual labour and the goals of the CCF – preserving the freedom of culture against the dangers of totalitarianism – it is unsurprising that Dutch intellectuals did not consider it important to join the Congress.

LIVE AND LET LIVE

A lively climate of public debate is a condition for a healthy and inspiring intellectual life. Yet in the 1950s there was hardly any tradition of a public debate as a consequence of the Dutch system of religious and cultural segregation. Since the nineteenth century Dutch society had been strictly divided or segregated into four pillars, based on religion or *Weltanschauung* – the Roman Catholics, Protestants, socialists and conservative-liberals. In the course of time, confrontation between these 'pillars' was avoided as much as possible, in order to keep the nation together. Among other things, this prevented the development of a tradition of confrontation in public debates and the development of a tradition of 'rhetoric'. The principle of 'live and let live' overruled the intellectual challenges of a nationwide discussion. Intellectual debates took place within the separate pillars and were mainly constructive.

This characteristic of the Dutch intellectual climate differentiated it from that of the US and other Western European countries. The way American, German, French or Italian intellectuals argued and defended their political opinions while attacking those of their opponents, often in public, was unheard of in post-war Dutch society. These differences in intellectual practices were another reason why the Dutch were not eager to participate in the CCF – an organization like the CCF and its practices did not fit into their intellectual traditions.

AN AMBIVALENT PERCEPTION OF AMERICA

For decades, since the beginning of the twentieth century, but in particular after 1945, Dutch intellectuals had a critical and dualist perception of the United States. Like the rest of the Dutch population they were grateful for the American participation in the liberation of their country, and for the

American food and Marshall aid later in the 1940s. Social democratic intellectuals were also in full support of the Netherlands joining NATO. And of course, they admired the freedom and democracy of the American system. But, on the other hand, the Dutch intellectual elite was worried about the new international role of the US. They feared that American influences would hasten the decline of European culture and civilization. Western Europe was still considered to be the foundation of Western civilization, and Western European intellectual elites felt slightly superior to their American colleagues.

This attitude was not new. Before World War II, Dutch intellectuals like the historian Johan Huizinga and the writer/journalist Menno Ter Braak had written of their concern over the placidity and vulgarity of American culture and its influence on European culture and civilization. At the same time they admired the dynamics and pragmatic energy of the Americans. After the war, most Dutch intellectuals maintained this ambivalent attitude. They found it hard to accept that post-war Western Europe had sunk to a second-rate status in international relations. For the Dutch it was extra hard because of the recent loss of their colonial possessions in the East Indies. This frustration, in combination with a strong Dutch tradition of high culture, had prevented the intelligentsia from adapting their perceptions of American culture. One might even say that the Dutch intellectual anti-Americanism was an act of resistance against the changed post-war world order. More than anybody else, they regarded the American successes during and after the war as a failure on the European side. While Americans had shown themselves to be very succesful in adapting policies to changing circumstances, Europeans had lacked the American dynamics and vitality and had failed to adjust themselves to a changed international situation. This devaluation of Western Europe to a second rank had caused an identity crisis among Dutch intellectuals, which made them extra-critical towards American cultural and intellectual activities. They focused on criticism of American (mass) culture in order to emphasize European superiority. They could not stand the idea of being a second-rate continent because of the impotence of European culture to renew itself. This context makes the Dutch intellectuals' opinions on American politics and culture a reflection of their struggle with changing values and situations and of their fear of losing pre-war traditions and relations. No doubt, this attitude played a major role in the Dutch reaction to the CCF.

CONCLUSION

Next to the failure of the CCF to approach the right Dutch intellectuals for establishing a Dutch branch, four possible explanations for the lack of engagement of the Dutch with the Congress have been discussed here: the relatively isolated position in society of the few intellectuals who had short-lived relations with the CCF, the lack of a tradition of political engagement among Dutch writers or artists, the lack of a lively climate of public debate in the Netherlands, and the ambivalent, often negative perception of American culture and society. Together, these explanations suggest that national cultural contexts and traditions exercised more influence on the intellectuals' position concerning the CCF than the Cold War policy of the Dutch government or their individual political opinions.

Situating the Congress for Cultural Freedom and Cold War intellectuals in their national cultural contexts and traditions offers a different perspective to the grand narratives of the CCF organization, its main members and its activities that have been published so far. The apparent unity in opinions and actions of the Congress might actually appear to have been more diverse if studied from different national perspectives. By focusing on the CCF in this way, the Congress's dominant image as an organization that attracted the membership and participation of every self-respecting, anti-communist Western intellectual during the 1950s, is brought into question. The non-interest of Dutch intellectuals to join the CCF shows once more that in international networks, national traditions can play a decisive role.

NOTES

1. *Proceedings. The 'Congress for Cultural Freedom'*, (1950) IACF Papers, Series III, Box 1, Folder 1, p.1.
2. 'Manifesto of Intellectual Liberty', IACF Papers, series III, Box 1, Folder 1. The Manifesto was signed by, among others, James Burnham, Reinhold Niebuhr, Lionel Trilling, Arthur Schlesinger, Jr., Peter Viereck, Raymond Aron, and Hendrick Brugmans.
3. Secretly the Congress was sponsored by the CIA, as was disclosed by *The New York Times* in 1966. See in particular Christopher Lasch, 'The Cultural Cold War: A Short History of the Congress for Cultural Freedom', in B.J. Bernstein (ed.), *Towards a New Past* (New York: Knopf 1968) pp.322–59, and Frances S. Saunders, *Who Paid the Piper? The CIA and the Cultural Cold War* (London: Granta Books 1999).
4. Brussels also lacked a CCF office.
5. Hendrick Brugmans, director of the College of Europe; A.N.J. den Hollander, sociologist; Pieter Geyl, historian; Abraham Hammacher, director Kröller-Möller Museum; J.H. Bavinck, theologian.
6. A. van Staden, 'American-Dutch Political Relations Since 1945: What Has Changed and Why?' *Bijdragen en Mededelingen betreffende de Geschiedenis der Nederlanden* 97 (1982) pp.470–86; D. Hellema, *1956: De Nederlandse houding ten aanzien van de Hongaarse revolutie en de Suezcrisis.* (Amsterdam: Mets 1990); D. Hellema, *Neutraliteit en vrijhandel* (Utrecht: Het Spectrum 2001).
7. Lasch, 'The Cultural Cold War' (note 3) pp.322–59; Peter Coleman, *The Liberal Conspiracy: The Congress for Cultural Freedom and the Struggle for the Mind of Postwar Europe* (New York: The Free Press 1989); P. Grémion, *L'intelligence de l'anti-communisme. Le CCF à Paris, 1950–1975* (Paris: Fayard 1995); Saunders, *Who Paid the Piper?* (note 3)

8. 'De vrienden van de vrijheid. De strijd tegen de "vredespartisanen" voor onze beschaving', *Het Vaderland*, 12 May 1951, p.3.
9. Letter from M. Josselson to A.A.C. van Ruiten, 9 September 1952, IACF Papers, Series II, box 249, folder 8.
10. L.A.V. Metzemaekers, *Alfred Mozer, Hongaar, Duitser, Nederlander, Europeaan* (Den Haag: Europese Beweging Nederland 1970) p.27. Also: A.Mozer-Ebbinge and R. Cohen (eds.), *Alfred Mozer: 'Gastarbeider' in Europa* (Zuthpen: De Walburg Pers 1980).
11. Frits Rovers, *Voor Recht en Vrijheid. De Partij van de Arbeid en de Koude Oorlog 1945–1958* (Amsterdam: Stichting Beheer IISG 1994) p.77.
12. Gerard Mulder and Paul Koedijk, *Léés die krant! Geschiedenis van het naoorlogse Parool.* (Amsterdam: Meulenhoff 1996) p.395.
13. At this founding conference another Dutchman was present: J.H. Bavinck, professor in missiology at the Theology Seminary, Kampen and the Free University Amsterdam. Later, Bavinck became an active member of the CCF 'Committee on Science and Freedom', which focused on the defence of academic freedom and on the moral/ethical questions raised by scientific research.
14. H. Brugmans, *Levend in Europa: Ontmoetingen en herinneringen* (Alphen a/d Rijn: Sijthoff 1980); H. Brugmans, *Wij, Europa. Een halve eeuw strijd voor emancipatie en Europees federalisme* (Amsterdam: Meulenhoff 1988).
15. Henri Brugmans, 'Chaos of orde? Europa's eigen taak' (1947), in Walter Lipgens and Wilfried Loth (eds.) *Documents on the History of European Integration*, Vol.3 (Berlin/ New York: De Gruyter 1988).
16. H. Brugmans, *Schets van een Europese samenleving* (Rotterdam: Ad. Donker 1952).
17. Ibid. 112-4.
18. Henri Brugmans, 'La Guérison par l'Esprit/Cure through the Mind'. IACF Series III, Box 1, folder 4.
19. Ibid.
20. CCF Secretary Bondy corresponded later in 1950 with Brugmans on a possible future cooperation between the CCF and the College of Europe. IACF, Series II, Box 41, Folder 1.
21. The Dutch sociologist A.N.J. den Hollander and the economist Jan Tinbergen were also invited. Tinbergen declined. IACF, Series III, box 7, Folder 3.
22. De Ruiter, *A.M. Hammacher: Kunst als levensessentie* (Baarn: De Prom 2000) p.348.
23. A.M.Hammacher, *Stromingen en persoonlijkheden – schets van een halve eeuw schilderkunst in Nederland, 1900–1950* (Amsterdam: Meulenhoff 1955).
24. A.F. van Oudvorst, 'Intellectuelen en de wereld na 1945', *Maatstaf* 37, nr.8/9 (1989) pp.38–51, quote on p.38. In the 1950s exceptions were novelist W.F. Hermans and the avant garde poet group De Vijftigers.
25. Ibid. p.39.
26. Hans Redeker, Anna Blaman, W.F. Hermans, A. Romein-Verschoor, Simon Vestdijk, Anthonie Donker, W.H. Nagel, Victor E. van Vriesland, Siegfried E. van Praag and R. Blijstra. Later in 1950 this issue was published as *Schrijvers voor de keuze: Getuigenissen over de cultuurtaak van de schrijver* (Den Haag: Daamen 1950).

PART V

High Culture as Political Message

15

'How Good Are We? Culture and the Cold War

JESSICA C. E. GIENOW-HECHT

For the last few years it has become commonplace to preface a paper, book or workshop intertwining culture and diplomacy with a few general remarks on how the field has changed and how today intellectual, artistic, ideological, philosophical, and numerous other connections have expanded our understanding of what constitutes 'foreign relations'. The essays assembled in this section all provide first-class examples for this exciting and dynamic change. As they show, today the history of American foreign relations is characterized by an intense pluralism, an intense sensibility of the significance of cultural factors, and an increasing awareness that the state is only one out of many principal actors in the international arena.

These papers also address an issue that, in the weeks following the attacks of 11 September 2001, has attracted renewed interest among policy-makers and the public alike. Why are foreign people and governments often so critical of and occasionally even outraged about the effects and the preponderance of US culture abroad? How has this perception affected the course of America's relationship with the world? And how have official and non-governmental US propaganda responded to such criticism?

In the years following the end of World War II, scholars, opinion leaders and politicians discussed these issues primarily in the context of anti-fascist re-education programs and Western Europe's commitment to the transatlantic partnership. Today, the camps have changed as the most visible and outspoken critics of the American Way of Life and its effects on the outside world live and operate in the Middle East. But the criticism itself has remained in place. And once again, public leaders call for governmentally-organized programs to teach the people around the world about the essence of American democracy and culture. In our quest for the answers to the challenges of 11 September and despite all the obvious differences, this is the time to consider the ideas of the men and women who half a century ago set out to shape a new image for the United States for audiences around the world.

This essay addresses, first, the existing scholarship on cultural policy and mass cultural transfer before turning to what I perceive as some of the most daunting research challenges.

AMERICAN CULTURAL POLICY

In the United States, the bulk of the publications on the interplay between culture and foreign relations has focused on the Cold War, including the papers in this section. Part of the reason is that most US diplomatic historians work on the post-1945 era anyway. It is during the Cold War that the United States became a global participant and leader; hence the scholarly interest. More importantly, after World War II, American diplomats began to believe that the United States needed to sell the American way of life abroad. Public figures encouraged the authorities to exert more influence through culture outside of the United States. '[W]e would be decadent people', Arthur W. Macmahon in the Department of State marveled in 1945, 'if we did not wish others to know about American standards and American techniques ... that demonstrably have contributed to human happiness'.[1]

US policy-makers subsequently grew interested in imparting the American Way of Life to others because American culture seemed to be resistant to autocracies on the left or the right. The belief in the ideological strength of American culture emerged from the writings of intellectuals like Arthur M. Schlesinger Jr. and Louis Hartz.[2] Scholars and policy-makers alike hoped that the promotion abroad of an enterprise-based culture would foster democratic values around the world and destroy fascism, communism, and other unsavory foreign ideologies.

Equally important, in the 1950s many Americans increasingly deplored what they thought was their worsening reputation in the international arena, an arena that they had really just entered.[3] Publications such as Franz M. Joseph's and Raymond Aron's *As Others See Us* described how foreign people detested America's industry, mass production, race-relations, superficiality, industrial barbarism, and 'the intellectual fodder offered to the American masses, from scandal magazines to digests of books'. The conclusion international observers drew from their analyses of the American Way of Life did not look good. Notwithstanding its fight for democracy and all the good things the nation had done for others, America seemed to be a giant with the head of a child.[4]

Such negative assessments covered aesthetic aspects of American culture as well. Public opinion polls taken between 1945 and 1950, for example, revealed that Germans feared the adaptation of democratic values at the expense of their cultural heritage: communists read the classics, spoke different languages, and listened to the nineteenth-century romantics. Democratically-inclined audiences, in contrast, paralyzed their brains with cartoons, pop music, and an avalanche of consumer products.[5]

Communists throughout Eastern Europe and the Soviet Union used much of this criticism as the cornerstone of their own propaganda: Americans were stupid, they had no culture, or at least nothing significant to write home about. But their power threatened to extinguish the cultures of other, more 'advanced' nations. Thus, when communist propagandists devised their advertising campaigns, the celebration of 'Old World culture' and especially German *Kultur* formed a central point to it. The government of the German Democratic Republic, for example, relentlessly attacked representations of American culture as manifestations of a corrupt democracy.

It was this animadversion that US officials found hardest to rebut. Most importantly, the arguments presented were not exactly new. They had been the standard fare of European political publishers for several decades and no American had ever made much effort to refute them. European conservatives had begun to resent what they perceived as the menace of American culture already in the nineteenth century, notably in France, England and Germany. William Stead, D. H. Lawrence, and Adolf Halfeld were among the most prominent early twentieth-century critics to give a voice to all those fears that have since become so commonplace around the world. Fears that US culture, standards and way of life would overrun everyone else's. Fears that American consumer products would erase other countries' cultural independence. Fears that American culture would extinguish local identities. To many observers, American civilization was not just different but formed a subversive threat to European culture.[6]

To respond to such fault-finding, in the years following VE-Day the US government founded a number of organizations and programs, such as the United States Information Agency and the Fulbright exchange program that sought to export American culture abroad. Cora Goldstein's article on US art programmes in the present volume presents a most interesting case study for these political programs. The 'Campaign of Truth', devised in 1950 in response to the Korean War, explicitly targeted public opinion leaders and other 'multipliers' with books, brochures, exhibitions and lectures.[7]

The cultural and information programmes thus devised in Washington were then implemented abroad by a variety of administrative programmes and divisions, the most prominent of which was the United States Information Service (USIS).[8] Likewise, Eisenhower's 'President's Emergency Fund for Participation in International Affairs' allotted, from 1954 on, five million dollars per year for some sixty musical tours abroad, including Robert Breen's musical *Porgy and Bess* which is the topic of David Monod's contribution in this collection.[9]

When responding to animadversions, US propagandists remained unspecific in their definition of American 'culture'. Take, for example, a look at the programmes of the United States Information Agency under the guidance of Theodor Streibert, designed in 1953 to convince people abroad that US goals were in harmony with their hopes for freedom, progress and peace. But these programs also underscore the Agency's uncertainty. Laura Belmonte, for example, has shown that USIA's programs focused on artifacts that were regarded as typical for American culture and society, including consumer products, high living standards, and the advantages of a free market economy.[10]

In the 1960s, however, as scholars as well as the public became increasingly critical of US cultural propaganda, the USIA moved away from the State Department and became, as cultural officers like to say, a more independent agency, responsible only to the President of the United States. Programmes and country plans assumed a more long-term perspective with little attention to actual events and next to no co-operation with the State Department. And if you talk to cultural officers today, they collectively believe that this was a smart thing to do. It gave them more power while simultaneously defying common domestic and international accusations of 'political propaganda'.

Nonetheless, the critical arguments raised against US cultural and information programmes that were first put forward in the 1960s and since repeated a million times around the globe are worth hearing. For they eventually triggered a second research trend that has almost superseded the one on cultural policies and that today dominates the field of culture and the Cold War. As Paul Hollander observed, in the 1960s a surge of anti-Americanism stigmatized the United States. It included, not surprisingly, an aversion to American culture at home and abroad, and an outright rejection of US foreign policy. A nascent leftist movement identified expansive capitalism as both the driving force behind the bipolar conflict between East and West, and as representative for a host of things describing twentieth-century society, such as consumerism, modernity, organization, and the conflict between society and the individual.[11] These arguments prepared the way for the study of US consumer culture and its influence around the world.

Much of the scholarship on American Cold War culture abroad since the 1960s has focused on the media in the broadest sense, because the media relate most obviously to current political issues. Information technologies, the news, movies, cartoons, books, and, most recently, the internet have been at the heart of this research trend. For over 20 years, scholars like Herbert Schiller, his students and followers, and many others have poured out an abundance of books in which they portrayed the American media as the essence but also the villain of modern culture, a kind of giant hypermarket with zillions of screens but no exit. Either one culture dominates another by exporting its media, or scholars detect the spread of a media-dominated culture the world over.[12]

What is interesting about this line of thought is that the United States government plays a rather subordinate role in this scenario. Its agents are primarily private American entrepreneurs, large anonymous corporations, and independently wealthy media tsars who either act on their own or, occasionally, conspire with secret services and governments in order to control foreign minds and foreign markets in their search for ever more consumers and profits.

While this is not the time or place to revisit revisionism or dependency theory, we need to remind ourselves that it was the New Left that severed the obligatory ties between governmental records and 'diplomatic history'. Even though these scholars focused very much on capitalist ideology and the link between private groups and the government, their thinking has alerted us to the fact that what is commonly defined as 'cultural exports' or 'cultural propaganda' refers to a highly heterogeneous and complex group of governmental and non-governmental agents, actions and motivations. Governmental exports focused increasingly on highbrow exports such as book and art exhibits; manifestations of popular culture were only admitted if they revealed a specific educational purpose. Non-governmental actors split into those who exported material goods (corporate enterprises) and those who were more interested in the exchange of people and ideas (unions, women's group, foundations).

Researchers writing on culture and diplomacy during the Cold War in the 1970s and 80s still very much focused their research on culture as an underlying force of diplomacy, an instrument of state policy ('cultural diplomacy'). Notably during the last decade of the Cold War culture increasingly developed into an all-inclusive category replacing the term and the meaning of ideology. 'Culture' seemed to offer historians as well as scholars in neighboring fields such as anthropology and cultural studies a path out of the dead-end Marxist analysis of economic domination.[13]

Since the 1990s, a new generation of younger scholars on both sides of the Atlantic has assumed a much more pragmatic and less ideologically blinded approach to the study of culture and international history. Many of these younger scholars were originally trained in neighboring fields such as social history, cultural studies, and anthropology. They have expanded the meaning of culture to include social affinities, comparative analysis, cultural conceptions, psychological influences, local traditions, and unspoken assumptions. And they have become increasingly fascinated with the peculiarity of individual cultures in the context of a non-bipolar world. Under the influence of resurfacing nationalism the world over, scholars have studied the periphery in greater detail, producing analyses of individual communities that came into contact with American (or Western) culture after World War II. They have shifted the centre of research from the intention of cultural transfer to, for example, the audience of TV programmes like *Dallas* or films such as *Gone With the Wind*.[14]

The contributors in this section on culture and the Cold War are very much part of this new generation. They all do not restrain their research to the planners in Washington but expand their inquiries to the agents of transmission, such as cultural officers or theatre directors, and the reactions of local audiences. I am hesitant to announce that today we have completed the analysis of American culture abroad, if only because each generation of academics claims to have finally discovered the philosopher's stone. But we certainly have a more multi-faceted, fuller and fairer picture than we did a dozen years ago. Which finally brings me to the question where the scholarship of American culture and the Cold War in Europe could turn next.

RESEARCH DIRECTIONS

The most under-investigated and simultaneously most promising approach, it seems to me, is American officials' gradual rapprochement with the high cultural scene. In the early years following VE-Day, information officials in Germany, for example, were tremendously reluctant to make any concessions to the quality of German *Kultur*, believing that such acknowledgment would echo Joseph Goebbels' propaganda tune that 'Americans are money-hungry barbarians with no cultural life of their own'. Such concessions, US propagandists feared, would then reinforce the Germans' 'national feeling' that their life and culture was superior to any other way of life. In Munich in 1945, for example, the head of the American Information Control Division, Robert McClure, went so far as to scold the editors of the official organ of the US Army for the local population, the *Neue Zeitung*, for dedicating three-quarters of the literary section to German authors. When the chief editor discovered Carl Sandburg and John Steinbeck in the inventory, he pointed out that both belonged to the writers' elite in the United States. McClure was perplexed: 'That's right', he said, 'but Sandburg and Steinbeck have German names – the Germans will take them for Germans.'[15]

In contrast, Soviet officials had realized early on – earlier than their US counterparts – that Europeans identified strongly with their high culture. Soviet and East German propagandists had made *Bildung* (knowledge, education) and *Kultur* (high culture) central points of their own advertising campaigns. For example *Tägliche Rundschau*, the Red Army paper in the Soviet occupation zone, regularly published reports on the popularity of Goethe and Beethoven among culture-loving Russians.

Public opinion polls taken by the American military government in Germany between 1945 and 1950 revealed that Germans feared the adaptation to democratic values at the expense of their cultural heritage. Numerous letters to the US radio station RIAS in Berlin showed that it lost many listeners due to its 'western' music program. The conflict between political principles and cultural criteria created an 'aesthetic syllogism' for many Germans who reflected that 1) I do not like jazz; 2) I associate American democracy with jazz; 3) I do not like American democracy. Communists, they concluded, at least, liked and listened to Beethoven and Tchaikovsky. Democratically-inclined audiences, in contrast, seemed to numb their minds with jazz.[16]

As US propagandists gathered more information on German cultural preferences and the significance of high culture in European society, they began to understand the failures of their early approaches and adjusted their programmes accordingly. Officials like Shepard Stone grasped that the United States' cultural programme should not only refute Soviet charges and inform German audiences about American society and culture. A transatlantic political partnership could only flourish if it rested on cultural ties as well.[17] To revise their unfavorable impressions of US culture, aside from all past military and diplomatic conflicts, Germans needed to learn more about US academic and high cultural achievements. And they needed to be reminded of their elective affinity with the United States that had tied the countries together for over a hundred years. In other words, the United States had to cease telling the Germans how to be more like Americans; instead, programs should reveal how much the United States and the Federal Republic resembled each other on the cultural level.

Stone knew that cultural bonds not only preceded but had shaped the German-American political partnership. American and European cultural elites had been interacting intensively since at least the late nineteenth century. As Jürgen Heideking and others have shown, German scholarship and science dominated the American university canon until the eve of World War I.[18] German and American academics embarked on a vibrant exchange program in the early 1900s. Organized by the Prussian cultural ministry and with the explicit support of the German Kaiser, German professors went to teach at Harvard, Johns Hopkins, and Columbia University, among others, while a trickle of American professors taught in Berlin and Göttingen. German artists frequently visited US studios in order to exchange ideas with their American peers. German entrepreneurs, manufacturers and bankers established branches of their respective institutions in the metropolises along the Eastern Coast and throughout the Midwest. Such phenomena do not fit into your typical immigration story; instead, these men and women shuttled back and forth across the Atlantic, often several times a year and more frequently than any German diplomat.

MUSICAL BRIDGES

Nowhere, it seems to me, did German and American cultural interests interact more intensively than in the field of music. Between 1850 and 1918, serious music (eighteenth, nineteenth and early twentieth century music, or 'classical') composed in German-speaking countries as well as German musicology and music pedagogy virtually monopolized the American music scene. An armada of German musicians, conductors, and composers visited, toured, and sometimes even moved permanently to the United States, in order to 'bring our rich treasures of our great masters there to the world of the future and help that they conquer the world'.[19] Driven by an almost missionary zeal they introduced orchestral music, notably Wagner as well as the symphony, to both metropolitan and rural audiences. They founded or helped to found the first and most important symphony orchestras in the nation (including the New York Philharmonic, the Chicago Symphony Orchestra, and the Boston Symphony Orchestra) as well as numerous conservatories. Because of their actions, at the end of the nineteenth century music became synonymous with German; indeed, to be German meant to be musical.[20]

The German musicians' success in the United States created an emotional elective affinity between the two countries that would survive two world wars and almost 50 years of nuclear antagonism. In the 1920s, 30s, and 40s, movies, cartoons, and musical theaters provided a new arena for the display of classical music that fused the power of the orchestra with socio-political messages and the popular appeal of fairy tales, criminal stories, and melodrama. Take a look at Walt Disney's 1940 production, 'Fantasia', that was designed to make movie audiences virtually 'see' and appreciate the power of music. Starring Mickey Mouse, famous conductor Leopold Stokowski, and the Philadelphia Orchestra next to dancing notes and surreal pictures matched to the music of Bach, Beethoven, Schubert, and others, 'Fantasia' sought to visualize the power of symphonic music and to bridge the gap between modern pop culture and European *Kultur*. In retrospect, the merger of popular and high culture reaffirmed the cultural bonds between the two continents (though this had not necessarily been the producers' intention).[21]

During the Cold War, many of these cultural ties and activities were suddenly subordinated and manipulated by the policy-making process. Men like Shepard Stone very much understood and built their programmes upon this preexisting high cultural bond. Sponsored by the prodigious funds and cultural anxieties of the Cold War, they created a multitude of cultural programmes designed to convince foreign audiences that Germans and Americans shared a common dedication to classical music.

From exchange programmes and trade treaties to concert trips and artistic visits, geopolitical strategy began to dictate and to fund where students, artists and business men went in their search for enlightenment, profit, and human encounter. Students who were looking for a 'study abroad' programme now looked to the Fulbright Commission, while artists took advantage of new programmes and funds created by the ideological pressures of the bipolar division of the world. Performing artists, in particular, eagerly applied for governmental funds that would enable them to travel to distant places and play in front of foreign audiences despite a lack of revenue.

The man who scored one of the highest points for American musical diplomacy during the Cold War was the pianist Van Cliburn. In April 1958 the 23-year-old Texan travelled to Moscow where he won the first prize at the Tchaikovsky International competition with an interpretation of Rachmaninoff's Piano Concerto No. 3 which catapulted him overnight to world-wide fame. Nikita Khrushchev, as well as composers Dimitri Shostakovich and Kiril Kondrashin, were among the first to congratulate the young pianist. When Cliburn returned to the United States for a triumphant ticker-tape parade in Manhattan, the first one ever accorded to a classical musician, the mayor of New York proclaimed the day of his return 'Van Cliburn Day'.[22] In the geopolitical struggle for Germany and Europe, Cliburn proved that an American could play classical music just as well if not better than a European artist. More importantly, his performance bore testimony to America's respect for and mastery of high culture, a point doubted by the German people and disputed by communist propaganda.

Van Cliburn's success inspired cultural officers to further explore the potentials of orchestral music in their quest for German (and West European) sympathies. Yet while officials believed they were merely using cultural products for political ends, the truth was that they did precisely the opposite: set in the geopolitical landscape of the early Cold War, their actions affirmed cultural bonds that had been existing way before political alliances came to be established. In 1959, President Eisenhower sent Leonard Bernstein and the New York Philharmonic on a mission all across Europe, to convince millions of listeners of the cultural compatibility between Europe and the United States. At the end of the trip, the Philharmonic played at a workshop at the Moscow Conservatory where the charismatic Bernstein exclaimed in front of hundreds of sober-looking

FIGURE 1

Pianist Van Cliburn with adoring fans in Moscow, April 1958.

Van Cliburn Foundation, Fort Worth, Texas

FIGURE 2

Van Cliburn's ticker tape parade in New York, 1958.

Van Cliburn Foundation, Fort Worth, Texas

Russians: 'Your music and ours are the artistic products of two very similar people who are natural friends, who belong together and who must not let suspicions and fears and prejudices keep them apart'.[23] Ideological and diplomatic differences notwithstanding, Bernstein implied, Europeans and Americans were bound together by the emotional bonds of their common cultural past and preferences.

The tales of Bernstein, Van Cliburn and the New York Philharmonic show that high culture provided the basis for Cold War propaganda as much as the Cold War manipulated representations of high culture. The fundamental preconception motivating the USIA's musical programmes in Germany originated in an elective affinity between the two countries that had already existed since the second half of the nineteenth century. Competing against communist claims that America had no high culture, US Cold War programmes invoked previous instances of high cultural exchange. In doing so, they sealed a cultural partnership that had been in existence for almost a 100 years.

Culture and cultural influences are their own form of power, not just mere tools of political propagandists. This is not to suggest a form of cultural power without any politics involved. Yet in the context of Cold War historiography, scholars interested in the nexus of culture and international affairs all too often focus on the political motivation for cultural programmes without considering the broader context and the influence of cultural images on these programmes, their reception, and their ultimate success – or failure.

Indeed, often cultural affinity and political antipathy develop hand in hand. This is a point I would urge you to remember when you read the following papers. There is an increasing tendency to view cultural relations in the context of and as a reaction to the political environment, in this case in the framework of post-war politics. But in the case of Germany, indeed in the case of all of Europe, cultural relations and exchanges had been in place before, both on the level of high and popular culture. The Cold War highlighted, formalized and politicized these ties. It triggered programmes to finance individual interactions that would otherwise not have been taking place. But it did not inspire new cultural affinities, least of all between Germany and the United States. Those had been in place before and they remained in place thereafter.

CONCLUSIONS

It seems to me that this insight – the fact that the success of cultural programmes depends on a pre-existing cultural affinity, and that even cultural sympathies are no guarantee for political compliance – is of enormous importance to us today. There is a fine line between the socio-economic position of 'You, too, can be like us' (as reflected in the European Recovery Program), and the plea for the recognition that 'we are the same as you' (as implied in countless USIA programs in the 1950s). Researchers and policy makers need to be aware of these subtleties and differentiate cases accordingly, when referring to 'Americanization' in the context of Western Europe.

Consider, for example, two recent statements following the attacks on the World Trade Center and the Pentagon, on 11 September 2001, that mesmerized the European media, one by the Russian president, Vladimir Putin, and one by his US colleague, George W. Bush. When lobbying for Russia's admission to NATO Putin exclaimed before the German Bundestag:

> Russia always had special feelings for Germany.... Today I will allow myself the courage to give the larger part of my speech in the language of Goethe, Schiller and Kant – in the German language.[24]

Less than three weeks later, President Bush wondered aloud during a press conference at the White House how to respond when confronted with such 'vitriolic hatred for America' in some countries:

> I'm amazed that there's such misunderstanding of what our country is about that people would hate us. I am – like most Americans, I just can't believe it because I know how good we are. And we've got to do a better job of making our case.[25]

Bush's effort to 'explain' downplays the significance of a common cultural ground and the necessity of listening to the other side. We should applaud the American President for his faith in cultural information programmes. Increasingly soft-pedaled and curtailed after the end of the Cold War, these programmes may perhaps experience a vigorous revival in new target areas around the globe. At the same time, we should be well aware of the boundaries of those very activities. First, the success of these programmes is limited, in particular as target groups may appreciate a country's culture while at the same time rejecting its political system and leadership. Second, cultural programmes have proved most successful in areas where locals already felt attracted to the United States and vice versa; that was the case even, indeed especially, for Nazi Germany. That is to say, unless there is a cultural framework in place that creates the foundation for a dialogue and a consensus on values such as individual liberty, the power of aesthetics, middle-class homes, or how to spend your leisure time, and unless governments employ culturally sensitive agents to mediate such a dialogue, it is very difficult to convince others of 'how good you are'.

NOTES

1. Arthur W. Macmahon, *Memorandum on the Postwar International Information Program of the United States* (New York: Arno Press [1945] 1972) p.2; Henry L. Luce, *The American Century* (New York: Farrow & Rinehart 1941) p.23; Benjamin Floyd Pittenger, *Indoctrination for American Democracy* (New York: Macmillan 1941).
2. Daniel J. Boorstin, *America and the Image of Europe: Reflections on American Thought* (Gloucester, MA.: Peter Smith [c.1960] 1976).
3. Laura A. Belmonte, 'Defending a Way of Life: American Propaganda and the Cold War, 1945–1959', PhD dissertation, University of Virginia 1996; Walther L. Hixson, *Parting the Curtain: Propaganda, Culture, and the Cold War, 1945–1961* (New York: St. Martin's Press 1997); Reinhold Wagnleitner, *Coca-Colanization and the Cold War: the Cultural Mission of the United States in Austria after the Second World War* (Chapel Hill: Univ. of North Carolina Press 1994).
4. Franz M. Joseph and Raymond Aron (eds.), *As Others See Us: The United States Through Foreign Eyes* (Princeton UP 1959) pp.65, 101, 112–23, 260, 346–53; William J. Lederer and Eugene Burdick, *The Ugly American* (New York: Norton 1958) pp.271–85.
5. D.G. White, *US Military Government in Germany: Radio Reorientation* (Karlsruhe: US European Command, Historical Division 1950) pp.114–17. For an extensive analysis of Soviet cultural policy in occupied Germany see David Pike, *The Politics of Culture in Soviet-Occupied Germany, 1945–1949* (Stanford UP 1992).
6. D.H. Lawrence, *Studies in Classic American Literature* (New York: Viking Press 1950) [Original: Thomas Seltzer Inc., 1923] pp.9–21; Adolf Halfeld, *Amerika und der Amerikanismus. Kritische Betrachtungen eines Deutschen und Europäers* (Jena: E. Diederichs 1927); Mary Nolan, *Visions of Modernity: American Business and the Modernization of Germany* (New York: Oxford UP 1994); Frank Costigliola, *Awkward Dominion: American Political, Economic, and Cultural Relations with Europe, 1919–1933* (Ithaca, NY: Cornell UP 1984) pp.19ff, 167–83, 264ff; Alexander Schmidt, *Reisen in die Moderne. Der Amerika-Diskurs des deutschen Bürgertums vor dem Ersten Weltkrieg im europäischen Vergleich* (Berlin: Akademie Verlag 1997) pp.163–9.
7. Howland H. Sargant, 'Information and Cultural Representation Overseas', in Vincent M. Barnett Jr., *The Representation of the United States Abroad* (New York: Praeger 1965) p.73f; Hansjörg Gehring, *Amerikanische Literaturpolitik in Deutschland 1945–1953. Ein Aspekt des Re-Education-Programms* (Stuttgart: Deutsche Verlags-Anstalt 1976) pp.93, 112; Gary E. Kraske, *Missionaries of the Book: The American Library Profession and the Origins of United States Cultural Diplomacy* (London: Greenwood Press 1985) pp.246–9.
8. Terry Deibel and Walter Roberts, *Culture and Information: Two Foreign Policy Functions* (Beverly Hills, CA: Sage Publications 1976); John W. Henderson, *The United States Information Agency* (New York: Praeger 1969); Thomas Klöckner, *Public Diplomacy – Auswärtige Informations- und Kulturpolitik der USA: Strukturanalyse der Organisaton und Strategien der United States Information Agency und des United States Information Service in Deutschland* (Baden Baden: Nomos 1993); Hans Tuch, *Communicating with the World: U.S. Diplomacy Overseas* (New York: St. Martin's Press 1990).
9. Charles A. Thomson and Walter H. C. Laves, *Cultural Relations and US Foreign Policy* (Bloomington, IN: Indiana UP 1963) p.123; John Harper Taylor, 'Ambassadors of the Arts: An Analysis of the Eisenhower Administration's Incorporation of "Porgy and Bess" Into Its Cold War Foreign Policy', PhD dissertation, Ohio State University 1994.
10. Laura Belmonte, 'Defending a Way of Life'; Hixson, *Parting the Curtain* (note 3); Klöckner, *Public Diplomacy* (note 8) pp.82–9; Michael L. Krenn, '"Unfinished Business:" Segregation and US Diplomacy at the 1958 World's Fair', *Diplomatic History* 20 (Fall 1996) pp.591–612.
11. Paul Hollander, *Anti-Americanism: Critiques at Home and Abroad, 1965–1990* (New York: Oxford UP 1992) pp.54–7, 337, 339.
12. For more on the historiography of American culture abroad after 1945, see Jessica C. E. Gienow-Hecht, 'Shame on US? Academics, US Cultural Transfer, and the Cold War', *Diplomatic History* 24 (Summer 2000) pp.465–94.

13. Richard Rorty, 'The Intellectuals at the End of Socialism', *Yale Review* 80 (1992) pp.1–16.
14. Bill Ashcroft, *The Empire Writes Back: Theory and Practice in Postcolonial Literatures* (London: Routledge 1989); Patrick Williams and Laura Chrisman, *Colonial Discourse and Postcolonial Theory: A Reader* (New York: Columbia UP 1994).
15. Jessica C.E. Gienow-Hecht, *Transmission Impossible: American Journalism as Cultural Diplomacy in Postwar Germany, 1945–1955* (Baton Rouge: Louisiana State UP 1999) p.85.
16. White, *US Military Government in Germany* (note 5) pp.114–17. For an extensive analysis of Soviet cultural policy in occupied Germany see Pike, *The Politics of Culture in Soviet-Occupied Germany* (note 5).
17. Volker R. Berghahn, *America and the Intellectual Cold Wars in Europe: Shepard Stone between Philanthropy, Academy, and Diplomacy* (Princeton UP 2001).
18. Jürgen Heideking, Henry Geitz, and Jürgen Herbst (eds.), *German Influences on American Education to 1917* (Cambridge/New York: Cambridge UP 1995).
19. Henry Albrecht, *Skizze aus dem Leben der Musik-Gesellschaft Germania* (Philadelphia: King and Baird 1869) p.9, translation in Nancy Newman, 'Gleiche Rechte, gleiche Pflichten, und gleiche Genüsse: Henry Albrecht's Utopian Vision of the Germania Musical Society', *Yearbook of German-American Studies* 34 (1999).
20. Abram Chasins, *Leopold Stokowski: A Profile* (New York: Hawthorn Books 1979) p.xv.
21. Ibid., p.174; John Culhane, *Walt Disney's Fantasia* (New York: Abradale Press/Henry N. Abrams 1983).
22. Artist Files, Van Cliburn, Academy of Music Archives, Philadelphia, Pennsylvania.
23. Leonard Bernstein in 'Leonard Bernstein and the New York Philharmonic', produced by Robert Saudek, taped on 12 Sept. 1959 at the farewell concert in the Moscow Conservatory, videotape, New York Philharmonic Archives.
24. Vladimir Putin, 25 Sept. 2001, Berlin, 'Auszüge aus der Rede Putins vor dem Bundestag', available online <www.tagesschau.de/archiv/2001/09/26/aktuell/meldungen/putin_rede.html>.
25. Bush's Press Conference, The White House, 11 Oct. 2001, available online <http://www.nytimes.com/2001/10/11/national/11WIRE-BUSH-TEXT.html?pagewanted=>

16

The Control of Visual Representation: American Art Policy in Occupied Germany, 1945–1949

CORA SOL GOLDSTEIN

Much of the literature on art and art policy in post-war West Germany underestimates the role that the United States played in the development of German art after 1945.[1] The resurgence of modern art in West Germany is more often depicted as a grassroots phenomenon, an explosion of intrinsically German artistic creativity after 12 years of totalitarian repression.[2] In this paper I show that the development of the fine arts in post-war West Germany was influenced by the Office of Military Government for Germany, US (OMGUS). Starting in 1946, OMGUS developed a fine arts policy to encourage the emergence of a new West German aesthetic paradigm in the Cold War context.

RE-EDUCATION

The American occupation of Germany in the immediate post-war period entailed more than the control of the economy and the reconstruction of political institutions. OMGUS initiated a cultural revolution in Germany. Washington's initial strategic objective was to ensure that Germany would not cause another world war. The short term solution was the total destruction of Germany's military and industrial potential. The long term solution called for a radical change of the norms and values of German society. The Americans viewed re-education as the way to change the Germans' tenets and behaviour, and make them accept a non-totalitarian world view, open to the influences of Western liberal democracy. The American re-education programme was based on the assumption that Nazism was a psychological malady that could only be eradicated through changing the way that Germans understood and interpreted the world.[3] To combat the 'warped German mentality', Germans had to be taught new moral and political categories by which to make sense and organize their views of reality.[4]

OMGUS waged a 'war of ideas'.[5] Its Information Control Division (ICD) regulated the ways and means, as well as the content, of the information that reached the German public in the American Zone.[6] Through ICD, OMGUS policed the boundaries of the acceptable and the desirable in the cultural fields. ICD controlled the media – which included the oral and written press, film, theater, literature, and music – and monitored German cultural life in the American Zone. OMGUS political and cultural officers encouraged cultural activities that were seen as politically healthy and democratic, and weeded out those associated with Nazism, nationalism, and militarism. ICD censored and licensed film, radio, and the press, and the political screening of people and projects excluded individuals and ideas deemed politically unacceptable.[7] All public cultural activities and entertainment were designed to re-educate the German population, combating Nazi legacies and implanting new ideas.[8] Through ICD, OMGUS introduced new narratives about Germany and America to the German public.

Initially, OMGUS did not regard the fine arts as a means of re-education, and its cultural policy ignored the potential usefulness of art as a political instrument. ICD cultural officers did not take into account that the fine arts were a central element of German *Kultur*, and ignored the pedagogic role that the fine arts had played in the Nazi period. Although OMGUS did not consider art as a medium of re-education, the Americans did have what amounted to a 'negative' art policy. Captain Gordon Gilkey, US Army, was charged with the task of eliminating 'Nazi or militaristic' art from museums and other public spaces, as instructed by the Joint Chiefs of Staff Directive 1067. Gilkey's iconoclastic campaign, carried out under the provisions of the Denazification Program, resulted in the sequestration of approximately 8,000 German works of art, and their shipment to military repositories in the Pentagon.[9] ICD ensured that the art exhibited in the American Zone and in the American Sector of Berlin did not contain Nazi propaganda. To gain access to art supplies and have the right to exhibit, artists had to complete *Fragebogen* (political questionnaires), and only those exonerated (from the status of Nazi) received *Erlaubnis* (authorization) to be registered and work as artists. Analogous clearances were necessary to open galleries and deal in art, as well as to publish art journals, produce exhibition brochures or posters, or even to issue invitations for art showings.[10] Since ICD did not have a Fine Arts Section, licensing was the responsibility of the Theater and Music Section.[11] The Museum, Fine Arts, and Archives Section (MFA&A) belonged to the OMGUS Economics Division, and initially it dealt solely with the recuperation and restitution of art collections stolen by the Nazis in occupied countries.[12] Until 1946, American cultural officers paid little if any attention to the German art scene.

The American indifference towards the development of a new German fine arts movement contrasted markedly with the attitude of the Soviet military government. Soviet intelligence officers knew the importance of the fine arts as a medium for political indoctrination and mass re-education, and understood the political relevance of the fine arts in Nazi Germany.[13] The 1945 decree on the restoration of German cultural life in the Soviet Zone called for the 'mobilization of art as part of the struggle against Fascism and of the re-education of the German people in the spirit of true democracy'.[14] To this effect, the Soviets immediately implemented an active cultural programme to support and encourage the development of the post-war German fine arts. The Soviets created cultural centres for German artists, provided them with means of sustenance and work, and organized exhibits of German art. At the same time, Soviet intelligence officers developed an active cultural programme to disseminate Soviet conceptions of art. Until 1947, Soviet fine arts policy was characterized by aesthetic tolerance and relative openness. In 1946, Lieutenant Colonel Alexander Dymschitz, the principal Soviet cultural officer in Germany, published a series of articles in *Tägliche Rundschau*, the Soviet newspaper in Berlin, explaining that Socialist Realism was not a 'canon' or 'dogma', and that it was 'open to all forms of art and all themes'.[15] With the beginning of the Cold War, this trend was reversed and Soviet cultural officers started an aggressively conservative campaign, demonizing modern art and glorifying Socialist Realism. In November 1947, Dymschitz proclaimed, at a conference held at the *Haus der Kultur der Sowjetunion* in Berlin, that art was part of a larger cultural battle between communism and capitalism. According to an American intelligence officer, Dymschitz declared that art 'must be realistic. Surrealism and abstraction have no right to exist. All art that does not fit the specifications is ... decadent, individualistic, capitalistic'.[16] This assault on modern art was followed by a new series of articles in *Tägliche Rundschau*, where he attacked 'formalist' tendencies in German painting as evidence of 'bourgeois decadence.'[17] The principal allegation was that 'formalist' art concerned itself with aesthetic issues at the expense of content, and was therefore contrary to the Socialist objective in Germany.[18] German art that was not Socialist Realist was labeled pathological and anti-aesthetical.[19]

The shifts in Soviet cultural policy in Germany reflected the new strategy of the USSR and the important changes in the international situation that it engendered. By 1947 the possibility that the Soviet Union and the United States would collaborate to reconstruct post-war Europe had evaporated. In May 1947, General George Marshall, the American Secretary of State, had proposed that the European states – the USSR included – should participate in a plan (financed by the US) to reconstruct

Europe. The Soviets rejected the agreement, and denounced the Marshall Plan as a ploy to isolate the Soviet Union and further the aims of American imperialism. Simultaneously, Stalin moved to replace the Comintern – that had been dissolved in 1943 – with the Cominform, the communist Information Bureau charged with forming a liaison with the foreign communist parties. Officially announced in October 1947, the Cominform rigidly controlled the national communist parties.[20] With the Cominform, the idea of indigenous roads to socialism was bypassed, and Moscow engineered a unified 'socialist camp' to fight against American 'imperialist aggression'. In the subsequent months the Soviet Union consolidated its hold over Eastern Europe, and the cultural and ideological struggle between the Soviets and the Americans for the control of Germany intensified.

FIGURE 1

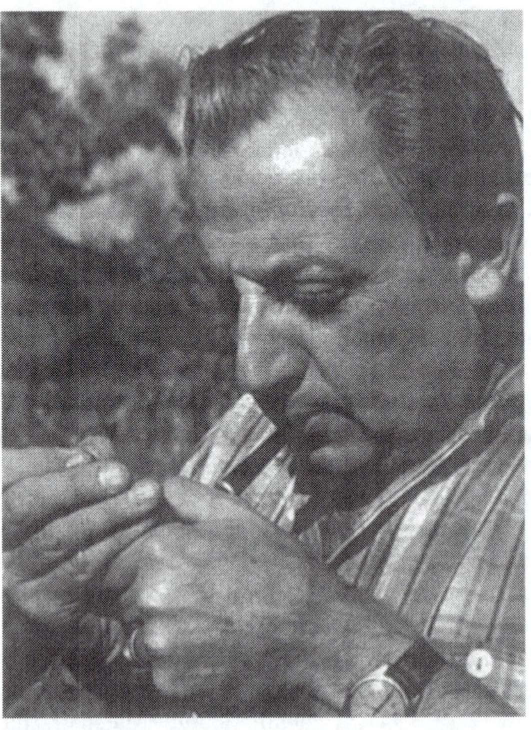

Hellmut Lehmann-Haupt in the 1950s.

Bezirk Steglitz, Berlin

HELLMUT LEHMANN-HAUPT AND MFA&A'S ART POLICY

Hellmut Lehmann-Haupt, an intelligence liaison officer with MFA&A, closely followed the Soviet military government's evolving cultural agenda, and proposed that an American art policy was essential. German by birth and educated in Germany, he belonged to a small group of American art experts that had studied the innovative political utilization of the fine arts by the Nazi regime.[21] Lehmann-Haupt insisted on the danger of leaving the public visual sphere under the control and influence of two major rivals, namely the Nazis and the Soviets. The fine arts were an ideal space for establishing clear cut differences not only between the new West Germany and its past, but also between the USSR and Eastern Germany. It is likely that Lehmann-Haupt's ideas were adopted because they fitted into the evolving West-East confrontation in the context of the incipient Cold War. MFA&A's role in Germany was transformed. By 1947, MFA&A officers were not solely involved in the restitution of looted art, but organized art exhibitions, provided exhibition space, established art contests, invited international speakers to lecture on art, created art appreciation groups, purchased work by and channeled funds to German artists, and connected German artists to American museums and art patrons. Formal and informal, overt and covert networks were established to encourage German painters and sculptors in the context of an expanding network of German-American cultural relations.

The primary objectives of the MFA&A's art policy were to overcome the cultural isolationism of the Third Reich and to link West Germany to the West, and these aims coincided with the new American conceptualization of Germany and of German-American relations. By 1947, the cultural reconstruction of Germany became an explicit political directive.[22] OMGUS cultural officers selected the elements of Germanness which they considered to be adequate for the development of a new democratic West German collective identity, and supported their diffusion. The 'Long-Range Policy Statement for German Re-Education', prepared by the Education and Cultural Relations Branch of OMGUS in 1947, announced that 'a program for the reconstitution of German cultural life has been initiated'.[23] The notion of 'cultural revival at a national scale' was considered integral to the long-terms goals of reeducation. The German cultural tradition and German 'contributions to civilization' were to provide a source of national pride and 'German self-respect'.[24] It is important to realize that OMGUS officers did not engage in a coarse exercise of 'Americanization.'

The OMGUS art policy promoted the revival of modern art in Germany, but its political role transcended aesthetic considerations. During his extended trips throughout the American Zone as OMGUS Arts Liaison in 1946 and 1947, Lehmann-Haupt interviewed many of the leading figures of

German art life and concluded that there was a marked tendency towards cultural nationalism and isolationism. The most reliable indicator was the prevalent rejection of modern art. In the immediate post-war period, art history professors continued to discourage students from studying modern art, few students enrolled in courses taught by modern artists, modern artists struggled in vain to get commissions from German authorities, and both private and public innuendos against modern art were commonplace.[25] After being exposed for 12 years to a defamation campaign against modern art, even bland exponents of modernism were often perceived with distrust and antagonism by the public.[26] The modernist works at the exhibit *Maler der Gegenwart*, held in Augsburg in December 1945, provoked violent outbursts among the viewers, and some of the canvases were mutilated.[27] The most negative reactions came from the young people, who in some cases asked that the abstract artists be 'stuck into concentration camps' or 'gunned down'.[28] Three-fourths of the 75,000 visitors at the *Allgemeine Deutschen Kunstausstellung*, a huge show of German modern art that opened in Berlin in 1946, were reported to have disliked what they saw.[29] The press was also often critical. An article in the *Berliner Zeitung* criticized Heinz Trökes, a painter who had been labeled as 'degenerate' by the Nazis and who had developed into *the* surrealist of the post-war period, with arguments that mirrored the older Nazi arguments: 'What we need is clarity and cleanliness, not this artistic glorification of the irrational and perverse.'[30] The negative attitude towards modern art was interpreted by Lehmann-Haupt as having serious political connotations. It was seen as an indicator of the continuing strength of Nazi prejudice and ideology. The rejection of modern art, particularly emanating from students and young people, was taken as a rejection of democratic culture and a failure of re-education.[31]

COLLABORATION

In November 1946, a small group of OMGUS functionaries stationed in the American Sector of Berlin, Hellmut Lehmann-Haupt, Beryl Rogers McClaskey, Charles Baldwin, and Paul Lutzeier, founded the group *Prolog*, an unprecedented experiment in American cultural politics. *Prolog* was a cultural covert operation because the OMGUS officers that conceived and developed the project operated as if acting in their private capacity. This 'informal' organization of Americans living in Berlin selected a group of modern German artists and met regularly with them.[32] The idea was to find potential future cultural leaders who were sympathetic to the American project for the democratization of Germany, and to encourage and guide their personal and professional development. Although *Prolog* did not claim any connection with OMGUS, the Americans who took the initiative were

FIGURE 2

Exterior of art gallery hosting the 1945 exhibit: 'Freiheit der Kunst'.

Bezirk Steglitz, Berlin

FIGURE 3

Interior of the art gallery.

Bezirk Steglitz, Berlin

acting within the framework of the OMGUS re-education agenda. Preserving the image of *Prolog* as a private initiative was crucial, since the differentiating motto of American policy was cultural freedom: the US, contrary to the Soviet Union and the Third Reich, rejected government intervention in culture.

Prolog aimed at 'increas[ing] understanding between democratic-minded Germans and Americans'.[33] In the short term, *Prolog* strove to help German modern artists survive the difficult post-war years, providing food, clothing, art materials, and friendship. In the longer term, it aimed at creating links between the American and the West German cultural establishment, thus catalyzing the cultural reintegration of West Germany into the Western community of nations. *Prolog* was a partnership of Germans and Americans, and the organizers claimed that the group was 'accelerating understanding between our two countries and encouraging democratic institutions.'[34] The Americans informed the artists about cultural developments in America about which the Germans had been kept in the dark by the tight Nazi censorship. Their Berlin homes became art salons, where they entertained the German artists, exhibited their work, and helped them to sell their *oeuvre*.[35] The American *Prolog* partners became aesthetic and political arbiters, discussing specific artists among themselves and deciding whom to sponsor. Through *Prolog*, OMGUS backed German artists considered to be aesthetically and politically acceptable, and encouraged their reinsertion into the German art scene.

Prolog did more than offer German artists the possibility of networking within German and American cultural circuits. The German artists were treated as friends and colleagues, and this made them feel as if they were overcoming the status of pariahs. Lehmann-Haupt wrote that *Prolog* gatherings 'were full of a special excitement and a thrilling fresh spirit of co-operation', and the German artists involved agreed.[36] In a situation where the boundaries between conqueror and conquered were very evident in daily life, *Prolog* was a space that allowed both the intellectual and the personal relations between Americans and Germans to flourish.[37] Of course, *Prolog* did not erase power differentials. The Americans had the structure of OMGUS behind them and the connections with America, and the German artists were dependent on the assistance. However, not unlike other subcultures developing in post-war Germany, *Prolog* made collaboration between Americans and Germans possible and fruitful.

Prolog was a symbol of the partnership between Americans and the 'good' Germans, the artists victimized by Nazism. In the *Prolog* catalogue of 1947, German modern artists are depicted as icons of resistance to fascism, even though none of the artists in *Prolog* had been part of the anti-Nazi resistance or former concentration camp inmates.[38] In a context so barren of heroes, of protest, and of resistance, the figure of the alienated modern artists gained political relevance. The tendency to treat the surviving modern artist as the embodiment of resistance and moral courage continued into the Cold War debates, where the enemy was no longer Nazism but rather communism and the Soviet Union. *Prolog* was smoothly integrated into the anti-communist rhetoric:

> Just as in 1848 when Berlin's cultural leaders fought side by side with their fellow citizens for basic human rights and freedom of expression, today's artists...are again in the vanguard of the fight for democracy and freedom. This was evidenced, particularly, to American personnel who resided in Berlin during the days of the Blockade and were associated with the *Prolog* Group.[39]

Later on, this perspective was reinforced by the West German authorities. For instance, in 1950, the 'Western Sector City of Berlin' established an annual award of DM 5,000 for outstanding artists in 'recognition of the roles these cultural elements play in the resistance of the people to dictatorial forces and totalitarian ideology'.[40]

COLD WAR TENSIONS

The increasing tensions between the Soviets and the Americans created a space for Germans to negotiate alternatives. In November 1948 a group of about 1,600 German artists made a collective presentation to OMGUS/Berlin, announcing that if they did not receive support from the American authorities they would be forced to accept, albeit unwillingly, a Soviet offer of monetary and artistic aid channeled through the 'Free Trade Union', a Soviet controlled artist organization. The artists' position was clear and amounted to a *chantage*: either OMGUS provided the goods requested, or the artists would join the Soviet controlled art union, thus shifting political allegiance.[41] OMGUS took the document very seriously, because a massive flight of artists to the East would have been an embarrassment, most likely to be used by the Soviets as proof that intellectuals preferred life in the Soviet Zone. Tom Hutton, Acting Chief of the Information Services, OMGUS/Berlin, decided that a positive response was necessary to 'achieve both important economic and *political* objectives'.[42] Granting the petitioning artists financial and institutional support would be a way to appease them and would serve to boost the appearance of personal freedom and intellectual opportunities in the American Zone. The operation, referred to in the OMGUS files as the 'Political Project: Graphic Artists in Berlin', was managed as a political, rather than an artistic, operation. Nonetheless, 'some upper-bracket artists and art patrons of Berlin' – both American and German – met to work out the details of the plan.[43] Of the people present at the meeting (American and German), several were associated with *Prolog*. The fact that Hutton's decisions were made in direct consultation with the Head of OMGUS/Berlin indicates that this matter was considered to be politically sensitive and strategically relevant.

Measures were taken to counter the exodus of artists to the Soviet sphere of control. It was decided that the artists would organize small exhibitions of work for sale, to be held in studios set up in OMGUS buildings and chaperoned by OMGUS personnel. It was agreed that rent would be free for three to four months, and then gradually increase. The sales would provide temporary economic relief, and the studios would serve as headquarters for the artists in the American Sector. The American proposal would result in 'a counter-inducement that would more than offset' the Soviet offer.[44] Did OMGUS sponsorship of German artists in West Berlin keep artistic freedom untouched? In other words, was American support a case of no-strings-attached aid? This was not the case. The artists were asked to submit confidential monthly reports to OMGUS, and to create a central employment bureau so that artists would be available immediately if OMGUS required their services. The project was to be *covert*, in fact this was made *a condition* of the agreement.[45]

Secrecy was needed because this explicit partnership between OMGUS and German artists went against the notion of artistic freedom at the core of the American value system. Admitting that OMGUS was providing counter-inducement to the artists – that is, playing exactly the same game as the Soviets and abiding by the same rules – would imply a similarity in strategy that undercut the American attempt to emphasize the moral and political differentiation between the American and Soviet projects. While sponsorship was an essential political move that ensured that artists would remain loyal, a covert policy was essential in order to hold the ethical high ground.

> The Russians are trying hard to win Berlin's artists over to their camp. They try to bribe them with fantastic offers, make unlimited promises and finally threaten them and their families. They invariably receive icy refusal. Berlin's artists are realistic; they cannot be bought. Although poor, often in debt, they refuse to accept promises of financial assistance by the Communists.[46]

The systematic breach of the emblematic American notion of 'freedom of culture' became, a few years later, the standard policy of the US in the international cultural field.[47]

PROMOTION

Meanwhile, American cultural officers encouraged the revival of German modern art through overt means. In 1949 Stefan Munsing, the head of the Munich Collecting Point and an officer in MFA&A, organized the first large modern art competition in post-war West Germany.[48] The event took place in Munich, the former Nazi capital of the fine arts. It was meant to foster the development of German modern art, and to encourage young artists. Blevins Davis, a New York theatrical producer, millionaire, and philanthropist involved in many overseas cultural ventures with the State Department, provided the funds.

The Blevins Davis Prize, the most prestigious art contest of the immediate post-war period in Germany, was a cultural turning point.[49] The Prize projected the image of America as a benefactor of the fine arts and a cultural leader. It was posited as 'evidence of [the] growing movement to narrow the gap between America and Germany'.[50] The contest had an international jury, the first prize consisted of $1,000 and a trip to the United States, and ten runner-ups were to receive cash prizes. The organizing committee received 3,700 entries, and 170 finalists had their works assembled in an exhibit at the Munich Collecting Point. According to Thomas Grochowiak, whose work was chosen for the exhibit, to be selected as a finalist was a significant achievement not only for the financial reward but also because the prize was American.[51] The contest integrated young German artists into the international art scene and it served to further German-American cultural relations.

For the first time in 16 years, the first prize of a significant German art contest went to a modern painting. The work selected, George Meistermann's *Der Neue Adam*, was a figurative oil painting with evident influences from Picasso's *Guernica*. What made this a landmark in German art was neither its aesthetic value nor its subject matter, but the fact that it was a modern painting with a title that suggested a religious metaphor of rebirth. Four years after the military and political defeat of the Third Reich, the Blevins Davis Prize went to a work that was radically different from what German spectators were previously shown as prototypical German art. Interestingly, the work did not make direct reference to the Nazi past or to the war. This was not an anomaly. The illusion that the American military government in Germany was not involved in the political control of the German fine arts was supported by the fact that OMGUS, unlike its Soviet counterpart, never encouraged politically engaged art. American cultural policy most often promoted artists whose work was mostly acontextual and atemporal (in the sense of being devoid of historical references to the recent past). This did not challenge the prevailing tendency among German artists to forget the horrors of the war. The artistic treatment of the Holocaust was not banned, but nothing was done to encourage artists that selected the Nazi genocide as their subject. The memory and the representation of the Holocaust were not subjects that fitted within the OMGUS conception of the cultural heritage of West Germany, and this coexisted comfortably with the German disinclination to remember Nazi crimes.

SHIFTING BOUNDARIES

The OMGUS campaign to further German-American relations in the cultural field met with certain resistance. The fate of *Ulenspiegel*, one of the most important satirical journals of the post-war period, illuminates how the limits of permissibility in visual representation changed as a function of the evolving political situation and the corresponding fluctuations in OMGUS tolerance.

Ulenspiegel was created by two anti-Nazi intellectuals, the graphic artist Herbert Sandberg (a former Buchenwald inmate) and the playwright and literary critic Gunther Weisenborn (jailed during the Third Reich for his resistance activities). Weisenborn, the literary editor, was a liberal democrat; Sandberg, the art editor, a communist.[52] In the chaotic and fluid situation of the first post-war months, there were contacts between communist intellectuals and American officers. In June 1945, Emil Carlbach, who had been the Communist Party leader in Buchenwald, introduced Sandberg to a group of American cultural officers. Carlbach had been licensed as an editor of the *Frankfurter Rundschau*, Frankfurt am Main, and Sandberg was offered one of the licenses for *Der Tagesspiegel*. Sandberg rejected the offer, and proposed instead the idea of a satirical journal. The OMGUS officers agreed, and the first issue of *Ulenspiegel* came out in December 1945.[53]

At a time when German artists avoided the representation of Nazism and the Holocaust, *Ulenspiegel* provided an alternative visual narrative. The journal reproduced work by famous modern artists that had been banned from Germany during the previous 12 years – for example, Chagall, Hoch, Nerlinger, Picasso, and Hofer. However, during its first two years in circulation, the main theme of the art work was Nazism and the camp system. The visual text of *Ulenspiegel* evoked the Nazi past in a systematic manner, creating an image of Germany that centred on the crimes of the Nazi leaders and the complicity of the German population. Strangely enough, a German magazine produced by two German intellectuals mirrored the directives of the Morgenthau Plan. The uniqueness of *Ulenspiegel* resided in its explicit anti-Nazi position, its denunciation and exposure of Nazi crimes and Nazi criminals, and its insistence on the collective responsibility of the German people.

After the first year, the thematic emphasis of *Ulenspiegel* slowly changed, and other subjects diluted the denunciation of Nazism. By late 1947, *Ulenspiegel*'s visual narrative concentrated on the mounting tension between the United States and the Soviet Union, reflecting the critical situation in Berlin. France and the UK faded away from its images, and the US and the USSR were pictured in caricatures as two giants struggling for control of Germany and the world. By the end of 1948, Germany was routinely depicted as a minor player, a powerless pawn in a much larger game. Simultaneously, the imagery took a marked anti-American slant.[54] Through illustrations, collages and caricatures, *Ulenspiegel* made a mockery out of the idea of German democracy and independence. The US emerged as a diabolical force that used wealth and power to mold a meek and compliant Germany into the shape desired by America. *Ulenspiegel* questioned the role of America as a true liberator from the Nazi past, instead positing denazification as a half-hearted attempt that ended in failure. This went against the prevailing message of the American-controlled press, that emphasized that the German-American partnership was developing a healthy German democracy. The image of the happy embrace between a partner with dollars and a partner with swastikas did not coincide with the notion of a transnational partnership that the ICD intended to disseminate.

In fact, *Ulenspiegel*'s anti-American slant developed simultaneously with the American decision to actively use the media in an information campaign to battle communism in Germany. In October 1947, OMGUS launched Operation Talk Back, a turning point in the American strategy towards the Soviet Union. Operation Talk Back used the mass media to counter Soviet anti-American propaganda.[55] From then on, anti-communist rhetoric became a central component of American propaganda, particularly in Berlin, where the Soviets and the Americans actually competed for the hearts and minds of one population. In this political climate, the *Ulenspiegel* critique of America's German policies clashed with OMGUS objectives.

As the confrontation between the US and the USSR escalated in Berlin, OMGUS cut the *Ulenspiegel*'s paper allotment and the circulation fell. This amounted to political censorship, and an internal memo from the ICD made the political nature of the decision explicit:

> Orders have been issued to reduce by one-half the paper allocation given to the magazine Ulenspiegel as a preliminary step toward inducing a change in editorial orientation of this publication or its replacement with a more effective medium.[56]

OMGUS paper rationing, which did not reflect actual changes in paper availability, was the method employed by the Americans to punish publications that they considered to be either threatening or subversive.[57] In

February 1949 Sandberg moved *Ulenspiegel* to East Berlin under a Soviet license, but the journal was soon terminated.[58] A new satirical journal edited by Gunther Neumann, *Insulaner*, was launched in the American Sector of Berlin in September 1948. It was an illustrated journal with bland caricatures, weakly political, and lacking direct references to the Nazi past and the Holocaust. The most common subjects in the cartoons were male/female relations, sports, and daily life. By July 1949 there was an increase in pin-ups and mild anti-Russian jokes, and the graphic treatment of the East–West conflict reflected a pro-American slant.

CONCLUSION

Although economic and political reforms are essential to achieve structural transformation in transitions to democracy, cultural policies are important in breaking the cultural isolation imposed by dictatorial regimes and redefining the boundaries of the permissible and the desirable. The post-war development of West German fine arts was the result of both the spontaneous revival of the German art scene, and the implementation of an OMGUS political agenda targeted at the use of art as a tool for political re-education. The American fine arts policy promoted certain aesthetic developments in the German art scene, and it also set constraints and boundaries. OMGUS removed art considered to be Nazi or militaristic from art museums in the American Zone, and banned all visual references to the Third Reich. At the same time, OMGUS did not encourage art that showed mass murder or mass atrocities, and did not strive to publicize images that reflected the experience either of the perpetrators or of the victims. OMGUS cultural officers protected, endorsed, and assisted German artists who were not primarily interested in the exploration of the German past and its horrors. At first, political caricature was tolerated, but with the emergence of the Cold War OMGUS suppressed anti-American visual messages. To neutralize the strong Soviet political offensive in the German cultural world (a policy based on material rewards and an aesthetic philosophy that fitted the tenets inherited from Nazi art), OMGUS developed overt policies and covert sponsorship programmes to help artists in the American Zone of Germany and the American Sector of Berlin. This helped construct a structural bond between West German artists and the United States. The Soviets had placed the fine arts in the forefront of their cultural offensive, and the American military learned from, and reacted to, their example. The fine arts became an arena with which to manage both the memory of Nazism and the increasing tensions with the Soviet Union.

NOTES

1. I thank in particular Hans Krabbendam, Giles Scott-Smith, and David Caute for their critical reading of the manuscript. The support of the DAAD, the German Historical Institute, CASPIC, the Center for Arts and Culture, Daimler Benz, and the University of Chicago is gratefully acknowledged.
2. For examples of this trend, see Jutta Held, *Kunst und Kunstpolitik 1945–1949* (Berlin: Elefanten Press 1981); Gerda Breuer (ed.), *Die Zahmung der Avantgarde: Zur Rezeption der Moderne in den 50er Jahren* (Basel: Stroemfeld 1997); Hermann Glaser, *The Rubble Years: The Cultural Roots of Post-war Germany 1945–1948* (New York: Paragon House 1986); Yule Heibel, *Reconstructing the Subject: Modernist Painting in Western Germany: 1945–1950* (Princeton UP 1995).
3. Uta Gerhardt, 'A Hidden Agenda of Recovery: The Psychiatric Conceptualization of Re-education for Germany in the United States During World War II', *German History* 14/3 (1996) p.298.
4. Benno Frank, Deputy Director of Film, Theater, and Music Control Branch of ICD, 'No Bread and Circuses for Germany', *Military Government Weekly Information Bulletin* 30 (23 Feb. 1946).
5. *Occupation* (United States Forces European Theater, 1946) p.5.
6. ICD included elements from its two forerunners, the Army's Psychological Warfare Division (PWD) and the Office of War Information (OWI). Its director was Brigadier General Robert A. McClure, the former chief of the Psychological Warfare Division of the Supreme Headquarters, Allied Expeditionary Force (SHAEF). With the dissolution of SHAEF, ICD was transferred to OMGUS.
7. Marshall Knappen, *And Call it Peace* (Univ. of Chicago Press 1947) pp.157–8.
8. Benno Frank, Deputy Director of Film, Theater, and Music Control Branch of ICD, 'No Bread and Circuses for Germany', *Military Government Weekly Information Bulletin* 30 (23 Feb. 1946).
9. Gordon Gilkey, *German War Art* (Office of the Chief Historian Headquarters, European Command), 25 April 1947.
10. *Altes Rathaus Steglitz Archiv* (Berlin): Files on art exhibitions in the 1945–1949 period.
11. Ibid.
12. For a detailed account of the American effort to trace and restitute art stolen by the Nazis, see Lynn H. Nicholas, *The Rape of Europa* (New York: Vintage Books, 1995).
13. Bernard Genton, *Les Alliés et la Culture: Berlin 1945–1946* (Paris: Presses Universitaires de France 1988); David Pike, *The Politics of Culture in Soviet-Occupied Germany 1945–1949* (Stanford UP 1992); and Marilyn Rueschmeyer, 'State Patronage in the German Democratic Republic: Artistic and Political Change in a State Socialist Society', in J. Huggins Balfe (ed.) *Paying the Piper: Causes and Consequences of Art Patronage* (Urbana: Univ. of Illinois Press 1993) pp.209–15.
14. 'Decree of the Supreme Commander of Soviet Military Government (S.M.G.) and Supreme Commander of the Soviet Forces in Germany.' Berlin, No. 51, 4 Sept. 1945. Quoted in Erich Kuby, *The Russians and Berlin, 1945* (London: Heinemann 1965) pp.335–6.
15. Genton, *Les Alliés et la Culture* (note 13) pp.336–7.
16. Hellmut Lehmann-Haupt, 'German Art Today', undated essay. Museum of Modern Art Archives (MoMA): Lehmann-Haupt Papers, Box 4, Folder 16.
17. *Tägliche Rundschau*, 19 and 24 Nov. 1948. Quoted in Hellmut Lehman-Haupt, 'Behind the Iron Curtain', *Magazine of Art*, # 44, March 1951; Genton, *Les Alliés et la Culture* (note 13) pp.333–44; and Pike, *The Politics of Culture* (note 13) pp.318–30.
18. Hellmut Lehmann-Haupt, 'Art Under Totalitarianism' (Symposium, The Metropolitan Museum of Art, March 1952) pp.61–3.
19. Berlinische Galerie, *Zone 5: Kunst in der Viersektorenstadt 1945–1951* (Berlin: Dirk Nishen 1989) p.11.
20. Francois Furet, *Le Passé d'une Illusion: Essay sur l'idée Communiste au XX Siècle* (Paris: Robert Laffont 1995); Pike, *The Politics of Culture* (note 13).
21. See, for instance, Alfred H. Barr Jr., 'Art in the Third Reich — Preview 1933', Jacques

Barzun, 'Editorial and a Memorandum from Jacques Barzun', and Lincoln Kirstein, '1945', all in *Magazine of Art* 38/6 (Oct. 1945).

22. 'Military Government Regulation #1', 18 Aug. 1947. Quoted in Edith Standen memo to Craig Smyth, 13 Nov. 1947. National Gallery of Art (NGA): Edith Standen Papers, Box 1.
23. 'Long-Range Policy Statement for German Re-education', Landesarchiv Berlin: OMGBS Education and Cultural Relations Branch, Box 14–3, Folder 3, July 1947.
24. Ibid.
25. MoMA, Lehmann-Haupt Papers, Box 7, Folder 1; Lehmann-Haupt Papers, Box 7, Folder 2. See also 'Bavarian Reactions to Modern Art', *Information Control Review* 18 (1946).
26. Wolfgang Hutt, *Deutsche Malerei und Graphik im 20. Jahrhundert* (Berlin: Henschelverlag Kunst und Gesellschaft 1969); Markus Krause, *Galerie Gerd Rosen: Die Avantgarde in Berlin 1945–1950* (Berlin: Ars Nicolai 1945); and Hellmut Lehmann-Haupt 'Art in Post-war Berlin', undated essay; MoMA,: Lehmann-Haupt Papers, Box 1, Folder 16.
27. 'Bavarian Reactions to Modern Art', *Information Control Review* 18 (1946).
28. Yule Heibel, *Reconstructing the Subject* (Princeton UP 1995) p.58.
29. Hutt, *Deutsche Malerei und Graphik* (note 26) p.460.
30. *Berliner Zeitung* (25 June 1947), quoted in *Zone 5: Kunst in der Viersektorenstadt 1945–1951* (Berlin: Verlag Dirk Nishen 1989) p.67.
31. Lehmann-Haupt memorandum to Howard, 12 Feb. 1947. MoMA: Lehmann-Haupt Papers, Box 7, Folder 2; Edgar Breitenbach and Theodore A. Heinrich, 'Major Activities of Museums and Fine Arts Sections', 3 June 1949. National Archives: RG 260, Box 211, File MFA&A.
32. Beryl Rogers McClaskey (ed.), *Prolog 1: A Portfolio of Contemporary German Drawings and Prints Selected by a Group of American and German Residents of Berlin* (Berlin: Gebr. Mann 1947).
33. McClaskey letter to Smithsonian Institution, 16 Aug. 1947. NGA: Cultural Relations, RG 7, Box 10.
34. Ibid.
35. Paul Lutzeier letter to William Constable, 6 July 1949. Archives of American Art (AAA): Constable Papers pp.481; Ursula Bluhm, memo, 1 June 1950. AAA: Constable Papers pp.610–12.
36. Hellmut Lehmann-Haupt, 'A Letter from America', in *Prolog: A Gift in Friendship for Beryl Rogers McClaskey and Charles Baldwin* (Berlin: Brothers Hartmann 1948).
37. Friedrich Winkler, 'Letter from Berlin', *Prolog* (note 36).
38. Ibid.
39. Peter F. Szluk, Deputy Chief ER&S Branch, Personnel Division Office of Administration, HICOG, 'Freedom Prizes for Artists', *HICOG Information Bulletin* (June 1950).
40. Ibid.
41. Letter to Tom Hutton, Acting Chief Information Services Branch, signed by Hans. J. Gaedick, 5 Aug. 1948, (in English). Landesarchiv Berlin: OMGBS, RG 260, 4/12-1/18.
42. Italics mine. Tom Hutton memo 'Political Project, Graphic Artists Berlin', to Director, OMGUS Berlin, 16 Aug. 1948. Landesarchiv Berlin: OMGBS, RG 260, 4/12-1/8.
43. Tom Hutton letter to Director, OMGBS, 16 Aug. 1948. Landesarchiv Berlin: OMGBS, RG 260, 4/12-1/18.
44. Hutton memo 'Political Project, Graphic Artists Berlin' (note 42).
45. Ibid.
46. Charlotte Weidler, 'Art in Western Germany Today', *Magazine of Art* 44/4 (April 1955) p.135.
47. Frances Stonor Saunders, *The Cultural Cold War: The CIA and the World of Arts and Letters* (New York: The New Press 1999).
48. The Collecting Points were the deposits where OMGUS stored art objects stolen by the Nazis pending their return to their owners. Originally there were temporary collecting points, but by 1946 there were four central facilities located in Munich, Wiesbaden, Marburg, and Offenbach.
49. Klaus Honnef and Hans M. Schmidt (eds.) *Aus den Trümmern: Kunst und Kultur im Rheinland und in Westfalen 1945–1952: Aus den Trümmern – Neubeginn und Kontinuität* (Köln: Rheinland Verlag 1985).

50. Ursula Bluhm, memo, 1 June 1950. AAA: Constable Papers pp.610–2.
51. Thomas Grochowiak, 'Neuanfänger '45 aus der Sicht der Künstlers', in Honnef and Schmidt (eds.) *Aus den Trümmern,* p.181.
52. Weisenborn was arrested in 1942 and held at the Zuchthaus Luckau prison until his liberation in 1945. Sandberg was jailed in 1935, and in 1938 he was transferred to Buchenwald, where he remained until the liberation of the camp. Gilbert Merlio, *Les résistances allemandes à Hitler* (Paris: Éditions Tallandier 2001).
53. Herbert Sandberg, *Ulenspiegel: Deutschland vor der Teilung* (Oberhausen: Ludwig Institut Schloss Oberhausen 1990) p.140.
54. It is interesting to note that in books about *Ulenspiegel*, which are basically a compilation of images from the journal, this anti-Americanism is most often weeded out, and the examples from the Cold War period tend to avoid explicitly anti-American images.
55. Author's personal communication with Harold Hurwitz, 9 July 1999. OMGUS brandished a combination of media weapons, relying heavily on two licensed publications, *Der Monat* and *Neue Zeitung*, and on the radio via RIAS, to 'broaden the intellectual and cultural horizons of the Germans' and to disseminate an anti-communist message. 'Monthly Report of the Military Government', September 1948, no. 39. Landesarchiv Berlin: OMGBS, RG 260, 4/1-3/9. For discussion of *Der Monat* in the context of Operation Talk Back, see Michael Hochgeschwender, 'The Intellectual as Propagandist: *Der Monat*, the Congress for Cultural Freedom, and the Process of Westernization in Germany'. Conference at the German Historical Institute: 'The American Impact on Western Europe: Americanization and Westernization in Transatlantic Perspective' (Washington DC, 25–27 March 1999).
56. Information Control, 'Monthly Report', 3 May 1948. Landesarchiv Berlin: OMGBS, RG 260, 5/39-1/18.
57. Bernhard Jendricke, *Die Nachkriegszeit im Spiegel der Satire: Die satirischen Zeitschriften Simpl und Wespennest in den Jahren 1946 bis 1950* (Frankfurt am Main: Peter Lang 1982).
58. Weisenborn was opposed to taking a Soviet license, and when Sandberg did so, their collaboration ended. Sandberg's status in the GDR was complex, because he was both enshrined as an anti-Nazi hero and ostracized for his public defence of modern art and modern artists. In 1949 Dymschitz denounced Sandberg as a 'formalist' fallen under the influence of bourgeois decadence. Pike, *The Politics of Culture* (note 13) pp.613–9.

17

'He is a Cripple an' Needs my Love': *Porgy and Bess* as Cold War Propaganda

DAVID MONOD

Champagne corks were popping in the Bristol Hotel that September night in 1952. The American Ambassador, Llewelyn Thompson, had invited 549 people out to the opening of *Porgy and Bess* at the Volksoper and then back to the Hotel for a party that lasted much of the night. Almost everyone of importance was there: the Allied High Commissioners, the chiefs of all the diplomatic missions, the Federal Chancellor, ministers of the Austrian government and prominent people in Vienna's art and business communities. 'The effect of *Porgy*'s opening night in Vienna was electric', the public affairs officer at the Embassy chortled, 'not only did the entire press carry rave notices; the impact of the premiere was carried far and wide by word of mouth'. Or, as the *New York Times* reporter announced more pointedly, if rather less excitedly, as an instrument of psychological warfare *Porgy* 'was worth several divisions of troops in the Cold War'.[1]

The State Department made no effort to conceal its intentions in sending *Porgy and Bess* to Europe. In a release to the press three months before the trip, the Department announced that the opera company was going to counteract 'propaganda of two kinds related to the United States: First, that this country has no real culture, [or] native artists of creative vitality. Second, that the colored people have no opportunity to develop their abilities beyond a slave status.' In order to achieve its goal, the Department spent big money – just under $100,000 plus DM 120,000 and over 400,000 Austrian schillings – to send the Gershwin opera to the front line cities of Vienna and Berlin. The show received such largesse, according to one of the State Department's officers, because it offered such a 'unique vehicle for exploitation'. *Porgy* was a manifestation of the American melting-pot: its African-American cast sang words and music written by New York Jews who had based their opera on a novel by a Southern white. Its company was assembled for no other purpose than to go to Europe, and they had, according to their government patron, 'an underlying sense of mission'; its sets were constructed at taxpayers' expense and the government paid the company's travel costs, the Gershwin Estate's royalties, and the show's advertising, profit margin and salaries. In short, *Porgy* was an opera which, 'while admittedly good art', had been re-fashioned by the Department of State to serve as 'even better propaganda'.[2]

Still, for all that, *Porgy* was a great musical work which remained wondrous in its possibilities. Culture serves authority in complicated ways: while it can defuse challenges to the order it encapsulates, in so doing, in revealing subversive powers, it can also make volatile that which it upholds. Art which opens wounds in order to suture them may still draw attention to the wound. Dissident expressions which are circumscribed and marginalized as art can nonetheless heighten awareness of dissent. As Frederic Jameson has written, even though cultural works seek to make their logic inevitable, their unchosen paths of narrative might still be explored for the alternatives they present. The challenge for cultural historians is to understand how the tensions implicit in these contradictory aspects of art are negotiated by creators and their audiences.[3]

Understanding this is difficult enough when studying one society, but even more complex when dealing with international contacts in which the power structures and cultural messages are multiple, interactive and not always complementary. I would like to approach the problem by asking two sets of questions: first, what was *Porgy*'s master narrative (did the Department of State control it) and what alternatives did the show contain? Second, how was the opera understood by those observing it? How were the master narrative and competing subtexts deciphered by peoples living in Berlin and Vienna in 1952?

MASTER NARRATIVE AND ALTERNATIVE READINGS

From the start, the State Department struggled for, but never achieved, mastery over *Porgy*; there were just too many other voices. Today we think of Gershwin's opera as a familiar classic, but such was not the case in 1952. The work had first been performed in Boston and New York in 1935, but it was not revived until 1942 and then not again until the show that went to Europe a decade later. Those making the decisions to send *Porgy* overseas certainly knew the hit songs – *Summertime* and *Bess, You Is My Woman Now* – but none of them appear to have seen the opera. Two months before the show was to be performed in Europe, officials there still had not received the libretto or even a plot summary and they were unclear about what they were getting.[4] What the decision-makers in Washington and Europe had known was that *Porgy* featured African-Americans, that

Gershwin's music was familiar to Europeans (in part because of army radio broadcasts), and that the composer had attained an iconic status as America's best.[5] It also helped that the show's producers were already well-connected to the foreign policy establishment. Robert Breen, co-producer and director, had helped co-ordinate and manage cultural programmes in Germany after the war when he worked as General Director of the American National Theater Academy, the State Department's liaison agency within the American arts community. Blevins Davis, the other producer, was one of President Truman's Missouri friends, a profligate millionaire and producer of the Ballet Theater, an ensemble that had already undertaken a government-subsidized European tour. Given what was known of the show and the quality of the people behind it, *Porgy* promised to be a perfect introduction to American high culture and a potential revelation of the progressive, democratic and multi-racial dimensions of American art.

Once the decision to send *Porgy* overseas was announced, voices of caution began to be heard. The public affairs officer in Vienna, when he finally got the libretto, discovered that the show 'deals with the seamy side of American life – a tatterdemalion community of Negro paupers and outcasts, often held in the grip of crime, vice and mob hysteria'.[6] In fact, *Porgy* is a story about love and hardship among poor Gullah fishermen and dock workers in South Carolina. Crown, a crude though superhuman force, murders a man during a crap game and is forced to go into hiding. His girlfriend, the beautiful but cocaine-addicted Bess, is left behind and finds shelter with a crippled beggar named Porgy. Under the influence of Porgy's love, Bess becomes a 'good' woman and the community opens to her. But then Crown returns for Bess and Porgy is arrested after he kills her former lover by knifing him in the back. Bess, abandoned once again, is seduced by her former cocaine dealer and, when Porgy gets out of prison, he finds she has gone to New York. Porgy, ever faithful in his love, follows her in his goat cart.

The unexpected brutality of the story posed a real challenge to diplomatic officers, but they worked hard to contain the potential damage by shifting attention away from the opera and onto the cast. As Penny von Eschen has shown, in the early 1950s the idea was emerging that the talents of individuals could be marketed as a way of deflecting charges regarding the African-Americans' collective inequality. The *Porgy* tour was presented as evidence 'that the Negro artist in America has reached a high degree of skill, acceptance and fame … and will demonstrate their achievement as American citizens not only on stage but off'. The very brutality of *Porgy* would further allow officials to 'demonstrate that the United States is assessing realistically the true importance of Soviet propaganda as far as our ethnical [*sic*] problems are concerned … and claims an appreciation of art above politics.'[7] This was the message American officials tried to present in Europe and they did so by controlling access to the show and choreographing its participants through newsreel footage, tourist walkabouts, invitations to go out in the company of locals and solo performances by cast members in clubs and private homes. The opening night party in Vienna and the free tickets were simply another form of damage control. Of course, something also had to be said about *Porgy* itself and news releases stressed the opera's 'cultural terms of reference'; which meant pointing out that it no more provided a real portrait of America than *Madame Butterfly* did of Japan.[8]

Still, no matter what public affairs officers tried to do, they could only parenthesize what went on in the theater. Unfortunately, the intentions of those mounting the production were only partially in harmony with those of the State Department. The idea to tour *Porgy* had come from Bob Breen, a New Deal liberal and self-proclaimed champion of African-American equality. He conceived of *Porgy* not as an ersatz work composed by the Gershwins, but as a real piece of *African*-Americana, a transcription.[9] Breen's belief that the opera might provide a *real* portrait of Gullah life inspired him to rewrite parts of the libretto in order to better reflect what he took to be the cadence and character of black speech. In a further bid for authenticity, he filled the stage with life – a ceaseless to-ing and fro-ing of characters, and a constant background noise as actors whistled and hooted, ad-libbed and gesticulated. According to one awe-struck contemporary, the stage was 'alive, it glitters and sparkles with color and movement.' In the first moments of the show, while Clara sang *Summertime* to her baby, 'children are playing. One woman prepares a scanty supper for her husband. Another is knitting a jumper. A tiny boy, helping his family, carries a sack of coal he has gathered somewhere. Between a husband and wife there occurs one of the small quarrels over two or three cents which she is missing from her wages. Two girls are learning new steps from a new dance … Men who have returned from their work are playing dice.' Breen's goal in all this was to break down the distance between audience and stage and, contrary to State Department assertions, provide the impression that what one was watching was 'real'.[10]

And yet, what Breen offered could only be a caricature. He failed, for all his good intentions, to overcome the limitations of his own New Deal liberalism. To him, African Americans were exotic and different, undoubtedly deserving of eventual freedom, but not yet as a group advanced enough for full democratic rights. His production of *Porgy* emphasized their Otherness - the superstitions, the exoticism of African American religion, the clannishness of community structures, the childlike innocence and waywardness of the people, the noble savagery of the heroes, the licentiousness of the sleazy. And most of all he considered black people sexually uninhibited and he portrayed that primitive freedom on stage, most notably in his graphic staging of a rape that turns consensual.[11] To be fair, Breen did see *Porgy* as more than simply an anthropological artifact, and he did stress the love story; but his *Porgy* was nevertheless a far cry from what the Department of State thought it was getting when it decided to send America's best-known opera to Europe.

But this is only a part of *Porgy*'s complexity. Theater is a collaborative work in which actors are crucial contributors, and black cast members had their own interests to project. Some of them clearly sought distance from the image Breen created for them. William Warfield, in particular, tried to make his Porgy into a more traditional operatic hero: noble and brave and even refined in his sensibilities. He wanted to sing recitals when in Berlin and Vienna in order to display his vocal credentials and secure future contracts, and it is significant that what he kept on singing were Schubert lieder. Other cast members also saw *Porgy* as a way of displaying their talents as serious performers, and they knew that race made what they were doing especially important. Many were apparently uncomfortable with the director's approach, and while accommodating themselves to his vision, sought to convey their professionalism on stage and their refinement when off. As Maya Angelou recalls, her fellow cast members interpreted their success in racial terms and acknowledged themselves to be 'the greatest array of Negro talent [we] had ever seen.'[12]

Beneath all these messages, of course, was the Gershwins' text. After all, the Gershwins' voices were being heard too and they had not conceived of their opera as a vehicle for propaganda. What George Gershwin believed he was writing was a 'combination of the drama and romance of *Carmen* and the beauty of *Meistersinger*', an operatic masterwork in a traditional mould. In this sense, he did not want to write a piece of folklore or a snippet of racial reality. To Gershwin, *Porgy* was a classic tragedy revealing the struggles of the individual against community, humanity against nature, love against fear.[13] These were universal themes and not things narrowly American.

If nothing else, *Porgy*'s multiple meanings – surely a feature of all art – suggest that we would be oversimplifying the case if we see the 1952 *Porgy* solely, or even principally, as the handmaid of American power. Here was no scheming State Department twisting culture to advance American influence. Rather, here was an overblown bureaucracy making expensive decisions with little understanding of the complexities involved in using art as propaganda. Which leads me to the second set of questions. Even if cultural exports speak in more confused and less direct ways than we sometimes imagine, their's remain American voices. For all the multiple meanings of what went on on stage, are we not still dealing with the cultural reach of a superpower? The question is a valid one, but if we conceive of American power in more indirect, less mechanical terms, don't we also have to ask if it was being perceived? Unfortunately, what audiences understand is not necessarily what artists and promoters communicate, or at least it is refracted by the various prisms of perception and understanding through which it must pass. This is especially true when we are dealing with cross-cultural contacts. Language, culture, history, tradition, all these and more serve as interpretive filters. Of course, artists can and must communicate, and it would be foolish to assert that messages cannot penetrate cultural barriers, but nuance is often lost and, more importantly, the significance of what is seen – how it is used and re-assimilated into people's lives – will change in different times and situations and cultures.[14]

EUROPEAN PERCEPTIONS

So what was seen in Vienna and Berlin? Were the messages which State Department officials hoped to communicate – that the talents and successes of individual African Americans disproved Soviet propaganda and that the US was not itself without 'high' culture – really understood by European theatre-goers? Which was paramount? Breen's vision of the black Other – the *authentic* African in America, different and exotic and tribal – or the cast's demonstration of their sophistication as a signifier of either individual or collective power? Or Gershwin's own sense of a people torn between modernity and tradition, community and individualism, crime and religion? Though we can never answer these questions with assurance, because all that we have are the writings of the critics who saw the show and not the views of the mass of the public, the evidence remains revealing: it represented at least part of the local response and it helped to shape collective opinions, especially for that majority which did not see the show. Although critics do not necessarily represent the views of average opera-goers, looking for commonalities in journalistic opinions can still help identify points where the show's voices and broad cultural expectations collided and merged. And so what was seen in Vienna and Berlin? Clearly not what State Department officials had expected.

Critical reaction to *Porgy* shows that the various messages different stake-holders were communicating were received, interpreted and re-prioritized. And if the process allowed any single voice to ring out, it was – not altogether surprisingly – the director's. Contrary to what the State Department hoped for, and what the cast struggled to express, critics felt they were not just experiencing Americana, but America itself. Even State Department officials recognized that despite their efforts to place *Porgy* in historical context, 'the very vigor and immediacy of the drama can well leave the critical viewer the impression that it portrays social conditions that still disfigure American life'. As the *Weltpresse* critic announced, the show reveals the 'poor and destitute that have sunken low and are defiled by poverty and dirt … [I]n these streets … reality stares one in the face … There's drudgery and privation, laughter and jibes, love-making and ready brutality … one is fascinated by the drastic reality.' Breen's realism was well understood; as the *Kurier* asserted, 'so much Negro reality was created [on the stage] that the invented figures finally became reality itself.'[15]

The impact of this was that the opera was generally taken by critics as 'little more than straight reporting'. Life in Catfish Row 'rises unadorned in its poverty before our eyes, [together] with the quickly changing joys and sorrows which are especially associated with people close to nature.' In this last comment, the reviewer for *Der Abend* was identifying another of Breen's points: the primitive innocence of black Americans. Here Breen's direction meshed with and reinforced prevailing attitudes. Personally unused to contact with African-Americans, especially out of uniform, Germans and Austrians retained stereotypes – as we have seen, not peculiar to themselves – concerning black primitiveness. Some critics, however, carried this past Breen's own fauve sense of the natural man, to a real emphasis on savagery. Crown was described by a critic as 'a mighty King-Kong, a creature of the primeval forest, with a set of teeth and arms of a gorilla', Porgy was a 'primitive', Bess was a 'will o' the wisp … who craves many men,' and African-Americans, as a whole, were a people capable only of 'high flaming and downcast feelings'. Berliners, this critic concluded, 'don't have race prejudices … [we] have open understanding of the folk art of the black singers and actors'.[16]

Not all critics were quite so crass in their correlation of the primitive and the savage, but all accepted as true Breen's portrait of African-Americans and most moved it further down the road to the jungle. To Friedrich Luft, a great man of the theater and hardly one hostile to America, the actors were 'graceful brown people' who glided over the stage 'without any restraints'. Unfortunately, he also felt them so good because they are 'on an earlier, more innocent artistic level' – they didn't 'act' they 'lived'. Kurt Westphal, the *Kurier* critic, concurred: 'Nobody seems to act, but to bring to the stage his own nature, his unique temperament, his vital existence.' The people of Catfish Row, announced the *Der Abend* critic, 'are playing themselves'. Even though he and everyone else admired the 'quality of the voices' and 'the explosive vitality of the acting', very few seemed to realize the artistry and refinement the actors communicated. The great American soprano, Leontyne Price, playing Bess at the very beginning of her career, was most admired for her 'fascinating voluptuousness', and only H. H. Stuckenschmidt had the prescience to notice that she was also 'a dramatic soprano of purest sound … technically the most perfect'.[17]

All of which would also suggest that George Gershwin's deep hope that he was writing an opera, universal and transcendent, was not materialized in this production. According to *Die Neue Zeitung*, *Porgy* 'certainly [was] not [an opera], if judged by the standards of Wagner and Debussy.' Heinz Ritter of the *Telegraf* agreed, 'it is no opera in itself, but naturalistic musical theater'. Interestingly, while there were those who liked the music and those who didn't, they almost all did so for the same reasons. All that separated them was the degree of their affection for 'musical theater'.[18]

Though some Europeans had tried to re-work jazz as a classical form, the efforts were 'tentative', 'experimental and ephemeral'; not so here, thought one reviewer, as Gershwin had 'deeply fused' jazz, the 'ancient art of the people', and classical forms. Which should not, however, be taken to mean that the US had a culture. Friedrich Luft, who undoubtedly meant well, felt the opera presents the 'unsifted feeling' of an 'artistic Garden of Eden'. Breen's job, according to the *Berliner Anzeiger*, had been simply to 'bridle the wild temperament' of his actors. The *Wiener Kurier* said *Porgy* was the product 'of an aspiring culture' and went on to note that Gershwin's music 'appears as arranged rather than invented … it is not "worked out" in a European sense; there is no development, hardly a polyphony or formal logic'. Indeed, it was a work 'without any pretensions to high art'.[19]

Remarkably, Public Affairs was delighted with these reviews and felt the opera 'has made its audience share a warm, figurative experience of American life.' This reading of the critical press made a certain amount of sense in view of the State Department's first objective, which was simply to offer Europeans an experience of American art, but it flew in the face of its second goal, which was to counter direct Soviet charges regarding American cultural backwardness and racial cruelty. Officials could only have felt vindicated by the reviews because they were either insensitive to the nuances of the critical reception or so dulled by attacks on American culture that they took the critics' ambivalence as high praise. True, audiences were enthusiastic and journalists did rhapsodize about the opera – they especially enjoyed the sex – but did that really mean they had gained a new appreciation of America? *Die Weltpresse*'s critic thought so, saying that the music had revealed to him an 'American life, throbbing with Gershwin's tunes, rhythms and harmonies – a life pulsating in the streets of the cities, on the bold bridges that span rivers and lakes, in the towering skyscrapers and the vast expanse of the cornfields in the Midwest and in factories, wharves and harbours.' And several critics shared the view of the *Arbeiter Zeitung* that the opera revealed 'the intelligence and humanity' of at least 'part of the American people'. But they also presented all of this as terribly foreign to European sentiments. The *Neue Wiener Tageszeitung*'s critic, while applauding 'this work as part of a free world,' also noted it was 'a far-off life that can be shown, but not transplanted.' The *Wiener Kurier* critic similarly found in it 'an overpowering and convincing strangeness.' Though he had felt, after years of American troops and radio and films, that he 'knew America', he was suddenly confronted in the theater by something 'never seen before or heard … a great unknown … [that], my God, we have never known, [that] we've never been able to picture'.[20] In comments such as these, the critics revealed no more understanding of America than they might have gained from gangster movies or Brecht plays.

MEASURING EFFECTS

If nothing else, all this should warn us against taking the assertions of the State Department or the excited fears of European intellectuals as proof of the effectiveness of America's propaganda offensive. Though the State Department, for its own quite obvious reasons, liked to boast of the strength of its cultural programme, and though many Europeans feared American power, the reality is more complex. In the *Porgy* case, there was never simply one sender and the messages were multiple and sometimes contradictory. Furthermore, values communicated by those on one side of the Atlantic were not always received as expected by people living on the other side. Though State Department officials at the time felt differently, art does not really make a reliable weapon of propaganda, if one has clear and precise objectives in mind. But it can serve positive and humane ends.

While *Porgy* may have failed to shake German and Austrian critics free of their preconceptions, it did, in its own way, open doors. Art creates possibilities, it raises questions and allows us to explore new terrain, and *Porgy* was no exception. Aesthetically, *Porgy* was part of a counter-reaction against the dominant trend of theater direction in the early 1950s, which was increasingly retreating from realism and embracing psychological ambiguities. One did not have to be a Zhdanov to resist this or to feel that theater needed not more abstraction, but a stronger dose of realism. *Porgy* was, for more traditional critics, a powerful assertion of stage possibilities. In particular, it seemed to them a revolution in opera. Neither romantic nor symbolist, Breen's approach, to many correspondents, would be well-suited for such hard-boiled modern works as *Lulu* or *Wozzeck*, or such potentially squalid classics as *Carmen*. The theater critic of the *Wiener Kurier* for example, ruminated that the show brings to opera what he thought was 'the salient feature of modern art … the image of human beings as they actually appear before our eyes in everyday life.'[21]

One might also note that the cast did not fail entirely in its task of communicating their enormous talent. If critics did not necessarily find them civilized, they nonetheless recognized them, as Fritz Skorzeny, of the

Neue Wiener Tageszeitung, observed, to be 'incomparable and great' and they praised their 'rhythmic fury and melodious gracefulness', their 'seriousness and humour', their 'grace and power', their 'deep-felt humanity'. Critics who probably had had minimal contact with African-Americans, and who shared, as we have seen, deep racial prejudices, nonetheless accepted, as did Robert Breen, that blacks might be fine and impressive human beings. *Die Welt*'s critic even believed that they could learn from Porgy and the way he materialized 'defiance of life and such delight ... with such naturalism and grace.'[22] Of course, the fact almost every critic felt they had to offer remarks like these reveals the extent to which blacks remained alien. But it was something.

Porgy also expressed to Europeans something singular about post-war America: the importance of spontaneity and immediacy. In these years, spontaneity – the ideal of improvisation – became the most important defining feature of American culture. Be-bop, with its self-conscious disruption of natural expectations; Bob Wills, who in the 1940s married swing to country music and insisted that his musicians never play a tune the same way twice; Leonard Bernstein with his wriggling and writhing conducting style; Little Richard and his explosive *Tutti Frutti*: all were examples of the desire to communicate a sense of music performance as an instantaneous, rather than a pre-planned or reproduced act. But the Culture of Spontaneity, as Daniel Belgrad calls it, extended well beyond music. This was the period of Jackson Pollock's splash and drip paintings, of William Carlos Williams' experimental, improvisational poetry, and of Gestalt psychology. Taken together, these artistic undertakings represented a revolt against the economics of mass reproduction. Art was not advertising because it drew attention to its own artificiality: the point of abstract expressionism was to highlight the brush strokes and paint smears and imagine the artist at work. In the same way, Be-bop was not swing; it challenged dancers, demanded concentrated listening and front-centred instrumental virtuosity. And in the classical idiom, John Cage's *4'33* turned audience members into composers and fixed attention on the act of creating through silence itself.[23]

This ideal of improvisation was clearly central to Breen's production of *Porgy*. In Austria and Germany, critics understood this and found it exciting. Improvisation was something about America that they had often derided as undisciplined, but were now coming to admire. Ultimately many young Europeans would strive to emulate this American spontaneity, and in their own variations of it would bring dramatic changes to European culture.[24] *Porgy* did not cause this to happen, obviously enough, but it was part of the sea change. And so, like all art, it worked subversively on certain cultural assumptions even as it served to reinforce others.

The difficulty which public affairs officials faced in deciphering these multiple and somewhat contradictory messages originated in part from expecting both too much and too little of their propaganda. The character of the post-war overseas programmes was shaped in Latin America and occupied Germany, places where officers confronted significant levels of cultural hostility. Propaganda employing the arts was largely designed, in these places, to present the United States as an open, complex and culturally sophisticated place. But the Cold War added new and pressing concerns, in particular the need to counter specific charges against the United States and to advance immediate foreign policy objectives. In *Porgy and Bess*, the government attempted to attract both broad cultural sympathy and to answer Soviet criticism regarding US race relations. But the two goals were not entirely compatible. Journalists and commentators in Berlin and Vienna expressed their excitement for the show in racist terms and they praised the production in measure because it confirmed their negative stereotypes. The production's own subversiveness – in challenging theatre conventions and harnessing the power of improvisation – was in turn left unexplored by US government officials because they did not see how these things were connected to America's foreign policy goals. Though overseas officers understood from the applause, the ticket sales and the newspaper reviews that *Porgy* had achieved something positive, they so needed to report tangible things back home that they misread and misrepresented much of the theatre criticism and tried to squeeze the complexity of local perception and reaction into the Cold War's binary conceptual categories.

Nonetheless, so successful were the American officials in their promotional reportage that the US government determined to enlarge its overseas arts project. *Porgy* was a major factor in the decision to expand the European cultural front beyond a few anti-communist intellectuals and to establish the President's Fund (with a $5 million annual budget, half of which went to exporting theatrical and musical productions) to subsidize non-political live entertainments. Ultimately, almost 60 individuals and ensembles would profit from the government's largesse between 1954 and 1956. Some of the projects – sending the Boston Symphony on a European tour or the Los Angeles Philharmonic to Japan – were relatively conventional undertakings, but others, such as Dizzy Gillespie's visit to the Middle East or native American actor Tom Two Arrow's tour of South East Asia, were acts of considerable imagination. Under the President's Fund program, *Porgy and Bess* would itself receive support for two further international tours, one to Latin America and the other to Mediterranean countries. By the mid-1950s, as one of Eisenhower's top psychological warriors, C. D. Jackson, observed, 'artistic and cultural development' had become an 'overt weapon in the war of ideas'.[25]

CONCLUSION

Still, performance art was employed as a form of Cold War propaganda without there being clear agreement on the point of sending it abroad or understanding of the complexity involved in presenting and receiving foreign cultural products.[26] And yet, though *Porgy* may not have achieved what the State Department had hoped for, it did serve to communicate some engaging messages about America. True, it did not break through cultural stereotypes, nor did it convince Europeans that Americans were a cultured people; but it did give audiences an exciting night of theater and it encouraged them to question some of their beliefs. Officials of the foreign service, still unsure of how to use art as propaganda, were insensitive to many of these possibilities and limitations. Like most bureaucrats with vested interests, they interpreted *Porgy*'s reception in the most positive of ways. We should be careful not to take their comments at face value. As for Robert Breen, he was certainly happy with how fully his directorial impulses had been appreciated and he kept *Porgy* on tour for the next three years. The cast also truly felt they were changing the way people saw African Americans and the Gershwin Estate made a good deal of money. And so, in the end, everyone was satisfied. As one Public Affairs official exclaimed, 'art … had mastered the matter, and in so doing had transformed and elevated [reality]'.[27]

NOTES

1. National Archives [NA], HICOG, Berlin Element, PAD, Box 2, Walter Dowling, 'Report on *Porgy and Bess*', 23 Sept. 1953. *New York Times*, 2 Oct. 1952.
2. NA, RG 59, IIA, IFI/E, Box 3, Mary French to Ben Crosby, 26 July 1952; Ohio State University [OSU], Breen Collection, F116, Press Release, 8 July 1953; NA, HICOG, Berlin Element, PAD, Box 2, Dowling, 'Report on *Porgy and Bess*' (note 1).
3. Walter Benjamin, 'The Work of Art in an Age of Mechanical Reproduction' in *Illuminations* (New York: Schocken Books 1968) pp.241–3; G. Lipsitz, *Time Passages: Collective Memory and American Popular Culture* (Minneapolis: University of Minnesota Press 1991) Chapter 5; F. Jameson, 'Reification and Utopia in Mass Culture', *Social Text* 1 (1979) pp.33–47; and *The Political Unconscious: Narrative as a Socially Symbolic Act* (Ithaca, NY: Cornell UP 1981). On international cultural transmissions and receptions: Rob Kroes, 'American Empire and Cultural Imperialism: A View from the Receiving End', *Diplomatic History* 23 (1999) pp.463–78.
4. H. Alpert, *The Life and Times of Porgy and Bess* (New York: Knopf 1990) Chapters 8–9; OSU, Breen Collection, F44A, Robert Schnitzer to Robert Breen, 31 July 1952.
5. OSU, Breen Collection, F106, Robert Breen to Robert Schnitzer, 11 Sept. 1951; NA, RG59, IIA, IFI/E, Box 3, Henry Kellerman memo, 11 July 1952; F44A, Robert Schnitzer to Mary French 30 June 1952; F44A, memo of phone call from Mary French, 6 June 1952.
6. NA, HICOG, Berlin Element, PAD, Box 2, Dowling, 'Report on *Porgy and Bess*'.
7. P. von Eschen, *Race against Empire: Black Americans and Anticolonialism, 1937–57* (Ithaca, NY: Cornell UP 1997); NA, RG 59, IIA, IFI/E, Box 3, Robert Schnitzer to W.J. Convery Egan, 8 Aug. 1952; Eisenhower Library [EL], OCB, Box 15, 007.2(6), Staff Study: 'Proposed Tour of *Porgy and Bess* in the Soviet Union and the European satellite countries', 20 Sept. 1955.

8. OSU, Breen Collection, F44A, Vienna and Berlin, 'For October 26 Broadcast over Red-White-Red Network'.
9. OSU, Breen Collection, F107, Robert Breen to Stefan Munsing, 17 Aug. 1952; RG 59 IIA, IFI/E, Box 3, Mary French [quoting Breen] to Ben Crosby.
10. EL, OCB, Box 15, 007.3 (6), U. Kovalyev, '*Porgy and Bess*' *Smena,* 29 Dec. 1955 (translation); E. Ziegler, 'The Black Manon', *Nowa Kultura*, 5 Feb. 1956; Morschikhin, 'American Opera in Leningrad' *Leningrad Pravda*, 5 Jan. 1956.
11. For more on Breen's approach to *Porgy* see D. Monod, 'Disguise, Containment and the *Porgy and Bess* Revival of 1952–1956', *Journal of American Studies* 35/2 (2001) pp.275–312.
12. M. Angelou, *Singin' and Swingin' and Gettin' Merry Like Christmas* (New York: Bantam Books 1976) p.251 and 127.
13. Cited in Alpert, *Life and Times,* p.89.
14. R. Kroes, 'Americanisation: What are We Talking About?' in R. Kroes, R. W. Rydell, and Doeko Bosscher (eds.), *Cultural Transmissions and Receptions: American Mass Culture in Europe* (Amsterdam: VU University Press, Amsterdam 1993) pp.302–18; L. Bredella, 'How is Intercultural Understanding Possible?' in L. Bredella and D. Haack (eds.) *Perceptions and Misperceptions: The United States and Germany* (Tübingen: Gunter Nass 1988) pp.1–25.
15. Dowling, 'Report on *Porgy and Bess*' (note 1); *Die Weltpresse* (Vienna), 9 Sept. 1952; *Wiener Kurier*, 8 Sept. 1952.
16. *Der Abend* (Berlin), 18 Sept. 1952; *Nacht Depesche* (Berlin), 20 Sept. 1952.
17. NA, RG 59, IIA IFI/E, Box 3, RIAS Radio Commentary by Friedrich Luft; *Der Kurier* (Berlin), 18 Sept. 1952; *Wiener Zeitung*, 8 Sept. 1952; *Die Neue Zeitung* (Berlin) 19 Sept. 1952.
18. *Die Neue Zeitung* (Berlin) 19 Sept. 1952; *Telegraf* (Berlin) 19 Sept. 1952; *Wiener Kurier*, 8, 9 and 11 Sept. 1952.
19. *Neues Oesterreich* (Vienna), 9 Sept. 1952; NA, RG 59 IIA IFI/E Box 3, RIAS Radio Commentary by Friedrich Luft; *Berliner Anzeiger*, 19 Sept. 1952; *Wiener Kurier*, 8 Sept. 1952.
20. Dowling. 'Report on *Porgy and Bess*' (note 1); *Die Weltpresse* (Vienna), 9 Sept. 1952; *Arbeiter Zeitung* (Vienna), 9 Sept. 1952; *Neue Wiener Tageszeitung*, 9 Sept. 1952; *Wiener Kurier*, 8 Sept. 1952.
21. *Wiener Kurier*, 8 Sept. 1952.
22. *Neue Wiener Tageszeitung*, 9 Sept. 1952; *Die Welt* (Berlin), 19 Sept. 1952.
23. G. Lipsitz, *Rainbow at Midnight: Labor and Culture in the 1940s* (Urbana: Univ. of Illinois Press 1994), 317; D. Belgrad, *The Culture of Spontaneity* (Univ. of Chicago Press 1998); G. Gillett, *The Sound of the City: The Rise of Rock and Roll* (New York: Da Capo 1996), 26; W.T. Lhamon, *Deliberate Speed: The Origins of a Cultural Style in the American 1950s* (Washington DC: Smithsonian Institution Press 1990) pp.179–86.
24. U. Poiger, *Jazz, Rock, and Rebels: Cold War Politics and American Culture in a Divided Germany* (Berkeley: Univ. of California Press 2000); K. Maase, *BRAVO Amerika: Erkundungen zur Jugendkultur der Bundesrepublik in den fünfziger Jahren* (Hamburg: Hamburger Editions 1992).
25. More on *Porgy*'s history and the President's Fund can be found J.H. Taylor, 'From Catfish Row to Red Square: *Porgy and Bess* and the Politics of the Cold War', *Theatre InSight* 7/1 (1996) pp.29–35 and in Taylor's thesis 'Ambassadors of the Arts: An Analysis of the Eisenhower Administration's Incorporation of *Porgy and Bess* into its Cold War Foreign Policy' (PhD Thesis, Ohio State Univ. 1994). Also of interest is Alan Woods, 'The Possibilities of Cultural Exchange: *Porgy and Bess* as a Cold War Weapon', paper presented to the American Popular Culture Association, 1989. For the US propaganda effort generally, see W.L. Hixson, *Parting the Curtain: Propaganda,Culture and the Cold War, 1945–1961* (New York: St. Martin's 1997).
26. This was occasionally remarked upon at the time: Eisenhower Library, C.D. Jackson Papers, Box 80, OIC file, Emmett Hughes, Rome Dispatch 122, 3 April 1947.
27. Dowling, 'Report on *Porgy and Bess*' (note 1).

Abstracts

Revealing the Parameters of Opinion: An Interview with Frances Stonor Saunders
W. SCOTT LUCAS

In 1999 Frances Stonor Saunders published *Who Paid the Piper? The CIA and the Cultural Cold War* (London: Granta) (American title: *The Cultural Cold War: The CIA and the World of Arts and Letters*). The book received much attention from the media and from academics, and triggered a renewed assessment of this important aspect of Cold War history. W. Scott Lucas interviewed Frances Saunders about the methods of the CIA, the role of the intellectuals in the political and cultural battles of the Cold War, the question of their autonomy, the need for financial support of cultural activities, and the debate about the principles of intellectuals.

Calling the Tune? The CIA, the British Left and the Cold War, 1945–1960
HUGH WILFORD

During the early Cold War period the United States Government covertly engaged in a variety of attempts to influence the politics of the British left. American 'labor diplomats' strove to fortify anti-communist elements in the trade unions; left-wing literary intellectuals were the target of the CIA's campaign in the 'Cultural Cold War'; Labour Party politicians became involved in CIA-sponsored ventures designed to promote greater European and Atlantic unity. However, it would be a mistake to conclude that the US 'called the tune' of the British left. Such a verdict overlooks internal problems in the American campaign and underestimates the complexity — and ingenuity — of the British response.

Beyond Freedom, Beyond Control, Beyond the Cold War: Approaches to American Culture and the State-Private Network

W. SCOTT LUCAS

Cold War historiography has been through several recognizable stages over the last five decades, and the increasing interest over the last few years in cultural themes has added an important extra dimension to this. Yet the focus on 'culture' has rarely gone beyond studies of government support for particular cultural events and programs. Rarely have historical studies attempted to address the issue that such political uses of culture were part of an overall ideological offensive in both the East and the West. Recognition that the foreign policy of the Soviet Union was ideologically-driven is one thing, but historians have generally avoided a similar posture regarding the United States. Yet without sufficient attention as to how the US government attempted to mobilize and utilize all areas of social activity for the greater good of confronting the Soviet Union, there can be no satisfactory understanding of what the Cold War really involved. In addition, this 'ideological impulse' has not disappeared with the end of the Cold War, as the reaction of the United States to the events of 11 September 2001 has demonstrated.

The Politics of Productivity and the Politics of Anti-Communism: American and European Labour in the Cold War

ANTHONY CAREW

The 'politics of productivity', an attempt to raise levels of industrial productivity in Europe by transcending class conflict and creating a consensus in society for economic growth, was a prominent element in Marshall Plan thinking. It constituted a central focus of the European Recovery Program's labour programme administered by American trade union officials who staffed the Marshall Plan's Labor Division. This programme was initially supported by the American Congress of Industrial Organizations (CIO), until hostility to collective bargaining in the local business community, combined with the unwillingness of senior Marshall Plan administrators to insist on collective bargaining as the price of receiving American assistance, blighted the project. This contribution contrasts the CIO's initial support for the productivity programme with the American Federation of Labour's (AFL) more direct strategy of combating communism at the level of organization and propaganda. It concludes by describing how the competing claims of these two American labour organizations for US government funding became a significant factor in American labour's conduct of Cold War politics.

Organizing Atlanticism: The Bilderberg Group and the Atlantic Institute, 1952–1963

VALERIE AUBOURG

The Bilderberg group, which originated in Europe in 1952, slowly organized an American participation in the following two years. After a first conference held in May 1954, it rapidly developed into one of the most successful private transatlantic organizations of the 1950s. The project for an Atlantic Institute, which dates back to 1953–54, took longer to develop into a concrete institution, and was formally created, after several years of preparation, in January 1961. Both organizations received funding and support from the Ford Foundation and became fully-established fora in the early 1960s. The study compares the two initiatives to see how they shed light on the more general context of a 'transatlantic culture' in the Cold War. Although the networks of personnel were of a different nature and drew on different circles and professions, one can observe some interlocking, and their joint success in the early 1960s was partly due to their importance in 'outflanking' Gaullism in France.

Putting Culture into the Cold War: The Cultural Relations Department (CRD) and British Covert Information Warfare

RICHARD J. ALDRICH

In 1943 the British Foreign Office created an obscure outfit called the Cultural Relations Department (CRD), to manage the growing organization of intellectual, cultural, social and artistic contacts designed to promote Allied goodwill. It became clear early on that the Soviet Union was already well-organized in this field, with many seemingly independent international organizations claiming to represent 'world opinion' yet operating as fronts for Moscow's foreign policy objectives. In the three years before 1948, when the more widely-known Information Research Department began its operations, CRD was the cutting edge of Britain's informational Cold War, focused very much upon the twin issues of culture and organized youth. This essay will examine this little-explored organization by focusing upon these twin issues and its neglected records in FO 924 in the Public Record Office, London.

From Stockholm to Leiden: The CIA's Role in the Formation of the International Student Conference

KAREN PAGET

This study contributes to the growing knowledge of CIA covert operations among non-governmental organizations during the Cold War by examining the formation of the International Student Conference (1950) and the creation of its Coordinating Secretariat (COSEC). The ISC objectives were global in scope — to organize the world's national student unions into a network that could deny the pro-Soviet International Union of Students its claim to represent the world student population. The CIA's reach depended heavily on the US National Student Association, which provided both a rationale for funding flows from the United States, and a steady stream of personnel. The structure of the relationship was complex and cumbersome, since the CIA had to work secretly through two organizations (NSA and ISC) whose legitimacy rested on democratic processes. This complexity suggests that issues of power and control require a more nuanced formulation than is usually presented in much Cold War political research.

Youth Organizations as a Battlefield in the Cold War

JOËL KOTEK

In the late 1960s it was revealed that ever since 1952 the CIA had financed and was still financing, by way of a whole series of 'screen' foundations, the overwhelming majority of youth and student organizations, not only in the United States, but throughout the free world. Non-governmental organizations (NGOs) as respectable as the International Union of Socialist Youth (IUSY), Pax Romana and the World Assembly of Youth (WAY) had benefited, at various times in their history, from the generosity and 'liberalism'of the CIA. The key to understanding this paradoxical American involvement in leftist organizations lies in the Soviet Union's policy of systematically infiltrating Western civil society and international organizations. Its constant aim, relentlessly pursued and never openly avowed, was to control Western opinion and further the goals of Soviet foreign policy. By 1950 the communists had succeeded in effectively controlling all the international mass organizations. This study deals with the crucial Berlin Youth Festival of 1951 and the East–West struggle for dominance in the World Federation of Democratic Youth (WFDY) and the International Union of Students (IUS).

The Memorial Day Statement: Woman's Role in the 'Peace Offensive'

HELEN LAVILLE

This contribution examines the gendered aspect of the American response to the issue of peace in the Cold War. In 1949, the US government accused the Soviet Union of launching a 'Peace Offensive', designed to represent the Soviet Union as 'peace-loving' whilst painting the Americans as 'warmongers.' In recognition of the undeniable appeal of 'peace' as a rallying cry, the United States sought to re-define the term in such a way as to illustrate the difference between what East and West meant by their commitment to the cause of peace. American women's associations had a particularly active role in US efforts to counter the Soviet 'Peace Offensive'. Leaders of US women's associations and policy-makers within the government were concerned that the 'Peace Offensive' specifically targeted women, on the basis of their special gendered interest in peace. They tried to convince women across the globe that Soviet-backed peace campaigns lacked sincerity and that women's special interest in peace was best represented by the United States.

The Cold War Culture of the French and Communist Parties

MARC LAZAR

This study is a comparative essay about the 'Cold War culture' of the two main communist parties of Western Europe, the French and the Italian, during the tense period of 1947–53. Both parties had a common Marxist ideology and used similar elements of propaganda: anti-imperialism, anti-capitalism, defence of 'national independence', defence of the Soviet Union, and the struggle for peace. However, while the French communist ideology was completely focused on the Soviet position, the Italians tried to maintain a limited autonomy for their parliamentary activity and their reactions to national issues. The reception and use of communist ideology and propaganda by some social categories of population, especially among the working classes, is then examined. The essay concludes with a reflexion on the notion of the 'culture of war' in France and Italy.

The Propaganda of the Marshall Plan in Italy in a Cold War Context
DAVID W. ELLWOOD

The study will highlight two key circumstances surrounding the workings of the Marshall Plan in Italy, namely the immediate Cold War context (e.g. the 1948 elections) and the fact that Italy was the country where communism had the most serious chance to come to power via the ballot box. The analysis will suggest that the European Recovery Program (ERP) propaganda effort largely failed in its short-term objectives. Left-wing strength continued to grow in various forms, and the quick-fix revolution in the customs and practices of the moderate parties, industry, and the state, as demanded by the Americans, was hopelessly unrealistic. However, the psychological boost to confidence that the ERP (and NATO) gave to the very weak ruling classes was as significant in Italy as it was elsewhere in Europe. In contrast, the Plan's long-term legacy is much more nuanced and hard to calculate. After fascism's failure, the United States offered a vision of modernization which was unprecedented in its power, internationalism and invitation to emulation. The ERP was one of the main ways that this modernization was expressed. How Italian society built mechanisms to adapt, translate, resist and domesticate this challenge had a lasting effect on the nation's development over the subsequent decades.

The Congress for Cultural Freedom in Denmark
INGEBORG PHILIPSEN

The Danish section of the Congress for Cultural Freedom (CCF) was established in 1953 by Arne Sejr, a former wartime resistance leader. The Society for Freedom and Culture was formed as a part of Sejr's private anti-communist intelligence network, called the Firm. But Sejr did not understand the methods or goals of the CCF's work, since he was more concerned with political propaganda and information rather than cultural issues. During its early years the special circumstances of the Danish branch were ignored by the Congress HQ, but in 1957 Jørgen Schleimann, a Danish employee at the Congress office in Paris, set out to reform the Danish Society's work. Denmark's experience with the CCF provides a good example of the tension that could exist between the universal agenda of the Congress and particular national conditions. It also demonstrates the limitations of the CCF's purpose and therefore also the 'boundaries' to Cold War cultural manipulation in the West.

The Absent Dutch: Dutch Intellectuals and the Congress for Cultural Freedom

TITY DE VRIES

During the 1950s and 1960s the Congress for Cultural Freedom was one of the main stages for anti-communist American and European writers and intellectuals to discuss the communist threat to the freedom of intellectual and cultural life. Most Western European countries were represented at CCF conferences and had their own national CCF branches, but the Netherlands was an exception. Dutch intellectuals participated very rarely in the conferences, and all efforts to establish a Dutch branch of the CCF failed. Possible explanations (the socially isolated position of some intellectuals, no strong tradition of political engagement among Dutch writers or artists, no lively climate of public debate, and an ambivalent perception of American culture and society) for this absence of Dutch intellectuals show clearly how national traditions can play a decisive role in determining the development of international networks.

'How Good Are We?' Culture and the Cold War

JESSICA C.E. GIENOW-HECHT

This analysis addresses the question of how different levels of culture were used in the Cold War by political and civil institutions to influence public opinion in Western Europe, and, more specifically, in Germany. It illuminates how what are commonly defined as 'cultural exports' or 'cultural propaganda' refer to a highly heterogeneous and complex group of governmental and non-governmental agents, actions and motivations. While governmental exports focused increasingly on highbrow products such as book and art exhibits, manifestations of popular culture were only admitted if they revealed a specific educational purpose. It can be argued that high culture provided the basis for much Cold War propaganda as much as the Cold War manipulated representations of high culture. Competing against communist claims that America had no high culture, US Cold War programs invoked previous instances of high cultural exchange, particularly with Germany. In doing so, they sealed and politicized a cultural partnership that had been in existence for almost 100 years.

The Control of Visual Representation: American Art Policy in Occupied Germany, 1945–1949
CORA S. GOLDSTEIN

The development of the fine arts in post-war West Germany was influenced by the Office of Military Government for Germany, US (OMGUS). In mid-1946, a small group of OMGUS officers proposed the development of a fine arts policy aimed at neutralizing the Soviet cultural offensive. They were also interested in overcoming the cultural isolationism inherited from the Third Reich, and in strengthening the link between Western Germany and the democratic West. In 1947 the Monuments, Fine Arts, and Archives Branch (MFA&A) of OMGUS began to develop an active fine arts policy. Its officers organized art exhibitions, provided exhibition space, established art contests, invited international speakers to lecture on art, created art appreciation groups, purchased work by German artists, channeled funds to German artists, and connected German artists with American museums, universities, and art patrons. Formal and informal, overt and covert networks were established to develop German-American artistic relations in the context of a cultural policy emphasizing collaboration.

'He is a Cripple an' Needs My Love': *Porgy and Bess* as Cold War Propaganda
DAVID MONOD

In 1952 the Department of State sent a touring production of *Porgy and Bess* to Berlin and Vienna in an effort to counter Soviet charges that America was a cultural wasteland and socially backward in its race relations. The tour was both the culmination of efforts by the US government to bind Germany and Austria to the West and the first attempt to use entertainment as a way of fighting Soviet communist ideals. This study explores the goals of those involved in the *Porgy* tour and assesses the success of their efforts to use art as propaganda. It concludes that, although the tour was deemed a great success, State Department officials were numb to the complexities of theatre production and reception and that *Porgy* never escaped the prejudices and misperceptions it was dispatched to counteract.

About the Contributors

Richard J. Aldrich is Professor of Politics, University of Nottingham, and co-editor of the journal *Intelligence and National Security*. His recent publications include *The Hidden Hand: British and American Cold War Secret Intelligence* (London: John Murray 2001) and *Intelligence and the War Against Japan: Britain, America and the Politics of Secret Service* (Cambridge: Cambridge UP 2000). His current project is to examine the practice of secrecy in statecraft since 1648.

Valerie Aubourg is a Teaching and Research Assistant at the Department of History, University of Bordeaux 3, and in 2002 she completed her dissertation at the Sorbonne in Paris. Recent publication: 'The Atlantic Congress of 1959: An Ambiguous Celebration of the Atlantic Community', in Gustav Schmidt (ed.), *A History of NATO: The First Fifty Years* (Basingstoke: Palgrave 2001) pp.341–57. Present research interests include civil society Atlantic organizations in the 1950s and 1960s, and cultural diplomacy in the Cold War.

Anthony Carew is Reader in International Labour Studies at the School of Management, University of Manchester Institute of Science and Technology. Author of, inter alia, *Labour under the Marshall Plan: The Politics of Productivity and the Marketing of Management Science* (Manchester: Manchester UP 1997) and, with Dreyfus, Van Goethem and Gumbrell-McCormick, *The International Confederation of Free Trade Unions* (Oxford: Peter Lang 2000). Currently writing a comparative study of the international labour programmes of the American Federation of Labour and the Congress of Industrial Organizations and researching a history of the British Trade Union Congress in international affairs.

David W. Ellwood is Associate Professor in International History, University of Bologna (since 1990), and Professorial Lecturer, Johns Hopkins University, SAIS Bologna Center (since 1979). He completed his PhD thesis at the University of Reading on *Allied Occupation Policy in Italy, 1943–45* (published editions available in Italian and English). His recent publications include: 'The 1948 Elections in Italy: A Cold War Propaganda Battle', in G. Tocci (ed.), *Ripensare il 1948. Politica, economia, società, cultura*, (Ancona: il lavoro editoriale, 2000); D. Ellwood (ed.), *The Movies as History: Visions of the 20th Century* (London: Sutton Publishing/History Today 2000). His current research interests involve a wide-ranging study of the politics of American modernization policies in twentieth century Europe, to be published by OUP.

Jessica C.E. Gienow-Hecht is an affiliate of the Martin-Luther-Universität, Halle-Wittenberg, and a fellow of the Charles Warren Center at Harvard University. Her field of expertise is the interplay between modern cultural and international history, with a particular focus on American-European relations. Her book, *Transmission Impossible: American Journalism as Cultural Diplomacy in Postwar Germany, 1945–1955* (Baton Rouge: Louisiana State UP 1999) was co-awarded the Stuart and Myrna Bernath Prize. She is currently co-editing a collection of essays entitled *Culture and International History*, and is preparing a study on the history of emotions in the United States.

Cora S. Goldstein received her PhD in Political Science from the University of Chicago in 2002. She attended the University of California at Berkeley (BA, Political Economy of Industrial Societies), and earned her MA in Political Science at the University of Chicago. She is Assistant Professor at California State University, Long Beach.

Joël Kotek teaches at the Free University of Brussels (ULB) and at the 'Ecole supérieure de Journalisme' of Lille (ESJ). He is the author of *Students and the Cold War* (Basingstoke: Macmillan 1996) His latest book *Le Siècle des camps* (*A Century of Camps: Imprisonment, Detention and Extermination – 100 years of Radical Evil*). (Paris: Jean Claude Lattes 2001) received le Grand Prix d'histoire Chateaubriand and will be translated into English and other languages. Since 1993 he has been secretary general of the CEESAG, *Centre Européen d'Etudes sur la Shoah de l'Antisémitisme et du Génocide,* based in Brussels.

Hans Krabbendam is assistant Director of the Roosevelt Study Center in Middelburg, the Netherlands. He is the author of *The Model Man: A Life* *of Edward W. Bok, 1863–1930* (Amsterdam: Rodopi 2001) and the co-editor of nine books dealing with European (Dutch)-American relations. He is working on a history of Dutch immigrants in the United States.

Helen Laville is Lecturer in American and Canadian Studies at the University of Birmingham. Her current research focuses on the international work of American women's associations in the early Cold War. Her book on this topic, *Cold War Women*, is currently in press with Manchester University Press. She has written articles on this subject, including 'CIA funding of Women's Organisations in the Cold War', in R. Jeffreys-Jones and Christopher Andrews (eds.), *Eternal Vigilance: 50 Years of the CIA* (London and Portland, OR: Frank Cass 1997) and 'Making Friends and Influencing Nations: American Women's Organisations and the Re-education of German Women', *Over Here* (Spring 1997). She is currently researching the use of gender within Cold War propaganda, focusing on the representation of Soviet women in American film.

Marc Lazar is Professor of Political History and Sociology of Western Europe at the Institut d'Études Politiques of Paris, and Dean of the Graduate School of Sciences Politique. His latest publications include: *La gauche en Europe depuis 1945. Invariants et mutations du socialisme européen* (Paris: PUF 1996); Ilvo Diamanti and Marc Lazar (eds.), *Politique l'italienne* (Paris: PUF 1997); Ilvo Diamanti and Marc Lazar (eds.), *Stanchi di miracoli. Il sistema politico italiano in cerca di normalit* (Milan: Guerini e Associati, 1997); Patrick Moreau, Marc Lazar, Gerhard Hirscher (eds.), *Der Kommunismus in Westeuropa. Niedergang oder Mutation?* (Landsberg/Lech: Olzog 1998); Stéphane Courtois and Marc Lazar, *L'histoire du parti communiste français* (Paris: PUF 2000). His present research topics include the history of communist and social democratic politics in Western Europe, and the history and sociology of politics in Italy.

W. Scott Lucas is Professor of American and Canadian Studies at the University of Birmingham. His recent work includes *Campaigns of Truth: Ideology and the U.S. Crusade against the Soviet Union, 1947–1956* (New York UP 1999); *The Lion's Last War: Britain and the Suez Crisis* (Manchester UP 1996); *Divided We Stand: Britain, the US, and the Suez Crisis* (London: Hodder and Stoughton, 1991; reissued in paperback by Sphere, 1996). He is currently pursuing further research into the importance of culture and ideology in the practice of American foreign policy.

David Monod is Associate Professor of History at Wilfrid Laurier University, Canada, where he teaches American History and Post-War European History. He is the author of *Store Wars: Shopkeepers and the Culture of Mass Marketing, 1890–1939* (University of Toronto Press 1996) and various articles on music and foreign relations: 'Verklärte Nacht: Denazifying Musicians under American Control', in A. Riethmüller and M. Kater (eds.), *Music and Nazism* (forthcoming, Laaber, 2002); 'Disguise, Containment and the Porgy and Bess Revival of 1952–56', *Journal of American Studies* (August 2001).

Karen M. Paget is a political scientist who has spent 30 years in government, philanthropy, and academia. She is a Contributing Editor to *The American Prospect*, a public policy journal. She is currently working on a full-length study of the CIA-student relationship and is the recipient of an Open Society Institute Fellowship.

Ingeborg Philipsen studied at the University of Copenhagen, Department of History. She has published the article 'The Congress for Cultural Freedom i Danmark– Selskabet for frihed og kultur', *Arbetarhistoria* (October 2001) and is currently working for the PET commission investigating the history of the Danish Police Intelligence Service.

Frances Stonor Saunders is author of *Who Paid the Piper? The CIA and the Cultural Cold War* (London: Granta Books 1999), which won the Royal Historical Society's Gladstone Memorial History Prize in 2000. She is currently Arts Editor of the *New Statesman* and contributes articles to a range of newspapers and journals.

Giles Scott-Smith is a post-doctorate researcher at the Roosevelt Study Center, Middelburg, the Netherlands. He has published several articles and the book *The Politics of Apolitical Culture: The Congress for Cultural Freedom, the CIA and Post-War American Hegemony 1945–1955* (London: Routledge 2002) on the Congress for Cultural Freedom. His present research focuses on public diplomacy and the State Department's Foreign Leader Program in the Netherlands and Western Europe.

Tity de Vries is Assistant Professor of History and American Studies at the University of Groningen, the Netherlands, and presently Director of Studies of the History Department. She has published *Complexe Consensus. Amerikaanse en Nederlandse intellectuelen in debat over politiek en cultuur 1945–1960* (Hilversum: Verloren 1996). Recently she was one of the co-editors of *The American Metropolis: Image and Inspiration* (Amsterdam: VU UP 2001), and she has published articles on Dwight Macdonald, the New York Intellectuals, and the Cold War information policies of the United States in the Netherlands. She is currently researching the representation of national identity in historical theme parks.

Hugh Wilford is Lecturer in American History at the University of Sheffield and the author of several publications in the field of modern American intellectual history, including *The New York Intellectuals: From Vanguard to Institution* (Manchester UP 1995). More recently his research interests have focused on US diplomacy in the early Cold War period and, in particular, its impact on the British left. He has published *The CIA, the British Left and the Cold War*: *Calling the Tune?* (London and Portland, OR: Frank Cass 2003).

Index